Canaris

by the same author

Portrait of André Malraux
The Kennedy Americans
The Last Year of Vichy
Pétain at Sigmaringen
1918; Why Victory?
The S S
Hitler and the Black Brotherhood

Canaris

*The Biography of Admiral Canaris,
Chief of German Military Intelligence
in the Second World War*

André Brissaud

Translated and edited by Ian Colvin

GROSSET & DUNLAP
Publishers, New York

First published in the United States in 1974

by Grosset & Dunlap, 51 Madison Avenue, New York 10010

Copyright © 1970 Librairie Académique Perrin and

André Brissaud

First published in France 1970

English translation copyright © 1973 Weidenfeld and Nicolson Ltd

First published in Great Britain in 1973
Library of Congress catalog card no. 73-15133

ISBN 0-448-11621-9

Printed in the United States of America

Contents

Acknowledgements

I could never have written this book without the efficient help of former officers of the *Abwehr* and friends of Admiral Canaris. I am deeply grateful to them for their guidance in narratives and documents. I would especially mention Dr Gert Buchheit, General Gerhard Henke, Admiral Patzig, Dr Kaltenhäuser, Colonel Oscar Reile, Colonel Franz Seubert, Colonel Otto Wagner, and General Cesare Amé of the Italian Intelligence Service.

I must also acknowledge my indebtedness to those who have not lived to see this book published, Frau Hans von Dohnanyi, General E. P. von Bentivegni, General Erwin Lahousen, General Hans Piekenbrock. Colonel Willy Jenke, former adjutant to Admiral Canaris, gave me some valuable material, as did Colonel Breithaupt, Colonel F. W. Heinz, and Colonel Helfferich, Captain Leissner and Captain Franz Liedig of the German Navy, Major Paul Leverkühn and Colonel Friedrich Rudolph.

I have to thank those French friends and colleagues who have helped me, especially Monsieur E. A. Amaury, my friends Raymond Lacoste, René Dunand and Colonel Gilbert Rémy, as well as my co-editors, Hélène Bourgeois and Marcel Jullian, and the staff of the Librairie Académique Perrin.

Introduction

It has been of absorbing interest to me to translate and prepare the English edition of André Brissaud's biography of Admiral Wilhelm Canaris, former Chief of German Military Intelligence. The first question that I had to resolve was whether this was a serious historical work or a product of scholarly and imaginative reconstruction, written round the life and death of a legendary and little known personage.

About the author it may be said that Monsieur Brissaud has to his credit several books already on the National-Socialist era, *The Last Year of Vichy*, *Pétain at Sigmaringen*, *The SS, Hitler and the Black Brotherhood* among them. He is thus steeped in his subject, and his service abroad as foreign correspondent for an important group of French newspapers enabled him to collect at first hand further evidence on Canaris and to meet many witnesses of events among retired *Abwehr* officers and other survivors of Hitler's holocaust.

What is immediately apparent is that André Brissaud uses a style of narrative in which his principal character, Canaris, is quoted in direct speech on many private and secret occasions. His interlocutors are men of the German opposition since massacred by Hitler or who have died in the twenty-five years of what may be termed the second world peace. Other conversations quoted take place with the sinister few at the top, Himmler, Heydrich, Marshal Keitel and Hitler himself. Canaris, as Chief of German Military Intelligence, very seldom mentioned in newspapers during his lifetime, was bound to be a reserved and secretive person outside his own confidential circle. His main collection of diaries, we are told, were destroyed by the *Gestapo* on the orders of Adolf Hitler about the same time in 1945 as the Admiral was hanged in Flössenburg and his corpse burned on a common funeral pyre. The Nazis wished evidently to destroy every trace, physical and literal of their enemy. The recent setting up of several military archives in Germany and the production of many official papers that were classified secret twenty-five years ago, has made more documentary material available to M. Brissaud; though all but a few pages of the Canaris diaries are not in that documentation. Whence then, the reader will ask, these intimate talks and meetings that he now describes? My first concern was to discover from M. Brissaud whether his *Canaris* was a serious work of modern history.

M. Brissaud has been forthcoming in replying to my enquiries and I therefore set forth my questions and his answers on the authenticity of these conversations. My attention quickly fastened on such highly secret meetings as that between Canaris and General Ludwig Beck, Chief of German General Staff in November 1937, at which they discussed the now famous but then ultra-secret Hossbach memorandum on Hitler's plans.

Since the International Military Tribunal sat in Nuremberg much has been written and published about the fateful meeting on 5 November 1937 in the Reich Chancellery, at which Hitler explained to a small circle his grand policy of aggression. Marshal von Blomberg, General von Fritsch, Admiral Raeder, Baron von Neurath, Hermann Göring and Colonel Friedrich Hossbach, adjutant to Hitler, were there, so that a live reconstruction of the scene from the evidence and interrogation reports of the five survivors was perfectly possible. However, it is another matter when we come to the meeting in General Beck's study, at which only the Chief of General Staff himself and Canaris were present and the unauthorized Hossbach memorandum about the Chancellery meeting was privily read. There was nobody else present, as far as we know, and both Beck and Canaris perished in the aftermath of the unsuccessful military coup of 20 July 1944.

Yet M. Brissaud is able to describe the scene as if he had been himself close to General Beck's desk in the Bendlestrasse. Such vivid glimpses certainly illuminate the book. There are intimate talks with Marshal Keitel and we are offered a conversation that occurred on 1 April 1939 in the *Tiergarten* between Erich Kordt, Ribbentrop's assistant in the Foreign Ministry, while out riding with Canaris and General Franz Halder, then Chief of General Staff. Their spoken views on Mr Chamberlain's policy of alliance with the Poles are here recorded.

Intimate conversations between Canaris and General Franco about military aid and Spanish independence are vividly given, although it is fairly certain that the Spanish *Caudillo* has not imparted anything about his relations with Canaris to foreign historians.

There are, moreover, a whole series of lively encounters described with Heinrich Himmler, the *Reichsführer SS* and with Reinhard Heydrich, Chief of the *Sicherheitsdienst*, to which the same question might be applied. How comes our author to be possessed of these dialogues of the dead?

M. Brissaud has been happily frank in his explanations. It appears that his original manuscript in French was annotated with his sources to such a copious extent that the French publishers (Librairie Académique Perrin) considered these numerous references to be an obstacle to the flow of the narrative. M. Brissaud therefore removed them from his text, though keeping a master copy of his sources. He also chose, while resorting to direct speech in his rendering of events, to do so in the French edition without the use of inverted commas. After due consideration, I have felt unable to follow this half-form in the English translation and so have given inverted commas to all his conversations of this kind. There is thus no difference in the English edition between the presentation of a *recorded* conversation and a *reconstructed* conversation. I feel that there can be no compromise in presentation and that M. Brissaud's methods are workmanlike enough to warrant going the whole way.

M. Brissaud assures me that there are no imagined conversations in this work. Everything has its attribution and most are based on more than one source.

'My quotations', he tells me, 'are generally based upon the account of a witness, a written document transposed into direct speech, a record of evidence from one of the post-war trials of major war criminals, or a blending of these three sources. I have nowhere invented the words attributed to the characters in this book.'

So the cavalier exchanges in the *Tiergarten* between Canaris, Erich Kordt and General Halder are, according to this system, reconstructed from personal conversations with Erich Kordt, the narrative of Colonel Hans Pieckenbrock, (Chief of Section I) to whom Canaris related the substance of his talk with Kordt, and statements by General Halder in the trial of the Foreign Ministry officials at the Nuremberg International Tribunal.

General Hans Piekenbrock, whom Canaris made his Head of Section I (Espionage) in 1935, was an intimate and trusted friend.

M. Brissaud has had recourse to him on this and many other episodes and he lists an imposing number of *Abwehr* officers who have helped him in his work of reconstructing the story. These include General Egbert von Bentivegni, Chief of Section III (Security); Colonel Willy Jenke, adjutant to Canaris; General E. Lahousen; Major F. Seubert; General Alexander von Pfuhlstein; Colonel Oscar Reile, Chief of Counter-Espionage in occupied France; Colonel Friedrich Rudolph, *Abwehr* Chief in France; Captain Franz Liedig and many others. Where *Abwehr* papers have survived in the hands of the Western Allies and have been passed on to the Munich and Freiburg military archives, he has had access to them, and these have included the Oster papers, the personal Canaris Service file, the diary of Lieut.-Colonel Helmut Groscurth, Chief of Section II (Sabotage), the War Diary of Section II, and the report of Colonel Wilhelm Heinz on the *Abwehr*. As far as an expertise can be done, M. Brissaud has done it.

In the case of the *Tiergarten* chat, two of those present, Halder and Kordt, survived to repeat their recollections of what was said and they were respectable witnesses.

We can rely on no surviving witnesses of the occasion when Canaris went to see Beck and was allowed to read the ominous Hossbach memorandum, but André Brissaud explains that Canaris at the time repeated to Colonel Piekenbrock and acted the scene over again, which was characteristic of his way of retelling an event. It was Piekenbrock who repeated the episode to the author. The same version of the Canaris visit to Beck is to be found in the personal papers of Major-General Hans Oster (Head of his Central Office). These are in the Institute for Contemporary History at Munich. Oster was certainly one of the intelligence officers in his immediate entourage to whom the Admiral would orally have confided his grave discovery.

The private conversation between Marshal Tuchachevsky and General Gamelin, which figures on page 58, is taken from the evidence of Gamelin himself before the French Parliamentary Commission of Enquiry on the Second World War and may be read in the Bibliothèque Nationale. Gamelin gave the same version of this meeting to the Riom tribunal in 1941. The conversations between Canaris and Keitel are based partly on a few surviving pages of the Canaris diary, on evidence in the War Crimes trials and on some interrogation reports.

M. Brissaud offers two sources for the conversations between General Franco and Admiral Canaris related in Chapter 12. Colonel Piekenbrock received a verbal account of them from Canaris himself at the end of the audience. His account is borne out by Herr von Stohrer's dispatch in the Spanish volume of the German Foreign Ministry documents.

We find tense and intimate conversations between Canaris and Heydrich on the respective duties of their two Departments, the *Abwehr* and the *SD*, and these are traceable to resumés written afterwards, or briefings by Canaris of his Heads of Section, several of whom, Piekenbrock, Lahousen and Groscurth among them, and the adjutant, Willy Jenke, survived to relate their recollections to M. Brissaud. Another source of close hearsay about Heydrich and Himmler and their versions of encounters with the *Abwehr* Chief was Walther Schellenberg, the Head of the Foreign Branch of the *SD*. Brissaud found him in ailing health during his last years in Italy and questioned him at considerable length shortly before his death. He does not regard Schellenberg as a trustworthy witness in every respect, but useful in what concerned the respective responsibilities and rivalries of the *SD* and *Abwehr*.

It may be asked how the very grimaces and gestures of Canaris on many private occasions could be described by M. Brissaud. He refers me again to a Canaris habit of re-enacting a scene to his colleagues, pacing up and down, his face reflecting the emotions of the moment. His gifts as an actor were considerable, or he would never have survived detection by the Nazis for so long. He also used those dramatic gifts for other purposes than deception. One was to impress on the minds of his Chiefs of Sections the seriousness of certain acts or decisions in a way that a frankly written memorandum in the Third Reich could not have done without enormous security risk. So it is from the memories of his friends that the author has received many sayings and sketches of Canaris, serving to make up a mosaic portrait, showing the marks of repair but not distorted, of this 'exceptional man', as M. Brissaud calls him.

In 1938 and 1939 I made a study in depth of the mentality of the German generals and the hesitant men of the Canaris circle. Utterances and evidence of outlook that fit entirely with the Brissaud portrait came to me at that time in Berlin by a direct link. Although I began by reading M. Brissaud's story of Canaris with the wary eye of one who claims some authority on the subject, I was unable to discover anything in it that was not inherently probable in the circumstances that I knew personally in the Third Reich. Much of what he tells about the enigmatic Admiral I knew from other sources to be true.

My own small book on Canaris, written about 1950, in the mainstream of prejudice against Germans of all sorts and during the aftermath of war propaganda, did not enjoy the propitious time for publication that M. Brissaud's *Canaris* has had in France today. In 1950, it was also not easy to publish everything in the circumstantial detail that it deserved. The German documents were still not fully available and Allied personalities were alive whose official capacity continued to be secret. I wished to avoid embarrassment to them.

My own impression that Canaris was much more than a garrulous intriguer or double dealer was founded on a personal recollection to which I have hitherto made only a slight reference in *Chief of Intelligence**. In relating it here in full, I think it may serve to support and verify the immensely painstaking and scholarly work that M. Brissaud has done, drawing on but adding to Karl Abshagen's pioneering work of 1948†, more than twenty years later in a definitive way.

Twenty-three years ago, when Abshagen's, the first biography of Admiral Canaris appeared in Germany, the name of Canaris was practically unknown to the German public, though the names of other generals, air marshals and admirals had become household words. My own biographical study of him, *Chief of Intelligence*, so excited the publisher, Victor Gollancz, that he asked the rhetorical question on the dust-jacket whether he had acted for the British – was he a British agent? André Brissaud evidently disapproves of such an eye-catching interpretation of the man; for Canaris, though a proven enemy of the Nazi regime, was no common spy, no double agent and in his high position orchestrated the score rather than peddled secrets himself. Nevertheless, it was at times essential to the dangerous game that he and other far-seeing men in Germany were playing, that the Allies should know what was about to happen.

We have indications that Canaris men in the latter stages of the war played closely with Allen Dulles of the American Central

*Chief of Intelligence, Ian Colvin (Victor Gollancz, 1951 and McGraw Hill, 1952).

†*Canaris*, Karl Abshagen (Union Verlag, Stuttgart).

Intelligence Agency. We shall never be told how close at times the contact was between Canaris himself and the British Chief of Intelligence; but I am able to add here a detail, unrevealed in my own book twenty years ago, as it was still too sensitive then for publication.

Major-General Sir Stuart Menzies, the wartime Head of British Intelligence, to whom in his Westminster office in October 1942, I explained my theory that his opposite number in Germany was in reality working against Hitler with the object of shortening the war, interrupted the conversation, saying with a smile: 'I think I know what is going on in his mind. Would you like to meet Canaris?'

I was surprised to realize from this direct question that an *Entente* of a sort must already exist, and when I declared myself ready to meet the Admiral, General Menzies went on to say: 'I should have to send a more senior man with you. You would not mind that? I don't doubt your capability, but you are a young man and I would wish him to think that I was taking him seriously.'

The matter was left that Sir Stuart required a week or two to obtain official approval for myself and one of his staff to meet Canaris. Such permission would probably come from Sir Alexander Cadogan, then Permanent Under-Secretary of the Foreign Office, his superior in foreign political matters. When I next saw Sir Stuart, however, he appeared disturbed and embarrassed by some awkward press reference that had been made in the interim to Admiral Canaris by the British propaganda services. It had been reported in a London newspaper that the Admiral was a disaffected anti-Nazi.

'Every time we build something up,' said Sir Stuart sadly, 'something like this happens and destroys what we have built.'

He then went on to say that he could no longer proceed with the plan for a meeting with Canaris. 'It has also been pointed out to me,' he explained, 'that you are a friend of Winston Churchill. We have to protect the old man and we have to be very careful not to offend the Russians.'

I remember thinking it odd at the time that these British leakages about Canaris should occur at the very time when the Admiral was becoming a factor in British political thinking. I could not have known then that Harold Philby, the industrious Russian agent, was at that time employed in the very Department to which I put my views on Canaris. Sir Stuart could hardly have suspected the presentable young public-school type in his Secret Service, but he could have added up quite a number of British undertakings that seemed to go unluckily wrong at the last moment. We are all sadder and wiser after the event.

Three months went by and Mr Roosevelt's declaration in Casablanca in January 1943 about unconditional surrender made it unlikely that any Allied representative meeting Admiral Canaris thereafter would have a subject of importance to discuss with him. In after years I once alluded to this incident on meeting Sir Stuart Menzies again, but he revealed no more then than he had found it necessary to reveal when he received me in his Whitehall office in October 1942. This had been enough, however, to establish without any doubt in my mind that Admiral Canaris was playing, as Sir Stuart described it 'an extraordinary game. I think I can read what is in his mind.'

M. Brissaud has evidently been imbued with the same conviction and has brought to his work an immense effort of concentration. The challenge for him has lain, not in making a novel out of a career that in some aspects resembled already a novel about spies. He has sought to reconstruct out of fragments a life that Hitler wished to efface as completely as he effaced the outlines of Lidice.

It has taken M. Brissaud years of research, as the documents became available, meeting people who knew Canaris, noting and comparing their versions of his actions and sayings, verifying where possible and reconstructing his story on the best evidence available with such documentation as remained after the vengeful orders of Hitler and the *SS* had been carried out to burn and scatter the ashes of the man and destroy his diaries.

I find the Canaris depicted by Brissaud a credible, human and convincing personality, who seems not to overact or to overreact to the desperate situation in which he found himself. How near his conduct came to high treason – that is conspiracy against the Head of State – and how near he was to *Landesverrat*, treason in the form of intelligence with the enemy or frustration of the higher direction of the war, we may at times glimpse in these pages without arriving at an ultimate conclusion. M. Brissaud, who relies much upon the recollections of surviving officers of the *Abwehr*, reproduces the inscription on a tablet placed in Flössenburg concentration camp in 1965 to commemorate Admiral Wilhelm

Canaris, 'without sentence and without reason murdered by the National-Socialist Government'.

Howbourne
October 1972

IAN COLVIN

Canaris

I
Myth and reality

At 5:30 AM on Monday 9 April 1945, the noise of tramping boots and raucous orders sounded in the dark. Prisoners were being wakened in Flössenburg Concentration Camp. Like many others this camp consisted of grim barrack huts surrounded by a perimeter of electrified barbed wire. It was built on the side of a wooded hill not far from Germany's frontier with Czechoslovakia.

Arc lamps lit up the courtyard of the central bunker, where executions generally took place. In cell 21 was Lieutenant Colonel Hans Mathiesen Lunding, Head of the Danish Army Intelligence Service. He heard the call, 'Cell 22!', the grating of the key in the lock, the door creaking open and the curt order, 'Out!' The prisoner in cell 22 appeared, chained hand and foot. Colonel Lunding recognized him easily. He had often met him, without being able to exchange more than a few words with him, in the courtyard of the central bunker where the prisoners who were not compelled to do hard labour were allowed occasionally to walk around. The prisoner in cell 22 was a little man with white hair and a red complexion, whose eyes were a piercing blue and who had a kindly smile. He had not been dressed like other inmates in the infamous striped uniform, prison cap and clogs. He had been permitted to wear his own clothes, a dark grey suit and a heavy tweed overcoat which he clasped round him. He stooped as he walked, but when an SS man spoke to him, he would straighten up in a lively and proud fashion. Everything about him suggested that he was accustomed to command, though his manner was quiet. His voice was low, almost inaudible, but firm and sometimes ironic. This little man seemed possessed of great force of character, exceptional intelligence and a high sense of dignity.

A long crack in the wood of the door of cell 21 gave Lunding a view of most of the corridor and through a window opposite the courtyard of the bunker as well. Lunding saw the pale face of the man in the next cell as he passed by. His nose and right cheek showed traces of bruises. An SS guard removed his manacles and irons which fell clanking to the floor. The little man gently rubbed his wrists. His expression was for an instant one of disdain when the *SS* man shouted at him: 'Move! Quick!' and pushed him towards the end of the corridor and the office of the Camp Commandant.

The guards continued to yell the numbers of cells, five in all. The doomed men passed before Lunding's eyes. All held up their heads as the *SS* yelled at them. Then, after a silence lasting no longer than five minutes, during which their sentence of death must have been read to them, Lunding heard the brutal words: 'Get undressed!' The *SS* took their victims naked to execution. 'Outside!' The words cracked like a whip. Lunding, through the crack in the door, saw astride the corridor window a spectral figure, white haired, naked, his cell neighbour, in the half light of dawn and the arc lamps that lit the execution square. So he would be the first to die. Lunding held his breath and listened for the sound of a shot. He knew that the condemned man was an officer and that the *SS* usually allowed them death by shooting, though not by a military firing squad. There was no sound, and this silence meant hanging. 'Next!' came the harsh shout. 'Outside!' came the response from the Commandant's office. A second man came naked to his fate in the grey morning, and so it went on for half an hour.

Prince Philip of Hess, Flössenburg inmate, was cleaning up about 6:30 AM in the room next to the Commandant's when he found a pile of clothes and two books, a volume of Goethe in which was inscribed the name of Dietrich Bonhoeffer and a copy of *Frederic II, Hohenstaufen*, by Ernst Kantorowicz, inscribed with the name of Wilhelm Canaris. Prince Philip was about to remove them when an *SS* man rushed forward, saying that these must be burnt like the corpses and all their other possessions: 'they have just been hanged and burnt on a pyre, Admiral Wilhelm Canaris, General Hans Oster, Pastor Dietrich Bonhoeffer, Dr Karl Sack and Captain Theodor Strünck.'

Half an hour later another prisoner, Dr Joseph Müller, noticed smoke eddying past his cell window. His recollection is that he 'nearly fainted at the sight of shreds of human tissue drifting in the air – my last sight of my friends, Oster and Canaris.'

So died Admiral Canaris, grand master of German espionage from 1935 to 1944, one of the most mysterious men of his age. What was the reason for this hanging ordered by Hitler, then shut up in the Berlin bunker which was to be his tomb a month later? Why such an atrocious death? Was Canaris guilty of high treason, of treason, or of passing intelligence to the enemy? Colonel Lunding asked himself these questions on 9 April 1945, and they may still be asked today.

Some years ago my friend Colonel Gilbert Rémy, whom General de Gaulle once described as 'the topmost secret agent of Free France', told me a curious story. He spoke with affection of an elderly man whom he had known in London in 1942, and whom he used to call 'Uncle Claud', Colonel Sir Claud Dansey, one of the heads of the British Secret Service directed by Sir Alexander Cadogan, Permanent Under-Secretary of State at the Foreign Office. Uncle Claud, responsible for all that was 'ultra-secret', was shy and reticent, working in charge of a multitude of agents whose service was in an honorary capacity 'for king and country'. Dansey went quietly about his business, and the only ambition that Colonel Rémy could discover in him was that he hoped to meet some day after the war the enemy whom he most respected – and whom he resembled in several characteristics – 'I mean Admiral Wilhelm Canaris, Chief of the German *Abwehr**'. Several months earlier I heard Allen Dulles, Chief of the Central Intelligence Agency, talk of him in almost identical language. Dulles told me:

Admiral Canaris was a very extraordinary man and a leader of genius. I had opportunity to see this when I was stationed in Berne from November 1942 to the end of the war and I operated with a secret anti-Nazi group of the *Abwehr*. This strange and enigmatic man still intrigues the Allied intelligence officers. I would have liked to have known him.

Around this person a web of fact and fiction has been woven for the past twenty-five years. A film was made about the life of Canaris, but it was far from being historically authentic. I remember a television debate in January 1969 after the showing of this film on the French television service, and the extraordinary number of telephone calls received by Paris television for ninety minutes afterwards. A year later, in February 1970, I took part in another panel discussing a Czechoslovak film on the assassination in Prague of the formidable Chief of the *SS*, Reinhard Heydrich. I was even more surprised to find that more than half the viewers

*Military Intelligence Service.

who telephoned wanted to know about Admiral Canaris's rôle in this affair. They were right to ask. So much has been written, right and wrong, about this man, that it is impossible to form an opinion about him without going into the subject in depth. He has become the man with a thousand faces. Some have seen him as an anti-Nazi nationalist; others as an anti-Communist patriot, opposed less to Hitler's aims than to his methods; yet others see him as an old fox, a master of the double game, servant of Hitler and conspirator against him, the victim of his own machinations. The mystery of his real personality remains, but nothing happened on the international scene between 1935 and 1944 without the silhouette of the little white-haired Admiral appearing somewhere in the corner of the picture.

2
Sailor and secret agent

In the Schlachtensee villa on the outskirts of Berlin, where Admiral Wilhelm Canaris and his wife Erika lived during the Second World War, there was a large portrait in oils hanging in the hall, that of Constantin Kanaris, hero of the Greek War of Independence, wearing national costume and brandishing a scimitar. Admiral Canaris was not averse to his visitors believing that he was descended from this moustachioed warrior. This was a foible of his, but there was no Greek blood in his veins. His family archives show that his ancestors were Italians from Sala Comacina near Lenno on Lake Como. They moved into Germany at the end of the eighteenth century and set up in commerce and mining in the Rhineland.

Born on 1 January 1887 at Aplerbeck near Dortmund, Wilhelm Canaris was the youngest of the three sons of Carl Canaris, an intelligent and wealthy man who was director of a foundry at Duisburg. Wilhelm Canaris spent his childhood and most of his adolescence in the vast patrician home at Duisburg-Hochfeld. He played tennis and rode, liked to roam the large garden with pet dogs, and showed himself apt in managing animals. At the age of fifteen his birthday present was a splendid mare. High spirits, gifts for mimicry, humour – 'we always laughed when Wilhelm was there', as one of his elder sisters recalled – marked the character of young Canaris. His sisters spoiled him; he was the favourite of his father, who despite his stern and reserved ways often found it difficult to remain serious when Wilhelm was up to his pranks. His mother, Augusta-Amalia, could not resist his disarming manner when she scolded him and he murmured: 'Mama, you look through me like an X-ray'.

His playmates called Wilhelm 'the peeper',* because of his gifts of observation and his insatiable curiosity. The religious outlook of the young man conformed to Christian principles, though Canaris tended to be undenominational – at one time of life he

*Der Kieker.

5

used to take his wife and two daughters regularly to the Dahlem Protestant Church to hear Pastor Martin Niemöller. He was also deeply impressed by the mysticism of the Roman Catholic monastic orders. The family was originally in the Roman Catholic Church until his grandfather adopted the Protestant faith on his marriage to a Protestant woman. At Duisburg high school Canaris excelled at languages, being fluent in French and English. He showed great interest in history and had a phenomenal memory.

In 1904 at the age of seventeen Wilhelm Canaris lost his father, who suffered a fatal stroke during a spa cure at the age of fifty-two. From the deep admiration that he had always felt for his father, Canaris seemed to have inherited his patriotism, his social conscience and a strong aversion to violence. The Canaris family were Liberal-Nationalists, admirers of Bismarck rather than of Wilhelm II, strongly anti-Marxist, but concerned about and attentive to the needs of their employees. There was no military tradition in the Canaris family – even an aversion to the Junker component of the army and a preference for the navy as the less feudal service.

At the age of eighteen, in 1905, Wilhelm ended his secondary-school studies, obtaining the equivalent of the Advanced level General Certificate of Education (*Abitur*), and received the assent of his mother to his choice of a naval career. At Kiel his intelligence and officer qualities singled him out, and after a short infantry course and three months as a cadet at sea in a training ship he became Midshipman. On leaving Kiel Naval College he did a naval artillery course and in the autumn of 1907 was posted aboard the cruiser *Bremen* in South American waters, becoming Lieutenant in the following year. He had by then added fluent Spanish to his languages, and when he left the *Bremen* in December 1909 his commanding officer, Captain Hopmann, described him as 'possessed of presence of mind, resourceful and suitable for delicate missions requiring tact and diplomacy'.

Canaris transferred to a torpedo boat in the North Sea and in the autumn of 1912 to the cruiser *Dresden* which visited the Eastern Mediterranean to watch over German interests during the war that broke out between Turkey and the Balkan states. This was a formative period for him, and he was detached while in the area to study the question of the Baghdad Railway. He was promoted to the rank of First Lieutenant and remained with the *Dresden* when in 1913 she was sent from Germany to Central and South America.

In July 1914 the *Dresden* was lying off the coast of Haiti to meet the cruiser *Karlsruhe*, due to replace her on the South American station. Instead of returning to Germany, therefore, the *Dresden* was ordered to attack Allied shipping along the South American coast and in October joined the squadron of Admiral Count von Spee in the Pacific, taking part in the German naval victory of Coronel. But the British Admiralty reacted quickly and a fleet of superior strength came up with Count von Spee's squadron off the Falkland Isles, an action in which all German warships except the *Dresden* were lost. All through the southern summer of 1914-15 the German cruiser managed to elude the British in bays and inlets, sometimes short of victuals and coal but always replenished by Canaris's skill. One of his fellow officers said of him later that 'we would have never been able to hold out until March 1915 but for the imaginative arrangements made by Canaris'.

On 9 March 1915, the *Dresden* was lying off Mas a Tierra in Chilean waters to take on coal when the only British ship to have escaped from the battle of Coronel suddenly appeared, the formidable cruiser *Glasgow*, more heavily armed than the *Dresden*. The *Glasgow* opened fire with her main armament, but ceased fire to allow a parley. The Captain of the *Dresden* sent Lieutenant Canaris on board the *Glasgow* to protest that the *Dresden* was inside Chilean territorial waters.

'I am ordered to destroy the *Dresden* wherever I find her,' replied the British captain coldly. 'The diplomats of Great Britain and Chile will settle the incident.'

No sooner had Canaris returned on board the *Dresden* than the *Glasgow* opened fire again, and under her heavy salvoes Captain Lüdecke decided to scuttle his ship. The Chilean Government interned the crew on Juan-Fernando Quiriquina island. This did not suit the young Canaris, who decided to escape. He was not the only German wishing to do so, but he was the only one who spoke perfect Spanish and could pass in a South American crowd. He found a boat and crossed to the mainland, then crossed the Andes, partly on foot and partly on horseback, passing from Mendoza to Cordoba and on to Santa Fé, boating down the Parana River. By Christmas 1915 he had reached Buenos Aires, taking eight months to cross from the Pacific to the Atlantic coast, and spent the last days of the year with a German family, named von Bülow, scheming his next move. It was disguised as a young Chilean widower, Reed Rosas, returning to Europe to inherit a property in the

7

Netherlands, that Canaris left Buenos Aires. He took passage on board the Dutch-Lloyd steamer *Frisia* and found that he was agreeably accepted by the British passengers, to whom he related that his mother had been British, asking them to help him improve his English. At Plymouth the *Frisia* entered the British naval control, but the young Chilean aroused no suspicion, though he sighed with relief as the ship left for Rotterdam. With a Chilean passport he had no difficulty in crossing into Germany, where the German navy sent him on a well-earned leave.

At the end of his period of leave his career took a decisive turn towards the strange sphere of espionage and counter-espionage. Nobody knows whether this was his own wish, but before proceeding abroad he had to attend a course in military intelligence directed by Colonel Walter Nicolai, the renowned head of German Military Intelligence, whose saying was that 'the Intelligence Service is the domain of gentlemen. If it is left to others it will collapse.' This was a lesson that Canaris took to heart.

How he avoided the Allied blockade is also not known, but in November 1916 Canaris arrived in Spain in his same identity as Reed Rosas and called on Prince Ratibor, the German Ambassador in Madrid. He met the Counsellor, Count Bassewitz, and the Legation Secretary, von Stöhrer, who became German Ambassador in Madrid during the Second World War. Canaris was introduced to the Military Attaché, Colonel Kalle, who was directing the network of German agents in France, and finally to Captain von Krohn, the Naval Attaché, under whom were to be conducted his own secret-service activities: the surveillance of Allied naval forces and particularly the British Mediterranean Fleet and its base at Gibraltar. He was to concentrate on British naval control there, with a view to finding targets for German U-boats. He had to arrange with agents to replenish German U-boats and surface raiders with provisions in neutral ports. His agents had also to report on the movements of Allied shipping and the bar gossip of Allied crews. Having to recruit merchants to refuel and revictual German U-boats, Canaris was therefore less often in Madrid than in Barcelona, Valencia, Algeçiras, Cadiz, Vigo, Bilbao and Santander. With his neutral passport and perfect knowledge of Spanish, Wilhelm Canaris in 1916 and 1917 began to establish friendly relations with other young men who would be in leading positions in Spain twenty years later, though I have not been able to confirm the possibility that Francisco Franco was among them.

His love of Spain became a permanent factor in his thinking and, as we shall later see, of consequence in history. I must correct a legend of this period that has found its way into some books: that the German agent Mata-Hari (Margarethe Gertrude Zelle) was Canaris's mistress. She actually left Spain for France in December 1916 and Canaris only arrived in Spain at the end of November 1916. A romance with the spy, who was arrested early in 1917, sentenced to death in July and shot in October 1917, seems improbable.

During the summer of 1917 Canaris suffered from malaria which he had caught in South America. At his age, just thirty, he wished for more active service and with the support of Captain von Krohn succeeded in obtaining a recall to Germany. He applied for a permit to cross France into Switzerland on the pretext of going there for treatment for tuberculosis. With a Spanish priest as his companion he set out by rail via Hendaye, Toulouse, Marseilles, Turin, Milan, but at Domodossola the Italian Security Service acted on information supplied by the British and French about the activities of Reed Rosas in Spain. Both travellers were put in gaol and interrogated, though the Italians had no knowledge of his real identity. Canaris provided some evidence of a tubercular condition by biting his lips and spitting blood in his cell, and in Madrid his identity as Reed Rosas, a Chilean whose mother was said to be English, was strongly reaffirmed to the Italian Embassy. However the Italian Government refused to allow the two men to proceed to Switzerland and put them on board a Spanish merchant vessel bound from Genoa to Carthagena via Marseilles. Canaris realized at once that French counter-espionage would be better informed about him than were the Italians. He decided to tell the Spanish Captain the truth, that he was indeed a German and that a call at Marseilles might be fatal for him. The Spaniard thereupon sailed direct to Carthagena, where Canaris landed safely, though feverish from his malaria and pale and thin from his days in gaol. No sooner was he restored to health than he reapplied for a transfer to active service. The chance came in the autumn of 1917 when the German U-boat U35, commanded by Arnauld de la Périère, touched at Carthagena, lying two miles off the coast at dawn on 2 October. Canaris and two other Germans, who had been waiting two days for a signal from the U35, jumped into a waiting Spanish boat and reached the submarine which set course for Pola on the Austrian coast.

Canaris

In the winter of 1917-18 Canaris was on a course at Kiel, having applied to serve in submarines. During this period of retraining he met Erika Waag, friend of a sister of one of his fellow officers and daughter of a Pforzheim industrialist, Carl Friedrich Waag. Erika, young and beautiful, gifted in music and the arts, made a deep impression on Wilhelm Canaris, but he concealed his feeling, knowing that he would soon be exposed to the daily perils of death at sea. After further training in Eckernförde, Canaris received command of a submarine in the spring of 1918, sailed from Kiel, down the English Channel into the Atlantic and through the Straits of Gibraltar. He arrived safely at the Austrian submarine base of Cattaro, and though the Great War was drawing to its close he made a number of successful attacks on Allied shipping in the Mediterranean. Cattaro was not a secure submarine base for much longer, with Serbs and Croats in insurrection against the Hapsburg Government and with fuel and munition supplies interrupted. In mid-October 1918 the German Flotilla Commander ordered his submarine officers to return to Kiel. Eleven U-boats of the Flotilla sailed into Kiel on 8 November. From the conning tower of his U128 Canaris saw that mutineers had hoisted the red flag to the masts of the Grand Fleet. On 9 November the Kaiser fled to Holland and on 11 November the armistice was signed.

The Kiel mutiny, the flight of the Kaiser, Red chaos in Germany, all this affected young Canaris deeply. He had no political prejudices and believed that the Social-Democrat Defence Minister, Gustav Noske, was well able to restore order. In the first fortnight of 1919 he was in Berlin, where the Spartacists were manning barricades with machine-guns. Noske's Free Corps of officers and volunteers was moving in to retake and clean up the capital. Canaris went to the Eden Hotel, where the headquarters of the Guards Cavalry Division had been established under General von Hoffmann and operations against the Spartacists were being directed by Captain Waldemar Pabst. Pabst sent Canaris on a mission to south Germany to organize a Home Guard movement (*Einwohnerwehren*). He left Berlin by train on the night of 14-15 January, determined also to ask the girl whom he had met at Kiel in 1917, Erika Waag, if she would become his wife. They became engaged at the end of January. He returned to Berlin and late in February was attached as liaison officer to the National Assembly at Weimar, then to the newly formed Löwenfeld naval brigade at Berlin.

On 16 January 1919, while Canaris was in south Germany, the two Spartacist leaders Karl Liebknecht and Rosa Luxemburg were murdered. They had been arrested on the night of the 15 January and escorted to the Eden Hotel for interrogation by Captain Pabst, who ordered them to be taken to Alt Moabit prison. There are several versions of what happened next. Rosa Luxemburg and Karl Liebknecht were shot down on the way there in the *Tiergarten* Park and Rosa's body was thrown into the Landwehr Canal, where it remained until 31 May. An official statement declared that, 'Karl Liebknecht was shot while trying to escape and Rosa Luxemburg was killed by an unknown person while being taken to prison'.

The Provisional Government ordered an inquiry and then a court martial to try those officers held responsible for the killings, one of whom was a Lieutenant Vogel. Lieutenant Canaris sat on the court martial, which acquitted four officers of the killing of Liebknecht and sentenced the principal offender in the killing of Luxemburg, Lieutenant Vogel, to a light prison sentence for 'disciplinary failings and abuse of powers'. The exact proceedings of fifty years ago are significant, because Canaris was subsequently the target of serious allegations. He certainly shared the general opinion of the officer corps at the time, that Liebknecht and Luxemburg, active Communists, were their arch-enemies, but it did not follow that he had organized their murder. This accusation quickly circulated but was soon dropped. There was a second criticism, that as an officer of the court martial he had shown partiality for the accused, a criticism rather than an accusation. For years afterwards it was further alleged that Canaris had helped Vogel to escape a few days after his sentence. The newspaper *Die Freiheit* accused Waldemar Pabst, Canaris and a Lieutenant Suchong of complicity in this escape. The three officers were held after an inquiry but then left under open arrest. It being then established that Canaris was absent from Berlin at the time of the escape, he was released without any restriction. On 23 January 1926, a Parliamentary Commission of Inquiry sitting on the events of the attempted mutiny of 1917 and the mutinies of 1918 heard accusations against Canaris. A Social-Democrat Deputy, Moses, supported by an Independent Deputy named Dittmann, accused Lieutenant-Commander Canaris of complicity in the murders, which led to violent press attacks on him as, 'murderer, reactionary, imperialist lackey'. An official communiqué of the Reichswehr Ministry, however, exonerated Canaris, though in 1931 when Chief of Staff of North Sea bases, Commander Canaris was again subject to similar accusations which were once again officially declared unfounded.

Better known is his part in the attempted *Putsch* by Dr Wolfgang Kapp in Munich in March 1920, when Canaris was a staff officer in the office of the Reichswehr Minister, Gustav Noske. President Ebert's Republic was threatened in the winter of 1919-20 by both Spartacist and monarchist forces. The Erhardt brigade of volunteers acted on 13 March 1920, marching down the Unter den Linden avenue in Berlin, installing Wolfgang Kapp as head of a 'patriotic government' and ousting Chancellor Scheidemann. Gustav Noske retreated with the legal Government to Stuttgart. Canaris chose to remain in Berlin, then in the hands of the Erhardt brigade, but the proclamation of a general strike and the refusal of the *Reichswehr* to back the *coup*, enabled Chancellor Scheidemann and his Government to return to Berlin on 18 March. Noske was bitter against those of his officers who had wavered in their loyalty to the civil power. Canaris was among those who spent several days in the cells of police headquarters, but Scheidemann did not wish for a prolonged quarrel with the military and they were released without charge. Canaris, who had married Erika Waag at Pforzheim on 20 November, 1919, returned to naval duties.

His immediate future was associated with the efforts of the German navy to continue development of naval weapons out of reach of the Allied Control Commission, especially in keeping the submarine in being by means of co-operation with the navies of Holland, Spain, Finland and Japan. He was convinced that a modern and powerful navy would one day be necessary if Germany were again to take her place among the world powers.

In the summer of 1920 Canaris was appointed a naval staff officer on the Baltic station. Two years later, aged thirty-five, he became First Lieutenant of the training cruiser *Berlin*. His attention was drawn by a singular and impressive young man, tall, slender, blue-eyed, with a long bony nose and a cold, even sinister, expression. This was Reinhard Heydrich, future deputy to Heinrich Himmler, Chief of the *Gestapo* in the Third Reich. What made Canaris first notice Heydrich was that he played the violin. Erika Canaris, herself an accomplished violinist, invited young Heydrich to their home and was surprised at his musical talent.

He soon became a regular guest at her Sunday musical parties, taking part in Haydn and Mozart string quartets. He listened eagerly, too, to the stories Lieutenant-Commander Canaris told about his war adventures and the more recent events of 1919 and 1920. This friendship lasted two years until Canaris was promoted to Commander and left the cruiser *Berlin* for another appointment. In May 1924 he was sent on a special mission to Japan, probably in relation to submarine construction on German lines, in the Kawasaki yards. In October he was appointed to the naval staff in the *Reichswehr* Ministry, closely associated with naval planning and policy. During the next four years he travelled often to Spain, Holland, Finland, Italy and the Argentine. In June he became First Officer of the battleship *Schlesien*. On 1 July 1929, he was promoted to Captain and in October 1930 made Chief of Staff of North Sea bases at Wilhelmshaven. In November 1929 he spent fifteen memorable days of winter holiday in Corfu with his wife, the occasion of finding and bringing home with him the portrait of the Greek national hero, Constantine Kanaris. In December 1932, at the age of forty-six, he took command of the battleship *Schlesien*, an old warship but an important command. Exactly two months later there was a fateful event in the history of Germany. President Hindenburg named Adolf Hitler as Chancellor of Germany.

3
The Nazis in power

How did Wilhelm Canaris view the new Government of 30 January 1933? There were to begin with only three National-Socialist members, Adolf Hitler as Chancellor, Hermann Göring, Minister of State without portfolio, Commissioner for Aviation and Minister of the Interior for Prussia, and Dr Wilhelm Frick as Minister of the Interior.

Canaris shared the opinion of Winston Churchill: 'We cannot say whether Herr Hitler will be the man who unleashes a new war, in which our civilization will founder irretrievably, or whether he will appear in history as a man who restored honour and peace of mind to the great German nation and brought her back calm, benevolent and strong into the first rank of European peoples'. Canaris was not opposed to the Nazis, though he did not share the enthusiasms of the younger officers and the other ranks. It was certain that the National Socialists would release Germany from the limits imposed by the Treaty of Versailles and restore the navy to its proper place. They would also neutralize the Communists whose attempts to gain power in Germany had since 1918 always disquieted him. SS Group Leader Werner Best described his attitude thus: 'As a Nationalist, Canaris was convinced that the new government was better than that which preceded it, and saw no other course than to follow it. This attitude did not prevent him from criticizing . . . and the more so because he wished to see a German national state with clean hands'. Despite his clarity of mind, his scepticism, his repugnance against brutality, Canaris was unable to see immediately the course of events after Hitler's succession to power. He was not the only one.

One man really alarmed Canaris in the new government, Werner von Blomberg, Minister of Defence, who was regarded as a follower of President Hindenburg but was already secretly allied to Hitler. Canaris knew that Blomberg lacked decisiveness and wondered what would happen to the Reichswehr under his leadership. Hitler soon showed more or less openly that he intended

14

to reject the restrictive clauses of the Versailles Treaty. He was obliged to wait until 16 March 1935 before announcing the law on conscription, but during the previous two years he had secretly prepared the rebirth of the armed forces. Blomberg, who had been Chief of the Military Delegation to the League of Nations Disarmament Conference, was useful in this process; but Hindenburg was mistaken in supposing that Blomberg was non-political, while Field Marshal Gerd von Rundstedt said of him later at the Nuremberg Tribunal that he was a person whom his fellow officers never really understood and did not like. Blomberg addressed the army on 1 June 1933, saying that: 'the time when the army was not concerned with politics is no more. Now it must serve the National-Socialist movement with absolute devotion'. Colonel Walther von Reichenau, Military Secretary in the Defence Ministry, had long been in personal contact with Hitler and was considered by his fellow officers to be a National Socialist himself. Hitler, who lacked military experience, carefully let Blomberg and Reichenau take the decisions that they thought necessary, even in the making of appointments. This was also the case when General Werner von Fritsch was appointed Commander-in-Chief of the Army in January 1934.

The first two years of Hitler's power were marked by a mounting antagonism between him and Ernst Röhm, Commander of his Storm Troops, the brown shirts. It was a grim and ramified struggle, with alternating reconciliations and quarrels, culminating in the bloodbath of 30 June 1934, known as the Night of the Long Knives. Hitler announced the withdrawal of the German delegation from the Disarmament Conference on 14 October 1933, which placed the military question at the top of the agenda. Whose was to be the new army, and who would command it? Röhm regarded his brown shirts as the nucleus of the new army and the Prussian generals as 'reactionaries' and 'crusty old men', while his men were really 'the army of the people'. He was, however, he let Hitler know, ready to settle if he was made Defence Minister. The generals were scandalized by the pretensions of this homosexual Captain. The tramp of brown-shirt boots became louder in the spring of 1934, and Ernst, Commander of the Berlin-Brandenburg Division of the Storm Troops, declared that, 'twelve years of combat have given us victory. We will not let Germany fall asleep again'. Hitler did not lose his nerve. Attending the spring manoeuvres in April 1934 in East Prussia, his main concern was with the imminent death of President von Hindenburg and support from the military for his own claim to the succession. In return he offered the army and the navy confirmation of their right to be the only armed units in Germany. In May General von Fritsch told Hitler that the generals supported him as a body. Sure of their support Hitler acted against the Storm Troops, and the Chiefs of the *SS*, Himmler and Heydrich, were his local executioners, while on 1 July the dying Hindenburg sent him a telegram of approval and esteem for the action taken against 'mutineers and traitors'. Blomberg and Reichenau then drew up a form of oath of loyalty to Hitler in his future capacity of Führer of the Reich, pledging the life of every soldier to his service. When the death of Paul von Hindenburg was announced on 2 August 1934, Blomberg at once gave the order for the entire armed forces to be sworn in to 'Führer Adolf Hitler'. The generals imagined that the oath would establish a loyalty that would be mutually binding like that form of fidelity between the Kaiser and his troops. One of them, however, General Helmut Stieff, observed to fellow officers that the oath did not appear to him to rectify the madness of a one-party system and therefore did not satisfy him. A certain number of high officers shared Stieff's view, but Captain Canaris, although like Fritsch a monarchist, was not among them, and on 2 August took the oath with his officers and men on board the *Schlesien* lying alongside at Hamburg. Four years later Canaris came round to Stieff's adverse opinion.

The *SS* had emerged the real victor from the Night of the Long Knives. Hitler had given them the device 'My honour is in loyalty'. Heydrich, the former naval cadet and pupil of Canaris, had now become Group Leader of the *SS*, his promotion dating from the Night of the Long Knives when he had won Hitler's confidence. The *SS* was reorganized from a strength of 100,000 to 200,000 men in three formations, the General *SS*, the Command *SS*, and the Security *SS*, only the first two categories wearing steel helmets and carrying arms identical to those of the *Reichswehr* infantry. These three branches became the instrument of totalitarian rule, watching over every aspect of national life from the philosophy of its rulers to the lowest gutters of criminal activity. The *SS* were everywhere, and active in their leadership was Reinhard Tristam Eugen Heydrich.

His father, Bruno Heydrich, had been Director of the Conservatory of Music at Halle on the Saale and a composer of opera. His mother, *née* Elisabeth Krantz, was the daughter of a Dresden professor. Reinhard Heydrich was born on 7 March 1904, at Halle. He showed considerable talent at school for music and sport and became one of the best fencers in Germany. His naval career began in 1922 but was brusquely ended nine years later when he was dismissed from the navy in April 1931 for 'unworthy conduct'. The daughter of a close friend of Admiral Raeder, Chief of Staff of the navy, accused him of being the father of her child. Heydrich rejected the accusation; he was already engaged to a blonde beauty, Lena Mathilde von Osten. A naval court recommended his dismissal from the navy, and, pushed by Lina, a fanatical Nazi, he entered the *SS* after a meeting on 14 June 1931, with Heinrich Himmler, the *Reichsführer SS*. His career was rapid, and he reached the rank of *Oberführer*, equivalent to Brigadier, by March 1933. At his death in 1942 he was *Obergruppenführer* or full General, being Himmler's deputy and even nursing ambitions to succeed Hitler himself. Heydrich was a perfect technocrat, in love with power, and he contrasted strongly with Himmler, whose Nordic-myth language bored him. They were opposites: Heydrich elegant, athletic and a great womanizer, but with a mind as sharp as a razor and as systematic and controlled as a machine, all personal feelings kept firmly in their place. It is difficult to sort out their exact relationship, but Heydrich was certainly the dominant character, subtly insinuating his ideas into the mind of his more stolid Chief Himmler. Walther Schellenberg, Chief of the *SS* Intelligence Service, confessed to:

strong apprehension when I arrived at the *Gestapo* building where Heydrich had his office. When I first entered his office Heydrich was seated behind his desk. He was a big man with an expressive face, an abnormally high forehead, small and shifty eyes, cunning as those of an animal and strangely arresting. He had a long, beaky nose and large thick lips. Altogether a fine face, but his full lips gave him a feminine appearance which was even more sinister. His voice was shrill for a man of his size, nervous and abrupt. I left his office impressed by the force of his personality.

In the summer of 1931 Himmler spoke to Heydrich about a Security Service that he wished to organize, and within a few years Heydrich became Chief of the *Sicherheitsdienst* (*SD*) setting up a series of networks through which his confidential agents (*V Männer*) reported on every aspect of national life. 'We must get the maximum information about people', said Heydrich. Above all, he amassed such details as could be used against an individual or an institution. Nothing in the private lives of the leaders of the Reich escaped him and his *SD* Foreign Service extended their activities into Europe, gathering information that provided him with a very powerful instrument.

As for the Military Intelligence Service, it had slumbered from 1919 to 1929, its activities being restricted by the Treaty of Versailles and the Allied Control Commission. It was nothing like Colonel Walter Nicolai's intelligence service in the First World War. At the end of 1929 General Kurt von Bredow was directed to reorganize the Military Intelligence Service, whose very name of *Abwehr** had been a concession to the Allied demand that it should exist for preventive purposes only. Von Bredow was a kinsman of Bismarck, courageous, intelligent and forthright; he was also a great friend of General Kurt von Schleicher, who became Chancellor in 1932 and Defence Minister in the Government of Hans von Papen, a Nationalist who both intrigued with and against the Nazis. In May 1932 von Bredow became Military Secretary to the *Reichswehr* Ministry in the Schleicher Government, handing over the Military Intelligence Service to his friend Captain Conrad Patzig, a naval officer with little aptitude for this work who remained Chief of Intelligence till 1934. Patzig was disturbed to see von Reichenau take over as Military Secretary in 1933 from his friend von Bredow. Patzig disliked von Reichenau's ruthlessness and was horrified, in the spring of 1934, to find himself working with Reinhard Heydrich, who had moved his Security Service from Munich to Berlin and wished to extend his surveillance to the activities of the *Abwehr*. The *SD* thus began to operate inside the *Abwehr*'s field of military security, though its terms of reference were, 'to combat the ideological enemy inside the State'. This led to interference with foreign agents, who were without doubt the concern of the *Abwehr*. Patzig began to collect a dossier on Heydrich himself, which soon made him a direct enemy of his rival. His inquiries centred upon the Night of the Long Knives, in which Generals von Schleicher and von Bredow had both been murdered because they knew too much about Himmler and his adjutant, Heydrich. Von Bredow's assassins searched their victim's apartment without success for the confidential documents on the Nazi leadership which he had collected, but which had been deposited in a bank. It seems that these did not pass into Patzig's

*Signifying counter-espionage (*abwehren* means to ward off).

18

hands but General Erwin Lahousen, deputy to Canaris, avers that Canaris may have had them after 1937. Patzig gathered information about Heydrich, and Heydrich knew it, but he could not yet make a frontal attack on the *Abwehr* and so provoked a series of incidents with it to undermine Patzig's position. In the autumn of 1934 Patzig told his friend Canaris plainly that he intended to leave the *Abwehr*, as he had too many difficulties with the *SS* and especially with Heydrich.

The *SS* Chief has found a pretext to get rid of me. We have made a few aerial reconnaissances over Poland and now there is a diplomatic note of protest from Warsaw that these flights are a violation of the non-aggression pact of 26 January. The matter would have remained on the diplomatic level if Heydrich had not heard about it and run to General von Blomberg with the complaint that this incident was harmful to the good name of the National-Socialist Government. Blomberg turned a deaf ear, but Heydrich came back to Reichenau and complained again. This time Blomberg called me in and reprimanded me.

Blomberg spoke to Admiral Raeder about this friction between *SD* and *Abwehr*, saying: 'Captain Patzig's presence at the head of the *Abwehr* is incompatible with the aims of the National-Socialist Party'. Raeder asked Patzig for his views. He replied that he could no longer ignore Heydrich's outrageous behaviour and would welcome a return to naval duties. The serious problem then arose of finding a suitable replacement. As the new Chief of the *Abwehr* must be a man who could collaborate with the *SS*, Blomberg might have selected a senior army officer and indeed had one in mind who was on good terms with the Party, but Admiral Raeder argued: 'Patzig's predecessor, General von Bredow, was an army officer, and the reason for choosing Patzig was that a naval officer has special knowledge of foreign countries, which is essential in directing the Intelligence Service. It is preferable that the Chief of Intelligence should be a naval officer.'

Patzig himself suggested Captain Wilhelm Canaris, who had just given up command of the *Schlesien* and been appointed to command the naval station at Swinemünde. Patzig emphasized the suitability of Canaris, but Raeder was unimpressed, not liking him personally and mistrusting the man's versatile and ambivalent character. Memories of the 'Canaris legend' still persisted in his mind: 'there is something Balkan about him'. They examined the qualifications of other officers, but Patzig brought the conversation back to Canaris. 'He is the only one who is really qualified for the appointment. Don't forget that he was trained by Colonel Nicolai and that his activity in Spain in the last war was so effective that the network he created is still in existence there. He knows the outside world, speaks several languages and has personal friends that are valuable to us'.

He placed before Raeder Rear Admiral Bastian's report on Captain Canaris while still in command of the *Schlesien*, recommending him 'for a command requiring gifts of observation and diplomatic skill, and giving scope also to his considerable intellectual qualities, formed by a rather extraordinary career'. Patzig insisted to the reluctant Admiral that 'The acute mind of Canaris, his skill in managing people, will compensate for his lack of recent experience in the intelligence service. Maybe you know that he knows Heydrich quite well, and that Heydrich was one of his cadets on board the training cruiser *Berlin* for two years. Young Heydrich used to be invited by Frau Canaris to musical evenings in their house. This personal relationship may assist relations between the *SD* and the *Abwehr*'.

This argument proved effective and Raeder decided to put forward Canaris's name to Blomberg. After a meeting with Patzig, Canaris, who had imagined that Swinemünde was to be his last naval appointment, was summoned by General von Blomberg and found General von Fritsch, the Commander-in-Chief, present when he called. Canaris was told little at this interview about his duties as future Chief of Intelligence, but emphasis was laid on the need for 'frank and friendly' collaboration with the *SD* and specially with Reinhard Heydrich. Canaris asked for a short time to reflect on this offer, promising his reply before Christmas.

4
The ten commandments

It was snowing in Berlin a few days before Christmas 1934 when
Canaris visited the *Reichswehr* Ministry for an interview with
Captain Patzig before taking over from him. A cold east wind was
blowing along the grey Wilhelminian façade of the building in the
Bendlerstrasse facing the Landwehr Canal. Their conversation,
Patzig recalled later, began with his own serious description of the
encroachments of Nazi organizations on the special field of the
military.

'I have just explained to you the strained relations between the
Abwehr and the *SS*, and my views on Heydrich's hunger for power
and Himmler's limitations. Doesn't this disturb you?' asked Patzig.

Canaris, already white haired at the age of forty-seven, replied
with a calm smile: 'On taking over I feel well disposed to these
youngsters'.

Patzig sighed deeply and then, as if succumbing to the fatalistic
and ironic mood of his friend, exclaimed: 'Let us hope that this
trial of strength can be sustained to the end!'*

Canaris committed Patzig's warnings to memory, but meanwhile
he had to achieve a *modus vivendi* with Heydrich. Only after that
would he be free to reorganize and modernize the Intelligence
Service. He first met Heydrich again on neutral territory in a Berlin
restaurant and the meeting had every appearance of being friendly.
Heydrich was evidently pleased to meet again the chief whom he
had admired in his youth. But Heydrich had developed greatly
and tended cynically to regard people in two categories, those
who had to be handled carefully until he had become more powerful than them, and others who had to be destroyed somehow and as
quickly as possible. He believed that he had sized up 'the little
Admiral', knowing him to be influential and intelligent, but Heydrich considered him to be easy going and inclined to inactivity,
and thought that he could deal quite easily with him in the jungle
of the Third Reich where he himself ranked among the largest of

*Admiral Patzig is my source for this narrative.

the beasts. His own aim was clear, to limit the scope of the *Wehrmacht* in the field of intelligence and security and extend the scope of the *SS* instead. He realized that the *Wehrmacht* was obliged to co-operate with the *SS* in security matters, arrests and searches, having no executive force of its own. He knew moreover that the senior officers of Canaris, von Blomberg and von Reichenau wished at all costs to avoid a clash with the *SS*. They expected their new Chief of Intelligence to find common ground with the state police, and Heydrich therefore thought himself in a strong position. However, he began by underestimating his adversary and when he had fuller opportunity to see him at work, he took care to warn his officers against the *Abwehr* Chief as 'an old fox to be treated with great caution'.

Canaris behaved towards Heydrich with the cordiality of a senior officer of the same service, and this was effective with Heydrich, who smarted still under the ignominy of his expulsion from the navy and disliked military officers in general. Canaris soon saw that Heydrich had changed very much since the days when he was a cadet on board the cruiser *Berlin* and had become formidable. He found Heydrich's intelligence both fascinating and repellent, and is said to have felt an almost physical fear of his cold, reptilian eyes. He saw that he must be extremely careful, and was aware that he must remain very much on his guard, if he was not to fall prey to this creature. On the day that he assumed his new appointment Canaris made a note in his diary that has been copied elsewhere and so preserved from the general destruction of his papers. 'Heydrich is a barbarous fanatic with whom it will be very difficult to collaborate in a frank and loyal manner'. He soon realized that at the *SS* Headquarters in the Prinz Albrechtstrasse the real master was not Himmler but Heydrich. The former he regarded as a demented civil servant, drunk with power, cruel and treacherous, but also stupid and cowardly. Himmler would be easier to outwit, he thought, than Heydrich.

Hans Bernd Gisevius, a Counsellor in the Ministry of the Interior, whose duties were with the criminal police, soon provided some evidence of the encroaching nature of *Gestapo* policy. He was opposed to any direct liaison between the *Gestapo* and the *Reichswehr* Ministry, and sought out Canaris soon after his appointment as Chief of Military Intelligence to put to him the point of view that the *SS* was a criminal organization. Canaris was cautious in his rejoinders and sceptical in his manner, which was as well, since his own Chief of Section III (Counter-espionage), Colonel Rudolf Bamler was present at the meeting and mentioned afterwards to Heydrich that the two men had met. There was a furious telephone exchange between Heydrich and Gisevius, who reported the incident to the Minister of the Interior, Dr Frick. Informed of this, Canaris drew his own conclusions; that the *SS* was well informed, swift in its reactions but less powerful than it would like to have others believe. For although it kept watch on Gisevius it did not feel able to take action against him. Canaris decided to avoid further involvement with Gisevius while the man's open antagonism to Heydrich remained a source of friction and uncertainty. He did not see him for more than a year after this incident.

Meanwhile, a decree of 21 May 1935 confirmed Hitler's position as Supreme Head of the *Wehrmacht*, or armed forces, in which the former name of *Reichswehr* was replaced by *das Heer*, the army. It was more than ever necessary, Canaris thought, to use diplomacy in negotiating with Heydrich. He abandoned one by one the less important positions but stubbornly resisted on the more vital ground. Canaris and Heydrich finally settled on ten points, which later came to be known as the ten commandments. The *Abwehr* was to retain its control of counter-espionage, while the *SD* was to be concerned with all actions resulting from judicial decisions. In the long term no improvement in relations between the two services resulted, as counter-espionage was not defined, and would in fact have been difficult to define exactly. The mistrust that existed and would increase simply reflected the great tension between the *Wehrmacht* and the *SS*, which quickened as soon as Himmler began to create *SS* military formations (the *Waffen SS*) to rival the *Wehrmacht*. *Gestapo* surveillance of political suspects also brought it frequently on to the fringes of the counter-espionage.

The *Abwehr*, according to the ten commandments, kept espionage to itself, but at the demand of Heydrich was to confine itself to the military field. The *SD* was to pass over to the *Abwehr* any military information gathered in the field of foreign intelligence. It was almost impossible to draw a line between military and political intelligence. Nor was Canaris mistaken in believing that Heydrich would intrude into military intelligence before the ink was dry on his signature. Heydrich wanted information about the *Wehrmacht*'s senior men and Canaris could not do without diplomatic and political intelligence. He collected this at the same time as he went about his military intelligence business.

The cosmopolitan side of Canaris's character which Raeder disliked, was, curiously, what attracted Hitler as soon as the two men met. The Führer was impressed with this soft-spoken, white-haired little man who showed a sense of realism in international questions. The attacks on Canaris from the Left for his rôle in the Kapp *Putsch* and his supposed rôle in the Liebknecht-Luxemburg affair had given him the appearance of being politically reliable. Moreover Canaris, whose technique of observation was highly developed, was an admirable listener. Hitler, the talker, noticed and appreciated this. He also wanted to have a secret service that would rival that of the British, and Canaris had no difficulty in persuading him to a policy of expanding the *Abwehr*. Hitler's confidence in Canaris did not falter until the very end.

There were in all seven intelligence services in Germany which so deluged Hitler with information that in the end he could believe none of it. Apart from the military *Abwehr* and Himmler's *SD*, Hermann Göring had created in 1934 a service for the surveillance and deciphering of foreign diplomatic codes, whether sent by telephone, telegram or radio – the Research Office (*Forschungsamt*) which was part of the *Luftwaffe*. Admiral Raeder possessed a naval intelligence service, attached to the Naval High Command. Alfred Rosenberg, the Nazi party philosopher, had his Foreign Political Office attached to the Foreign Organization of the *NSDAP*. Himmler had a special service based on the Head Office for communication with *Volksdeutsche*, the German minorities abroad. Finally the Foreign Ministry had its own intelligence service which, under Herr von Ribbentrop, in 1938 was named the *Henke* Service.

Canaris soon became one of the best informed of all German personalities on the politics of foreign countries. In this field he worked with the Ministry of Foreign Affairs. Patzig had attempted to form a common front of non-Nazi intelligence services with the Foreign Ministry, but the latter had remained aloof. The Foreign Minister, Baron von Neurath, had a prejudice against military organizations. Canaris succeeded in establishing close and confidential relations with Baron Ernst von Weizsäcker, Director of the Political Section, who became Under-Secretary of State in 1938, remaining in this key Foreign Ministry post until 1943, when he went as Ambassador to the Holy See. This former sailor, like Canaris, was not hostile to Hitler, but disliked the behaviour of the *SS* and *SA*, the Hitler policy of expansion by force, and Rosenberg's fantastic philosophy of the German race. So Canaris and Weizsäcker developed the art of passive resistance to Hitler's madder schemes, and notably the development of an atomic bomb. Between Ribbentrop and Canaris, however, there were frequent scenes of jealousy as the Admiral trumped the diplomatic service with secret intelligence from his independent sources.

Canaris had other cards in his hand, such as the use of business intelligence, employing for the purpose a strange Levantine known as Baron Ino, director of the big Berlin export-import firm, Transmare. It seems that Canaris had known Ino for many years, perhaps since his Great War service in Spain; for the two men were on familiar terms and Canaris valued highly the information that Ino brought him. Baron Ino put through many commercial and financial deals for the *Abwehr* and helped place *Abwehr* agents abroad as businessmen.

Canaris formed a series of special relations with influential men of his time, strengthening his hand by personal correspondence and meetings with them. Among these were Marshal Mannerheim in Finland, the Japanese Ambassador in Berlin, Baron Oshima, Cesare Amé, Chief of the Italian *Siguranza*, Admiral Horthy, President of Hungary, King Boris of Bulgaria, General Franco, and such shadowy figures as the Grand Mufti of Jerusalem, Amin Husseini, and the Indian revolutionary Subhas Chandra Bose. With such allies he would conduct his personal and mysterious diplomacy, sometimes in opposition to that of his own government.

5
Reorganization of the *Abwehr*

Admiral Canaris summoned his closest colleagues to his office early in January 1935 as soon as he had become Chief of Intelligence. They were asked to introduce themselves by name and Canaris memorized the appearance of each. He had yet to get to know them and assess their qualities. When they were all assembled he addressed them in these terms:

Gentlemen, the *Abwehr* is a subordinate service of the General Staff. We are going to try and make it into a complete intelligence service: counter-espionage, security and espionage, so that the *Abwehr* can establish an independent identity. We will adopt the motto of my renowned predecessor, Colonel Nicolai: 'the Intelligence Service is the domain of gentlemen'.

An officer present on that occasion has described to me the powerful impression made by his words and appearance.

There was instantly a strong contact between us. I regarded the man sitting there as my chief and felt that we were going to do good work together. I had the feeling that the Admiral was more than just another senior officer. He was a personality. In the course of the lively conversation that followed I realized that his sense of duty was not dictated to him by his appointment, but by his conscience, by his own idea of the interests of his country. He saw Germany in full expansion becoming little by little the leader of a peacefully organized Europe. It was strange to hear these ideas at a time when Germany was rearming to the hilt. There was a discrepancy between what he was saying and the propaganda of Dr Goebbels. I had a presentiment that it would not be long before Canaris became opposed to Hitler's policy of aggressive expansion. I was thankful at the thought of being able to work with a man who appeared not to believe at all in the vaunted superiority of the German race and who showed himself far more interested in human problems than in military matters. When he said of the *Abwehr* that 'it will be the domain of gentlemen', I was persuaded that it would be so and that we had a prince in charge of us.

Canaris was in fact founding his service on a spirit of absolute confidence between 'the old man' and his colleagues, and on standards of moral integrity. He said:

'The *Abwehr* will have to conform to the prevalent rules of intelligence services in other countries. We must have a high idea of the rights of man, of international law and morality. I need gentlemen in the *Abwehr* and not unscrupulous gangsters.'

Colonel Oscar Reile wrote after the war of the *Abwehr* that

> all its activities were conducted in the gentlemanly style of its Chief, Admiral Canaris. Cruelty revolted him and it grieved him when he could not prevent it. Woe betide those of his subordinates who resorted to brutal or dishonourable methods! The responsible officers of the *Abwehr*, strongly under his influence, were careful to keep to his rules.

Colonel Rémy in his preface to the French translation of Colonel Reile's book *The German Counter-espionage in France*, wrote in confirmation:

> Basing my opinion on the experiences of those of my fellow officers who fell into the hands of the *Abwehr*, I have several times said in public that the officers attached to Admiral Canaris knew how to respect the laws of war, laws which are certainly stern, but which would have been applied in the same way in the same circumstances by French officers. I understand and share the admiration of Colonel Reile for Admiral Canaris.

I have been impressed by common sentiment of devotion to his memory in all those officers of the *Abwehr* whom I interrogated after the war. It pervaded Würzburg during a reunion between 8 and 10 April 1970, when the former *Abwehr* officers gathered to commemorate the twenty-fifth anniversary of the death of their chief. It moved me deeply on this occasion to hear the tributes paid to his memory by the sixty survivors of his service.

The *Abwehr* in 1935 did not dispose of large resources. Its officers, according to Dr Karl Heinz Abshagen, author of the earliest work on Canaris, were a mixed collection of men. Some had been trained before 1918, some in General von Seeckt's army under the conditions imposed by the Treaty of Versailles; others had been recruited during the first period of military expansion; finally there were those who began their careers as officers under Hitler. Abshagen notes that there was a large gap between the outlook of the first three categories and that of the last. Canaris had a delicate problem in recruiting the sort of men he wanted, realizing that the military mind is not always suited to intelligence work nor does discipline in the various arms of the service necessarily equip a man for it. He preferred naval officers, provided that they responded to special training. He had, however, long ago rejected the idea that competence was directly related to the insignia of military rank. This is why after 1939 he enlisted a large number of men from civil life, professors, lawyers, doctors, engineers and even clergymen. He required his candidates to know well the country assigned to them and to know foreign languages, but he also insisted on high standards of intelligence and probity. Sometimes he was mistaken in his choice. He was apt to make instant decisions according to his own likes and dislikes, but to judge from his choice of close collaborators, his instinct guided him well.

There is one who deserves special mention, Major Hans Oster, Head of the Central Section of the *Abwehr* which dealt with personnel and the secret register. Born in 1884, Oster was the son of a Protestant clergyman. In the First World War he had been a cavalry officer and remained in the army during the period of the Weimar Republic. In December 1932 he provoked a scandal by associating with the wife of a senior officer and was obliged to resign his commission. General Franz Halder, who had a high regard for him, was able to arrange for his return to the intelligence service, first under General von Bredow and continuing under Captain Patzig. Oster was thus an old hand in the Service when Canaris rejoined it. There was only one year's difference in their ages but in other respects they were not alike. Oster was active, impulsive, often rash in his actions. He was an elegant, good-looking man, who sported a monocle and never ceased to be interested in women. His courage was faultless and as a strong monarchist he detested National-Socialism, feeling himself still bound by his oath to the Kaiser rather than by that which he had been obliged to give to Hitler. He deeply admired General von Bredow, and when the General was brutally assassinated by order of Himmler and Heydrich on 30 June 1934, the Night of the Long Knives, the result was to make a determined rebel of Oster.

Canaris was soon aware of his opinions and sentiments. He did not yet share them himself and closed his eyes to them. Oster had the qualities that he needed and he made him first his Chief of Staff and later the Chief of the Central Section. They would never become complete friends, though they worked together and trusted each other. Hans Gisevius, who worked closely with Oster in the conspiracies against Hitler, attests his ability and his indifference to the risks that he ran. 'He did not seem to see the jungle that surrounded him and he faced up to obstacles and surmounted them like the ardent cavalry officer that he was, never defeated, trusting in God.'

The two periods of great expansion of the *Abwehr* were 1935-8 and 1938-41. When Hitler replaced the War Ministry in 1938 with a High Command of the *Wehrmacht* directed by General Wilhelm Keitel, the *Abwehr* was organized in five sections: the Foreign Section; Espionage; Counter-espionage and Security; Sabotage and Political Action; and the Central Section.

The Director of the Foreign Section (*Abteil Ausland*) was Captain Leopold Bürkner, 'a loyal and energetic sailor', as Canaris called him. The duties of this section were liaison between the War Ministry and the Foreign Ministry.

At the Head of Section one, Espionage, Canaris put the man who was to become his closest friend, Colonel Hans Piekenbrock. He was a Rhinelander, a tall, distinguished, amicable man, intelligent, humorous and acutely analytical. Canaris called him 'Piki', and trusted him with his most intimate thoughts and cares.

Piekenbrock repeated to me Canaris's instructions concerning the reorganization of Section one.

We must push recruitment and training of operational agents [said Canaris] they are the spearhead of any intelligence service worthy of the name. Without them we are reduced to collecting bits and pieces, looking through the press, and waiting at our desks for intelligence to be handed to us on a silver platter. But the foreign agents, gentlemen, are not the only ones. There must be specialists to sift their harvest. These specialists are the brain of the Intelligence Service; for it is not enough to have understood, analysed and collated the information that we receive. The specialists must know what questions to put and they must look ahead. What we need in the Intelligence Service is men and not machines. We need executives, intelligent and upright if that can be, and we need men in charge who are able to play a game of chess.

These words recall those of General L. Rivet, the eminent head of the *Deuxième Bureau* (the Intelligence and Counter-espionage Service of the French army), related to the military historian Michel Garder.

The art of intelligence does not lie in its aims, which are easy to discern, nor in its disconcerting methods. Its double aspect of seeking information and seeking it in secret leads to the use of all the qualities and vices of man, all his venality and all his disinterestedness. The basis is a sort of pact between two men, the officer and the agent, a director and an executive. The result is an infinity of special cases, which are of intense human interest. The multiplicity of sources, the need to protect them, the continuous redirection of their activities to meet the needs of the moment. That is the sacred duty of the intelligence officer.

Paul Leverkühn, a Hamburg lawyer recruited by Canaris to work in Turkey during the war, related in his book, *German Military Intelligence* the way in which after 1935 Canaris extended his network of secret reconnaissance across Holland and Belgium and down the coast of France to cover all objectives and targets in France of strategic interest, working from Spain as well as from Germany. He adds:

> We had to organize slowly and laboriously a network of agents who for the most part were not of French nationality. Men of various nationalities were recruited and put through a rigorous intelligence training at an *Abwehr* centre. We had usually to use adventurers for this kind of work. They did not have to be indoctrinated and usually volunteered their services, but it was essential to success that their officer-instructors should be on terms of mutual trust with their agents. Money could not achieve this, only the human element. Canaris was careful to forbid the use of pressure or threats and only in exceptional circumstances would he approve the use of *agents provocateurs*. He was relentless in punishing any disobedience of these rules.

As for women in the *Abwehr*, the rule was that although many volunteer agents were women, there should be as few as possible in the Service itself. The *Abwehr* did not like using a woman for an important mission. Yet a woman can obviously be as courageous, discreet and determined as a man and if she is clever and beautiful she can move more easily into strange surroundings. It was only the war that brought women into the corridors of the *Abwehr* building, and this either as secretaries or non-established agents. Colonel Oskar Reile affirms that 'no German woman agents were used for espionage activities in enemy-held territory. Some were used, and some foreigners too, inside Germany or in areas occupied by our troops on small duties such as the surveillance of security suspects'.

Canaris was not averse to women in his service, but he was prudent. Colonel Franz Seubert recalled to me the Admiral's saying:

'Women can be very useful in the intelligence service. That is true. They can be used, but you must not go to bed with them. Those who do so will be dismissed from the *Abwehr*.' Canaris was very strict on this precept. Colonel Reile recalls the case of Captain Jurek Sósnowski, the Polish intelligence officer who arrived in Berlin in 1935 and passed himself off as a wealthy man, seeking to be received by families whose daughters worked in the War Ministry. By means of seduction, promises of marriage, and even threatening them with pornographic photographs that he had taken of them, he was able to obtain from his mistresses certain *Wehrmacht* secret documents. The conspiracy was discovered and two of Sósnowski's women were condemned to death and executed with the axe, still protesting their abject devotion to Sósnowski; the third was condemned to a long prison sentence. Sósnowski was exchanged for several German agents whom the Poles had arrested. When Canaris heard the details of Sósnowski's behaviour, he exclaimed in Colonel Reile's presence: 'if one of my officers has recourse to these methods, I will proceed against him with the utmost severity.'

Section II (Sabotage and Subversion) had the task of working in the rear of the enemy. Although its work was important in time of war it was numerically the smallest of the five sections. It had to attack the enemy lines of communication, oil supplies, etc., and encourage subversive activities behind the front, spreading defeatist propaganda and aiding guerilla movements.

Canaris was sceptical about the use of sabotage and did not think that in wartime it could be really effective. He estimated that sabotage was also counter-productive and he disliked the excessive risks that it entailed to defenceless civilians. This was the basis of his criticism of the activities of the British and American Special Service Commandos. However he did not oppose the use of sabotage, considering it his duty to exploit all means at his disposal in the service of the German Armed Forces. His ruling was, however, that the laws of war must be observed. If Hitler or the High Command insisted on action contrary to these laws, Canaris avoided putting their orders into effect. In the annals of the Third Reich this was a unique instance of disobedience, usually punishable by death. Canaris selected ruses suitable to each case of non-execution, sometimes he put up arguments against such orders; sometimes he procrastinated; sometimes again he went through the motions of obeying an order and in reality did nothing, as in the cases of General Weygand and General Giraud when he was ordered to procure their removal by assassination.

Until the beginning of 1939 Section II was directed by Colonel Helmut Groscurth, a tall, fair-haired, quiet man with special gifts as an organizer. When he returned to field service he was succeeded by General Erwin Lahousen, an Austrian who had joined the German army in 1938, and who was in turn succeeded by Colonel Wessel von Freytag-Loringhoven in 1943.

Section III, Counter-espionage, was of capital importance to Canaris, who told a meeting of his heads of sections in January 1935:

The counter-espionage service is vital to Germany. Any short-comings in this service would lay our country open to foreign agents, with serious consequences. All our military secrets – and there are more than is generally supposed – all our industrial or scientific secrets would be directly threatened. Do not be misled – the French *Deuxième Bureau* and the British Secret Service have many agents here watching our rearmament. We must be in a position to do big cleaning-up operations, and must therefore expand counter-espionage to its maximum. It is a slow and difficult business, but, I repeat, indispensable. All our own efforts are useless if we cannot defeat the enemy's intelligence. We cannot rely on other services. We must act on our own. I shall see to it that Section III is intensively developed.*

Until the outbreak of war in 1939, Major Rudolf Bamler directed Section III, an appointment made by General von Reichenau. Bamler was an admirer of the National-Socialist system and his close collaboration with the *SS* Security chiefs, Heydrich, Ohlendorff, Schellenberg, Müller, Arthur Nebe (Chief of Police) and Best, did not please Canaris, who feared nothing more than interference by the *SS* in *Abwehr* business. He took the first opportunity of getting rid of Bamler, releasing him from the *Abwehr* when he asked for an active command at the outbreak of war.

When Canaris took over the *Abwehr* in 1935, counter-espionage was confined to frontier control and the surveillance of military suspects inside Germany including, in certain cases, their correspondence and telephones. There were strict regulations for the security of military and naval establishments, of the courier service, of airfields and industrial installations, but there was a shortage of counter-espionage personnel and *Abwehr* activities were confined

*Record of Colonel Oskar Reile.

to Reich territory. Colonel Reile relates that in 1935 Canaris added a new section to the *Abwehr*, charged with recruiting personnel to watch suspects abroad and penetrate enemy intelligence systems. A further development was the systematic feeding of hostile intelligence services with false information.

This placed the centre of gravity of our counter-espionage abroad, on the same lines as the British intelligence system which operated through MI5 at home and MI6 abroad. The aim was twofold, to find out as accurately as possible what dangers threatened the Reich, and provide against them; also to provide protection for foreign agents (*V-Männer*) operating abroad. In 1914 the British had arrested in one operation the entire network of German agents in England. It is a long and difficult operation to set up an intelligence service in time of peace and nearly impossible in time of war.

This survey is necessary to avoid the impression that the *Abwehr* was nothing but an organization collecting documentary material on the crimes of the Nazis or conspiring to resist Nazism, though it did that also. The espionage and counter-espionage work of the *Abwehr* was more important than has been allowed by any of the books written about it, except Gert Buchheit's *The German Secret Service*. It would require several volumes to relate the successes and the failures of 'the Admiral's outfit' in espionage, sabotage and counter-espionage between 1935 and 1944. It will suffice to give a few examples illustrating the degree to which Admiral Canaris exerted his influence over his subordinate officers, and how they had at last to make the painful choice between serving the State or their country.

6
The war in Spain

Admiral Canaris was not surprised when civil war broke out in Spain on 18 July 1936. He had expected it for a long time. In the spring of 1936 the situation was so explosive that civil war could be said to exist already, with widespread crimes and assassinations. He learned from his excellent sources that arms were being delivered to the Republican militia of the extreme Left, who were openly preparing to 'defend the Popular Front and bar the way to Reaction', with the ulterior aim of supplanting the Spanish Liberals and Socialists and setting up a Communist republic. Canaris was also informed that the army chiefs, expecting a Communist coup on 29 July or 1 August, were planning to take preemptive action.

Such was the situation when, on 13 July at dawn, special police arrested at his home and murdered the Deputy, José Calvo Sotelo, leader of the Monarchist opposition in parliament. This act brought home to many the fact that Spain had become an inferno, where it was either fight for your life or lose it. General Sanjurjo on 17 July called for an insurrection against the Republican Government; the ensuing war was to last three years at the cost of a million lives.

The army fought successfully against the Republic nearly everywhere. In Old Castile, as in Navarre province, the Nationalists won and united under General Mola. It was the same in Aragon, Alava and Galicia. The rest of Spain remained under the control of the Republican Government, except for Seville, Cadiz, Cordoba and Grenada. The military insurgents had grave setbacks in Madrid and Barcelona, but the army in Morocco was firmly under the control of General Franco, who arrived at Tetuan on 19 July. This army in Africa could have attacked in the south and marched on Madrid, while General Mola advanced from the north to take the capital in a pincer movement, but General Franco's army lacked ships and transport aircraft to cross the Straits of Gibraltar. The Spanish air force had mostly declared for the Government, and in the navy the crews, mainly Communist, had massacred seventy per cent of their officers. The navy, led by the battleship *Jaime I*, moved menacingly towards Tangiers, and at this critical moment General Sanjurjo was killed in an aircraft accident on his way from Portugal to Burgos, a grievous loss to the insurgents.

Pinned down in Spanish Morocco, General Franco organized a small airlift between Tetuan and Seville, using five old *Bréguet 19*s, a *Potez*, a *Douglas* and several small *Dornier* seaplanes. He sent Legionaries and Moorish troops across the Straits in fishing boats, thus reinforcing by 2,065 men the little force of 130 with which General Queipo de Llano had taken Seville, but this was only a stop-gap.

'What shall we do if we cannot get the Army of Africa across?' asked Lieutenant-Colonel Saenz de Buruga.

'We shall do everything that is possible and necessary', replied Franco, 'but not surrender'.

He could not ask France for arms, as the French Government was already supplying the Republican Government. Great Britain had also no inclination towards the Spanish Nationalists. There remained Italy and Germany, and Franco first sent his friend Luis Bolin, London Correspondent of the newspaper *ABC*, to Rome. Here he was sympathetically received on 25 July by the Italian Foreign Minister, Count Ciano, but Ciano explained that his father-in-law, Mussolini, had received direct from Tangiers a request from General Franco for twelve aircraft and had scribbled in blue pencil on the telegram, 'No'. Bolin and his fellow delegates recalled earlier promises of assistance from the Duce for the Spanish Monarchists, but the reply from Mussolini remained negative. One of them, Antonio Goicoecha, insisted that Mussolini must be mistaken in his view of the situation, since Monarchists, Carlists, Falangists and Franco were all intent in setting up a corporate state like that in Italy. Ciano went back to Mussolini, who was persuaded to provide twelve *Savoia-Marchetti 81* aircraft, but these were not sent until 30 July and even then two landed by mistake in French Morocco and a third crashed into the sea. At the same time as this attempt to obtain military assistance from Italy, General Franco approached Hitler.

He began through Colonel Juan Beigbeder Atienza, a former Spanish Military Attaché in Berlin, who asked the German Military Attaché in Paris, General von Kühlenthal, for ten heavy-transport aircraft, to be privately supplied on a commercial basis and delivered by German pilots. Concurrently, General Franco asked a German businessman in Tetuan, named Johannes Bernhardt, a member of the Foreign Organization of the Nazi Party, to call at his headquarters, with Group Leader Adolf Langenheim, Nazi Party Chief in Spanish Morocco. Franco explained his problems and requirements to them, and on 22 July Bernhardt and Langenheim flew to Berlin in a Lufthansa aircraft, accompanied by a Spanish representative, Captain Francisco Arranz.

The German reaction was cool. Herr Dieckhoff, Director of the Political Department of the Foreign Ministry, explained to them,

In my view it is absolutely imperative that the German authorities and the Party maintain a complete reserve in the present state of affairs. Deliveries of arms to the rebels would very soon become known. The German community in Spain, as well as our merchant shipping and navy, would be heavily compromised if it became known that we were supplying the rebels.

He referred to the request already made by Colonel Beigbeder to General von Kühlenthal in Paris for a secret delivery of aircraft, describing it as 'impracticable and not to be visualized at all. But we might consider allowing Franco's representatives to make agreements here now for when they have attained power. Even if that eventually happens, the German authorities must, for the present, remain at a distance from the whole affair'.

On a Minute to this effect, the Foreign Minister, Baron von Neurath, added comments in his own handwriting: 'Exactly' and 'Yes'. But the Foreign Ministry and the Party were not at one. Gauleiter Bohle of the Party Foreign Organization sent three Party officials with Bernhardt, Langenheim and Arranz to Bayreuth where the Führer was attending a Wagner opera festival.

Adolf Hitler arrived back from the opera house on the night of 26 July to receive a letter from Franco and meet his emissaries. After a short meeting with them, despite the late hour, he summoned Hermann Göring, Marshal von Blomberg and Admiral Canaris, who were all three at Bayreuth. Ought aircraft to be sold to the rebels? Should they be aided and have arms delivered to them? Hitler was very hesitant, preferring to wait and see. On the other hand this military uprising was Nationalist and anti-Communist. Blomberg avoided giving an opinion. Göring was unfavourable to the idea. Germany having reoccupied the Rhineland without too much disturbance, would now risk serious differences with France and Great Britain in taking sides with the rebels. As for Admiral Canaris, he favoured support for the rebels and explained why. He knew Spain and the Spaniards well, he told Hitler, and he had been following the political evolution of that country very closely. It was evident that Stalin had made and was still making great efforts to support the Spanish Communist Party and bring it to power. If this movement succeeded and there was a Communist state in South-west Europe, taking orders from the Kremlin, this would be a serious threat, first to France which already had a Popular Front Government, and then to all European countries lying as Germany did between Soviet Russia and Soviet Spain.

Canaris explained that in the course of his numerous visits to Spain he had met the civil and military leaders of that country and General Franco among them. He then drew an attractive portrait of the Spanish Nationalist leader, for whom he expressed esteem. He spoke of him as a man of high qualities and character, a firm believer in discipline and order, with a strong sense of duty. Franco was an imperturbable leader, he said, with extraordinary physical courage, and at thirty-three years of age the youngest European General since Bonaparte. In every promotion course in the Spanish army he had found himself the youngest cadet of the class. He was efficient and prudent as well as brilliant, said Canaris, and a rigid self-disciplinarian. Franco did not drink or smoke and avoided involvement with women, he added, relating these characteristics of austerity to suggest a similarity to Hitler. He recalled how Franco had told his officers in Morocco: 'I want neither women here, nor drinking bouts, nor masses celebrated', not wishing for the Church to impose its rituals on the severe military code, though Franco himself was a devout Roman Catholic.

What Canaris took care not to tell Hitler was that Franco disliked National-Socialism and its racial laws, did not consider Italian Fascism as anything to be imported into Spain, and was fiercely isolationist. He succeeded in this way in inspiring a sympathy for Franco in the minds of Hitler and Blomberg. Göring said that he was prepared to sell aircraft to Spain and that it would interest him to test them out there in war conditions, though he thought the military insurrection too precarious to support openly. Hitler remained undecided, but was coming round to the idea of discreet and limited aid to Spain.

Canaris returned to the subject with Hitler on the political plane. Having said that earning foreign exchange by arms sales 'was not a negligible factor' and that Spain 'could be an excellent experimental station', he added that the success of the rebels would depend on the aid that they received and that Mussolini, he had just heard, was favourably inclined towards supplying the Spanish insurgents with aircraft. The meeting broke up at 4 AM, but the same day Blomberg, Göring and Canaris met the Spanish delegation. After 27 July though Göring showed some signs of irritation, Canaris became the indispensable link, managing relations between the Third Reich and Franco. The German leaders had to rely on his knowledge of the country and personal relations with Franco, and felt obliged to send him to Spain whenever there were problems to smoothe out. In the process the Head of the *Abwehr* won the unbounded confidence of Franco, but incurred the annoyance of those German authorities who saw him going over their heads on the Führer's orders.

Keitel, Göring and Canaris quickly agreed with the Spanish delegates on a programme of aid for the nationalists. A commercial firm entitled Hisma Ltd was founded (Hispano-Marroqui Transport Company) headed by Johannes Bernhardt. A second company was founded with the participation of Göring and called Rowak (Raw Materials and Wares Purchasing Company). In 1937 when other companies had sprung up, Bernhardt grouped them in a new holding company, Sofindus, the Sociedad Financiera Industrial Ltda.

Bernhardt, Langenheim and Captain Arranz hurried back to Tetuan to tell Franco the good news. Captain Arranz carried a personal letter from Canaris to Franco in which the Head of the *Abwehr* expressed his hopes for his friend's success and informed him that Hitler would send Colonel Walther Warlimont to represent the German Armed Forces in Spain. Canaris added that he hoped soon to meet Franco on Spanish soil and that he wished to accredit to him one of his best men in the *Abwehr*, Commander Leissner.

Franco had already been told by Luis Bolin that twelve Italian aircraft were on the way. Now he could expect twenty *Junkers 52* and six *Heinkel 51* fighters. Langenheim sent an important message through the German consul in Tangiers to Göring and Canaris:

According to my instructions I have to report that I have had a conversation with General Franco. The future Nationalist Government of

Spain will consist of a Directorate of three generals, Franco, Queipo de Llano and Mola, the President being Franco. Our conception of future commercial, cultural and military relations coincides entirely with the wishes and intentions of General Franco. Heil Hitler!

Franco was less concerned with setting up the new Junta of the Provisional Government than with getting his troops across the Straits. He stepped up his airlift with the *Junkers* and the *Savoia-Marchettis* to a rate of 500 men and 15 tonnes of military supplies a day. By the end of August a force consisting of 15,000 men of the African Army, legionaries and Moors, the best of the Spanish troops, had been transported into Spain. Neither Queipo de Llano nor Mola possessed such hard and disciplined men, and this established Franco's claim, in fact if not in title, to the supreme command. Throughout this long and bloody Civil War Franco would never forget the invaluable help that Canaris offered him at the moment when his destiny hung in the balance.

Early in October 1936 Admiral Canaris left Berlin by air for Salamanca where Franco was staying. The aircraft flew from Stuttgart over France at a high altitude without an intermediate landing. Canaris was provided, in case of an accidental landing in France, with a passport in the name of Juan Guillermo, citizen of the Argentine. His seat was in a stripped-down cabin among petrol cans, carried to give maximum range.

When he arrived in Spain Canaris was invited to lunch with General Franco, who had established his headquarters in the palace of the Bishop of Salamanca. His wife, Doña Carmen Franco, was present at this lunch, as well as General Luis Orgaz, Director of Military Training, and Nicholas Franco, brother of the General and Political Secretary in the Foreign Ministry of the Junta. The table conversation was about an offensive which Franco had decided to launch against Madrid on 5 November, later postponed till 8 November, under the command of General Mola. The Spanish Nationalists were full of hope after the capture of Toledo on 27 September by General Varela, the fall of Oviedo and successes on the outskirts of Madrid between 6 and 29 October. Canaris reserved his opinions until he was alone with Franco.

He then informed Franco of the total aid supplied to the Republican Government, according to *Abwehr* reports, by foreign governments. It was a disturbing report. The Soviet Union, the Comintern and European countries had been active, and an estimated 50,000 volunteers had arrived in Spain for the International

Brigades. Military trucks, guns, machine-guns, tanks, aircraft and ammunition were flowing in from France and Russia. Canaris named 8 Russian supply ships which had passed through the Dardanelles. Among these, for example, the *Kurak* had brought from the Black Sea to the port of Barcelona 40 trucks, 12 armoured cars, 6 pieces of artillery, 4 aircraft, 700 tons of ammunitions and 1,500 tons of foodstuffs. The *Komsomol* by the same route brought 50 trucks, 5 aircraft, 8 tanks, 2,000 tons of ammunition and equipment, 1,000 tons of food, and 100 tons of medical supplies. Admiral Canaris urged that this was a considerable quantity and that General Franco should appeal for aid to Rome and Berlin. Franco realized that the International Brigades and the flow of foreign arms had created a new situation.

This began [he said] as a reaction of the army against anarchy, the Popular Front and the threat of a red revolution. Now international mercenaries are trying to impose on Spain a foreign ideology and the rule of Moscow. We have so far fought this war with the existing army, the Carlists and the Falangists. Now I must conscript an army in the provinces that we govern.

Canaris observed that Franco could only equip this new army from Italy and Germany. He felt that Franco was ill at ease and that this determined Nationalist was anxious not to accept or ask for a larger effort by Italy and Germany. He hastened to assure Franco that while Hitler might ask for some economic concessions in return for his aid, he would insist on nothing that might impinge on Spanish independence. He interpreted the German Government's view to Franco as follows: 'In Berlin, since Franco-Soviet support for the Republicans is growing, we do not think that your troops are fighting on land or in the air in an effective fashion. The *Wehrmacht* considers that this hesitant and methodical conduct of battle, failing as it does to exploit favourable circumstances, weakens your gains.'

'I cannot exterminate the other side or destroy towns, agriculture, industrial installations or means of production', replied Franco. 'That is why I cannot hurry. If I made haste, I would be a bad Spaniard. If I made haste, I would not be a patriot and I would be behaving like a foreigner.'

'I know,' agreed Canaris, 'but in Berlin they do not reason in that way. A swift seizure of Madrid would be politically decisive, because it would soon lead to recognition of the National Government by Berlin, Rome and certainly Lisbon and would be the one result that would justify to Hitler comprehensive military aid.'

'Give me aircraft, give me artillery, give me tanks and ammunition, give me your diplomatic support and I will be very grateful,' replied Franco. 'I have already said this to the Italians and I repeat it to Herr Hitler. But above all, do not require me to hurry. Don't force me to win at any cost, because that would mean a larger number of Spaniards killed, greater destruction and consequently a less firm basis for my government. I will occupy Spain town by town, village by village, and one railway line after another. Nothing will oblige me to change the pace of my programme. There may be less glory in it, but there will be a greater peace at the end of it. We are sure to take Madrid soon, but if we don't succeed we will try again later and we will succeed then.'

Admiral Canaris shared this outlook and knew that Franco was haunted by the horrors of civil war. This programme of reclamation and consolidation seemed to him more humane and wise and more beneficial in the long term. For the duration of the Civil War, as we shall see, Canaris supported Franco's policy, even against the Nazi leadership and the Italians when they threatened to abandon Franco if he did not accept their demands.

At that time Canaris explained to Franco the German conditions for increased aid in the air. He said that Göring intended to send to Spain the following military formations: one group of bomber aircraft; one group of fighters; one squadron of long-range reconnaissance aircraft; one squadron of short-range reconnaissance aircraft; two signals companies; two companies of engineers; three batteries of heavy anti-aircraft. The German proposal was:

a) That the German formations in Spain be placed under a German commander, who will be the sole adviser to General Franco in matters concerning the German air corps and responsible to General Franco only for its entire activities. Outwardly the appearance of a Spanish command would be preserved.

b) That all German units already in Spain be attached to this German air corps.

c) That the German air bases in Spain be adequately protected, if necessary, by infantry reinforcements.

d) That the conduct of both land and air operations be more regular, active and co-ordinated, having in view a more rapid occupation of the ports which Russia might utilize to increase its reinforcements.

e) If General Franco subscribes to these conditions we intend to increase German military aid.

Admiral Canaris explained that Hitler was willing to create this German air corps, which would be known as the Condor Legion and would be commanded by General Hugo Sperrle, but there would be no question of sending army 'volunteers' for the war on land. Marshal von Blomberg was opposed to that and had succeeded in convincing Hitler on that point. Canaris assured Franco that as soon as Madrid fell, Germany would recognize the Nationalist Government and would send a Chargé d'affaires whom Hitler had already nominated, Lieutenant-General Wilhelm Faupel. Canaris added: 'Faupel is a soldier in the Prussian mould, an entire believer in National-Socialist ideas. He has been chosen for this mission principally because in the Great War he commanded the Bavarian regiment in which Hitler served as a corporal.'

The result of these conversations between Franco and Canaris was not long awaited. The Condor Legion took shape, though it was not completely formed till the end of December 1936. On 18 November, although Franco had suffered a setback and had not been able to take Madrid, the German and Italian Governments nevertheless recognized his Government, and General Faupel was sent to Salamanca on 28 November to establish diplomatic relations after the withdrawal of the German Chargé d'affaires in Madrid.

The first contact between Generals Franco and Faupel was not a success. Canaris had hinted that although Faupel spoke Spanish he was not a man with an affinity for the Latin races. Franco mistrusted this 'Prussian Nazi', and with reason. Faupel was a man of limited outlook, arrogant and without finesse. Faupel came away from his first audience in a pessimistic frame of mind, reporting that Franco was 'an engaging personality, whose open and courteous manners were attractive, but whose military capacity and experience are not equal to the conduct of operations at the present juncture.'

According to the report which Faupel sent to the Ministry of Foreign Affairs in Berlin on 10 December he had given a series of lectures to Franco: 'the Spaniards must look after their weapons better', . . . 'the training of officers, NCOs and other ranks, which is very bad, must be energetically organized', . . . 'we must ask for a combat unit to be sent to Spain which could act as a spearhead before the enemy rallies'. When Field-Marshal von Blomberg showed him this report, Canaris frowned. He knew Franco well and realized that this would not improve German-Spanish relations. He would have to return to Spain to put things right, though this would not be easy.

Canaris had just returned from a converence in Rome with the Italian Foreign Minister, Count Ciano, on 6 December, at which General Roatta, the Intelligence Chief, and the Chiefs of the Armed Forces and Fascist Militia were present. Canaris with the German Military Attaché in Rome represented Germany. The object of this conference had been 'to examine events in Spain and work out a methodical and effective programme for the future'. In the course of the meeting it had been agreed that neither country would send major formations to Spain, but Faupel was now putting forward a recommendation 'that Franco be urged to take at least a German division and an Italian division'. After another discussion with Blomberg, Canaris let Faupel know that the Condor Legion would be sent to Spain but not a combat division as well. Italy, however, was to go further than Germany and ignore the Rome decisions. After the second week in December Mussolini began to send well-equipped Fascist militia to co-operate with the Spanish army. These were volunteers, of whom about half had seen action in the Abyssinian war. By 15 January 1937, these troops had the numerical strength of one infantry division.

The work that Canaris had to do in the period of German-Spanish co-operation was of a delicate and complex character. It was not only a matter of providing Franco with the Condor Legion. Arms had also to be bought for Nationalist Spain in Czechoslovakia, the United States and other places. Sometimes Germany had to extend foreign credits to the Nationalist Government, which repaid them through London, where Franco had some financial backing.

Some of this business was handled between Canaris and the Spanish Embassy in Berlin, with the counsellor, Señor Vargas, and the military attaché, Count Roccamora, old friends of his, or with Franco's arms agent in London, Augusto Miranda, also an old friend. The friendship between Franco and Canaris deepened at this time and was ultimately to play a significant rôle during the Second World War.

7
Setting up the intelligence

Admiral Canaris expressed surprise on taking over command of the *Abwehr* at the complete void in overseas intelligence, especially in the United States. He put his views to Colonel Hans Piekenbrock, Head of Section I, Espionage.

'When the United States decided to support the Allies in the Great War their powerful war potential was decisive. I am convinced that it would be just as effective if they intervened in a Second World War. We must therefore build up a reliable network at the earliest moment in the United States. I attach great importance to this. The officers charged with this network will have to set it up without haste and with the greatest care, choosing appropriate people and giving them a thorough training.'

'It will take years,' sighed Piekenbrock, 'to choose the right people and get our communications right by messenger and radio.'

'I know, but that is why we must not lose time.'

'Then Admiral, I suggest Lieutenant-Commander Erich Pfeiffer on the staff of the North Sea Command at Wilhelmshaven.'

'I agree. He is the man we need. Let him make a visit of technical reconnaissance to the United States and inform himself on the American navy and air force. After that I have no wish that Pfeiffer should remain at Wilhelmshaven. It is a small town, a cantonment. Move him to Hamburg.'

In fact there were *Abwehr* intelligence branches in Hamburg, Bremen, Kiel and Wilhelmshaven, all instructed to obtain information on five points:

1) Are the United States taking measures in their armed forces, in industry or elsewhere that suggest preparations for a war?

2) Are there in existence any secret agreements between the United States and other powers directed against Germany or that could work to the detriment of Germany?

3) What weapons and new devices do the American armed

forces possess? What are their newest aircraft and warships in service and what new designs do they have?

4) Reconnaissance of naval bases that would be important in time of war.

5) Close reconnaissance of the American armed forces, their organization, effectives, equipment and dispositions.

Piekenbrock, Groscurth and Bamler selected naval officers for preference to work in America. Canaris gave them these directives:

It will take several years to create this network. Having regard to the multiplicity of targets our agents must be up to the mark and must have already or expect to have access to secret material. They must be particularly discreet. It is quality not numbers that counts.

They must be of as high a social standing as possible.

The same applies to couriers acting in liaison with important sources, the more so since they will not have recourse to invisible inks or use of the post.

I wish above all that staff officers, agents and couriers receive intensive training. They will not know each others' identities unless that is made unavoidable by their duties.

Remember that the recruited personnel will come to us with no idea of secret-service work nor of the risks that they run from other intelligence services. They must be taught rules of general behaviour and what their conduct should be in special circumstances. They must be given a sense of security so that they go about their work in a calm atmosphere.

You will only employ Germans or German women with their free consent.

See particularly that our handlers gain the entire confidence of their agents. Those who do not succeed in this are to be removed.

Concentrate in Germany on those who go frequently to America or who have relatives there, such as sailors, artists, industrialists and businessmen. These will open our activities in America among friends in the German-American community.

When I speak of America, I do not only mean the United States. I want centres in Canada, Mexico, Brazil and the Argentine, without running into serious difficulties and without risks for the participants. These centres will offer better opportunity for recruiting agents in the United States than will those in Germany.

We must find men in countries neighbouring the United States who can visit the United States often, even in time of war. The best of these must be couriers.

We must find in Canada, Mexico, Brazil and other countries men who will act as post-boxes. It will be essential that in time of war our agents in the United States can send their reports to addresses in neutral countries, who can then by post or courier forward them to us. These will be indispensable in wartime unless we can set up a radio transmitter network. I have already asked for a study of this problem.

I hope and wish that there may be no war and especially not with the United States. You know that the agents of both East and West swarm in Germany and cases of treasonable intelligence have been numerous in the past two years. We must make out a picture of the military potential of the great powers as a matter of urgency, as our Government has no very precise ideas on this subject.

It is deplorable, for instance, that our intelligence knows nothing exact about the armed forces of a great power like the United States.

Devote yourselves entirely to this task. We can perhaps within two years possess at least an embryonic intelligence service on a world scale. The danger of the present vacuum in intelligence is the greater since we cannot, because of it, put our own government on its guard against a policy of risks.

The vacuum did not last for long and by 1937 Canaris was able to present a fairly satisfactory picture of the American armed forces, though the efficiency of the *Abwehr* was handicapped by duplication of activities. Colonel Reile notes that despite the agreement reached between Canaris and the Reich Security Office, other German organizations began to encroach into the field of espionage in America – the *Gestapo*, the *SD*, the Organization of Germans Abroad, the Labour Front and special agents of the Air Ministry. Some of these worked with a blind zeal, came to know each other and so compromised their own security. This situation brought about setbacks and some tragic results, when agents of the *Abwehr* paid with their lives for the indiscretion of others. These setbacks did Germany great harm in the foreign political field.

However, one notable success was achieved by the *Abwehr* through an operator in Berlin known by the name of Dr Ranken, who worked with a South African agent in New York called Frederick Joubert Duquesne. Duquesne, established there as a specialist in aeronautics, was utilizing the stewards of the Norddeutscher Lloyd Steamship Line as his secret couriers. It was one of these stewards in fact who made the acquaintance in a New York bar of a German-American working in the Norden optical instrument factory. This man furnished Duquesne with two blueprints of the Norden bomb-sight, a highly secret instrument being developed for the US air force. Although at first sight in Berlin these blueprints were pronounced to be a fraud, Dr Ranken, who knew that no money had been demanded for them, determined to investigate further. He made a voyage to New York and met the technician in question, Hermann Lang, who was working on US air force projects. The upshot was that a series of blueprints reached the *Abwehr* in Berlin, out of which it was possible to copy to perfection the Norden bomb-sight and put its advanced design at the disposal of the *Luftwaffe*.

The result of this espionage operation was an instrument described to Canaris by General Udet of the Air Staff as 'of inestimable value to us'. Hermann Lang was persuaded by his *Abwehr* contacts to take a summer holiday in Germany during 1938, so that he could in security answer a long series of technical questions on the Norden bomb-sight for the *Luftwaffe* experts. At the end of this visit he declined an offer of employment in Germany and returned to the United States. Canaris described Lang as a man who was not a traitor, but whose original German nationality had asserted itself more strongly than that which he had adopted. Lang would not take money for his services.

But Canaris thought that treason was evident in the case of another agent who brought in highly valuable material, the French naval cadet, Henri Aubert. This case was handled by Dr Fritz Unterberg Gibhardt, who in October 1937 was called into the office of his Chief, the senior *Abwehr* officer in Bremen. He entrusted Gibhardt in the strictest secrecy with the task of meeting and reporting on a man who had approached the German Embassy in Paris with an offer to sell 'certain secret documents of great interest'. The case had been referred to Canaris by the Ministry of Foreign Affairs, which feared its diplomatic personnel becoming involved with an *agent provocateur*. Henri Aubert, the man in question, was a French naval officer, aged twenty-three. Canaris's intention was that this unknown person should be contacted in a neutral country, where the documents which he was to offer could be safely examined and valued against the high price that he was asking for them. Lieutenant Commander Gibhardt decided to offer Aubert an appointment at an hotel in Antwerp, which took place at 11 AM on a Sunday morning late in October 1937.

A subsequent report by Gibhardt records in detail his impressions of this man, whom he was told to observe closely, in case the affair proved to be a deception. He was at first surprised to find a second person in the hotel where they met. Aubert was a tall young man of good appearance, but beside him stood a young woman, whose hard face and possessive, dominating behaviour made it plain that she was the real manager of the affair. Aubert himself showed every sign of nervousness at the gamble in which he was risking his life. He finally produced two suitcases, opened them and invited the German Intelligence Officer to examine their contents – French official papers, most of which were marked *secret*. These were service reports of the French navy, and the statistical material included the report on the trials of the submarine *Surcouf*, the most modern of its kind. The German produced the money that had been demanded for these papers by Aubert, discussed the possibility of a second delivery of the same sort and outlined the precautions to be taken for a second meeting. Aubert and his companion quietly left Antwerp for Paris. The suitcases of papers were taken to the German Consulate-General in Antwerp for safe transfer to Germany.

Early in November 1937 Lieutenant-Commander Gibhardt was called from Bremen to Berlin to report. An *Abwehr* officer met him at Tempelhof airport and accompanied him to the Defence Ministry buildings. As soon as they were on their way into Berlin, his companion exclaimed:

'Congratulations! Do you know what Admiral Canaris said when he was informed of the value and interest of the documents that you obtained in Antwerp? He said – "Gibhardt can take a year's leave. He has brought us in documents, whose value is equivalent to a year of research".'

Canaris was beaming with satisfaction when he received them in his office and wanted a closer account of the operation. 'Who is this naval cadet who is willing to betray his country?' he asked.

When he had heard the circumstances, his face clouded and he said with a gesture of disdain:

'Let us be glad that this young woman exists: for without her the young man would never have come to us. But as a naval officer I am disgusted. This is what women do to a man and you can understand why I do not want women among our agents.'

The operation continued. Henri Aubert brought in quantities of documents after a visit to the Far East, then after being posted to Toulon more material, and finally he provided through a post-box address in Belgium, a few pages at a time, the French naval cipher book, until the *Abwehr* realized that it was in possession of the entire French naval code.

Aubert was at last discovered to be a traitor by the French Deuxième Bureau, arrested, tried before a court martial, and condemned to death for treason. He was executed by a firing squad at Toulon. The case of Aubert was long remembered by Admiral Canaris and cited by him as a classic instance of the pernicious influence of a woman on a man of weak character.

I have mentioned these two cases – it would be possible to fill several volumes with the case histories of the *Abwehr* – to show what many historians appear to forget. Admiral Canaris was head of an intelligence service and as such was active on behalf of the German armed forces. He was not merely the drawing-room conspirator that some have made him out to be. At the same time, it is evident that politics and diplomacy after 1938 began increasingly to preoccupy his thoughts, and that he tended after that date to leave the conduct of espionage and counter-espionage to his Heads of Sections, though never ceasing to interest himself in their activities.

8

The Tuchachevsky affair

At the beginning of his career as head of the *Abwehr* Canaris found himself a house to rent in the residential quarter of Dahlem in South Berlin. A few houses away in the Dollestrasse lived Reinhard Heydrich, while Himmler was only a quarter of a mile further off. Erika Canaris was delighted to meet the former naval cadet again and became a friend of Lena Heydrich who recalls the musical evenings that were resumed at both houses.

My husband and the Admiral never spoke of politics in my presence. When we were all together it was literature, philosophy, the arts, travel and above all music that was discussed. My husband and Madame Canaris could talk for hours about Haydn and Mozart and this was a real relaxation for Reinhard who worked day and night finding only a little time off for fencing, riding and flying.

She did not allude to his habit of frequenting Berlin night-clubs.

In the spring of 1936, the year in which the German army marched into the Rhineland, Canaris bought a small villa near the Schlachtensee Lake in the suburb of Zehlendorf. The Heydrichs found Zehlendorf very pleasant and they too moved into the same district. Several other personalities lived not far away. Among them were Colonel Hans Oster, Count Wolf Heinrich von Helldorf, Police Commissioner of Berlin, Hans-Bernd Gisevius of the Ministry of the Interior, Arthur Nebe of the Criminal Police, and the Chief of the *SD* Foreign Branch, Walther Schellenberg.

I found and questioned Schellenberg in Italy a few months before his death. He was a man of good family, intelligent and well educated; he had been an athlete, handsome and elegant, and attractive to women. He had become a close friend of Lena Heydrich and discussed with her his own sentimental attachments, while she found him a better listener than her volatile husband. This friendship led to a terrible scene with Schellenberg, when Heydrich's ferocious jealousy erupted after Lena had gone out boating alone with Walther on one of the Berlin lakes. Schellenberg gave his solemn oath that there was no cause for complaint, but thereafter he avoided being alone with Lena Heydrich, though continuing to play bridge with the pair of them and going with them to concerts and theatres. It was at the Heydrich villa that he met Canaris and was fascinated by the Admiral's personality. Schellenberg liked to play croquet on the lawns at Canaris's home, or to discuss service matters as they rode together in the morning in the *Tiergarten*.

At the beginning of January 1937, while out riding with him, Schellenberg turned the conversation to the existing relations between Berlin and Moscow. He discussed with Canaris Stalin's recent action in restoring traditional ranks in the Red Army and the creation of the title 'Marshal of the Soviet Union'. He mentioned the youngest of these marshals, Mikhail Tuchachevsky. Canaris said that he had never met Tuchachevsky, though he had heard a lot about him from German generals who had been his hosts when he visted Germany in 1922 with a group of Russian officers to watch the *Reichswehr* manoeuvres. Tuchachevsky had also done a staff course for Russian officers in the *Reichswehr*. Other German officers had met him in 1923 on a joint German-Russian military commission.

'Yes', said Schellenberg, 'Tuchachevsky knows our country well. He has been five times to Berlin between 1925 and 1932. He is on friendly terms with a certain number of our generals. He seems to be a Germanophil'.

'He made an excellent impression on Blomberg', remarked Canaris, 'probably less on account of his military ability than his manners, which are less crude than those of his fellow officers.'

Several days later Heydrich found an occasion to ask Canaris to dinner, after which he spoke about Russia, declared his own ignorance of its political and military institutions and said that he would like to be better informed, especially about the commanders of the Red Army. He knew that Admiral Canaris had easy access to the files of the General Staff, he said, and would like to borrow for a few days the files on certain Russian generals who had visited Germany before the National-Socialist era. Heydrich said that Tuchachevsky interested him particularly. Canaris pricked up his ears, remembering the conversation with Schellenberg. What were the *SS* looking for? Were they out to compromise some German generals known to be hostile to the Nazis? Canaris gave evasive answers, but Heydrich was pressing, and only his adroitness enabled Canaris to terminate the conversation without embarrassment. Yet Canaris could easily have satisfied Heydrich's curiosity with some fresh reports that he had received from London and Paris on the movements of Marshal Tuchachevsky. A year of official contact with Heydrich had taught Canaris to be wary of this twisted personality. Heydrich did not conceal his disappointment.

'I know, Admiral, that espionage and military counter-espionage are your exclusive field,' he said, 'but the Führer wishes to have precise information on the political plane about the Red Army commanders and he has ordered me to furnish him with this information.'

'I am sorry,' replied Canaris, 'but without an exact and mandatory instruction written by the Führer, I cannot make the files of the General Staff available'.

Heydrich looked suddenly cold with fury, after which he mastered his emotions and replied:

'All right, Admiral, I will report to the Führer'.

Canaris heard no more about the files on Russia for several days. Then he was told one morning that a fire had broken out on the previous night in the offices of the *Abwehr* and the General Staff Central Office, causing considerable damage and confusion. When he arrived at the Bandlerstrasse, Canaris saw to his astonishment that the fire had occurred in the Russian Affairs section, which contained the personal files on generals of the Red Army. The *Gestapo* were busy on an enquiry into the incident and the secrecy of the *Wehrmacht* records was evidently breached. There could be only one culprit, he thought, and that was Heydrich. Canaris was both furious and appalled. What could he do? Should he complain to Hitler and be disbelieved? He thought it better to wait and see.

Months passed and Canaris may have ceased to think about this incident when on the afternoon of 11 June 1937, he found on his desk the text of an official communiqué from Moscow:

Cases have been referred to a special tribunal concerning Tuchachevsky, Yakir, Oborevich, Kork, Eidemann, Feldmann, Primakov and Putna, arrested at various times by the Commissariat for the Interior.

The detained persons are accused of breaking their oath of military duty, of treason against the Soviet Union and its people and of treason against the Red Army of the workers and peasants.

In the course of preliminary hearings it has been established that the accused, together with Gamarrik who recently committed suicide, were engaged in activities against the state in concert with the military leadership of a foreign state that is politically opposed to the Soviet Union. Working for the military intelligence of that state, the accused were betraying to it military information about the Red Army and carrying out acts of sabotage to weaken Soviet armed strength and so prepare the way, in the event of military aggression, for the defeat of the Red Army and the re-establishment of big landed estates and capitalists in the Soviet Union.

All the accused have admitted that they are entirely guilty of the accusations made against them.

The hearing of this case will take place today, 11 June, *in camera* before a Special Tribunal of the Supreme Court under the chairmanship of the President of the Court, Ulrich. The Tribunal will consist of Defence Commissar Egorov, Chief of the Air Force, Alksnis, Marshal Budjenny, Marshal Blücher, Chief of General Staff, Chapochnikov, the Commanding Officer of the White Russia Command, Belov, the Commanding Officer of the Leningrad Command, Dybenko, the Commanding Officer the Caucasus Area, Kachirin, the Commander of the 6th Cossack Cavalry Corps, Goriatchev.

On the following day Canaris found another brief Moscow communiqué on his desk, stating that Tuchachevsky, Yakir, Oborevich, Kork, Eidemann, Feldmann, Primakov and Putna had been executed by firing squad. It was later said that they had been shot in the neck in the cells of the Soviet *NKVD*.

Admiral Canaris could not yet know the full truth, but he sensed a connection between the Russian communiqués and his own conversations with Schellenberg and Heydrich in January. What rôle might the *SS* have played in this affair?

How in fact was this most sinister police machination of our time set in motion? Canaris only knew a little of the background, but his suspicions about the Tuchachevsky affair corresponded with the truth. We know know more since the revelations made on 27 October 1961, by Alexander Chelepin and Nikita Khruschev at the 22nd Congress of the Russian Communist Party.

In 1936 Stalin was highly suspicious about the loyalty of the Red Army generals. On 20 November 1935, he had conferred the rank of Marshal of the Soviet Union on Voroshilov, Blücher, Budjenny, Egorov and Tuchachevsky, who at forty-two was the youngest of them all. But Stalin perceived among them, and especially in Tuchachevsky, also the most popular of them, a sort of class consciousness and independence of mind which much perturbed him. The Red Army did not seem to be sufficiently integrated with the Communist Party., Whe would happen if the marshals challenged his authority? Future relations between Soviet Russia and Nazi Germany were on the agenda of the Supreme Soviet. Stalin was inclined to seek an *entente* with Hitler, especially as he sensed the danger of an impending armed conflict. He wanted to turn Germany against the West and use that country as his ice-breaker against the capitalist world. It was therefore necessary to convince Hitler that he had less to fear from Russia than from the West. If he felt sure of Russia, Hitler would no doubt throw the *Wehrmacht* against Austria and Czechoslovakia and unleash a war of attrition with the West, in which Russia could intervene at a chosen time.

This was not, however, the reasoning of the Red Army chiefs, and Marshal Tuchachevsky wanted a preventive war against Germany. He did not conceal his anxiety at official conferences about the German rearmament programme and spoke up before the Supreme Soviet. Stalin was furious. Who was master of the Kremlin? Who directed Soviet policy? The Russian dictator feared a double threat: at home, a military coup; abroad, a preventive war against Hitler, which Stalin certainly did not want, as he thought it would tend to unite the capitalist countries with Hitler against the 'Bolshevist aggressor'. Stalin was particularly irritated by a recent pamphlet by Trotsky in exile containing this criticism of him: 'Stalin's fatal policy makes it easy for the Bonapartist elements. If there were a military conflict some Tuchachevsky would have no great difficulty in overthrowing the régime with the aid of all the anti-Soviet elements inside Russia'.

What could Stalin do? He was more and more convinced that certain 'Bonapartist' generals were plotting against him. He could not dismiss him, as the whole Red Army would side with Tuchachevsky. Stalin found the most cunning means to his end: he would have the army itself condemn Tuchachevsky after furnishing it with 'proofs' of his 'treason'. He would have to produce such incriminating evidence against Marshal Tuchachevsky that Voroshilov and the other army leaders would not defend him; he must therefore discover something like a conspiracy with Trotskyist elements and the German military chiefs.

Stalin began by reshuffling his police. He dismissed Yagoda and made Yagov Commissioner General of Secret Police (*NKVD*). He disclosed to him his suspicions of the Red Army in general and

Tuchachevsky in particular. He charged Yagov to proceed with an enquiry. 'I have had enough chatter', said Stalin. 'I want to see the truth. Be sure to realize one thing. If you want to retain this post, don't come to me and say that there is no such conspiracy. Bring me proof that it exists.'

Yagov had understood that to save his own life he must find the evidence Stalin obviously wanted. He turned to the Czarist General Nicolas Skoblin who was living in Paris with the former Petrograd ballerina, Nadia Plevitskaya, as his wife. Skoblin was the nominal adjutant to General Miller, Chief of the World Organization of White Russian Officers in Exile. In fact Skoblin had become vulnerable to Moscow: his wife had always worked for the Soviet Secret Police, though Skoblin remained a sworn enemy of the Red Army and especially of Tuchachevsky for having supported the Revolution. Skoblin, in furtherance of the idea that it would be possible to displace Stalin with German aid, maintained relations with Heydrich, and this was known to Yagov. At the beginning of December 1936 Yagov sent two agents to Paris to make a bargain with Skoblin. These two, Sarovsky and Spiegelglass, were to arrange for General Miller to be eliminated and replaced by Skoblin, who was to provide evidence of collusion between Tuchachevsky and the Trotskyists, and with certain members of the German High Command as well. Skoblin saw the chance of destroying Tuchachevsky and removing the best men from the army; the Germans, he imagined, could be convinced that this would improve their chances of defeating the Red Army. He aimed ultimately at a German-Russian alliance with himself at the head of a new government in Moscow. Skoblin drew up a tendentious report on certain conversations alleged to have taken place with British military leaders in London while Tuchachevsky was representing the Soviet Union at the state funeral of King George V, and in Paris where he met General Gamelin, Chief of the French General Staff. Skoblin went with this report to Berlin to meet Heydrich secretly in a private room at the Hotel Adlon. Schellenberg relates that after this meeting he was summoned by Heydrich.

I have never seen Heydrich looking so happy. He told me that he had received sensational reports, according to which Tuchachevsky had been discussing a preventive war against Germany with the British and French. Heydrich added that when the Führer was told of these reports he would be furious and would suspend all present attempts at a rapprochement with Moscow.... This report shows, though not absolutely clearly (we can always arrange that, however), that Tuchachevsky has been in close contact with certain of the *Wehrmacht* chiefs. We can show that these contacts have as their purpose a double military *Putsch*, in Moscow to get rid of Stalin, in Berlin to get rid of Hitler. We can kill two birds with one stone. We can decapitate the Red Army and eliminate those *Wehrmacht* men who are still opposed to National-Socialism. You have understood me, Schellenberg?

During his reconstruction of this episode Schellenberg told me:

At the time I did not grasp exactly what this conspiracy was that Heydrich was preparing, but Heydrich seemed to see quite clearly what he was doing. On Christmas Eve, Heydrich and Himmler went to see Hitler. Heydrich told me that Hess and Bormann were present when he unfolded his plan. This was to produce sufficient documents indicating that Marshal Tuchachevsky and certain of his comrades in the Red Army were conspiring with certain generals of the German High Command to take over power in their respective countries. A way would have to be found to place these documents in Stalin's hands. Heydrich told me that Hitler was quickly persuaded that this would be a useful operation, but insisted that the German generals involved must not be made to appear to be plotting against himself directly. Evidently Hitler did not want to have such an explosive proposition put on paper, even for the purpose of political deception.

Heydrich then gathered Schellenberg, the *SS* General Hermann Behrens, Wilhelm Höttl of the *SD* and Alfred Naujocks, another *SD* man of whom we shall hear more later. Heydrich expounded the outline of the plan and said that it was necessary, if documents were to be forged, to possess the General Staff files on past contacts between Tuchachevsky and the German generals. For that, it would be necessary to have the assistance of Admiral Canaris. Schellenberg was to make the first approach and Heydrich would follow it up. Behrens and Naujocks would then be able to prepare the documents and give them the appearance of authenticity. Heydrich concluded:

'Photocopies of these documents will be sold to the Russians at a high price, and we will make it appear that they have been stolen from the files of the *SD*. We will also create the impression that we are investigating the German side of the conspiracy, but without mentioning names, as the Führer is opposed to that. Stalin will break Tuchachevsky, because he will receive this dossier through his own Secret Service and will be convinced that it is authentic.'

What Heydrich did not suspect was that Stalin was not really the dupe but in fact the moving force behind the whole machination. As we have seen, Canaris did not comply with Heydrich's wishes and did not release the General Staff papers to him. Hitler had given orders that the General Staff were to be kept in absolute ignorance of the operation for fear that some German general would put Tuchachevsky on his guard. So Heydrich could not compel Canaris to produce the papers, but he organized instead a secret operation, breaking open the filing cabinets of the *Abwehr* and obtaining as many documents as they could find. The audacity of this action amazed even the dozen *SD* men taking part in it, who played the rôle of burglars. The team was formed in three sections, each with an expert of the Criminal Investigation Department. As soon as completed, the operation was to be camouflaged by a fire, that would cover the traces by creating the maximum disorder. The *SD* gangs were perhaps too conscientious; for the fire spread rapidly and a large quantity of documents was destroyed by the flames or the hoses of the Berlin fire brigade.

There are several versions of the next phase of the operation. The dossier consisted of more than a dozen pages of letters purporting to be the reports of a German counter-espionage agent directed to investigate the contacts between the German General Staff and the Red Army. They contained transcripts of faked telephone conversations between German staff officers; intercepted letters; fragments of coded messages. The choicest specimens were a letter appearing to have been written by Tuchachevsky himself and an imaginary report by Canaris to Hitler. Yagov would not have to rely on the apparent authenticity of the documents, which Voroshilov might doubt. He would be provided with a warning from a foreign personality whose name would carry weight in the Kremlin. For this purpose President Benes in Prague was misled by false reports from various agents and informed the Russian Minister in Prague, M. Alexandrovsky, of a conspiracy against his master. The warning and the forged documents thus reached Moscow about the same time.

The killing of Tuchachevsky was the beginning of a vast purge in the Red Army. Of the 9 judges who sat on the Special Tribunal which tried Tuchachevsky, 7 were shot in the course of the next few weeks, among them General Alksnis and Marshals Egorov and Blücher. The purge struck down 3 of the 5 marshals, 11 defence commissars and 75 out of the 80 members of the War Council, 13 out of 15 army commanders, 57 out of 85 corps commanders, 110 of the 195 divisional commanders, 200 of the 406 brigade commanders. It is estimated that 30,000 officers were slaughtered.

For a long time Admiral Canaris did not know the details of the operation devised against Tuchachevsky. But henceforth, partly aware of them, he ceased to regard the *SS* with anything but a severely critical eye. He was not astonished at the execution of Tuchachevsky knowing him to have been guilty of some sort of treason.

Admiral Canaris related to Lahousen that he knew from two reports that reached him from London and Paris that Tuchachevsky did not recoil from revealing secrets of Russian military strength to the British and the French in order to draw them on to the side of the Soviet Union in a preventive war against Germany. Skoblin's forgeries were not entirely devoid of truth, although the Czarist general had embellished his information. The British were amazed at Tuchachevsky's figures, which did not resemble the estimates of the British Secret Service. They listened to their Russian guest with polite scepticism. Canaris noted these occurrences in his diary and spoke about them to Major Oster, but did not inform Heydrich or Blomberg.

Tuchachevsky was also coolly received by General Gamelin in Paris, who declared that France would not forsake her defensive attitude until Germany had committed an act of aggression. He recorded Tuchachevsky's reply in his memoirs.

'But then it will be too late!' exclaimed Tuchachevsky.

'A preventive war would be contrary to the principles of French policy', replied Gamelin. 'It would not be approved by the majority of public opinion'.

Canaris told Lahousen: 'Tuchachevsky returned to Russia deeply disappointed. All his revelations to the British and the French had been of no avail. Stalin did not know exactly what game Tuchachevsky had played and had him shot for an offence invented by Heydrich'. This conversation with Lahousen took place in the spring of 1939, and Canaris added: 'There is no limit to the murderous folly of a frightened dictator. He will always find a sinister figure like Yagov to execute his enemies and an underling like Khruschev to applaud the deed. Take care, Lahousen. God knows if our "Emil"* will not one day act like Josef Stalin!'

---

*A precautionary name for Adolf Hitler.

9
Hitler's master-plan

Canaris was disquieted in the autumn of 1937 by growing discord between the German army and the National-Socialist Party. The atmosphere was like that on the Night of the Long Knives, 30 June, 1934. There was a storm in the air. He had heard on 6 November of an ultra-secret meeting called in the Reichs Chancellery on the previous day by Hitler, which lasted for four hours. Those present were Field-Marshal von Blomberg, General Göring, General von Fritsch, Admiral Raeder, Baron von Neurath, and Colonel Friedrich Hossbach, Military Aide to the Führer, and also his liaison officer with the *Wehrmacht*. It had evidently been an important meeting, but nothing said was known outside the small circle of those present twenty-four hours later. Canaris believed that serious military matters had been discussed. As Chief of Intelligence he ought to be informed, but Blomberg and Fritsch remained silent and grave-faced. Canaris could not hope for enlightenment from Admiral Raeder as they rarely met. He could not approach Göring and he did not feel that he knew Neurath well enough to question the Foreign Minister. Hossbach, he was aware, shared his own misgivings about Nazi policy, but his contacts with him were limited to service formalities.

On 11 November, six days after the mysterious meeting, Canaris was in the office of General Ludwig Beck. For several months he had been forming sympathetic relations with the Chief of the General Staff, whose wisdom, moderation and intellectual qualities he much admired. Canaris knew that this exceptional officer of the old Prussian school had expressed fears privately to a friend on becoming Chief of the General Staff that Germany was being dragged into a war for which she was not prepared.

Canaris did not find this outlook strange in a senior officer whose duty it was to be ready for a war of offensive or defensive character. He himself thought exactly the same. What is more, he knew that Beck was a man who kept a sharp eye on his country's foreign policy and did not look only at the military picture. As

Hitler transformed his government more and more into a dictatorship; as he forsook the legality and the morality of a civilized state; as the levelling of the National-Socialist party destroyed other organizations, Canaris saw Beck attempt to shield the *Wehrmacht* from Nazi influences. They had the same problems.

On 11 November, 1937, Canaris felt that Beck had something serious to tell him. Canaris was not so naive as to expose his own thinking before hearing that of the Chief of Staff. Beck, less subtle though highly intelligent, put an end to formality by uttering this key phrase: 'Hitler is leading Germany into the grave and he must be stopped before it is too late.'

Canaris then played a card himself: 'If Hitler's policy showed itself to be in favour of war and the German people knew as much, it would be easy to overthrow the government and change this régime. But does Hitler really want war? If the answer is yes, there can be no hesitation, and every effort must be made to remove him from power.'

The two men understood each other. Beck then drew a file out of his desk. He explained that it contained a report on the secret meeting of 5 November 1937, drawn up by Colonel Hossbach. The Colonel evidently thought Hitler's proposals far too serious to be kept secret from the Chief of the General Staff. Beck had been shaken by what he read and he begged Canaris to maintain absolute secrecy about the contents of the report. As Canaris turned over its pages his face became more and more serious. He re-enacted the scene soon afterwards to Major Oster, whose notes have survived, together with the Hossbach report itself. Hitler's preamble was explicit:

The subject of this conference is so important that in another state it would be the occasion for detailed discussion by the Council of Ministers. Because of its exceptional importance I have decided to confide in you alone, under the seal of secrecy.

What I have to tell you is the sum of intensive meditation and experience during the four and a half years since I assumed the direction of this country. My object is to define to you our long-term policy. That is why, if I should disappear, I ask you to regard these reflections as my testament.

Colonel Hossbach remarked: 'Each man held his breath and fixed his eyes on Hitler. Even Göring was tense. What would he tell us?'

Hitler spoke for four hours without pausing and without one of his subordinates thinking of interrupting with a question.

Firstly, he declared that it was necessary to annexe a large area of *Lebensraum* for eighty million Germans. The territory required by the Reich to ensure its self-sufficiency in agriculture could only be in Europe and not in the colonies, just as primary raw materials must be found close to Germany and not overseas. No territory could be acquired without risk and without breaking some resistance. For Germany the question was to know, 'where she can get the maximum of gain for the minimum of risk'.

Hitler then gave a long dissertation about Great Britain and France, the 'sworn enemies' of Germany, saying that the former was on the verge of decadence and could no longer defend its empire with its own resources but only with the aid of other nations. The position of France was less catastrophic as her colonial population could provide additional military strength, but France also had serious internal difficulties and might collapse. Hitler then declared: 'If it is well understood that we must use force, with all the risks that ensue, it remains to say when and how that force will be used.'

Hitler disliked talking from behind a desk. He got up, took several paces and then stood with his legs astride to continue his discourse. He saw three courses of action, he said:

I do not think Italy will seriously object to the elimination of Czechoslovakia. As for her reaction to the Austrian business, it is still too early to forecast that. This will depend mainly on the Duce at the head of the Italian government. The attitude of Poland will depend above all on the rapidity with which we act. She will hardly want to intervene against a victorious Germany with the Russian threat at her rear. We must act very quickly to prevent any intervention by the USSR, though such intervention is hypothetical, with Japan threatening Russia.

In the second instance, if France should be paralysed by social disorders the attack on Czechoslovakia would have to be immediate.

Hitler declared that if France became involved in a Mediterranean conflict, he had the firm intention of profiting by it, 'even in 1938'. As for Spain, 'from Germany's point of view, a complete victory for Franco is not desirable, as it would put an end to Italian intervention in Spain. As long as the Duce is occupied in Spain he will close his eyes to our intervention in Austria and Czechoslovakia. The Mediterranean situation will determine the hour of the offensive against Czechoslovakia.'

Hitler did not seem to envisage Italy as a military ally but aimed to exploit the Axis for a 'lightning attack' which would bring him sufficient territory to support six million more Germans after he had expelled two million Czechs and a million Austrians, including the active Jewish population.

When Hitler had finished speaking there was a heavy silence, so Hossbach noted, in the Führer's gilt and marble office. No one looked at his neighbour. Each knew perfectly well that no expression of doubts would be tolerated. Hitler had decided to solve with the sword what Professor Haushofer had called 'the problem of German's *Lebensraum*'.

According to the Hossbach report, there was then 'a fairly long discussion', lasting a quarter of an hour, 'which sometimes became quite violent, especially when General von Fritsch and Field-Marshal von Blomberg began to quarrel with Göring'.

They urged that it was essential under any circumstance to avoid France and Great Britain entering a war, nor did they exclude the possibility of an attack on Germany by France, even if France was simultaneously at war with Italy. Von Fritsch thought that France could leave twenty divisions on the Italian front and still launch an offensive against Germany with a strong numerical superiority. Blomberg emphasized the weakness of the German fortifications on the Western front, where Germany's four mechanized divisions were not operationally mobile. He thought the Czechoslovak frontier fortifications would make a German attack extremely difficult. Baron von Neurath objected that a war between Italy and France was not so imminent as the Führer appeared to believe, but Hitler retorted that 'in fact something of this sort could happen in the summer of 1938'. Although he waved aside their objections he was sufficiently impressed by them to repeat twice that he did not believe that Great Britain would make war on Germany to preserve the independence of Austria and Czechoslovakia, and therefore neither would France.

Göring at the end of the conference expressed the view that it would be opportune to reduce the German military component in Spain, and while von Blomberg and von Fritsch agreed with this, they thought that German support for Franco against Communism must continue for an indeterminate period. Angry words with Göring ensued until Hitler brusquely cut short all argument, ruling that 'a decision can be made at the proper moment'. Not once in the course of this conference was there mention of the United States and its enormous industrial power – an extraordinary omission.

Canaris finished reading the Hossbach memorandum. His expression showed Beck plainly that Hitler's plans appeared to him sheer madness. He said:

'Hitler will bring about a war in the worst possible conditions, because his whole argument is based on erroneous assessments.'

Beck sighed:

'It will be necessary to break the spell that Hitler has cast on the German people.'

'That is easier said than done', replied Canaris. 'I do not believe that an armed insurrection or a popular revolt has the least chance of happening. The police are in the hands of the *SS* and the Party controls the means of information and propaganda. The majority opinion is favourable to the Führer. How can we bring home to the German people, which wants peace, that Hitler's plans are leading them to the slaughter-house? A revolution from above, whether a conspiracy within the Party or by members of the government, industry and the administration, could not succeed. There remains action by the army, you will tell me, but I am sceptical.'

'You have reason to be,' said General Beck. 'The navy and the air force are strongly infected with the Nazi spirit. The army is less so, but most officers are drawn to the new régime by various considerations: their sense of discipline; their oath of loyalty; their conviction that the army must serve the state, no matter what sort of state. They remember that the Nazi movement saved Germany from Communism and unemployment.'

'We can add that the majority of generals and admirals favour rearmament and have no motive to oppose Hitler as he has so far obtained results. What then can be done?'

'I am going to draw up a memorandum for General von Fritsch,' replied Beck, 'and I will refute point by point the Führer's wild assertions. Then we will consider what is to be done.'

The memorandum, based on the Hossbach record, was presented to von Fritsch on 12 November 1937, but no word came back. This was not surprising. Dr Schacht, former President of the Reichsbank who resigned as Minister of Economics in December 1937, spoke to Canaris about General Beck.

'General Beck', he said, 'is a man of perfect integrity and high attainments, with a wide-ranging knowledge. As Chief of General Staff he has the confidence of the entire *Wehrmacht*. He is, however, more an intellectual than a man of action. I do not believe that he will take a line that might conflict with the Führer's plans.'

That was also the assessment made by Canaris, whose character, we must observe, bore a certain resemblance to that of Beck. He too had misgivings about Beck, but who else could deter Hitler from the path of mad adventure?

The opposition of some generals to Hitler, as Canaris knew very well, lay not so much in moral objections as in their disapproval of the line that he was following in foreign policy. The German generals held to the principles of Bismarck, with some additional lessons from General von Seeckt, regarding friendship with Russia and China, mistrust of Japan, contempt for Italy and a studied neutrality towards Britain and France. This was coupled with hatred of Poland and, to a lesser degree, of Czechoslovakia. In his foreign policy Hitler thought and acted in a different fashion from the orthodox military caste. He sought rapprochement with Poland, pacts of friendship with Japan and Italy, and intervention in Spain in disregard of Great Britain and France, against the Soviet Union. This was all stupid, the generals thought, both politically and in the military sense as well. Some day there would be a riposte from Great Britain or France. As the Soviet Union was the ally of France and both had pacts with Czechoslovakia, a war with Russia would be inevitable if the Western powers opposed Hitler. The generals saw again the spectre of a war on two fronts.

A hundred army officers with monarchist tendencies commemorated the birthday of Kaiser Wilhelm II at the garrison town of Stolp on 12 January 1938, by toasting the Crown Prince as Emperor of Germany. This gesture was symptomatic of a mood in the army. A few days earlier some generals called upon Marshal von Blomberg to acquaint him with their serious view of Hitler's policy. 'This is how the *Reichswehr* has acted in the past,' they said. 'We count on you to persuade him to more rational opinions.' The dummy lion, as Blomberg was called, understood this sort of language, but equally he knew that he would not even receive a hearing. Canaris was not astonished to hear that von Blomberg replied in a biting manner: 'Gentlemen, the *Wehrmacht* does not venture into this field. Its duty lies in obeying orders, not in discussing them. These are no longer the days when the army could rule the Chancellor. Take my advice and return to your duties and don't interfere with politics.' This acquiescence earned him many reproaches, but his attitude was not entirely unreasonable. His critics did not know the new situation that had developed. Blomberg shared Hitler's daring vision, but feared only lest it could not be achieved in the near future. This was the sole difference between his views and those of the Reich's Chancellor.

Hitler, however, was convinced that Blomberg, Fritsch and Neurath were irrevocably hostile to his policy. He resented particularly the attitude that he suspected in the two military men of being opposed to any military venture upon which Germany might embark. He regarded their objections as sorry evidence of an unwillingness to fight and said to Joachim von Ribbentrop, his Ambassador in London, who was shortly to become Foreign Minister: 'These eunuchs strut about in uniform, but they are incapable of taking the opportunity that I offer them of winning laurels on the battlefield'. 'The men in field grey with crimson-braided trousers have long since betrayed, forgotten or dispensed with the teaching of Moltke and Schlieffen,' said Hitler later to Gauleiter Hans Frank. 'This *Junker* caste is a collection of addle-pates . . . They dazzled me at first . . . They have one idea only in their heads and think they know everything. The General Staff is the last freemasonry remaining for me to dissolve.'

Since these gentlemen refused to believe in his infallible instinct, he would in future only call them together to hear his intentions. He would also find other generals of his way of thinking. He was waiting for an opportunity to get rid of von Blomberg and von Fritsch without too much uproar. Göring, Himmler and Blomberg himself would all play a part in making this purge possible.

10

Any means to an end

Colonel Piekenbrock remembered driving along icy streets across Berlin on 22 January 1938, with Admiral Canaris, who had just returned from a visit to the Teruel front in Spain. The Admiral had gone to the front with his friend Franco and afterwards to a conference in Rome on the 20 January with Count Ciano and the Italian Chiefs of Staff. Canaris was silent and seemed tired and preoccupied with his own thoughts about the winter campaign in Spain, but one piece of news from 'Picki' aroused his curiosity:

'Marshal von Blomberg has married again.'

'Ah, the dummy lion?'

'Yes, Hitler and Göring attended the ceremony. It was conducted in the greatest secrecy. General von Fritsch was only told by Blomberg at the last moment, and there were a few lines in the press.'

'Who is the new Madame Marshal?'

'I don't know. One Eva or Luise Gruhn, twenty-four years old and, they say, a jolly girl.'

Piekenbrock repeated what Wing-Commander von Boehm-Tettelbach, aide-de-camp to Marshal von Blomberg, had told him. The wedding took place in a big room at the War Ministry. Apart from the registrar there were only the three aides present when Marshal von Blomberg arrived in ordinary uniform and wearing his Iron Cross and *Pour le Mérite* orders only. His bride wore a grey costume and silk blouse with no jewels and carried a large bouquet of red roses.

Boehm-Tettelbach thought that the bridal couple were unusually tense and silent as they waited for Hitler, who arrived at noon with Göring. Hitler was wearing his brown storm trooper's uniform tunic but no swastika armband. He wore the Iron Cross. Göring was in the full-dress uniform of a general of the air force with all decorations. Blomberg presented Fräulein Gruhn to the Führer and Hitler handed to her a bouquet of yellow roses. Hitler and Göring sat as witnesses one on either side of the bridal pair as the

civil marriage ceremony was performed, after which all four
signed the marriage register. Then, in accordance with recent
custom, the Registrar handed a copy of Hitler's *Mein Kampf* to
the married couple as prescribed reading after marriage, while
Hitler looked on impassively. There was no reception and no
wedding breakfast. Boehm-Tettelbach saw Hitler and Göring to
their cars. When he returned to the War Ministry, he found the
copy of *Mein Kampf* still lying on the table, forgotten by Marshal
von Blomberg.

Canaris was amused by these details and, as it was a Saturday,
asked Piekenbrock to see him again on Monday at his office for a
further discussion.

On the morning of Monday 24 January, Oster related to Canaris
the rumours that were circulating in official circles in Berlin: It
appeared that Marshal von Blomberg's bride had a seamy past.
Was Hitler aware of this? Oster did not know, but there seemed to
him to be some disturbance going on in Göring's offices. Canaris
expressed his concern but Oster could give no precise details.

That afternoon Canaris had to go and see General Wilhelm
Keitel, Chief of the High Command, to settle various questions
affecting the *Abwehr*. He thought highly of Keitel's integrity and
capacity for hard work but he did not confide in him, as he knew
that Keitel was a model of docile loyalty to the Führer. Keitel's
uncritical outlook was, however, useful when there were points of
friction to be discussed with the Nazis. For his part he respected
the Admiral's qualities of intelligence and character.

During their conversation Keitel related to Canaris the rumours
circulating about Blomberg's bride. Count Helldorf, the Chief of
Berlin Police, had informed him that he possessed a dossier on the
humble origins of Fräulein Gruhn and did not know whether to
destroy it. Keitel had replied that Helldorf should be guided by
regulations, and Helldorf had proposed to refer the matter to
General von Fritsch who would determine whether there was any
need for a board of inquiry. Keitel shook his head and suggested
instead that Hermann Göring, who was, after all, one of the officer
caste, should be informed. Canaris was surprised that Keitel,
whose son Wilhelm was engaged to Dorothy von Blomberg,
daughter of the Field-Marshal, should not have gone directly to
von Blomberg to warn him of this treacherous affair. And why
bring Göring into a matter that the army ought to keep to itself.
He thought no more of the matter: after all an unfortunate

marriage meant rather less in the Third Reich than in the days of the Kaiser. Hitler and Göring, moreover, had been themselves invited guests at the ceremony and that would perhaps suffice to still the rumours.

On the following evening, 25 January, Canaris was again seized with anxiety. He met Colonel Hossbach coming away from General von Fritsch's apartments in the Bendlerstrasse. Hossbach said that 'things are more serious than you think and there is another scandal, this time concerning the Commander-in-Chief'. He then moved on before the perplexed Admiral could ply him with questions.

On Wednesday 26 January Canaris discovered that at the War Ministry the talk was of discreetly 'retiring' von Blomberg. Things appeared to have gone from bad to worse. Although the scandal was still secret it had somehow become more serious. At the War Ministry nobody seemed to know quite what were the reasons for this development or when it would become public. Canaris, who did not personally regret the prospect of Blomberg's going, was nevertheless disturbed by an idea that had occurred to him earlier – that somehow the *SS* had a hand in this affair.

At noon Canaris was in his office discussing the marriage with Oster and Piekenbrock when the Police Counsellor, Hans Bernd Gisevius, was announced. He had come from the offices of Count Helldorf and the Chief of Criminal Police, Arthur Nebe. There he had learned the enormity of the scandal. Rumours had begun to circulate early in the previous week when the wedding had first been announced in the press. A question had been asked about Fräulein Gruhn's character and one zealous, or inspired, police inspector had been rummaging about in the files of the Vice Squad and then in the pornography Section. The results were such that he had no alternative but to report to his superior officer, who in turn took the matter higher, until the Police-President of Berlin was informed. Count Helldorf was faced with the brutal fact that the wife of the War Minister had been a prostitute.

In 1914, Luise Margarethe Eva Gruhn was born in the Berlin working-class district of Neukölln, where her mother ran a shady massage establishment. Frau Gruhn had twice previously been sentenced for procuring and prostitution. The dossier showed further that Eva at an early age had several adventures which came to the notice of the vice squad. She was reported to have used her domicile for naked orgies in prostitution and was described as having posed for pornographic photographs with partners of both sexes; further she had made commercial transactions in the said photographs, five of which were included in the dossier. These reports related to Eva Gruhn in 1931 and 1932 at the age of seventeen and eighteen. There was another case on the file in which she lodged a complaint against a man who had paid her only sixty marks for her services.

Helldorf was thunderstruck. He was a man of the world, but he could not quite believe it all. Yet when he looked at the face of the nude girl on the photographs, there was no doubt in his mind. It was Madame von Blomberg. He thought that his duty was quite clear and that this was no longer a police matter – it was an affair of state. To whom should he refer it? He thought of Himmler, but he did not trust the *SS*. He had himself been one of the rival brown shirts. With great courage he decided to go direct to the War Ministry.

On Thursday 20 January, with the Gruhn dossier in his briefcase, Helldorf went to the Bendlerstrasse and saw General Keitel, the man closest to Marshal von Blomberg. Would Keitel pass on his revelations to the War Minister himself? At the end of their interview Keitel instead advised Helldorf to go to Hermann Göring, seeming not to realize that Göring was the principal aspirant for the post of War Minister if it should fall vacant.

On Friday 21 January, Count Helldorf telephoned to Arthur Nebe of the Criminal Police, whom he trusted, notwithstanding that Nebe was an *SS* general and as such nominally under the orders of Reinhard Heydrich. Helldorf asked Nebe to come to his office, feeling that he would have the fullest confidence in him.

Arthur Nebe had returned from the Great War of 1914–18 a Lieutenant-Colonel with the Iron Cross, First Class. He was a man passionately dedicated to the war against crime, and by 1933 at the age of forty he had already made a name for himself as a criminologist. He had created an efficient Central Office of the Criminal Police, and although in July 1936, when Heinrich Himmler was made *Reichsführer SS* and Heydrich became Chief of the Reich Security Head Office, the Criminal Police came under their orders, Nebe remained indispensable. Himmler and Heydrich did not feel quite certain about his ideological outlook and mistrusted him: with reason, for Nebe's professional eye had detected their own criminal aberrations. He was to suffer in silence for a time, serving a state that had become the incarnation of crime but eventually he ventured further into opposition to it. He related to Hans Gisevius what happened during his interview with Helldorf.

Nebe cast a cold eye on the pornographic material. Helldorf questioned him with some impatience. What did he think?

'It is evidently an attempt to destroy Marshal von Blomberg,' replied Nebe. 'It is a *coup*, well prepared and well executed, probably by the *Gestapo*.'

'But the *Gestapo* is not yet informed!'

'Do you really believe that Heydrich, who keeps files on everybody from Hitler and Göring downwards, including yourself and myself, did not know that Eva Gruhn was a prostitute? You may be sure that when the most important man in the German army marries, Heydrich knows all about the lady.'

'But then?'

'Then I would like to know who pushed this prostitute at the Field-Marshal.'

'What shall I do with this file – show it to Himmler or Göring?'

'Preferably Göring who will tell the Führer at once. Himmler might make use of it to blackmail von Blomberg.'

On Saturday, 22 January, Helldorf went to Karinhall, where he revealed the file's sordid contents to Göring. Göring had a real sense of drama, and he played a rôle of profound indignation. Some have suspected him of being concerned in the operation from the start, but the truth of that will never be known.

'The Führer must be told,' he exclaimed.

On Monday 24 January Göring called at the Reich Chancellery and spoke to Colonel Hossbach, rolling his eyes and groaning that he must discuss with the Führer 'the reputation of Madame Blomberg'. He then swept from the ante-room into Hitler's presence.

Not till the morning of the next day, Tuesday 25 January was Hossbach informed by the Führer of what happened at this interview. 'After having made me promise absolute secrecy,' wrote Hossbach, 'Hitler revealed to me that the War Minister had put him in a very embarrassing situation by failing to reveal to him what sort of wife he was marrying and asking him to be a sponsor at the wedding ceremony, although the woman had been under observation by the vice squad over a long period and had been sentenced several times. The Minister had never breathed a word about her bad reputation; he had confined himself to an allusion that she had a "certain past", and Hitler had taken this to mean that Blomberg was referring only to his wife's age.'

Hossbach knew enough already not to be astonished by Hitler's narrative, but he was appalled that the most senior officer of the *Wehrmacht* could thus wreck his reputation and inflict a heavy blow on the prestige of the officer corps. Hossbach had no doubt either that there would soon be another act in the drama. Another visitor, but one whom Hossbach much disliked, came to visit Hitler. *Reichsführer SS* Heinrich Himmler came and spent more than an hour with the Führer. When the man in the black uniform had gone, Hitler called in Hossbach. He was plainly in a highly indignant mood and shouted: 'After the indescribable behaviour of the First Marshal of the Third Reich I might have expected anything, but this is really too much!' Hitler explained that Himmler had come to bring him a dossier with the name of von Fritsch on it, according to which the Commander-in-Chief of the army was a homosexual and the victim of blackmail by a man wanted by the police. Hossbach said that he did not believe a word of it and that only a confession by General von Fritsch himself could convince him that it was true. Hitler handed the dossier to Hossbach who saw at a glance that the evidence in it was not conclusive. It even seemed to him to savour of clumsy manipulation. He said as much, but Hitler was too excited to pay any attention. He ended by formally forbidding Hossbach to say anything at all to von Fritsch. The Colonel replied that his conscience would prevent him from complying with an order of this kind.

Hossbach went the same evening to acquaint General von Fritsch with Himmler's monstrous accusations. The round head of General von Fritsch, had become scarlet in his high collar and then livid with indignation. He explained: 'Those are nothing but abominable lies. How can the Führer listen to such accusations? If he wants to be rid of me, he has only to say the word and I will offer my resignation.'

'I don't think it is as simple as that,' replied Hossbach. 'I have the impression that Himmler and Heydrich wish to attack the honour of the *Wehrmacht* as such, and having capped the Blomberg affair with a Fritsch affair, they want to reduce the rôle of the army to that of a mere instrument of their ambitions.'

'We must know whether this dirty game is being played by Hitler himself or others, perhaps Himmler and Heydrich,' said von Fritsch. 'I believe that the latter is the case. If he can only be shown proof that these accusations are without foundation, he will realize that he too has been the victim of an intrigue.'

'I will see the Führer tomorrow,' Hossbach reassured him.

But it was not with 'the Fritsch affair' that the meeting in the Canaris office was concerned on Wednesday 26 January, when Gisevius explained what he knew in the presence of Oster and Piekenbrock. They were still preoccupied with the case of Field-Marshal von Blomberg and amazed that a man in his position should have made such an enormous blunder. Canaris heard the account in silence and then silently left the room, almost on tiptoe, murmuring as he went: 'And now there's something about Fritsch too.' He said no more because at that time he knew nothing more, except Hossbach's haunting remark on the previous evening: 'and now there is a new affair, this time with the Commander-in-Chief'. We may wonder that the Chief of Intelligence was not better informed, but Gisevius has since explained: 'Schacht was a Minister. Wilhelm Canaris was Chief of the Intelligence Service. In these positions ought not men to have known what was going on? In reality a minister is today a person protected from rumours, and these ministers reach their high positions through passive qualities. These were no longer well-informed and responsible men but simply the salaried executives of Hitler . . . It may appear unbelievable, but the Chief of the Intelligence Service was the least well informed on internal politics. The *Abwehr*, after its ten-point agreement with Heydrich, was deprived of a political intelligence service . . . His bitter experience during this crisis convinced Canaris that he must disregard this restrictive agreement, if the General Staff was not to become the plaything of the *Gestapo*. From that time onwards Oster was told to set up a secret service section which would report what was going on in Hitler's Chancellery, in the *Gestapo* and in Göring's Karinhall.

The last days of January 1938 were dramatic and decisive in the Third Reich, determining the fate of millions of people for the next seven years. On the morning of 26 January Hossbach reported to Hitler that despite his warning, he had visited von Fritsch on the previous evening and was convinced of his innocence 'The Führer appeared very relieved,' said Hossbach. 'He even saw von Fritsch as successor to Blomberg in the War Ministry.' But a few hours later, after Himmler and Heydrich had conferred with him, Hitler remarked to Hossbach that the accusations against von Fitsch were unfortunately well founded. He commented:

'homosexuals, the highest and lowest alike, are all liars'. Hossbach then proposed that a tribunal of honour should sit to investigate the affair, but Hitler declined this proposal, saying that he had decided to suspend the General from his command. He directed Hossbach to call von Fritsch to the Chancellery the same evening, adding: 'It is not for von Fritsch to exonerate himself, as he will only tell lies. Our purpose is to confront him with a witness named Schmidt who is detained by the *Gestapo*.'

When the Commander-in-Chief arrived that evening at the Chancellery, he believed that he was capable of convincing the Führer of his innocence. He was met by Hossbach, who told him briefly of his own talk with the Führer and the sort of interview that it was likely to be. Von Fritsch in a tense mood entered Hitler's office, while Hossbach withdrew to a small oval ante-chamber. Göring was already in the room as von Fritsch entered. He announced to von Fritsch that he was accused under paragraph 175 of the penal code, that dealing with homosexuality. Von Fritsch rejected the accusation with fury and determination. Hitler said nothing, but ordered the witness to be brought in, and asked him whether von Fritsch was the man implicated in his statements to the *Gestapo*. The witness, Schmidt, assented without hesitation. He repeated that von Fritsch was indeed the man who four years ago had accosted a young homosexual near Lichterfelde railway station and committed an offence with him. He, Schmidt, had then approached the said person with a threat of denunciation and had obtained on the following day 1,500 Marks as hush-money.

Von Fritsch declared that this man was lying. He had never seen him before in his life. Hitler then ordered Schmidt to be removed and suggested to von Fritsch that he should 'disappear without any form of proceedings', each agreeing to preserve silence about this scandal. Von Fritsch refused and demanded instead his right to be allowed to appear before a court martial. Hitler did not accept this. He told the General that he was to consider himself on indefinite leave and that the Ministry of Justice would be instructed to open an inquiry into the case. General von Fritsch withdrew without a word.

Half an hour later, at midnight, General Beck was summoned to the Chancellery. The Chief of General Staff was told in Göring's presence about 'the Fritsch affair'. Astounded but never-theless unshaken in his belief in the Commander-in-Chief, Beck questioned the veracity of the *Gestapo* evidence and demanded a military inquiry. He also asked Hitler to allow him immediate access to General von Fritsch. The Führer assented. Beck drove to the Commander-in-Chief's residence, where von Fritsch gave him his word of honour that he was innocent. Beck returned to the Chancellery and reported the outcome to Hitler, who appeared to show no interest in what Beck was saying and cut him short with the demand that General von Fritsch was to be replaced. Beck politely but firmly refused this demand, saying there could be no question of disposing of General von Fritsch other than by a Court Martial.

On this same Wednesday 26 January, Göring deputized for Hitler at an interview with Marshal von Blomberg. Blomberg was stunned when Göring told him that he could not remain War Minister, because of the reputation of his wife. He retold to Allied officers in 1945 during his interrogation at Nuremberg much that related to this critical period. Göring had said nothing precise at the interview and had ended by adding that even if the marriage were annulled, von Blomberg could not remain at his post. Blomberg acquiesced in this decision. He went in plain clothes to the Chancellery on the next day, 27 January, to take leave of Hitler, who received him but skilfully avoided speaking to him of the reasons for his removal, inferring that the matter was already closed and begging the former Minister to make the transition easier. Blomberg did not seek to discover why he was being ousted and, flattered by the Führer's request, discussed his successor with him, proposing General von Fritsch.

'No question of that', replied Hitler, 'he is going too'.

Von Blomberg was startled but asked no questions, saying:

'In that case the choice must fall on Göring'.

It was Hitler's turn to look surprised.

'Not possible,' he replied. 'He has neither the patience nor the application to work'.

'In that case the Ministry of War must revert to the Führer himself'.

This may have corresponded with an ambition long cherished by Hitler. Before leaving, Blomberg recommended General Wilhelm Keitel for the post of Chief of the High Command of the *Wehrmacht*, a choice that would have serious repercussions. Hitler acted rapidly, as soon as von Blomberg had departed, calling for Keitel and telling him among other matters to take charge of the von Fritsch case.

I have confidence in you, you must always be at my side. You are my deputy and my sole adviser in Wehrmacht affairs. I regard command of the unified *Wehrmacht* as my sacred duty which I assume with your aid. I wish also to have a new ADC who will be in my confidence and yours and not the servant of other departments.

Keitel realized his immense debt to Hitler, who had promoted him the to highest rank in recognition of his organizing ability and capacity for hard work. He at once replaced Colonel Hossbach with a man of his own, Major Schmundt.

Keitel directed the Head of the Legal Department of the *Wehrmacht*, Dr Heinrich Rosenberger, to draw up a memorandum for submission to Hitler on the procedure for dealing with the accusations against von Fritsch. When Canaris heard what had happened during these past two days, even before he knew the full truth, he was appalled by the squalor of these intrigues and by the very human vulnerability of men such as von Blomberg and von Fritsch. His profession had made manifest to him that such men were seldom what they appeared to be, but he clung to the naïve idea that at the summit of human society, human failings are restrained by tradition. He had to admit that here was manifest evidence that rogues and weaklings existed everywhere. It was still difficult to see very clearly the entire ramifications of the von Fritsch affair, but the more he heard about it the more astonished he was that the Commander-in-Chief had been so little equal to the predicament in which he was placed. Was the rugged exterior of von Fritsch no more than a façade? Canaris in any case was attached less to the man than to what he represented, a front against the intrigue and subversion of the Party and the *SS*. His conclusion was that the entire game was in the hands of the *SS*, played by Himmler and Heydrich. Was Hermann Göring, as in 1934 on the Night of the Long Knives, their accomplice? Was he perhaps the originator of it all? As I have said, Canaris was still without full information on the von Fritsch case, but in the case of von Blomberg he was fairly sure that Göring had done everything possible to estrange Hitler from his Minister of War. Canaris knew that Göring dreamed of taking over that Ministry and commanding all three Services. He felt certain that Göring had known before the wedding who Eva Gruhn really was. Had he pushed her at Blomberg with the aid of the *Gestapo*? Had he heard of the liaison, and decided to exploit this *mésalliance* because he coveted the post of Minister of War? In either case Göring needed the connivance of Himmler and Heydrich. Canaris also suspected, though he had never seen the dossier on Fräulein Gruhn, that it had been 'salted' by the *Gestapo*. It appears that Göring had proposed himself as a witness of the marriage ceremony and pushed ahead with the date chosen for the wedding, suggesting 12 January, although von Blomberg would have preferred the spring, and urging Blomberg to invite Hitler to the ceremony as well. Whatever the degree of Göring's complicity, it seems that he did want Blomberg out of the way before Hitler began on his path of conquest.

A few days after explaining to Piekenbrock how he saw Göring's rôle, Canaris received some unexpected confirmation of his views. Arthur Nebe informed him that the police officer who set the Blomberg case in motion had worked in 1933 with Rudolf Diels, assistant to Hermann Göring who had just created the *Gestapo*. This inspector had left the Secret Police in 1936 to join the Criminal Police in Berlin. It seemed to Canaris that the police official had been acting under instructions and that this threw light on the obscure rôle of Göring.

'It is infamous', he remarked to General Beck when imparting the results of his research to the Chief of General Staff. Both men felt that they were serving a guilty régime that ought to be removed, but it was still unclear to them at this time whether Hitler himself was aware of the real truth. The sequel to the von Fritsch affair would make that plain too.

The thunderbolt fell on 4 February 1938. Hitler announced that the Minister of War, Marshal von Blomberg, had resigned for health reasons and that General von Fritsch, Commander-in-Chief, had asked to be relieved of his duties, also for health reasons. Nobody was deceived by this explanation of events, but there was complete surprise when he added the appointment of two Party members for key positions in the state. Dr Walther Funck was to become the Minister of Economic Affairs in place of Dr Schacht and Joachim von Ribbentrop, the Ambassador in London, was to replace Baron von Neurath as Foreign Minister. Finally Hitler decreed: 'As from today I will exercise personally direct command of all armed forces. The former General Staff of the *Wehrmacht* in the War Ministry will become the High Command of the *Wehrmacht*. It is to come directly under my orders and serve as my military staff.'

General Walther von Brauchitsch was named Commander-in-

Chief of the Army and General Wilhelm Keitel Chief of the High Command of the Armed Forces (*OKW*). Göring received the baton of a Field-Marshal of the air force, no real consolation for the War Ministry that Hitler had grabbed. Sixteen generals suspected of disaffection were retired, while forty-four others and many senior officers were moved to new posts.

The reshuffle was not so complete as the Tuchachevsky purge by Stalin had been, and Canaris had feared something worse than actually happened; but in taking over the supreme military command Hitler completed the work that he had begun by fusing the presidency and the chancellery four years previously. This added significance to the oath of loyalty to his person that the armed forces had taken at that time. From that day onwards his orders would be obeyed by men who shared his ideas and his outlook.

Hitler had nullified all the military manoeuvres against him, defeated, humiliated and abused the German army and brought it to heel. With few exceptions, such as Beck, Witzleben, K. H. von Stülpnagel, Halder and Canaris, the army generals thought that they could do nothing against the dictator, and General von Fritsch shared this spirit of fatalism.

Meanwhile the Minister of Justice, Dr Gürtner, had received the dossier on General von Fritsch. He advised the Führer 'not to take proceedings against General von Fritsch on the basis of this sort of documentation.' Later Dr Gürtner perceived that not all the papers in the dossier had been sent to him, which would have made his advice even stronger against taking any proceedings. Gürtner told Hitler: 'The evidence is very flimsy and the case should be seriously reviewed before any further step is taken'. Hitler disregarded this prudent advice.

Gürtner then proposed that two military judges, Dr Biron and Dr Karl Sack, and a Counsellor of the Ministry of Justice, Dr Hans von Dohnanyi should constitute a board of inquiry. The legal representative for General von Fritsch would be Count Rüdiger von der Göltz. Hitler accepted these arrangements but ordered the *Gestapo* to conduct a parallel inquiry. He also reserved for himself the right to suspend the inquiry and to confirm its findings.

The *Gestapo* seems to have rapidly gained the ascendant, having had time to prepare itself. Contrary to all rules of military procedure it began interrogations of all former ADCs and adjutants of the General to see whether the number of witnesses could be increased, but the only witness in support of the accusations remained the blackmailer Schmidt. The Ministry of Justice and the Military Board turned their attention to him.

It was easy in the first place to demolish some of the descriptive details given in Schmidt's evidence. The General had for instance never inhabited Ferdinandstrasse in Lichterfelde, did not smoke and never wore an overcoat with a fur collar. Then Count von der Göltz referred to an old street directory and discovered that a retired cavalry Captain named von Frisch, had lived in the Ferdinandstrasse in 1934. Schmidt appeared to have a story but to have confused the two names either by mistake or under direction. The matter did not long remain in doubt. The *Gestapo* knew that Captain von Frisch was a homosexual. When he appeared before the tribunal, he told them that a *Gestapo* agent had come to visit him in January 1938 and had questioned him at length about withdrawals from his bank account in 1934. He explained that he had in fact committed a homosexual offence near Lichterfelde station in November 1934 and that Schmidt had extorted 1,500 Marks from him as the price of his silence. When Canaris heard of this dramatic development, he exclaimed: 'No tribunal can now maintain this accusation against General von Fritsch.' Canaris did not yet know fully what the *SS* was capable of doing. Above all, he did not know Adolf Hitler.

When the Chairman of the Military Board of Inquiry, General Heitz, went to see Hitler with his assistant counsellors Biron and Sack, to inform him that they had discovered the real offender and that proceedings against the General would have to be terminated, Hitler declared: 'To my mind General von Fritsch remains suspect as long as Schmidt does not withdraw his accusations.'

So the struggle was to continue. It was now necessary to obtain a retraction from Schmidt. Canaris, Hossbach and the Military Board feared *Gestapo* intervention. It could act against General von Fritsch, against Captain von Frisch, or against Schmidt. It could arrange the apparent suicide of one of the three. Canaris told Dr Gürtner of his fears, and the Minister of Justice replied: 'Your fears are perfectly justified. The *Gestapo* recoils from nothing. You may be sure that I am not exaggerating.'

The *Gestapo* did in fact intervene. It arrested Captain von Frisch. Happily for him his evidence had already been given on oath to Judge Sack, registered and deposited with the Board's records. The Captain was nevertheless badly mistreated in an attempt to force him to retract his evidence. He did not give way. The blackmailer Schmidt maintained his own accusations against the General. At this stage of the proceedings it was hardly likely that any more evidence would emerge.

A military Court of Honour was to sit in review of the Board's findings on 10 March. Field-Marshal Göring would be the most senior officer on this tribunal. General von Brauchitsch would represent the army and Admiral Raeder the navy. Dr Biron who had hitherto sat on the Inquiry, would represent the prosecution, and the Minister of Justice with several legal experts would attend.

The first hearing was occupied entirely with the witness Schmidt, who persisted in his accusations against the General without the defence being able to shake him. After suspending the hearing Marshal Göring announced that the Court of Honour would have to adjourn its deliberations 'for reasons of state.' Hitler had just given the order to invade Austria.

If the *Anschluss* with Austria was not provoked by the von Fritsch affair, as some historians affirm, it is almost certain that 'the Austrian Solution' was precipitated by it, as the case was becoming most embarrassing to those who had engineered it. I entirely share the view of the German historian, Gert Buchheit: 'The invasion of Austria was to divert attention from the internal crisis with the army. Hitler hoped that the triumphal annexation of Austria would prevent the acquittal of General von Fritsch from becoming the pretext for a *coup d'état*. He was right in this assumption.'

The Court of Honour resumed the von Fritsch case on 17 March and ended on the 18th with an acquittal. A fresh interrogation of Schmidt obliged him to confess that he had lied and that he had been intimidated into making false statements. When asked who had intimidated him, he preserved a frightened silence. When the defence counsel insisted on an answer, Schmidt replied that Commissioner Meissinger of the *Gestapo* had told him that very morning that 'if I retract my evidence, I will go to heaven.' Dr Biron, for the prosecution, asked for the proven innocence of the accused General to be confirmed by the Court. The defence counsel asked for an acquittal and expressed himself in vehement terms about the way the case had been conducted against General von Fritsch. The *Gestapo* was confounded, but did not in the least alter its demeanour as a consequence. As for Hitler, his reaction after the acquittal of von Fritsch was revealing, and brought home to Canaris the Führer's complicity in this travesty of justice.

It might have been supposed that a public rehabilitation of General von Fritsch would ensue. There was neither a public declaration by the Führer, nor were proceedings taken against those in the *Gestapo* who had perverted justice. General von Fritsch was offered neither honourable reinstatement in the army, nor advancement to Field-Marshal in retirement. Hitler wrote a few lines to the General on 31 March to say that he was glad that his honour had never been publicly compromised. He added that the army's performance during the annexation of Austria was proof of von Fritsch's excellent work during his period of command. That was all.

The General accepted his fate in silence. In June 1938 he was named Colonel-in-Chief of the 12th Regiment of Artillery. At the end of August 1939, in a letter to his friend Baroness Schutzbar, he wrote: 'there is no place for me any more in Hitler's Germany, in time of war or in time of peace. I will enter this war with my regiment, but as a mere cipher, as it would be quite impossible for me to stay at home.' On the morning of 22 September 1939, General von Fritsch was killed outside Warsaw at the head of his regiment. He was given a funeral with full national honours, at which General von Brauchitsch paid a tribute to the fallen that contained a phrase deleted on higher orders from press and radio reports of the ceremony.

'The General has gone to join the Great Army. He will continue to live in us and in our acts, if these correspond to his aspirations.'

The witness Schmidt soon met his fate. The *Gestapo* did not forgive him for retracting. He disappeared in April 1938.

We will never know whether Göring was the instigator of the monstrous proceedings against von Blomberg and von Fritsch or simply the unwitting instrument of the *SS*. It is a secondary consideration whether Hitler and Göring were being deceived by others while believing that they were in control of the game. Canaris saw their conduct as that of guilty men, although the threads of the intrigue may have been held by Himmler and Heydrich.

11

The fall of Austria

While Canaris was still a horrified spectator of the machinations against von Fritsch in February 1938, another event that added to his cares, was the case of Austria. On 12 February 1938, Hitler received the Austrian Chancellor, Dr von Schuschnigg, at his retreat in the Obersalzberg, threatened him with a military invasion and raved at him like a madman. Canaris read through the secret record of these conversations on 13 February, exclaiming to Colonel Piekenbrock: 'Austria will become Nazi during the next few days'.

Canaris was not opposed to a union of Germany and Austria. He much regretted that the Allied powers had prevented such a union in 1919, but he considered an *Anschluss* to be preferably an aim of diplomacy, to be freely achieved without pressure from the mighty Third Reich. He was instinctively opposed to the use of force whether against individuals or against states. Nevertheless he was himself to be one of the instruments of the force exerted by Hitler against Austria. To have to act sometimes against his own conscience and inner convictions was part of Canaris's dilemma. At this time his sense of duty came uppermost and his own opinions and misgivings receded, as he played his part in what was the product of superior orders, a plan for the aggrandisement of the Third Reich.

At 4 PM on 13 February Canaris was called in to see Keitel in his official residence. The Chief of the High Command had just returned from Obersalzberg, where he had stood beside the Führer during Hitler's tirade against Schuschnigg. Keitel carried 'orders from the Führer'. He explained to General Jodl and Canaris that a plan must be prepared to simulate military pressure on Austria, so that President Miklas would be obliged to ratify the agreement signed between Hitler and Schuschnigg on the previous day, providing for certain Cabinet changes that would bring the Austrian Nazis into the Vienna Government. Dr Joseph Goebbels, Minister of Propaganda, joined them and the four men considered what they would do, deciding upon the following outline plan:

1) Take no actual measures in the army or the air force. No movements of troops or changes of dispositions.
2) Spread false information, appearing perfectly probable, which will cause it to be supposed that military measures have been taken against Austria,
   a) through our liaison agents in Austria,
   b) through our frontier services,
   c) through visiting agents.
3) Such rumours would include reports that:
   a) Leave has been suspended in the VIIth Army corps;
   b) military stocks have been assembled at Augsberg, Munich and Ratisbon;
   c) Major-General Muff, our Military Attaché in Vienna, has been recalled to Berlin for a conference – as is indeed the case;
   d) our frontier police have been reinforced on the Austrian frontier.
   e) The customs officers are to talk about imminent manoeuvres by Alpine units in the areas of Freilassing, Reichenhall and Berchtesgaden.

There must be increased military radio activity in the Bavarian frontier sector, to make it appear that troop concentrations are being moved up.

Keitel, Jodl and Canaris together with Goebbels completed the deception plan which was submitted to Hitler for approval by telephone that evening. At 2:40 AM Hitler's approval reached them in Berlin, and at dawn Canaris with Groscurth and Piekenbrock left for Munich, where they put the plan into operation with the senior *Abwehr* officer for that area, Lieutenant Colonel Rudolf von Marogna-Redwitz.

Colonel von Marogna-Redwitz, scion of an old Bavarian Roman Catholic family, was the official liaison officer with the Austrian Intelligence Service and friendly with Colonel Boehme, Chief of Austrian Intelligence, and Colonel Erwin Lahousen. He expressed his anxiety to Canaris:

'Could not our deception plan be mistaken for genuine military measures? I am not thinking of the Austrians as much as the British, French and Italian governments. That could be disastrous.'

Canaris was aware of the real possibility of an armed conflict but he said:

'In the present state of our *Wehrmacht*, with the High Command still being reorganized, I don't think the Führer would take a risk. Bluffing is one thing and you must have a few cards in your hand.

Hitler has none and the *Wehrmacht* is absolutely unready to face up to a declaration of war by Britain and France, especially if Mussolini took part.'

The Austrian drama heightened its pace till 9 March. Hitler's threats became louder and Schuschnigg's resistance feebler. Austria was succumbing to the powerful compulsion of the Reich and the Western powers were not willing to intervene on Austria's behalf. Believing that he could place Hitler in a dilemma and safeguard Austrian independence, Schuschnigg announced on 9 March a plebiscite for the following Sunday, 13 March.

'Idiotic man!' exclaimed Canaris when he heard of Schuschnigg's decision, 'he has signed his own death warrant.'

This was also the opinion of Mussolini who told the Austrian Military Attaché in Rome, Colonel Liebitsky: 'It is a mistake. He should have played for time and not precipitated things. Tell the Chancellor that he is handling a bomb which may explode in his hands. If the result of the plebiscite is not clear, it will be said to be indecisive; if it is a clear victory, it will be said to have been rigged.'

When Schuschnigg replied to Mussolini that it was too late to change the arrangements that he had made, Mussolini commented: 'Then Austria is no longer any concern of mine.'

Hitler exploded in wrath when he heard of the Schuschnigg plan for a plebiscite. He telephoned from the Berlin Chancellery to Göring: 'It is an intolerable challenge. This plebiscite must in no circumstances take place. Schuschnigg has violated all his agreements with us. 12 February at Berchtesgaden was his last chance. He did not understand. So much the worse for him!'

At 10 AM on 10 March, Hitler summoned Keitel to the Chancellery. After a short interview Keitel went to General Beck and told the Chief of General Staff: 'The Führer requires you to report to him immediately on the dispositions made for the *Wehrmacht* to enter Austria.'

'But we have made no preparation,' replied Beck. 'Nothing at all has been done.'

'What about Plan Otto of June 1937?'

'That was a contingency plan for preventing a Hapsburg restoration. It is not the same thing.'

Keitel shrugged his shoulders and took Beck with him to Hitler, where they were joined by General von Manstein and General Jodl. Hitler was emphatic: 'There is no reason to fear foreign intervention. Neither England nor France nor Czechoslovakia will move. Let us have no unnecessary comments and confine yourselves to carrying out my orders. Prepare Plan Otto for operation. It is entirely suitable for the present situation.'

General Beck pointed out that Plan Otto called for the use of an armoured division and of the VIIIth and XIIIth army Corps in Bavaria, but that no steps had been taken to mobilize them. Hitler exploded: 'Am I or am I not the Supreme Commander of the *Wehrmacht*?' he shouted. 'At a time when I need to act like lightning you tell me that nothing is ready, and that all must be improvised at the last moment. Do what you like but our troops must be in Vienna on 12 March!'

Keitel, Beck, Manstein and Jodl returned to the Bendlerstrasse and set the War Ministry in motion. Keitel called for Canaris and told him of the Führer's decision. General Beck, who was present in the room and had just given his instructions to General Guderian, Commander of the 16th Armoured Corps, said dejectedly: 'After all, if the *Anschluss* with Austria has to come, it must be recognized that the time is particularly well chosen.'

Canaris looked at him with surprise but made no remark. He left immediately for Munich and planned to arrive in Vienna immediately after Plan Otto had been put into operation.

On 11 March, at 8:45 PM after hurling at Schuschnigg an ultimatum to cancel his plebiscite, Hitler signed two documents, instructions which sounded the death knell of Austrian independence. Operation Otto I contained Hitler's political and military intentions and Otto II ordered the army to enter Austria since she had not accepted the German ultimatum.

At exactly 7:45 PM, an hour earlier, Chancellor Schuschnigg in the presence of President Miklas and some thirty high Austrian officials, broadcast to the Austrian people. He described the German ultimatum and the spreading of false rumours that there was bloodshed in Austria. Then he spoke slowly and distinctly: 'The Federal President charges me to announce to the Austrian people that we yield to force. As we have no desire, even at this grave hour, to shed German blood, we have ordered our army to withdraw without resistance and await the decision of the next few hours. I thus take leave of the Austrian people, saying from the depths of my heart – God protect Austria!' It was for the new Chancellor, Dr Seyss-Inquart, to form the first Nazi government of Austria.

Hitler was nevertheless worried. He was not afraid of French or British reactions. The Blum Government in France, after yet another ministerial crisis, would not be formed till 17 March. As for Britain, she had for several years been pursuing a policy of 'appeasement', which consisted of accepting every breach of a treaty by Hitler and signing behind the back of her French ally an agreement which permitted the German navy to construct submarines. Britain also declined to be associated with any direct action when Hitler reoccupied the Rhineland. Hitler was concerned, however, about Mussolini's reactions. He had not forgotten that during the Nazi *Putsch* of 25 July, 1934, in which Dollfuss was murdered, Mussolini had sent Italian divisions to theAustrian frontier. Italy was Austria's protector. It was true that Mussolini had warned Schuschnigg in one of their recent interviews not to regard him as more than a mediator in any future dispute with Germany, but his declarations, whether to Schuschnigg, Neurath or Ribbentrop, had nevertheless a certain ambiguity as to his final attitude. Hitler, knowing him to be impulsive, feared a sudden reversal of stance.

On the morning of 11 March Hitler gave Prince Philip of Hess a letter for Mussolini, informing the Duce of his decision to send the army into Austria. The Prince flew to Rome and was received that afternoon by Mussolini in the Venezia Palace. Hitler waited nervously for a reply. At last the telephone rang at 10:25 PM with Prince Philip on the line from Rome, saying that he had just returned from the Venezia Palace. 'The Duce has accepted everything in a very friendly way, my Führer. He sends you friendly greetings. He has been informed of the Austrian affair by Schuschnigg himself . . . Mussolini told him that Austria was not his concern.'

Hitler: 'Then please tell Mussolini that I will never forget what he has just done.'

Prince: 'Yes, my Führer.'

Hitler: 'I will never forget, no matter what happens. If he ever needs help or if he is in danger, he may be assured that I will stand firm beside him, no matter what happens, even if the whole world is against him.' Hitler had tears in his eyes as he put down the telephone. He knew now that he need fear no international opposition to his order to cross the Austrian border and so decided to go in person to his native land.

At one o'clock on the morning of 12 March Heinrich Himmler

and his *SD* Chiefs climbed into a large transport aircraft at Tempelhof aerodrome in Berlin and left for Vienna. Himmler had discarded his black *SS* uniform for field grey. He was accompanied by Walther Schellenberg, Chief of his Foreign Intelligence Service and by an officer of his anti-Jewish section, Adolf Eichmann. At 4 AM the aircraft landed at Vienna-Aspen airport.

The *SS* party leapt into a waiting car which drove them to the Bundeshaus, seat of the Austrian government, where there was a hum of activity, with conferences and little meetings being held continuously. With an enormous crowd outside in the square, excited groups were taking over the Austrian government offices. Austrian Storm Troops and *SS* wearing white armlets, had taken control of the building. In a corridor Schellenberg bumped into President Miklas and Dr Skubl, Austrian Minister of Police, who looked in a desperate mood and left the building without Schellenberg interfering. He knew that they would be arrested outside by Austrian *SS* who had orders to that effect. While waiting for Heydrich to arrive, Himmler and Schellenberg took urgent precautions against any resistance that might be aroused. Their targets were the Austrian Intelligence Service, their political opponents and the Jewish community.

The first operation was a partial failure. When Schellenberg found Colonel Ronge, then Head of the Austrian Intelligence Service, he was surprised to learn that Admiral Canaris and the heads of the German *Abwehr* had visited him a few hours earlier and that Canaris had taken away several dossiers that appeared to interest him very much. Beside Colonel Ronge stood a giant Austrian Lieutenant-Colonel, Erwin Lahousen, who smiled broadly at Schellenberg's anger. Yes, the *Abwehr* had got in first The five dossiers that so actively interested Heydrich and Schellenberg were those on Hitler, Göring, Himmler, Heydrich and Canaris, compiled by the Austrian Intelligence Service and now in the hands of their rival. Heydrich would be furious, thought Schellenberg. And so he was when Schellenberg told him an hour later what had happened; but the *SS* were consoled by finding other dossiers and by an offer from Colonel Ronge to work with them, though Colonel Lahousen curtly refused to do the same. A little later he joined the *Abwehr* and became one of the most valuable men in Canaris's service.

From their headquarters in the Metropole Hotel the excited *SS* launched a hunt for all enemies of National Socialism, whether real or imaginary, ordering the Austrian police to round up suspects, 'and so avoid reprisals by the populace'. In two days 76,000 people were arrested in the capital alone. The cellars of the Metropole Hotel contained President Miklas, Dr von Schuschnigg, Baron Louis de Rothschild, Dr Figl, the future Chancellor of Austria, Dr Skubl, the former Police Chief, Archduke Max, Prince Hohenberg, Princess Fanny Starhemberg, the financiers Krupnik and Sigismund Bosel, as well as many others. The full total of executions, running into many hundreds, will never be known. Adolf Eichmann set up the structure of the Central Bureau for Jewish Immigration, with the object of expelling 250,000 Jews.

Operation Otto rolled along as Hitler intended. Small infantry detachments of the German army began entering Austria at 3 AM on 12 March. Customs officials lifted some barriers; others were destroyed by civilians with axes. Women and children brought flowers to the German troops. Leading reconnaissance units of the 2nd Armoured Division crossed the frontier at dawn, followed by General Guderian with the main *Panzer* formations at 9:12 AM Sepp Dietrich and the Adolf Hitler Bodyguard of the *SS* brought up the rear. In his memoirs Guderian wrote that: 'the Austrian people knew that we came as friends'. The 2nd Division did not reach Linz till noon, hampered by icy roads and the failure of their fuel supplies to keep pace with the advance.

Hitler flew from Berlin to Munich and watched in operational headquarters there the advance of his toops into Austria. Then at 3:50 PM he crossed the frontier into Austria at Braunau, his birthplace, at the head of an imposing motorcade accompanied by General Keitel, Gauleiter Bürckel, Dr Dietrich, and his ADCs of the three services, escorted by thirteen lorry loads of police and *SS*.

There was a short halt outside his childhood home. Without entering the house Hitler looked at it with emotion, and moved on to Linz, where more than 60,000 people crowded the market place, shouting '*Sieg Heil. Ein Volk! Ein Reich! Ein Führer!*' Swept away by the impulse of the moment, Hitler proclaimed on the spot that Austria would be simply annexed, a decision which he had hesitated to take a few hours previously. On the balcony of the town hall he exclaimed in harsh tones: 'Providence called me forth from this town to fulfil my mission. Now that Providence has made me Chancellor of the German Reich, the mission for which I have lived and fought is going to be fulfilled. I am going to bring the country of my birth back to the German Reich.' When he stepped off the balcony, once more tears streamed down his face.

On the afternoon of 14 March, 1938, Hitler made his triumphal entry into Vienna to the ringing of church bells. What a change from his departure on 24 May 1913, when, with fury in his heart, he left Vienna, writing of that time in *Mein Kampf*: 'I felt a real revulsion for the mixture of races that I saw in the capital. The more I lived there, the more I hated the mixture of peoples beginning to take over this old centre of German culture'. He rode on this day through a sea of faces and through buildings draped in the German colours. He could claim that ninety per cent of the people were yelling with joy, to the stupefaction of foreign journalists and diplomats, and that this was no annexation, but a real *Anschluss*, a union of peoples drawn together, not a rape but a marriage.

After a massed military parade on 15 March, Hitler left Vienna for Berlin on 16 March and was received by a delirious crowd. Until a referendum completed the attachment of Austria to the Reich, both countries lived in a state of exaltation while a stream of decrees and ordinances aligned Austrian institutions with those of Germany. In the referendum of 10 April, Hitler reaped 99.08 per cent of the votes in Germany, and in Austria the figure announced was 99.75 per cent – or ten thousand only out of four million opposed to union. Austria was German and the *Anschluss* was complete.

Canaris chose as head of the *Abwehr* in Vienna Colonel Rudolf von Marogna-Redwitz, whom we have already met as head of the *Abwehr* in Munich and in whom he had the fullest confidence. He was to play an important rôle in the future, as the activities of the *Abwehr* in Vienna radiated into the Balkans. Count Redwitz, an anti-Nazi, often succeeded in thwarting the extreme activities of the *SD* and *SS*. The *SS* hated him and were to take their revenge in 1944. H. B. Gisevius, in writing of the German resistance to Hitler and National Socialism, pays a high tribute to the Colonel's part in the liberation movement as 'a European in the best sense of the word'. Sentenced to death by the Peoples' Court after the conspiracy of 20 July, Colonel Marogna-Redwitz was executed on 12 October, 1944.

Twelve days after taking up his *Abwehr* appointment in Vienna, Colonel von Marogna-Redwitz addressed to his Chief a secret report on the demented behaviour and excesses of the *Gestapo* in

Austria. 'The *SS* are criminals,' commented Canaris to Pieken-brock after reading the report.

According to Piekenbrock Canaris's outlook was exactly as described by his German biographer, Karl Heinz Abshagen:

A few days after the *Anschluss* Canaris began to feel that this conquest, although no blood had been shed and no European power had seriously protested, was nevertheless pregnant with danger for the future. He had sensed with a sort of physical revulsion the symptons of delusions of grandeur that Hitler displayed during his speech after entering Vienna. This easy success, he augured with certainty, would drag Hitler into new dangers. As for a resistance to him in the higher ranks of the army, that would diminish progressively. The idea that 'the Führer will find a way out' and 'the others will not interfere' had received confirmation. This explains why Canaris remarked brusquely to an Austrian officer presented to him at this time, 'it's your fault, you Austrians, Why didn't you shoot?'

12

Victory in Spain

Coming from Berlin a *Lufthansa* airliner landed on the snowy airfield of Salamanca on Tuesday, 11 January, 1938. The Secretary of the German Legation, Herr Striele, met Canaris when the Admiral disembarked from the aircraft. Canaris had an appointment to meet General Franco, but the diplomat told him that Franco had been obliged to go urgently to the Teruel front and had asked the Admiral to join him there. Canaris was not pleased at the idea of a long drive on icy Spanish roads, but he consoled himself with the prospect of seeing something of the battlefront. Before taking the Aragon road he lunched with his old friend Eberhard von Stohrer, now German Ambassador, who gave him a gloomy account of the Nationalist position, later recorded in the German Foreign Ministry archives:

On the Teruel front the Reds have quite unexpectedly shown themselves strong enough to maintain their positions, they retook the whole of the town last Friday (7 January) and are now making other attacks on the Nationalist front in the west and north of the city. The battle for Teruel is still in progress. These are the results of an offensive spirit instilled in the Red forces during past Months by foreign officers and organisers so that they have again taken the offensive.

'So the Nationalist position, which improved after the northern front was won, has become considerably more serious,' commented Canaris.

'It is serious, though not yet dangerous,' replied von Stohrer. 'For my part I do not believe that Franco is capable of striking a telling blow at the Reds in the near future. I question whether he can gain the upper hand. When we consider the aid that the Reds are receiving from abroad and will receive on an even larger scale after their success at Teruel, it seems that Franco can hardly succeed with no more than his own resources.'

'So we Germans, and the Italians, too,' said Canaris, 'have to decide whether we add to his fighting strength.'

'Exactly! It is a case of Franco making great sacrifices to achieve a victory or to avoid a negotiated peace which would amount to "a pink solution" of the Spanish problem. The German and Italian military have recommended emphatically that such aid should be given.'

Canaris said nothing to the Ambassador of Hitler's unwillingness to provide more aid. Having received Colonel Hossbach's account of Hitler's military conference on 5 November 1937, at which the Führer has revealed his grand strategy, Canaris had no illusions.

Hitler's attitude towards Franco was not dictated by ideological questions, nor yet by sentimental feelings; it was formed by his own plans for territorial expansion in the direction of Austria and Czechoslovakia. Hitler had declared in the course of this conference, as we know: 'a total victory for Franco is not desirable in the German interest, and we have a greater interest in the war continuing and in tension persisting in the Mediterranean'. This was a clear and precise definition.

Canaris had no doubts that the line of Hitler's policy in Spain was to offer limited military aid to Franco, enough to deserve his gratitude (thus permitting the Germans to strengthen their influence in the Iberian peninsula); enough to prevent the Republicans from winning; but not enough to ensure a rapid victory for Franco. Hitler's desire for tension in the Mediterranean served a double objective. It focussed world attention on that area while Hitler settled his two most urgent problems elsewhere, in Austria and Czechoslovakia. At the same time it involved Mussolini more and more in the Spanish Civil War, obliging him to increase his stakes there and so diminish his Continental strength, until he would be constrained to accept the absorption by Germany of Austria and then of Czechoslovakia. The fact that Mussolini was driven to massive intervention deprived him of freedom of action and placed him in a dangerous relationship with Britain and France. Hitler could thus hope that sooner or later the Duce would realize that it would be prudent to align himself with Germany in face of the Western powers. His knowledge of Hitler's secret thinking prompted Canaris to listen to the proposals that von Stohrer made without revealing his own ideas.

'Suppose that Franco is determined to prosecute the war more energetically than in past months,' said von Stohrer, 'it would seem to me insufficient to give him military superiority in the form of material aid only.'

'I agree.'

'Germany and Italy would have to give him a much larger number of technical personnel and trained staff officers. But our men would have to be assured of a more important, perhaps a decisive, rôle in the conduct of the war and execution of orders from the high command. It would be understood that Franco would retain command as in the past. I know and you know that given the Spanish mentality there would be some serious difficulty over this. Tact as well as firmness would be needed. As for the international factor, this tends to make time work against Franco, and so the proverb applies – "who gives quickly, gives twice over".'

Canaris calculated that Hitler would not want to give anything, and that even if he did accept the Stohrer idea, staff officers for Spain would certainly be refused by von Blomberg. 'I will inform the Führer of your ideas,' he replied to von Stohrer.

After lunch Canaris took the road into Aragon to meet Franco. Temperatures were as low as six degrees Fahrenheit, and after he had spent the night at Almazan between Catalayud and Monreal del Campo a violent snowstorm slowed down his progress. It took him the best part of a day to reach the Teruel area, where Franco received him at his field headquarters, consisting of four railway coaches attached to a locomotive which provided steam central heating.

General Davila, who commanded the Teruel sector, General Varela, in charge of the troops from Madrid, and General Aranda, who commanded the Huesca-Saragossa sector, made their reports on the military situation, which was in reality not as bad as von Stohrer imagined. Franco explained to Canaris that he had rushed to the rescue of the Teruel garrison for two reasons – typical of his way of thinking. The first was a military reason: he wished to seize the opportunity to destroy an important Republican force. The second reason was psychological and humane; he had sworn that he would never let a city which had rallied to the Nationalist cause fall back into the hands of the Republicans, who would take reprisals on the population. He also did not consider that the Nationalist army ought ever to accept defeat, even though it could not advance all the time. His adherents must not be placed in the same danger of a collapse of morale as threatened the Republican front.

The year 1937 had been marked by a skilful political unification of Franco's forces and the acceptance of himself in supreme authority. He had tactfully and firmly put the Falangist and Carlist leaders in their places. His brother-in-law, Serrano Suñer, husband of his wife's sister, played a decisive rôle in this unification. Having escaped from Madrid, where his two brothers had been executed by the Republicans, Suñer arrived at Salamanca at the end of February 1937 and in a few weeks supplanted Nicholas Franco as polital counsellor to the Caudillo.

A decree establishing the new form of authority had been published on 19 April, emphasizing Franco's totalitarian ideas.

Our state will be a totalitarian instrument pledged to the service of national unity. The entire Spanish people will take part in the forward movement of the state, by family, by municipality and by 'syndicates'. Nobody will participate in this movement through a political party. We abolish the system of party politics and all that goes with it: the loose knit suffrage system, representation by parties in strife, and a parliament of a kind that we know all too well.

To remove any remaining doubts, Franco declared:

As initiator of the historic epoch in which Spain will fulfil its destiny, while realizing the purposes of the Movement, the Caudillo will exercise absolute authority.... The Caudillo is responsible to God and to History.

Despite a shortage of military material compared with the growing supplies of the Republicans, Franco had succeeded by June 19 in taking in the north of Spain all those places still in the hands of the Republicans: Oviedo, Santander and Bilbao. One of the best of the Nationalist leaders, General Mola, had been unfortunately lost on 3 June in an aircraft accident near Burgos. This tested the morale of Nationalist troops, especially as there were some fierce engagements on the Madrid front between 7 and 26 July to contain the big Republican offensive. The year 1937 had ended with another big Republican offensive, this time at Teruel.

In the diplomatic field Franco had many problems over his German and Italian supporters, and Canaris acted as watchdog to keep supplies of military material moving. He had also been instrumental in replacing the inept Faupel as Ambassador at Salamanca with his own old friend of 1916, Eberhard von Stohrer. The new Ambassador was an agreeable personality, who was less inclined than his predecessor to become involved in intrigues, and who concentrated on improving economic relations between Spain and Germany. The pace was not, however, fast enough for Hermann Göring, who began to take a personal interest in Spain and told his subordinates that 'his special assistance to General Franco' . . . gave him the right 'to ask for special safeguards for Germany's war prizes'. He proposed to send an envoy to Salamanca 'to hold a pistol to Franco's breast.' Bravado, perhaps! Nevertheless Hitler, when he knew of Göring's mood, sent Canaris to Salamanca 'to clarify relations between Germany and Nationalist Spain.'

During their talks at Teruel, Franco told Canaris that the Junta would soon be replaced by a real government. He told him secretly about the subtle mixture of diverse elements out of which his government would be formed, so that no faction dominated. Suñer would be Minister of the Interior and General Count Gomez Jordana the Foreign Minister, one Falangist and one Monarchist at the top. He proceeded down the scale to name his various ministers and their affiliations, specifying those who were unconditionally loyal to himself.

When Canaris asked whether such a government could be viable, Franco replied with a smile:

'I am the Caudillo. All my ministers will swear an oath of loyalty to the Caudillo.'

'If I have understood you properly, Spain will be a kingdom without a king, and you will be a king without a crown.'

'That is exactly so.'

'But are there not in this totalitarian form of yours risks of a sort that I have already detected in Germany?'

Franco rummaged among the papers on his desk and by way of reply handed Canaris a copy of the weekly *Noticiero de España* for 8 January 1938, asking him to read a scholarly and tolerant article about the Jews by the writer Pio Baroja. This rejected the anti-Semitic theories of Hitler and Rosenberg, though without mentioning them by name.

This attitude of mind did not surprise Canaris, who knew his friend well. Franco's biographer, Brian Crozier, remarks that, having need of German arms to win the Civil War, Franco knew that it was good policy to found a party of Nazi appearance and to take the title of Caudillo, 'but this did not mean that he accepted that the Nazis should dictate his behaviour and still less that he should subscribe to their anti-Jewish theories'.

Canaris did not conceal from Franco what he knew of Hitler's intentions with regard to Spain. He added that not all the German leaders shared those views absolutely. The German-Spanish policy that it would be best to pursue, he suggested, would be to avoid pressure on the high command of the Nationalist forces, such as the Italians were always recommending in Berlin. They should work instead for a steady mobilization of Spanish manpower with German and Italian support.

'If you agree,' he concluded, 'I will expound this idea when I call on Count Ciano in Rome next Thursday.' Canaris related Franco's reply afterwards to Colonel Piekenbrock and recorded it in a subsequent report.

I do agree. This is a possible solution and the only one worthy of the future government and the Spanish people. At the same time do not conceal from Count Ciano or from Hitler that I am unable, in view of the defensive effort here at Teruel, to mount an offensive of any size in the next few months, either on the Madrid front or in Catalonia. Perhaps in spring. As for the military advice heaped upon me by the Italians, you know what I think of it. You must explain to Count Ciano that Italian military assistance is valuable to me, but not so valuable as to make me agree about everything with the Italian representatives here.

In Rome, where he arrived on 20 January Canaris perceived that the Italians, and especially Mussolini, were very dissatisfied with Franco and his method of making war. They were prepared to renew their promises of aid, but not beyond four to six months, said Ciano. Canaris argued the case for Franco, but Ciano retorted:

'There must be more efficient organization of the Spanish army and better co-ordination of its various components. It will not be possible to support Franco further, if our efforts come to nothing.' Canaris had some difficulty in calming the Italians down. He said to Ciano:

'General Franco, having cleaned up the Teruel region, will confine himself to small isolated operations to shake the morale of the enemy and give battle experience to his own forces. He assures me that in the spring his big offensive will take place. In order to make that offensive he will meanwhile consolidate his hold on the Teruel front, in order to be able to defend it with reduced numbers and concentrate the rest of his forces for attack. He is already enlisting 40,000 conscripts. He has hardly any anti-tank guns or heavy weapons for the infantry.'

'I had the impression that Franco was shrinking from a decisiv
attack,' replied Ciano, 'and that this check might mean losing th
war or at least make a victory impossible. I hope that this impres
sion is wrong.'

When Canaris reached Berlin on 22 January he took one day o
rest before briefing the military and the Foreign Ministry on th
results of his visit to Spain and Italy. Soon, however, Spain cease
to be his main preoccupation; for the crisis with von Blomber
and von Fritsch was at hand. The crisis over Austria followed fast
It was 4 April before he visited Spain again.

It was raining in torrents when he arrived in Petrola, twenty
four miles north-west of Saragossa, where Franco had set up hi
headquarters in a sumptuous palace put at his disposal by th
Duke of Villahermosa. A wide smile lit up Franco's face when h
received his friend. He explained his reasons for hoping now fo
total victory.

Since yesterday my forces have occupied the big hydro-electri
installations at Tremp, cutting off the Catalan industries from thei
electricity supply. We have taken Sort, Balaguer, Frage, Flix, Gandes
and Morella. We are forty miles from Vinaroz and Castellon. We hav
entered Lerida and are at the gates of Tortosa. I am pushing forwar
the Tortosa offensive, as it is the key to the Ebro valley and Vinaroz a
well as Castellon and Valentia. In a few days we will have reached th
Mediterranean, and the Republicans will be reduced to two area
(Catalonia, Madrid and Valentia), cut off from each other. The days o
the Barcelona Government are numbered and our victory is near.

Canaris was sincerely glad at the success of the big offensives in
Aragon, launched by Franco on 9 March with five army corps
under the command of General Davila. Franco's optimism was so
great that he opened 'discreetly' with Canaris the question of withdrawing the German Condor Legion, explaining that 'the insistence of the Non-intervention Committee and the sensitivity of the
British and French representatives made it advisable to withdraw
foreign volunteers on both sides.' For his part he was willing to
study ways and means of withdrawing the Condor Legion and
likewise the Italian volunteers. He wished Canaris to go into this
matter with General Veith, the German military adviser, who would
agree on details with General Kindelan, the German Commander
of the Condor Legion. As for personnel, Franco argued that he
now had fifty trained Spanish aviators who could take over the
German aircraft. He needed specialists and technicians rather than

German airmen, and, for his navy, he told Canaris, 'a few German naval officers as instructors'.

Canaris asked Franco not to bring Veith into this matter for the time being and on 5 April 1938, sent a telegram to the Ministry of Foreign Affairs in Berlin. Herr von Ribbentrop reacted immediately to the telegram and, 'considering that the moment has come to define with Franco the system of future political relations between Spain and Germany,' he prepared a plan 'for a treaty of friendship' with Spain and presented it to Hitler. Hitler commented that he 'would prefer a commercial treaty to this proposal, which *really* has no great value'. He added that in view of the telegram from Admiral Canaris, it would not be a bad thing to his mind to withdraw German forces and especially the air force. Naturally a withdrawal would have to be agreed with the Italians.

Although the position of the Nationalist forces steadily improved, Franco remained anxious about the massive material aid still reaching the Republicans through France, which alone enabled the Red forces to prolong their resistance. For this reason at the beginning of May 1938 he asked the Germans to agree 'to leave the volunteers at his disposal until further notice'. Von Stohrer sent a telegram to Herr von Ribbentrop informing him of this request and adding: 'Franco has promised to inform me frankly in good time when he considers from his point of view that the withdrawal of the Condor Legion can begin.' In fact this withdrawal did not take place until after the Nationalist victory.

Franco's primary concern was of a political, not a military, nature. Among the storm-clouds over Europe, the most threatening was the Sudeten-German crisis that Hitler had conjured up at the end of the summer. A widespread conflict was not impossible and Franco feared that the victory which seemed within his grasp might yet elude him.

German military supplies were suddenly cut back after the beginning of September 1938, as Germany needed all available material in Central Europe. Franco realized that in the event of a major conflict, Spain would be left to her own resources. He would remember this in 1940. He had moreover to consider the risk of France invading Catalonia and Spanish Morocco in the event of war. He took his own precautions and began to build fortifications along the Pyrenean frontier and in Morocco. The French Government, supported by Britain, waged a war of nerves against Franco. General Gamelin, however, sent him a message that if Franco undertook not to enter the impending European war on the side of Germany, France would send no aid to the Republicans and would observe strict neutrality in the Civil War. Franco had, in fact, already decided that if neutrality could save his government, he would be neutral, whatever the Germans might think of his 'ingratitude'. The message from Gamelin was carried to Franco by General Ungria, Chief of the Nationalist Intelligence Service. The Caudillo gave him a direct look and exclaimed: 'Good! Tell the French that in the event of a war Spain will remain neutral as long as they keep their word not to intervene in our own struggle.'

This pledge would weigh heavily on Franco's relations with Germany. Hitler would not forgive him for his promise to remain neutral in a general war. On 2 November, 1938, after an interview with the Spanish Ambassador in Berlin, Herr von Weizsäcker, the German Secretary for Foreign Affairs, noted:

When Senor Magaz alluded to the continuity of Spanish policy, I observed to him that we had nevertheless been somewhat astonished at the haste with which Spain had promised France to remain neutral in the critical days of September 1938. The Ambassador sought to excuse his government by reason of the very critical situation in which it found itself at that time, but I did not accept his excuses.

Several days later Admiral Canaris was instructed to visit Franco again to 'clarify German-Spanish relations'. The Caudillo wished to obtain more supplies from the Germans, but the German Minister of Foreign Affairs would only consent to this at the price of economic concession to Germany which Franco had so far refused. Ribbentrop's idea of getting him to sign a political treaty had already been rejected by Hitler, but it was nevertheless necessary to get answers to several questions on the future of political relations between Franco and Germany. Before leaving Germany for San Sebastian, where he was to meet Franco, Canaris had a conversation with Herr von Ribbentrop, who told him:

The political problem of our relations with Spain is as follows. Firstly, do we wish to give aid to Franco until he achieves final victory? If so, he will need considerably more material than he is receiving from us at present.

Secondly, do we simply seek to keep Franco's strength equal to that of the Reds? If so, he will still need military aid from us, and the material that he would receive would be a useful amount.

Thirdly, if our aid to Franco is limited to the Condor Legion, he cannot expect more than a compromise peace with the Red Government. This is the problem to broach with Franco. Finally, if we do furnish him with more material he must expect counter-demands from us. Moreover the Führer wishes you to examine the conduct of military operations with the Caudillo. The view of Lieutenant-Colonel von Funck (our Military Attaché) as a German staff officer is that Spanish military organization is very faulty. However, the Führer believes that you must not make demands but rather suggest a reorganization.

At San Sebastian Canaris as usual discharged his mission in the best interests of both parties, especially helping Franco to resolve his difficulties with Berlin. He reported to Herr von Ribbentrop in a telegram of 27 October 1938:

Franco declared that he would resume the offensive, but gave no date for this action. He also said that he would not begin offensive action without receiving the war material that he had demanded from Germany and Italy. He did not think that he needed more manpower. Franco tells me that in this way he can bring the war to a victorious end, the more readily because the strength of the Red forces has been substantially reduced for lack of trained reserves, food and means of payment... I consider Franco too optimistic in his estimate of his chances of military victory if he receives from us all the new war material that he has asked for, and also in his judgement of the Reds' failing strength. It seems unlikely that the war will be ended by a purely military victory. I believe nevertheless that it is very important for Franco to receive all the war material that he has asked for, so that he can achieve important successes and so convince the Reds that it is useless to continue the war. Without this, a war of attrition is inevitable. Although certainly not without hope for Franco, it would hold certain dangers, because of internal conditions on the Nationalist side and the probable aid that will reach the Reds in foodstuffs and perhaps arms as well. . . .

This telegram was signed Guillermo, a code name used by Canaris. Herr von Stohrer affixed his own signature in approval.

Despite the able work done by Canaris, a shadow began to fall on the deep friendship that he had built up with Franco: that shadow was the purge in Nationalist Spain. Canaris was aware of the numerous atrocities committed by the Republicans since the beginning of the Civil War, but he knew also that Nationalist reprisals in the 'liberated' territories had been frightful. He had no sympathy at all for General Martinez Anido, Minister of Public Order, whose repressions were comparable with those of the *Gestapo* or the *Ogpu*. When he sounded Franco on this human

99

problem, suggesting a wide amnesty, the Caudillo told him in passionate tones that 'there is a long list of Red criminals who must suffer their just punishment.' Canaris tried to explain that magnanimity befits the victor, but the Caudillo remained deaf to his arguments. 'If the situation had been reversed, Republican reprisals would have been murderous,' said Franco.

Canaris's profoundly humane character was distressed by this attitude: he detested violence and reprisals. But were these merely reprisals? For he realized that his friend seemed to think of the enemy whom he had already partly crushed as the anti-Spain, for whom there could be no pardon, and with whom no dialogue could be held; it had to be crushed. When the war of liberation was over, those leaders who had survived would still have to be exterminated, and the chasm between White and Red forces would only be bridged by repentance and submission, or those who remained Reds must perish. This distorted perspective caused Canaris anguish. He knew that Franco was not a butcher like Heydrich and Himmler, but that his strong sense of mission necessitated rigorous justice. With the Nazi example fresh in his memory, Canaris tried to put Franco on his guard against summary justice and rapid executions and also against the mass trials held during a state of emergency. Franco assured Canaris that only those who had committed crimes would be punished. Unhappily, these words were soon to be interpreted loosely and the number of victims in Franco's purges was large.

Fifteen days after this conversation at San Sebastian, the Republican armies on the Ebro front were put to rout. Franco launched his troops in a vast offensive against Catalonia on 23 December. Barcelona fell to him on 27 January 1939. On 6 February the men of the Republic, Azaña, Negrin, Martinez Barrio, together crossed the frontier into France on foot. On 21 February Franco reviewed his troops on parade in Barcelona and on 26 March he opened the offensive against Madrid, capturing it on the twenty-eighth. Valencia, Murcia, Alicante, Almeria, Jaen, Ciudad Real, Albacete, Cuenca and Guadalajara surrendered without a blow. On 1 April 1939, Franco published in Burgos his last war communiqué: 'Today the Red Army has been disarmed and made prisoner. The Nationalist troops have reached their last military objectives. The war is ended.'

On that day Canaris was in San Sebastian, the seat of government, but he was not able to see Franco, who, for the first time since the Civil War began, was sick, in bed with influenza. He had instead two meetings with Count Jordana, the Foreign Minister.

Canaris had come to Spain a few days earlier for the signing of a German-Spanish treaty of friendship and to persuade Franco to allow immediate publication of Spain's adherence to the Anti-Comintern Pact, secretly signed on 20 February. The Spanish Foreign Minister asked the Germans to be patient for a little longer, 'so that France can be persuaded to return the Spanish gold reserves removed by the Republicans and to hand over the military equipment of the Red forces and Spanish merchant ship'. As Canaris continued to insist, Franco sent word to him through Jordana that he required a delay of two to three weeks. When Ribbentrop was consulted, he commented that the Führer's opinion was that there was no real reason for postponing the announcement any longer: 'the French will hand over the Red equipment and the ships all the sooner if Franco takes up a clear position'. Canaris was asked 'to intervene with the greatest vigour and to agree with Jordana a date this week, perhaps 5 April, on which to publish Spain's adherence to the Pact'. Canaris obeyed, Jordana demurred, Franco in his sick bed conceded. It was announced on 7 April, a week after the Nationalist victory, that Spain had joined the Anti-Comintern Pact.

13
For state or country

A few days after the *Anschluss*, Lieutenant-Colonel Erwin Lahousen, hitherto Chief of Austrian Counter-espionage, turned over all his dossiers to his German successor, Colonel Count von Marogna-Redwitz. On the advice of Marogna-Redwitz and Major Groscurth, Chief of Section II (Sabotage) of the *Abwehr*, Lahousen applied for transfer to the *Abwehr*. The personality of Admiral Canaris, whom he knew slightly and admired much, attracted him. He was pleased to receive a written instruction from General Beck, attaching him to the *Abwehr* in Berlin, and a telephone call from Groscurth to tell him that 'the old man' was expecting him at his office on the Tirpitz Embankment.

When Lahousen entered Canaris's office, Groscurth was present. The Austrian officer quickly felt himself at ease. The *Abwehr* Chief gave him clearly to understand that this was no Nazi establishment. Lahousen told me: 'The Admiral's attitude pleased me all the better, since my own was the same, as he knew very well from Helmuth Groscurth.'

Canaris asked him whether there were any of his friends in the Austrian Intelligence Service who would work for the *Abwehr*. When Lahousen said that there were, Canaris continued: 'Let us understand each other, Colonel Lahousen. Above all do not bring any National Socialists with you. In your future position as Deputy-Chief of Section I (Espionage), directed by my friend Piekenbrock, to which I appoint you, you may not under any pretext admit to this section, to which I appoint you, or take on your staff any member of the *NSDAP*, the Storm Troops, or the *SS* or even an officer who sympathizes with the Party.'

The solemn Groscurth, a tall, fair-haired, bespectacled officer, smiled silently. The Admiral noticed this and seemed to be annoyed.

'Why are you smiling?' he exclaimed.

'Because Admiral, you seemed to be reciting the *Abwehr* creed

102

in the same way as a Nazi would recite the twenty-five points of the Party programme.'

'You must be joking! You know very well that no Nazi can remember a single point of that programme and that even our beloved Führer could not recall them all.'

This short dialogue in Lahousen's presence was proof that he was accepted by 'the old man'. The sympathy between the two men soon grew into solid friendship. Those who knew the likes and dislikes of the little Admiral were somewhat surprised to see him so quickly befriend the lanky Lahousen, who towered above him. Canaris had an instinctive mistrust for big men, but Lahousen walked with a slight stoop, which was perhaps for Canaris an attenuating circumstance. It may also be that Canaris was attracted to Lahousen by his charm of language and expression, a pleasant contrast to the mannerisms of the old Prussian type of officer. Whatever the reason, Canaris henceforth rarely went about without 'his tall friend' at his side.

When in later years I asked General Lahousen whether he considered himself an intimate friend of Canaris, he replied:

In the *Abwehr* offices Admiral Canaris had intimate friends and confidential friends. Among the first were Colonel Oster and Colonel Piekenbrock. I was one of the second category. Even so, I knew very well what my Chief's ruling ideas were and was able to determine my own actions by them, but I was not informed of his political designs. You know, Canaris was not a simple man. His intellect and personality were complicated, though his behaviour was, in contrast, forthright: he hated violence as such, and though this may appear strange in a military man, he hated war as a result. He hated Hitler, his philosophy, his system and to an even greater degree his methods. Let us be clear about this: he hated Hitler from the day that he had the opportunity to see what his methods were, and that National Socialism was an anti-Christian movement – an instrument of domination fated to plunge Germany into an aggressive war. Hitler's war was for Canaris a misfortune, a great catastrophe, the end of Germany as an independent nation. Yet there was for him something that could be worse still, and that was the triumph of the Nazi system as typified by Himmler's *SS*. That had to be prevented by every possible means.

Lahousen added:

The room where Canaris worked symbolized the man and his character. You could not but notice the simplicity of his surroundings. The floor had no carpet. There was no arm-chair, only upright chairs. On the walls there were maps and between them the portraits of former *Abwehr* Chiefs, among them the legendary Colonel Nicolai. There was a signed photograph of Franco, and a picture of Canaris's rough-haired dachshund Seppl, which he adored; another showed the Seppl successors named Kaspar and Sabine. These two dachsunds were inseparable from their master; even when he was working in his office they were always around his legs. Between the two windows was a beautiful engraving, a gift from Baron Oshima, the Japanese Ambassador, a close friend. In the centre of the room stood a very ordinary desk, of a sort seen in any government office, with numerous drawers. On top stood a scale model of the warship *Dresden*, his ship in the battles of Coronel and the Falkland Isles; also an unusual bronze paper-weight, another gift from Oshima, and the three Oriental monkeys that see nothing, hear nothing and say nothing: which as Canaris interpreted to his subordinates as 'seem to see nothing, seem to hear nothing and know how to keep silent'. A metal washstand with a jug and basin, a coffee pot and a spirit heater. A large safe and a table piled with books, for Canaris read avidly.

Dr Werner Best said of him after the war: 'No matter how much he worked, he never stopped reading, and he gave books to his friends at Christmas. I received theological works, history and philosophy.'

It was the room of an intellectual rather than a military man. No portrait of Hitler on the wall!

Having met his new Chief, Piekenbrock, Lahousen went on to Colonel Oster's office. 'I don't know what stupid impulse moved me', related Lahousen, 'but when I entered and saw Oster for the first time, I said: "*Heil Hitler.*" As if stung by a hornet, Oster bounded to his feet and exclaimed: "Lahousen, if I didn't know who you were and if Admiral Canaris had not told me a lot about you, I would throw you out. You must know that we never say '*Heil Hitler*'. You must realize that we have a criminal at the head of the Reich".' Lahousen continued:

Canaris was our spiritual leader. We were all enthralled by him and influenced by his personality. He was his own man, a man of very high intellectual and moral quality. There were two groups in the *Abwehr*, not gangs of conspirators, because that would have been contrary to Canaris's nature, but associations of men with the same convictions, though each man acted according to his own personality and all were not expected to be alike. Canaris chose for a particular task those whom he personally knew to be best suited for it.

In the first group, which we may call the Canaris circle, there were

Oster, Piekenbrock, Hansen and Helmuth Groscurth. My successor in Section II, Colonel von Freytag-Loringhoven, was one of the circle, as well as Colonel von Bentivegni. I should also mention a man who did not fully belong to it, but was informed about certain actions to prevent atrocities and the issuing of orders for assassination. This was Rear-Admiral Leopold Bürkner, Chief of the *Abwehr* External Office.

The second group was not so closely in contact with Admiral Canaris and moved round Colonel Oster. This group consisted of some *Abwehr* members and others actively planning against Hitler, men such as Hans von Dohnanyi and his brother-in-law, Pastor Dietrich Bonhoeffer, Pastor Eberhard Bethge, the lawyer Dr Josef Müller, the Ambassador Ulrich von Hassell, and also, we may perhaps add, Hans Bernd Gisevius, Arthur Nebe, Count von Helldorf, Otto John of the Lufthansa Airline and several others.

What was the attitude of Admiral Canaris in 1938 to the Oster group and its clandestine operations? Canaris knew fairly well what the Oster group was up to, but he kept his distance from those activities. As Baron von Weizsäcker of the Foreign Ministry said of him: 'Canaris had the cunning of a serpent and the innocence of a dove'. He liked to remain aloof, on the side-lines, although always ready to give a helping hand in case of need. Colonel Otto Wagner told me: 'Canaris's eyes were opened by the Blomberg affair. He became more and more preoccupied with the trend of events. His misgivings and his spirit of opposition were aroused. People with complaints about the Nazis came to him and he was given the nickname: "Father of the Persecuted".'

Fabian von Schlabrendorff, one of the activists of the opposition, a lawyer and army reserve officer, wrote this of Canaris:

Despite the hatred that he felt for National Socialism, Canaris did not feel capable himself of leading a decisive action against Hitler; but he protected Oster and allowed him to use all the resources of Counter-espionage that were at his disposal to organize, strengthen and extend the German resistance movement.

Such were his nervousness and his obsession for concealment and finessing with the enemy, instead of boldly confronting him, that 'the little Admiral', as one of his war-time officers Major Paul Leverkühn has written, 'preferred to avoid conspiracy, husband his energies and concentrate on the immense *Abwehr* organization that was his responsibility.' We may recall Canaris's words to his predecessor, Rear-Admiral Conrad Patzig, in 1934 about the *SS*: 'I am well disposed towards these youngsters'.

Canaris

Three years later, in December 1937, Canaris and Patzig were together again, lunching in a corner of Horcher's restaurant in Berlin. 'There's no better place to be at ease for a talk than a big restaurant,' said Canaris when he invited Patzig by telephone to meet him there. Admiral Patzig listened attentively as his successor, with cold anger, outlined in detail the obscure and bloody happenings contrived by Heydrich and Himmler during 1937, culminating in the Tuchachevsky affair.

'These men are criminals,' said Canaris.

Conrad Patzig nodded his approbation and then suggested: 'You cannot continue to direct the *Abwehr*. Submit your resignation from the service. As Chief of Naval Personnel, I will see that you get transferred to an important command.'

Canaris was moved, but he shook his head in reply, saying despondently:

'No, I cannot do that, because after me would come Heydrich.'

The tragedy of Canaris is contained in these two conversations, authenticated by Admiral Patzig. The Chief of the *Abwehr* faced the facts about the *SS*. There were for him two alternatives: the Nazi state or his fatherland, Germany; and in the struggle between these two forces he was to go to the gallows.

Some have described Canaris as having always been opposed to Hitler, knowing everything in advance, and even as being the centre of the 'Great Conspiracy'. The truth is both simpler and more complicated than that. As Colonel Otto Wagner has written, it was not until the end of 1937 or the beginning of 1938 that Canaris saw everything. To begin with he was merely defending his own service against the *Gestapo*; then, having seen the *Gestapo*'s methods in the Tuchachevsky affair and other cases, he realized that he was dealing with utterly unscrupulous men. The longer the régime lasted, the more he came to believe that Hitler and his band were contaminating the whole German people and must be eliminated. Canaris had not reached the limits of his opposition in 1938. He was still asking himself whether it was not more honourable and more useful to refuse to serve to Hitler and to resign from the *Wehrmacht*. The German historian Gert Buchheit is one of the few to discern that Canaris was faced with the agonizing alternative, state or country:

He found himself dragged into a moral conflict which destroyed his inner composure and made him continuously restless. Like the Wandering Jew, he went from place to place, and yet he should have been able

106

to resolve this issue, even in war-time, by resigning. But Canaris felt that he must remain at his post, because that mattered more than his opinion of Hitler and the Third Reich. He felt it was his duty to maintain this powerful organization, the *Abwehr*, with its thousands of agents, its network throughout the world and its enormous budgetary resources which he controlled. He wished it to be identified with a high conception of human rights, of international law and morality.

It must be recognized that if Canaris had resigned, it would have been a catastrophe, in that Heydrich could then have taken over the *Abwehr*.

Canaris was assailed by moral conflict on another plane too. He did not torture himself with qualms of conscience about opposing a totalitarian state. He found moralizing somewhat ridiculous. He had decided to venture into the vast political arena of war and peace, on humanitarian rather than moral grounds. Gisevius thought that, despite his deep religious feelings and his faith in a just and avenging God, Canaris's outlook was curiously inter-woven with a fatalistic belief in immutable destiny. Wilhelm Canaris lost his illusions as the years of his adventurous career passed by. After the von Fritsch case, he ceased to believe in the imminence of a just power. After the outbreak of the Second World War, he lost hope of a rapid and violent end to the Nazi tyranny. When he succeeded in overcoming his fatalism and his resigned outlook, it was in order to intensify his efforts to prevent barbarism, murder and other arbitrary acts, but no more than that.

14
A plot against Hitler

A month after the *Anschluss* with Austria, on 21 April, 1938, Hitler summoned General Keitel and charged him to put the finishing touches to Operation Green, as the Nuremburg Tribunal records now reveal, for the destruction of Czechoslovakia. 'I reject the idea of a sudden attack on Czechoslovakia without justification or clear motive,' he said. 'That sort of behaviour would provoke a hostile reaction in the world and the risk of serious consequences.' He would prefer 'an open attack, following an improvised incident, such as the assassination of the German Minister in Prague during an anti-German demonstration, which would appear as an intolerable provocation to the Third Reich, and would furnish, at least to some in the outside world, a justification for our military preparedness.'

So Hitler had no idea of negotiating a settlement of the Sudeten-German question. 'I will fix the date myself for the commencement of operations,' he said. Keitel questioned him on 20 May about Operation Green. 'There is no hurry,' replied Hitler, 'I have no intention of beginning military action against Czechoslovakia in the near future.'

What happened then? It may perhaps never be known, but on the next day the Czechoslovak Government announced that Germany had mobilized, that war threatened and that a number of Czechoslovak reservists had been called to the colours. The sensational news from Prague was taken up by the world press. In other capitals there was excitement, but the German Government remained calm because there was no truth in the report of imminent war. Why then these announcements? Did President Benes wish to provoke a situation in which Britain and France would mobilize too? If that was so, Benes would have reason to regret his false move, which in September 1938 would be remembered against him.

Hitler, attacked by the Western press and accused of having

been unable to carry out his aggressive intentions, was seized with violent anger and accepted the challenge.

Two days later he summoned Keitel again and dictated to him a series of military directives, since recorded in the records of the Nuremburg Tribunal, and beginning with this phrase: 'I have taken the irrevocable decision to crush Czechoslovakia by military action in the near future . . . the preparations must begin immediately . . . the new directives will take effect from October 1st at the very latest.'

Hitler had provided for everything, except the possibility that some of his most eminent generals might refuse to follow him. That was indeed to happen. He thought that when he was rid of Blomberg and von Fritsch that the other generals would remain at heel. This was not the case. An opposition to him was reborn, the more dangerous because the hour of decision was not far away, and also because this opposition centred round General Ludwig Beck, Chief of the General Staff of the army, who enjoyed great prestige among his fellow generals.

When Beck had learned from Keitel on 23 April of Hitler's intention to make short work of Czechoslovakia, he took up his pen and wrote a considered memorandum, dated 5 May 1938, in which he set forth his reasons for anxiety. His reasoning was that the policy pursued by Hitler was leading to war, and not to local war but to world war, the result of which could only be crushing defeat for Germany. This view was exactly the same as that of Admiral Canaris, to whom Beck showed the memorandum on 7 May before forwarding it to the Commander-in-Chief General von Brauchitsch. This memorandum now seems prophetic. Even if General Beck was mistaken as to the attitude of Britain and France in the case of Czechoslovakia, if the case of Poland is substituted for that of Czechoslovakia, the general's judgement is accurate.

The memorandum irritated Hitler, who exclaimed to von Brauchitsch: 'It is stupid. Instead of holding me back, my generals should be pleading with me to advance. After all, I don't ask them to understand my orders but to carry them out!'

Then, controlling his indignation, he asked von Brauchitsch: 'How many people have read this memorandum?'

'Very few, five or six at the most!'

Reassured, Hitler laid it aside and continued in a calmer voice. 'This man Beck is always the same. A year before the *Anschluss* this bird of ill omen warned me that if I touched Austria I would have to fight France, Czechoslovakia, Great Britain, Belgium, Russia, Poland, Lithuania and who knows what others. Well, what happened?'

Von Brauchitsch replied awkwardly: 'Nothing'.*

'Tell him from me to remember that!' concluded Hitler. He next called in Keitel to fix the date for action against Czechoslovakia as 1 October at the latest. After being told what the Führer had said, Beck went through his previous calculations again, but arrived at the same conclusion: 'a conflict under such conditions can only end in a catastrophe for Europe'. A second memorandum from General Beck dated 29 May met with rejection, as the first had done.

The Chief of General Staff then decided to have recourse to other means of persuasion. Time was short and the situation was becoming more and more critical. Hitler ordered the fortification of his Western frontier with France to be speeded up and he issued a decree forbidding the military attachés of foreign countries to visit the frontier zones of Germany. He asked for more exercises by the army on divisional and corps scale, with reservists taking part. All these preparations added to Beck's resolution that he must act. Admiral Canaris and Colonel Oster, who saw him frequently during this period, encouraged him in his resolve. On 16 July Beck sent von Brauchitsch a note in which he repeated and enlarged the arguments of his two previous memoranda, but his concluding words this time were of a summary character: 'I ask you immediately to take the necessary steps with the Supreme Chief of the Armed Forces to induce him to renounce his war preparations against Czechoslovakia until such time as the military conditions have radically altered.' When von Brauchitsch asked Beck what steps he supposed to be necessary to bring influence to bear on Hitler, Beck replied:

'All senior commanders of the *Wehrmacht* must be taken in a body to Hitler to force him to abandon his warlike measures.'

'And if he persists in his intentions?'

'In that case they must all tender their resignation.'

'But this is a collective act of insubordination that you are demanding of them,' exclaimed von Brauchitsch. 'It fringes on rebellion.'

Beck had expected this reaction and produced a flow of argu-

*Major-General Schmundt, who succeeded Colonel Hossbach as Hitler's adjutant, was a witness of this meeting.

ments to justify his views. General Schmundt, who was informed of these exchanges, has left this record of Beck's reply:

All sincere and responsible Germans, wherever they may be placed in high positions, must do their utmost to prevent a war with Czechoslovakia, which will lead to a world war and the end of Germany. The existence of our nation is at stake. History will regard all these men as criminals if they fail to act. Their duty of obedience ceases at the point where their knowledge, their conscience and their sense of responsibility forbid them to carry out an order. If their advice and warnings are unheeded, they have the right and the duty to resign. Acting together they can make war impossible. They will thus have saved their country from direst shipwreck. Exceptional times call for exceptional actions.

Von Brauchitsch was acquainted with his Chief of Staff's pessimistic outlook, but had never supposed that it would push him so far. He hesitated to follow Beck along this unprepared path towards an unforeseen outcome. He was also not wholly convinced that the Chief of General Staff was correct in assuming that military operations against Czechoslovakia would lead to a general war. Much to Beck's disappointment he asked for time to reflect.

What would the Commander-in-Chief do? Nothing! What would the senior generals do, Wagner, Stülpnagel, Manstein, Adam, Thomas, Witzleben, Olbricht and others? They agreed with Beck, but a general strike of military men would not take place.

Canaris was not surprised when Beck complained to him of his solitary position and his disappointment. The Admiral said calmly to him: 'You thought they would follow you. You attached importance to their talk. I know them well, they are serfs.'

In fact von Brauchitsch and several others preferred their careers to their country and would put the Fatherland at risk rather than quarrel with the state. At a conference on 4 August, when some twenty generals assembled around von Brauchitsch, all showed themselves opposed to a war with Czechoslovakia, but all – except Beck – appeared to follow General von Reichenau, who stood up against their general pessimism and declared:

'The question of knowing whether it is proper or not to make war does not concern us. That is the Führer's business. We must rely on him to choose the best solution.'

'All the more so', added General Busch, 'since nothing can release us from our oath of loyalty to the Führer. I know the weaknesses of our army, but nevertheless I would carry out his orders because any other course would be an act of indiscipline.'

When Beck repeated these arguments to Canaris and Oster, the latter exclaimed in anger:

'They are incorrigible. Rather than disobey "Emil" they would prefer to go to the slaughterhouse and drag millions of young Germans with them, perhaps the whole nation.' After a pause he said: 'Well, since they will do nothing, it is up to us to act before 1 October.'

Canaris said nothing. He did not believe that the conspiracy which he was allowing to form, with Oster as one of its principal movers, would really be efficacious. He knew that Beck was supported by General Adam (Chief of the Personnel Office, a key component of the army), by General Thomas (Deputy Quartermaster-General), by von Witzleben (Commander of the Berlin Region) and Frederick Olbricht (Chief of the General Army Office), but what of the others? Few in the army would follow them, and none in the air force or the navy would approve of a coup led by Beck. There were in addition some civilians who wanted a coup, but what could they do against the *SA* and the *SS*?

Some of them were valuable adherents, such as Count Helldorf, Chief of Berlin Police, Gauleiter Wagner of Silesia, Professor Popitz, former Prussian Finance Minister, Herr von Weizsäcker, Chief Secretary of the Foreign Ministry, Ulrich von Hassell, former Ambassador in Rome, Erich Kordt, Counsellor in the Foreign Ministry, Carl Goerdeler, former Mayor of Leipzig, Arthur Nebe and others hovering on the edge of opposition, like the subtle Dr Schacht, sometimes lending a hand and sometimes withdrawing scornfully from contact with intellects inferior to his own.

The conspirators drew up an outline of their plan with the knowledge of Canaris. He remained strongly sceptical without saying so openly, and paradoxically gave them what assistance he could.

Despite the signs of opposition from his principal generals, Hitler remained firm in his determination. On 15 August at the Jüterbog manoeuvres he told the attendant generals that he was more firmly resolved than ever to settle the Czech question by force before the end of autumn. General Beck drew the inevitable military conclusion that Hitler meant war. On 18 August he asked General von Brauchitsch to release him from his position as Chief of General Staff. Three days later Hitler gave his consent. He asked Beck, however, not to divulge it 'for a certain period', 'in view of considerations of foreign policy.' Receiving Beck's agreement to this, Hitler directed General Franz Halder to take over Beck's duties.

On the morning of 27 August the principal officers of the General Staff were assembled in the Chief of General Staff's office. Colonel Hossbach, in his memoirs, has described this scene. When the officers entered the large room looking onto the Landwehr Canal, Beck was standing beside his desk near the window, upright and motionless except for a slight nod of recognition in reply to his officers' salutes. Wrote Hossbach,

> His fine face had an ethereal look, his eyes fixed in the distance. He spoke to us for a quarter of an hour in classical style, profoundly wise: he explained to us that he had struggled to maintain the creative prerogatives of the General Staff, though with less success than he could have wished, as circumstances had not been favourable to him. He appealed to us to be independent in our judgement and firm in our actions, and that made a great impression on us. His character, talent and capability made him the last of the great German Chiefs of General Staff.

Before leaving Berlin Beck wrote on a separate page this addition to his July memorandum:

> To define clearly our position to the historians of the future and to preserve intact the reputation of the High Command, I wish in my capacity as Chief of General Staff to record that I have refused to approve the adventures in which National-Socialism may engage. It is impossible that Germany should have the final victory.

After Beck's departure, Canaris hastened to make contact with his successor who had hitherto been Deputy Chief of General Staff, a man with a military reputation, descended from a Bavarian Catholic family of soldiers. Aged fifty-four, General Franz Halder was a precise, sardonic man wearing a pince-nez whose military haircut gave him a bristly appearance. Halder shared Beck's views, but Hitler appeared not to have discerned this, though Halder had openly criticized Hitler's plans of aggression. Oster had served under him, knew him personally and arranged a meeting between him and Canaris with positive results. Halder favoured a *Putsch* against Hitler and with this in mind was already in touch with Schacht at the end of July. He quickly became a key figure among the conspirators.

Of Canaris's activities in the summer months of 1938, Abshagen has written in his biography:

> the Admiral worked on Halder with the help of numerous documents

received from abroad. He was tireless in his efforts to depict to Halder, Brauchitsch, Keitel and Raeder the dangers to Germany resulting from Hitler's bellicose plans against Czechoslovakia. He did not even shrink from describing the Western powers as stronger and more determined than he believed them in reality to be. He believed these exaggerations to be justified. He was so sceptical about the German generals that he despaired of arousing opposition to Hitler among them other than by predicting defeat in the event of war.

General Halder, closely linked through Colonel Oster to Admiral Canaris, prepared a plan to rid Germany of Hitler and his régime before it came to an armed conflict with Czechoslovakia '. . . with the sole aim of preserving peace at all costs and permitting, under the army's protection, a new government to be formed freely chosen by the German people.'

The following were ready to act: General von Witzleben, commander of Military Region III (Berlin), General von Brockdorf-Ahlefeldt, Commander of the 23rd Division at Potsdam, Colonel Paul von Hase, Commander of the 50th Infantry Regiment in Berlin, Count Helldorf, Chief of the Berlin Police, who would have his deputy, Count von der Schulenburg, with him, and Arthur Nebe, Chief of Criminal Police.

Their principal objectives would be to seize the Reich Chancellery by a surprise assault on its *SS* guards, and to occupy the communications centres of Berlin, the telephone exchange, the radio station, the telegraph office, and all others, which would prevent the Government from issuing counter-orders. Then the principal buildings of Berlin would be seized, with special attention to the *SS* and *SD* barracks. General Hoeppner with his armoured vehicles would seal off entry into Berlin so that no Nazi reinforcements could arrive from the provinces. A state of emergency, to be proclaimed immediately, would be no more than a transitory measure before general elections and parliamentary government.

The nerve centre of this conspiracy and the planning centre for the coup was, of course, the *Abwehr* office, where the threads were gathered together. Canaris was in agreement with the plan, but he believed that the Berlin garrison regiment should not be brought directly into the coup, lest it fell prey to conflicting emotions. It should only be called in once the military action was completed. Canaris also did not like the idea of the Chancellery being attacked by the Potsdam garrison. He urged that the Führer's arrest should be made as quietly as possible. A small number of young and resolute officers should be sent to the Chancellery on some plausible pretext, arrest Hitler and remove him from Berlin by the most rapid means.

To study this proposal, in the first half of September General von Witzleben visited Colonel Oster, in whose room were three *Abwehr* officers, Captain Franz Liedig, Lieutenant-Colonel Helmuth Groscurth and Major Friedrich Heinz, as well as Hans von Dohnanyi, judge in the Leipzig Supreme Court and an eminent member of the conspiracy against Hitler. It was agreed that Heinz would form a unit, twenty to thirty strong, which would accompany General von Witzleben to the Chancellery to arrest Hitler. Halder, Witzleben and Canaris refused on principle to accept the idea of assassination. 'The purge must not be a bloody one', they said. Heinz and Oster considered that Hitler alive was a stronger force than Witzleben's army corps and that it was preferable to shoot him immediately 'and so clear the decks'. This was obvious reasoning, but Halder, Witzleben and Canaris were unwilling to shed even a dictator's blood.

The great weakness of their plan – a fundamental one – was that it depended on political factors which the plotters could not control. In order to protect their rear in the foreign field, they wished to inform the British Government. Several emissaries were sent to London both to inform the British that a war was imminent and to obtain British reactions to a possible coup in Germany.

The first of these emissaries was an intimate friend of Canaris, Ewald von Kleist-Schmenzin, always an anti-Nazi, a sincere Christian and an ardent monarchist. Furnished by Canaris with false identity papers and a travel permit, von Kleist arrived in London on 18 August and returned to Berlin on the 23rd. During this short visit he had time to see Sir Robert Vansittart, Chief Diplomatic Adviser to the Prime Minister, and two eminent Conservatives who were not in the British Government, Lord Lloyd and Winston Churchill. But in London they were mistrustful of the German opposition. Nearly all the British leaders shared the same appreciation of the international scene and were agreed on their tactics towards Nazi Germany – reach a compromise with Hitler.

Winston Churchill was impressed by von Kleist and on 19 August wrote him this letter:

My dear Sir,

I have welcomed you here as one who is ready to run risks to preserve

115

the peace of Europe and to achieve a lasting friendship between the British, French and German peoples for their mutual advantage.

I am sure that the crossing of the Czechoslovak frontier by German armies or aircraft in force will bring about a renewal of world war. I am as certain as I was at the end of July 1914 that England will march with France, and certainly the United States is now strongly anti-Nazi. It is difficult for the democracies in advance and in cold blood to make precise declarations, but the spectacle of an armed attack by Germany upon a small neighbour and the bloody fighting that will follow will rouse the whole British Empire and compel the gravest decisions.

Do not, I pray you, be misled upon this point. Such a war, once started, would be fought out like the last to the bitter end, and one must consider not what might happen in the first few months, but where we should all be at the end of the third or fourth year. It would be a great mistake to imagine that the slaughter of the civil population following upon air-raids would prevent the British Empire from developing its full war power; though, of course, we should suffer more at the beginning than we did last time. But the submarine is practically mastered by scientific methods and we shall have the freedom of the seas and the support of the greater part of the world. The worse the air-slaughter at the beginning, the more inexpiable would be the war. Inevitably, all the great nations engaged in the struggle, once started, would fight on for victory or death.

As I felt you should have some definite message to take back to your friends in Germany who wish to see peace preserved and who look forward to a greater Europe in which England, France and Germany will work together for the prosperity of the wage-earning masses, I communicated with Lord Halifax. His Lordship asks me to say on his behalf that the position of His Majesty's Government in relation to Czechoslovakia is defined by the Prime Minister's speech in the House of Commons on 24 March, 1938. The speech must be read as a whole, and I have no authority to select any particular sentence out of its context; but I must draw your attention to the final passage on this subject – Columns 1405-6, *Official Report of the Parliamentary Debates 1937-8*:–

Where peace and war are concerned, legal obligations are not alone involved, and, if war broke out, it would be unlikely to be confined to those who have assumed such obligations. It would be quite impossible to say where it would end and what governments might become involved. The inexorable pressure of facts might well prove more powerful than formal pronouncements, and in that event it would be well within the bounds of probability that other countries, besides those which were parties to the original dispute, would almost immediately become involved. This is especially true in the case of two countries like Great Britain and France, with long associations of friendship, with interests closely interwoven, devoted to the same ideals of democratic liberty, and determined to uphold them.

May I say that, speaking for myself, I believe that a peaceful and friendly solution of the Czechoslovak problem would pave the way for the true reunion of our countries on the basis of the greatness and the freedom of both.

On his return to Berlin von Kleist received this letter, which had been sent after him by a safe route and was handed to his friend Fabian von Schlabrendorff. Von Kleist showed it to Canaris and Oster; copies were made for Beck and others; the original was returned to von Kleist who put it in the desk at his Pomeranian country home at Schmenzin.

Von Kleist's visit to London was not entirely fruitless, but the results were not conclusive, thought Halder, and he sent his own emissary, Hans Böhm-Tettelbach, a retired officer, who did not make a strong impression in London. A few days later, at the instigation of Baron von Weizsäcker, Theodor Kordt, the Counsellor in the German Embassy in London, informed Lord Halifax that the invasion of Czechoslovakia had been fixed for 1 October and that the conspirators had the firm intention of acting; but Mr Chamberlain had aleady decided to base his hopes of peace on a meeting with Hitler.

On 14 September Chamberlain announced that he was going to visit Hitler 'in order to arrive at a peaceful solution of the Czechoslovak situation.'

Canaris was at dinner with Lahousen and several other *Abwehr* when he heard the news. He was consternated.

'What, he is to visit that man!' he exclaimed, and repeated this remark as he strode up and down the room.

'Why send emissaries to London if this is the result?' he muttered.

There could be no question of a *Putsch* against Hitler after such an outcome.

117

15
Czechoslovakia must die

One of Frederick the Great's sayings was that 'the aggressor is he who obliges his adversaries to have recourse to arms'. This saying haunted Canaris; for in the two meetings between Hitler and Chamberlain at Berchtesgaden and Bad Godesberg on 15 and 22 September, two melodramatic encounters, nothing seemed to favour moderation or negotiation. Hitler's megolomania seemed to grow and thrust the world towards war. Canaris realized that he had been mistaken about the will of Great Britain and France to resist Hitler. He now saw that lack of preparedness was obliging Britain to avoid war, but that the British were not willing to admit their incapacity in this respect. As for France, she had been unable to react to the re-militarization of the Rhineland, was weakened by the Popular Front, and was being forced by her military leaders, after their inertia during the Austrian crisis, to avoid war and abandon the Czechs to Hitler's rapacity. But Canaris thought that France and Great Britain could not remain passive indefinitely and that one day or another they would resort to military action. He regarded this prospect fatalistically. General Halder himself said to him late in September 1938: 'Hitler has unbelievable luck. He succeeds in everything.'

The *Abwehr* Chief had several reasons for thinking that Hitler really did succeed in everything that he did. On his desk lay an ultra-secret report, a death-warrant for Czechoslovakia. This report by *Abwehr* Section I (Espionage), not yet published, collated the information that had come in from Prague, London and Paris:

Two days after the meeting between Hitler and Chamberlain in Berchtesgaden, the Czechoslovak President, Eduard Benes, called the French Ambassador, M. de Lacroix, to tell him that he could no longer maintain the same attitude as hitherto, that of conceding autonomy to the Sudeten-German minority without alterations to the frontier. He must show himself more conciliatory to Hitler, and was thinking of seceding certain segments of territory amounting to 8,000 square kilometres and containing nearly a million Germans. This might be a way to agreement with Hitler without a mortal blow to the Czecho-slovak Republic, as 'these territories lie in front of our fortified line'. The British Minister in Prague, Mr Basil Newton, was also asked to call and was told about the same proposed concession.

On the same day Benes sent to Paris his Minister of Health, Jaromir Necas, with a memorandum and a map showing the territory that could be transferred to the Reich. This memorandum was handed to M. Léon Blum, former President of the Council, who showed it to Edouard Daladier, the new head of government, who appeared amazed at the extent of the concessions.

Necas went on to London and showed the memorandum to the Foreign Office.

The French and British Governments are now fully informed of the intentions of President Benes, who is now no longer entirely opposed to ceding territory to the Reich.

Colonel Hans Piekenbrock, the author of this composite report, looked at his Chief, who sat with his elbows on the desk and his hands to his forehead. In an almost inaudible voice Canaris said:

Piki, the problem is well defined. Since Benes is ready to abandon one million Sudeten-Germans, a little more pressure will make him cede the remaining 2,300,000 Sudeten-Germans, to the great relief of Britain and France, who appear absolutely unwilling to save Czecho-slovakia. For that is what it amounts to. Hitler does not want merely to gather in the Sudetens; there will be a Slovak state and a Protectorate of Bohemia and Moravia, all at Hitler's orders. There is no other way. Paris and London will say to each other: 'Since Benes himself accepts such large concessions, we don't really see why we should risk a world war.'

Hitler was right. After a period of dangerous tension, following a general mobilization of all Czechoslovak armed forces, came the Munich conference of 29-30 September, of which Winston Churchill disdainfully said: 'His Majesty's Government had the choice between shame and war. They chose shame, and they will have war.'

Canaris thought exactly the same. The German generals, on the verge of revolt a few days earlier, threw their conspiracy to the winds and, though with some reluctance, saluted the man who could win wars without fighting battles.

As for the German people, it thought, like the other European peoples, that it had been saved from the spectre of war and that peace was assured for a long time. Dr Goebbels, at lunch with

119

Hitler on 28 September said to him: '*Mein Führer*, if you think that the German people would be happy to go to war, you are making a mistake. I was among the Berlin crowd yesterday when the troops marched past, and they were not enthusiastic. They were morose and fearful'. Hitler took no notice. To him the essential was that France and Britain had accepted his demands, and that must mean that they were tacitly agreed to leave him a free hand in the East in exchange for no demands in the West. It was the beginning of his dream of a thousand-year Reich containing 150 million Germans.

On 1 October Hitler signed instructions to General von Brauchitsch to occupy those areas that Czechoslovakia must evacuate. He named Konrad Henlein Reich Commissioner for the Sudeten-German territories. As they advanced, special army units of *Abwehr* II blew up the concrete fortifications on their route and dismantled the powerful Czechoslovak defence line.

On 3 October General von Reichenau sat in his command headquarters, newly installed in the Park Hotel at Karlsbad, and fortified himself with several bottles of champagne. Perceiving Major Helmuth Groscurth, Chief of *Abwehr* Section II, sitting on a large sofa in the lounge, the General, sprawling at ease, roared at him in vinous tones:

'What a mess! The signals don't work; the armoured columns are stuck for hours waiting for those idiots from the maintenance units. As for the louts who drafted Operation Green, they could not have made worse arrangements for revictualling. If the enemy only knew what a stew we were in! Benes is mad to have let himself be pushed around.'

Helmuth Groscurth watched the Nazi General, who erupted again: 'Any Czech peasant with a pitchfork could have held up our army. When one thinks that the Czechs could mobilize an army of 750,000 men and an air force of 1,360 machines, it's unbelievable that they let themselves be pushed around.'

Major Groscurth said nothing, and von Reichenau showed no surprise, knowing him to be taciturn even after several glasses of champagne. Groscurth, who had been reconnoitring the Sudeten-German areas after the army had crossed the frontiers, was just as upset as von Reichenau, but for different reasons. He was not concerned with the disorganized state of the army. He was scandalized by the behaviour of the *SS* Commandos, operating in the rear of the 4th Division. In a report to Admiral Canaris, Groscurth wrote:

The *SS* Germania Standard Regiment has dispossessed, pillaged and killed in the most bestial fashion. I have seen an unfortunate young girl that a band of these ruffians violated nine times. Her father was murdered. Her mother was locked in a shack and left to her miserable fate. This young girl was without doubt a Czech, and the troops perhaps believed the stories they had read of atrocities on our Sudeten kinsfolk. That was no reason to have set on fire the farm where this family lived. These depredations are inexplicable, since the farm was to have been taken over by a Sudeten-German who has now nowhere to live.

While General von Reichenau was emptying another bottle of champagne, muttering to an officer and signing papers for him, Groscurth recalled the events of that afternoon. He had first visited the wife of Konrad Henlein the Sudeten-German leader and found her nervous and anxious, fearing for her husband's life. 'They are doing all they can to get rid of him,' she said. 'He has as many enemies in the *Gestapo* as among the Czechs. Heydrich hates him; he is jealous of his influence here. I am afraid.'

Groscurth supposed that her fears were exaggerated, but on arriving at Eger, the ancient city of the Sudeten-Germans, he met Henlein's adjutant, Karl Hermann Frank, who also spoke to him of a shadowy feud against his Chief. He affirmed that the *Gestapo* were making massive arrests, so that Reich Germans could take over the empty premises not only of Czechs but of Sudeten-Germans too. Frank continued: 'Believe me, we have reached the conclusion that our struggle to gain liberty from the Czechs will be nothing compared with the struggle to keep our jobs and our lands from the Reich Germans.'

Groscurth noted in his diary:

I went to Marienbad. We had made contact with the General commanding the region and with Lieutenant-Colonel Koehler of Group Kommando XIII of the *Abwehr*. They are furious with the *Gestapo* for making numerous arrests among the Sudeten-German party in the Marienbad area. Karl Hermann Frank has already told us of his difficulties in Eger. He found two men of the German Security Service who were trying to rouse the public against Henlein. At Marienbad Headquarters we also met Gauleiter Frank, former General Staff Officer of the Austrian army, and he complained roundly of the *Gestapo* arrests. Gauleiter Frank said that Himmler's brutes were burning and killing as they went. The Gauleiter says that a new clique is forming against Henlein and there is a sordid struggle for power. We must inform the Chief of Central Army Group, General von Reichenau, and his Chief of Staff in Karlsbad.

121

But once in Karlsbad and looking across at General von Reichenau, Groscurth asked himself whether he could make his report to this man. The Chief of Staff was away and von Reichenau was at another bottle of champagne. While he still hesitated, von Reichenau intoned one of his favourite couplets and went on:

'Think of it, Groscurth. Czechoslovakia at our feet without firing a shot! It's not surprising that after that I regard our Führer as a genius. He doesn't know what fear is, even if to lose the gamble would mean war with the Western powers. If our Führer played poker, Groscurth, he'd win 100,000 Marks in an evening. But the stakes are higher than that,' he cried, emptying a glass of champagne with a laugh. 'The game has just begun. Shall I tell you a secret? In a short time the Führer will settle the whole Czech business. Not only the Sudeten districts. That won't be all. Just wait and see. You'll see that he will do some big things, not only this!'

General von Reichenau looked solemn. He screwed his monocle into his right eye. He stared at the *Abwehr* officer to make sure that his words had penetrated.

Groscurth ventured the idea that the Führer's aims were limited and that the integrity of the remainder of Czechoslovakia would be guaranteed under the Munich Agreement.

Von Reichenau, red in the face, interrupted him: 'They are incapable of doing anything. Shall I tell you what the Führer thinks of Chamberlain and Daladier? Chamberlain is an old dotard. The Führer in his own time will have him in his pocket. As for Daladier, he's a pastry-cook.'

Von Reichenau jerked his head up, seemed to be thinking and then added: 'I know all that. I am an optimist. I hate war, but there won't be a war. You can believe me, Groscurth.'

The major realized that this was no time to put in a plea for Czechs or even for Sudeten-Germans.

Back in Berlin, Major Groscurth related to Canaris and Oster his impressions of the progress of annexation in the Sudeten-German territories. The Admiral was tired, despondent, more pessimist than ever. With his elbows on his desk he stared at Groscurth and the others – Pieckenbrock, Oster, Lahousen, Bürkner and Jenke, saying softly:

Hitler has bluffed the world and yet the world had been warned. By refusing to take the least risk, by taking Hitler's word by feeling certain that he could keep the peace by accepting Hitler's demands, Chamberlain has made war inevitable. What happened yesterday (9 October, 1938) is characteristic: the British Prime Minister in London speaks of 'an era of peace and good relations in Europe'. Hitler declares in Saarbrucken: 'we will no longer put up with British tutelage'. Hitler is drunk with power. He thinks that he dominates the world. He defies Chamberlain: 'we ask these gentlemen to mind their own business and to leave us undisturbed'. I can tell you from a British source how the Prime Minister reacted when he heard about the Führer's speech. Chamberlain said simply to Sir Horace Wilson: 'we are on solid ground. Hitler has given me his word and I have confidence in him. We have saved the peace of Europe'. Despite the respect that I have for Chamberlain, I say this man is either mad or senile. How can he fail to see that the Sudeten affair is only a step on the way to the destruction of Czechoslovakia? Yet he knows that Hitler, speaking of the Munich Agreement and the rôle played by Chamberlain, said angrily: 'that brute prevented me from making an entry into Prague!'

The Admiral stopped talking. His companions sat silent too, dark thoughts turning over in their minds. In a few months, in a year at the most, there would be a war, a world war. Could it still be avoided? As if replying to this mute question, Canaris began to speak again.

'The German people do not want a war, but even the Führer's most determined adversaries do not see a way of ridding themselves of him.'

'We must begin all over again,' cried Oster vehemently.

'Yes, but with what? The *Wehrmacht* chiefs are losing faith in the Government because Hitler overestimates the strength of our armed forces, and this error of judgement will mean a catastrophe sooner or later. The High Commands of the army and the *Wehrmacht* have not changed their opinions, but they go about their duties with indifference and resignation. We must resign ourselves too, even if it is in anger. Do not forget that any action against Hitler is impossible for the time being. The troops are victims of a victory psychosis, as you have seen in the Sudeten areas. Hitler's prestige with the *Wehrmacht* has been enormously increased. Believe me, the time has passed when we could rid ourselves of "Emil", and if we had a half-hearted *Putsch* like the Kapp *Putsch*, there would be a frightful civil war. It is as if we are in a tunnel with a bend in it and we cannot see the light at the other end.'

On the day after this depressing meeting, Major Groscurth took a train to Karlsbad, where he had arranged to meet Konrad

Henlein. On arrival he learned that Hitler was to visit the frontier and inspect the captured fortifications in the Linz area between Czechoslovakia and Austria. On 16 October Groscurth went with Henlein to Linz.

They joined Hitler on the following day, and General von Leeb, commanding the Linz area, drove with them in a cortège of military vehicles in the direction of Ceské Velice. They stopped at a little village inn to lunch, and Groscurth found himself at the same table with Hitler, Henlein, Seyss-Inquart, and the two Generals, von Leeb and von Schobert, as well as some more junior officers and *SS* General Bruckner. The meal was simple, consisting of ham, sausage, fried potatoes and then pastries. They drank beer with a show of moderation, as Hitler himself drank only fruit juice and ate biscuits and Viennese cakes. The Führer was in a curious mood, sometimes raving about the British and then exulting over the defeats that he would inflict on them in the future. Groscurth noted in his diary:

At the beginning of the meal the Führer launched into a long dissertation on the political situation and its future perspectives. The door of the room stood open and drivers and villagers crowded outside, straining their ears. Their eyes were fastened on him, fascinated as his tones grew louder. I had a painful impression of it all, and of the great risks entailed.

Hitler did not go into the details of his plans. He confined himself to some savage threats against 'the enemies of National Socialism and the Third Reich'. The British were, of course, enemy number one. 'The English,' he said, 'it is always the English who criticize me. Decadent, led by degenerate aristocrats with no energy, or by old idiots like Chamberlain. And yet they dare to cross my path. I will not have it. I will attack them and I will destroy them. The French too . . . Latin dogs, parasites! All their politicians are venal in France, no matter what party! Jewish dogs. They will be trampled and crushed if they dare to bar my way!' Curiously, Hitler went on to abuse Hungary, virtually Germany's ally and certainly Fascist Italy's ally, but as an Austrian by birth Hitler has inherited much of Austria's dislike for its Hungarian neighbour; exacerbated no doubt by Hungary's hesitation to take up a hostile attitude to Czechoslovakia in the recent crisis. . . .

'Cowards, pigs, effeminate Slavs', yelled Hitler, telling his audience that he would have had something to show the Hungarians had they not had the luck to be under the protection of Mussolini, 'my good friend'.

'As for the Poles, . . . they also are Slavs', he continued, 'but they are a totally different people. I admire the Poles. They can be compared to the Yugoslavs. They are grand people, afraid of nothing. I can reach an understanding with the Poles. I must tell my friend their Ambassador Lipski that he can count on me'.

Groscurth then notes that he murmured to his neighbour, Major Gunther Blumentritt: 'no war with Poland this year!'

Two days later Groscurth, in Hitler's entourage, was still touring the fortifications along the mountainous frontier between Germany and Czechoslovakia. Fifty senior officers arrived from Berlin by train, among them Generals von Brauchitsch and Keitel, another tour was led round by General Warlimont of the High Command.

Once more they took their midday meal in a little country inn and Hitler relaxed and began to reveal the lines of his master plan:

I was cheated at Munich. They played on my sensitivity and my sentimentality, and they succeeded. [He said that the German people had been the accomplices of the Western powers showing the same feeble, humanitarian traits] ... Now I see things clearly. I was stupid to let them cheat me. It was a moment of weakness. Chamberlain's entreaties, the fears of the German people, the doubts of my generals ... I gave way. But that won't happen again. I am returning to my original plan. I have decided to incorporate Czechoslovakia within the Reich and to do so without delay.

I am convinced that this next step will not need the mobilization, the time or the expenditure that might be supposed. We don't need the army to take Bohemia and Moravia. The whole operation will be on the political plane.

He turned to Keitel and von Rundstedt, saying: 'All you have to do is to believe in your Führer and maintain the army in an operational condition.'

Major Groscurth noted further remarks in his diary.

Have confidence in me. The action we are considering will not end in war. I have now taken the measure of my opponents. They will not go to war in this cause. All I ask of you is to keep the army ready to act. No mobilization, no useless military activity. The Czechs may yell, but we will smother their yells for them, and who would be likely to go to their aid anyway?

Groscurth and Warlimont slipped away from the inn to take a short walk through the village in the pale sunlight. General von Rundstedt soon joined them and they walked in silence, overwhelmed by the words that they had just heard. Groscurth looked after von Rundstedt who was walking on alone to his car. He remembered that Canaris had repeated to him von Rundstedt's words when the *Wehrmacht* first entered the Sudeten-German areas:

'All this will come to a bad end, Canaris. How long must this comedy go on?'

Canaris had not replied, but he commented to Groscurth: 'I was tempted to reply to him: knowing the nature of National Socialism and the low calibre of Western leadership, the comedy will last longer than you think.'

It was a bad time for conspiracies. General Halder, still amazed at the capitulation of the Western powers at Munich, was more than ever inclined to be cautious. He was still prepared to put himself at the head of a *Putsch* 'if war is declared', but would have nothing to do with the preparatory stages. 'Hitler is acting in conformity with secret conventions that he has already agreed with London and Paris', Halder told Canaris. Baron von Weizsäcker also thought that 'the barometer points to peace, even in the East'. Dr Schacht, who wanted someone to arrest Hitler, talked but did not act. Goerdeler's activity was incessant but ineffective. General Beck remained aloof. Oster made a pile of documents designed to provide evidence that if Hitler overran Czechoslovakia, Britain and France, having offered guarantees to that country, would be bound to resist.

Hitler's intuition was to triumph once again. He knew that he could deal the death-blow to Czechoslovakia without a move from the Western powers, despite all advance warnings.

The Chief of the British Secret Service telephoned to Sir Alexander Cadogan on 11 March 1939, asking the Permanent Under-Secretary of the Foreign Office for an immediate interview. They met at the Foreign Office and 'C', as he was called, handed Sir Alexander a deciphered telegram containing this message:

On 15 March at 6 AM the German army will invade Bohemia and Moravia. In order to create a diversion – which should not be mistaken for the real operation – paramilitary forces will cross the frontier a few hours earlier. An ultimatum will be put to the Czech Government and armed forces, demanding that they lay down their arms, keep their aircraft grounded and remain in their barracks. The ultimatum will not be delivered till the last moment. The vital characteristic of the operation will be surprise.

It had been said that this warning came from Germany, but it may perhaps have come from Prague. Erich Kordt suggests in his memoirs that Oster sent it to the British. There is no means of confirming this, though it may be true. It is certain that if it was indeed Oster, Canaris was not told.

There was no British reaction. In his diary Sir Alexander Cadogan wrote that 'it was a hair-raising message', but what did he do? He showed it to the Foreign Secretary and the Prime Minister. They did not think to call a Cabinet meeting or inform the other ministers. Wait and see! Incredible but true.

Group-Captain Stehlin, French Air Attaché in Berlin, who had just flown over the area between Dresden and Czechoslovakia in his own aircraft and noticed significant troop movements, did not react vigorously either.

On 11 March at 7 AM in the waiting-room of a railway station at Turnov in Czechoslovakia, a few miles from the German frontier, there was a meeting that is significant in this period of events. A man in a grey overcoat with a Prussian haircut, sitting at one of the small tables, rose to greet another man wearing a heavy black fur-lined coat, who had just come in. They shook hands in silence and went out to a waiting motor-car. As they moved off, the German in the grey overcoat said:

'Captain Fryc, it's a good thing you came. I have something important to tell you, something dramatic.'

'My dear Steinberg, you always have something important to tell me whenever we meet.'

Captain Fryc was one of the best men working for Colonel Moravets, Chief of Czechoslovak Intelligence. He opened the door of the car and let Paul Hans Steinberg get in first. Steinberg was, he knew, an *Abwehr* agent from Dresden who had over the past two years provided information to the Czech Intelligence that was both sensational and accurate. The car moved off along the Prague road.

'What is happening?' asked the Czech officer impatiently.

'In Berlin the final decision has been taken. On 15 March at 6 AM the *Wehrmacht* will march on Prague. Hitler has decided that on that day Czechoslovakia will cease to exist. Bohemia and Moravia will be placed under a protectorate and Slovakia will be declared an independent state.'

Captain Fryc felt that he was suffocating and his breath came in gasps. He knew that this was the truth.

The car stopped at the secret offices of Czech Intelligence in the Brenov district of Prague. Steinberg, alias Voral, was known here as Agent 54. Several officers, among them the regional commandant of the Czech Intelligence, began to question A.54. The particulars that he gave were convincing. He was able to relate in detail the dispositions that would precede German action. He mentioned that on 13 March the Germans would provoke incidents in the Brno and Jihlava areas and in other towns with German minorities, and this in fact happened just as he had foretold. At the end of the interrogation A.54 made a written report before leaving by car for the city centre.

The Czech officers looked at each other in silence. A sentence of death had been pronounced on the Czechoslovak Republic. What could they do? As they pondered, they asked themselves: 'who is this extraordinary man, A.54?'

That question would be answered twenty years later. Colonel Frantisek Moravets, already apprised by the French *Deuxième Bureau* of German preparations, was not astonished by A.54's information. In view of the short time remaining, he went at once to the Kolovratsky Palace, seat of the government, with the Chief of General Staff, Bohuslav Fiala. Colonel Moravets, who revealed to me after twenty years A.54's identity, wrote a report on the ensuing interview.

We went to the Council of Ministers on the same day that A.54 arrived in Prague. We did not expect to receive the pre-arranged telegram informing us that the German army and other formations would be in action against us. This telegram did reach us next day. The Government was in session. We were received in the ante-room. The Minister of Foreign Affairs, Chvalkovsky, rejected our information, describing it as untrue and alarmist. He said:

'Colonel, I know you as a good intelligence officer in my estimation and in your own. But this time your agents have told you a tall story. If such events as you report were in preparation, as Minister of Foreign Affairs I would be the first to know. Keep calm and in future do not bring us this sort of information, which is only likely to provoke alarm and public unrest.'

Colonel Moravets spoke to the other ministers, entreating them to accept his agent's report, but they adopted the same attitude of disbelief.

The Minister of National Defence, General Syrovy, assured me that we need not fear a German invasion, except if our country was necessary to Germany for military purposes. According to him that time had not yet arrived. Another minister telephoned to our Embassy in Berlin, asked what news there was in the German capital, and if there was a noticeable change of attitude towards us. The Ambassador replied that all was calm in Berlin and that the Germans were on friendly terms with our representatives. The Counsellor could not report any sign of deterioration in our relations with Germany.

I decided, in view of this blind obstinacy, to save the Czechoslovak Intelligence Service. I went to see the British Air Attaché; Major Harold Gibson, representative of the British Intelligence Service in Czechoslovakia, joined the meeting. I told them what my information was, without revealing the source, and discussed with them how we could leave Prague with the greater part of our confidential files. A plan was quickly made. A KLM airliner flew over Prague on a regular route without making a stop there. On the afternoon of 14 March at the request of the British this aircraft landed at Ruzyne airport and took on board eleven men and a number of cases, taking off at 5:15 PM for London . . . What worried me was how to remove our most important archives, the lists and case histories of our principal secret agents, without the *Gestapo* and the *SD*, who had been watching us for two weeks already, perceiving what was happening. One of my officers, Alois Frank, who had recently moved house in Prague, was the only officer of Czech Intelligence who was not being watched by German agents. It was he who took over this job, using his own car to move part of our archives from Dejvice to a villa in Podbaba.'

After lunch on 14 March the intelligence officers selected by Colonel Moravets left their homes for the office as usual, without a word even to their families about what was to happen. At 4:15 PM, leaving the Defence Ministry offices by a back door, they travelled in three cars by different routes to Ruzyne airport. The cases of documents were already on board the KLM aircraft. Nobody in Ruzyne airport knew that the airliner leaving at 5:30 PM contained the Czech Intelligence staff and its most secret records. Colonel J. Kalla, the Czechoslovak Air Attaché, met the aircraft late that night at Croydon, and so began a new life for the eleven Czechs.

President Benes wrote in his memoirs of the 'extraordinary importance' of this escape. On their arrival in London they placed themselves at his service in a letter addressed to Benes in America and began at once to set up intelligence communications with occupied Czechoslovakia.

On the night of 14-15 March, on an order from Hitler after a nod of assent from the exhausted President Hacha, forced to sign the capitulation document, the German army marched on Prague, Pilsen, Olmütz, Iglau and other towns. At 9 AM, despite icy roads and snow-storms, the troops of General Blaskowitz entered Prague. Four hours later three German military vehicles drew up outside the Czechoslovak General Staff Headquarters. An Admiral of the German navy got out of his car and entered the building, followed by a dozen officers. Admiral Canaris, accompanied by two former Austrian Intelligence officers, thus took over the Czech Intelligence offices in Prague and installed the *Abwehr* there. In the courtyard an immense pile of ashes and charred remains of paper was already covered with a layer of snow. These had been the residual documents that could not be taken to London. The filing cabinets were empty.

'We've been fooled by these dirty Czechs', grumbled Major Himmer, one of the advance party.

The Admiral turned to him: 'Colonel Moravets was well informed.'

Colonel von Kornatski, who was to command the *Abwehr* in Prague, remarked: 'I wonder when the Czech Intelligence were informed of the *Wehrmacht*'s movements.'

Canaris gave a wry smile. 'As soon, maybe, as we knew ourselves!'

As night fell a small convoy of cars approached Prague and drove rapidly through its empty streets to the Hradschin Palace, residence of the President. At the gates Hitler's bodyguard were already in position and presented arms as Hitler alighted from his car and entered the Palace.

President Hacha's special train had not been allowed by Hitler to leave Berlin until late morning. It arrived in its turn, and Dr Hacha was stupified to find Hitler at his residence, giving orders to General Blaskowitz. Without leaving him time to recover from his surprise, Hitler asked Dr Hacha to summon his ministers and principal civil servants and present them to him. They filed past Hitler, silently, with bowed heads.

Hitler then entered the great banqueting hall, lit by countless candles, opened a window and walked out onto the balcony – a calm night but with snow still falling. The capital was plunged in a deathly silence, its lights dimmed, and it was bitterly cold. Hitler shuddered, re-entered the banqueting hall and shut the window He strode over to a large table heaped with Prague hams and cold meats of all sorts, game, cheeses, fruit and beer. Seized by an uncharacteristic impulse he raised a mug of beer and emptied it at a draught, grimaced and burst out laughing. This was the only time that he was seen to drink alcohol, as if to celebrate an exceptional victory, achieved without his enemies daring to lift a finger.

Admiral Canaris had entered the banqueting hall with Baron von Neurath, whom Hitler had appointed Protector of Bohemia and Moravia. They saw this incongruous action, and he told Piekenbrock afterwards: 'I looked at him and said to myself that this rampant tiger was not going to wait until his prey was digested – eighteen million new subjects of the Third Reich – but would spring forward anew. . . . This chain of actions, the *Anschluss* the Sudeten coup and then Prague, were leading us irrevocably into a world war – the worst of catastrophes for Germany.'

16
At the cross-roads

On 31 March, 1939, Mr Neville Chamberlain announced in the House of Commons: 'In the case of any action clearly endangering the independence of Poland and which the Polish Government would consider its vital interest to resist with its national forces, His Majesty's Government would consider itself bound to afford the Polish Government all the support in its power'.

Next morning in the *Tiergarten* Park in Berlin, Canaris was out riding with Erich Kordt of the German Foreign Ministry. They reined in their horses, the Admiral flushed by the vigour of his exercise, and he began to tell Ribbentrop's secretary what he thought about the events of the previous day in London. Kordt memorized their conversation and related to me his recollections twenty years later.

'What a blockhead Chamberlain is!' exclaimed Canaris. 'His announcement to the House of Commons will not change anything. On the contrary. Does he think that he can wave a threat in Hitler's face? Does he expect the Führer to capitulate and admit: "You have won . . . I don't want a war on two fronts" . . .'.

Erich Kordt smiled. The Admiral was in a bad temper that morning. He went on:

'Poland is not a second front. The Germans are not afraid of Poland. I have all the information that we need on Poland and I am passing it up to High Command. Poland is no threat to Germany. We can go in there like a knife into butter. What a bunch of idiots they are in London! If they want to encircle Hitler – and today it's the only way to stop him – they can't do it with daisy-chains. They will need walls of steel, not these Warsaw daisy-chains'.

General Halder rode up to join them and all three horsemen cantered to the end of the ride, returning to the stables at a trot. Handing over their horses to the grooms they walked on to the Bendlerstrasse and their War Ministry offices. Halder has recalled in his evidence to the Nuremberg Interallied Tribunal that he said to Canaris: 'I have the impression that our friend Kordt must make another visit to London. The British seem to think that their agreement with Poland will settle everything. They are wrong.'

'The British are the only ones who don't see that,' replied Canaris. 'What idiots! What dolts!'

'I have been thinking, and I'm not the only one to come to this conclusion. A pact with Russia would be a hard blow for us,' said Halder. 'It really would mean the encirclement of Germany. At the same time it is the only way that Hitler could be stopped. He has had a talk with Keitel and von Brauchitsch. Both have told him that he can go ahead as long as the British and the Russians are not in alliance. He won't think of moving if the Russians turn against us.'

The General turned to Kordt: 'You must tell the British that. I don't much like the idea of Germany caught between the pincers of the West and the Bolsheviks, but I fear it is the only way.'

'Can you get leave?' asked Canaris.

'Impossible at the moment,' replied Kordt, 'but I will speak to Weizsäker.' As it turned out, Kordt was not able to visit London until 15 June.

That evening, 1 April, Canaris returned to his office from the Chancellery, where he had been in conference with Hitler. Canaris pushed Oster and Gisevius ahead of him into his room, growling: 'I've just seen a madman. I can hardly believe it. He is mad, mad. Do you understand? He is mad.'

Oster and Gisevius looked expectantly at the Admiral and listened. Canaris told them that he had found Hitler foaming with rage and pacing up and down his study, drumming his fingers on the marble table and uttering a stream of curses. A strange light in his eyes, Hitler said threateningly: 'I will make the English swallow a devil's brew.'

Canaris had been much shaken by the experience. Oster and Gisevius calmed him down, saying 'it is just the trumpeting of a criminal.' They added that Hitler might bring about another war but that he had reached the end of his surprises and deceptions. He could no longer hoodwink the world.

It may appear strange today, but Hitler at that time did not want a war with Poland. A few days previously he had said, according to General von Brauchitsch: 'Some very important negotiations are afoot with Poland. They are concerned with removing all points of friction. I don't want to quarrel with Poland. I have not supported the Ukrainians in their aspirations. I have claimed neither west Prussia nor Silesia. I am optimistic about an agreement.'

Colonel Joszef Beck, the Polish Foreign Minister, was moving towards a break with Berlin and an alignment with the Western powers. He raised the pitch of anti-German feeling, and the Polish press was unusually violent. On 3 April Hitler called Keitel in and dictated to him his new directives for Operation White.

Poland's present attitude demands on our part military dispositions going beyond our normal frontier precautions. These dispositions will in the case of trouble put a definite end to any threats from that quarter. Germany's attitude towards Poland is still ruled by the desire to avoid any incident. Poland has hitherto followed the same policy. If she should change to a hostile attitude, a final settling of accounts would be necessary. The aim would be to destroy the Polish armed forces and create a situation in the East that would ensure our security. The Reich's political task is now to isolate Poland as effectively as possible, and so limit a war to that country. Operation White must not in any circumstances be considered as the prelude to a conflict with the West. The *Wehrmacht*'s task is to annihilate the Polish army, and for that purpose plans for open and rapid attack must be prepared.

These directives were accompanied by a letter mentioning 'Delay in preparation . . . According to the Führer's directive, Plan White must be prepared so that it can be put into operation any time after 1 September, 1939.'

Canaris, on receiving Plan White from Keitel, made these comments to Major Groscurth: 'The Führer is wrong if he believes that he can localize a war with Poland. Prague is the drop of water that causes the pitcher to overflow, and the British will this time not reply with Mr Chamberlain's umbrella but with the squadrons of the Royal Air Force.'

He shared General Ludwig Beck's opinion, that bilateral wars between nations in Europe ended with the nineteenth century and that any war begun by Germany now would involve the whole of Europe or become a world war.

Tension mounted in Europe: Mussolini abrogated the Rome agreements with France. Hitler denounced the Anglo-German naval agreement. Then on 28 April in a speech to the *Reichstag*, Hitler declared what his demands had been on Poland: 'Danzig, a Free State, rejoins the *Reich*; Germany is to have a motor road and a railway across the Polish Corridor, having the same extraterritorial character as the Polish Corridor.' In exchange Hitler offered to recognize 'all Poland's economic rights in Danzig, the extent of which rights Poland herself may define and access to which city will be completely open; to recognize and accept the present frontiers with Poland as being definitive; to conclude with Poland a non-aggression pact for a duration of twenty-five years – longer probably than my span of life.'

Then Hitler, after a short pause, told the *Reichstag*: 'the Polish Government has rejected my offer.' His complaints multiplied, firstly against the anti-German policy of the Warsaw Government and its attempts to negotiate a treaty promising aid from Britain. 'This time it is too much,' he roared. 'This agreement is in direct contradiction to the agreement that I reached with Marshal Pilsudski; with which only the Franco-Polish Pact was compatible.'

Colonel Joszef Beck reacted adversely to this speech, which nevertheless contained some reasoned proposals. On 5 May the Polish Foreign Minister refused any modification to the status of Danzig. Beck's memorandum to the German Government was written in an arrogant style that infuriated Hitler.

On 21 May 1939, Berlin was decked in the Italian colours and the swastika flag for a visit by Count Ciano. A sumptuous welcome was prepared for the Italian Foreign Minister, whose father-in-law, the Duce, had just signed the 'Pact of Steel' with Germany. Hitler was smiling, Göring beaming, Ribbentrop in transports of joy and Ciano swollen with self-conceit. Germany and Italy would now march hand in hand, but in what direction? Ribbentrop and Ciano said on the radio: 'from this day on, 150 million Germans and Italians will march together in defence of their indestructible right of existence. With their friends they form an invincible world bloc.'

Canaris was sceptical, knowing Italy and the Italians. His friend General Roatta, former Chief of Italian Intelligence, at that time Italian Military Attaché in Berlin, told him what was worrying the Duce. Mussolini feared that Hitler would drag him into an adventure against his will. Although he benefited from the Pact of Steel, Mussolini wished to avoid any attendant risks. He needed a long period of peace, 'at least three years', confided General Roatta. He wanted to build up his artillery, construct a number of warships and mechanize some of his army formations. He also wished to hold a world exhibition in Rome, a project dear to his heart. In this Pact of Steel it would be Hitler who brandished the steel while

Mussolini waved an olive branch. Mussolini wrote to Hitler on 30 May that, 'only after 1943 can a war effort have some chance of leading to victory. Fascist Italy, although convinced that war is inevitable, does not wish to precipitate events. In proportion to her population she can mobilize more men than Germany can, but her effective strength is limited by the shortage of war material.'

To this letter, brought to him by General Ugo Cavallero, Hitler replied instantly: 'Duce, have no fear. There will be no war before 1942-3. All disputes likely to arise before that will be settled amicably.'

On the evening of the signing of the Pact of Steel, '22 May 1939, the XVIIth year of the Fascist era', Hitler called Keitel to the Chancellery to tell him that he must summon a military conference for the following day. Hitler did not conceal from the assembled generals the grand lines of his policy.

I wanted to reach an understanding with Poland [he told them], but that is now impossible. The Poles are not just temporary enemies; they have always been ranged on the side of those who are against us. Despite pacts of friendship, they have always persisted in the intention of seizing any chance to act against Germany. Any growth of our strength disturbs them, and that is why they will always try to snatch victory from us. If we make war, it will not be for Danzig, but to extend our *Lebensraum* in the East and assure it for future generations.

The Führer sipped nervously at a glass of lemonade. His audience, according to the Nuremberg documents, consisted of Marshal Göring, Admiral of the Fleet Raeder, Admiral Schniewindt, General Keitel, General von Brauchitsch, General Milch, the Chief of Air Staff, General Halder, General Bodenschatz, three colonels and three naval officers. Hitler continued in a composed manner:

I doubt whether Poland is an effective barrier against Bolshevism. I have ceased to consider Poland a bastion against Asia, and that is why I have no further reason to indulge the Poles. The only question is what is the most favourable moment to crush Poland. We must not expect a repetition of the Czech proceedings. This time it will be a hand-to-hand affair. But it is essential at any cost to avoid a war with Poland leading to a simultaneous conflict with France and Britain. It must be localized. Success in localizing it will be of vital importance.

Your task will be to prepare operations so that we can deal the enemy a crippling blow at the onset of the campaign. My task is to isolate Poland, so that the Western powers do not come to her aid. This can be achieved only by clever policy. That is why I am reserving for myself the decision at what moment to order the final attack ... Nobody will force us to make war, but we will not be able to avoid it. Remember that the decisive element in our success is secrecy. Nobody must know our aim, not even Italy or Japan. Neither must it be revealed to the officers of the General Staff.

Hitler was not telling his military chiefs anything new, but they were now aware that war was not far away, depending on how long Hitler might need to achieve the isolation of Poland.

After three years of horror, the Spanish Civil War was drawing to an end with the hammer and sickle in the dust and Franco's red and gold flag triumphant. The International Brigades dispersed, the Italians withdrew from the Balearic Islands, the Condor Legion returned home. The German contribution had been 16,000 men, many of them civilians and instructors. The Condor Legion itself was no more than 6,000 strong consisting of 30 anti-tank units whose casualties amounted to 300 dead. This contribution to the war in Spain had cost the Reich £18 million. On 6 June the Berliners saw the Condor Legion march through the *Lustgarten*, reviewed by Field Marshal Göring, who said: 'We possess today a powerful *Wehrmacht* in a still more powerful Germany, because providence has given us an indomitable chief.'

Canaris was on the rostrum with the generals and admirals. He smiled as he remembered the obstacles that Göring had put in the way of aid for Spain in July 1936. Hitler spoke too, praising the victory which he had secretly hoped, in furtherance of his own schemes, might not have come quite so soon. After congratulating his troops on their achievement, Hitler exclaimed:

You know what would happen to our country if the Bolshevik hordes flowed over it. You have fought against this scourge beside your Italian brothers-in-arms under a valiant leader, who never despaired of victory, and under whom we wish the noble Spanish people a new life. Long live the Spanish people and their leader Franco! Long live the Italian people and their Duce Mussolini! Long live our people and the great German Reich!

Canaris, who stood beside General Halder, murmured: 'At least he didn't add, *Heil* Hitler!'

During the month of June 1939 the international situation deteriorated further. Europe began to accept that a war was inevitable. There was a flurry of meaningless statements, wild rumours and official denials, while the Polish press and Colonel Beck himself added fuel to the flames, bringing furious replies in the German newspapers. Hitler was possessed by one of his excessive rages that would end in an explosion.

Hitler's opponents in Germany had not yet lost hope of preventing a war. Goerdeler went to London in May, where he spoke to Churchill at length about the 'German resistance'. Dr Fabian von Schlabrendorff also visited Churchill. On 15 June Erich Kordt flew to London to meet his brother, Theo, of the German Embassy, who had arranged an interview with Sir Robert Vansittart. Britain's most senior diplomatic adviser was to behave with a regrettable lack of candour to the Kordt brothers, they complained.

Erich Kordt, at the beginning of the conversation, said to Vansittart that he was not speaking on his own behalf but as the mouthpiece of an important group of people in Germany, consisting of generals, an admiral and several statesmen (Beck, Halder, Canaris, Weizsäcker and Schacht), as well as high officials (Helldorff and Nebe), all opposed to Hitler's policy and convinced that he was leading them to war. All wished to reach an understanding with the British to frustrate Hitler's plans.

'To this end,' said Erich Kordt, 'they have urged Britain since before the meeting in Munich to give Hitler unmistakable warning that his policy of aggression in Europe would lead Britain to resist him, if need be, with force.'

'I am afraid that it is now a little late for that,' replied Vansittart. 'But haven't we already done so by the treaty of guarantee with Poland?'

'But in giving this guarantee,' answered Erich Kordt, 'you have left Poland *carte blanche* as to the definition of aggression. You have surrendered the initiative. There are some dangerous elements in Poland. Since you have given this guarantee to the Poles, my group fears that they will provoke some incident, the kind of incident that would give Hitler an excuse for attacking Poland. This guarantee is more a provocation than a deterrent to Hitler.'

'Why?'

'Because it enables him to shout about encirclement, and, rightly or wrongly, the encirclement of Germany will only frighten the German people.' Kordt added: 'The country that Hitler fears is the Soviet Union.'

Vansittart raised his eyebrows.

'Kordt went on: 'My friends and I do not doubt the peaceful

intentions of the British Government and its lack of aggressive spirit. Otherwise we would be disturbed by the overtures that Britain has just made to the Soviet Union. Having considered this problem and not without some hesitation our group approves of these advances, but what disturbs us is that having started these negotiations, the British have not yet achieved any result.'

Kordt paused for breath. Vansittart remained silent, waiting for the sequel. The German now came to the important point. 'We know from reliable sources that Hitler has taken steps to open negotiations with the Soviets. Ribbentrop is ardently in favour. But nothing that you have done so far has obstructed Hitler's plans for the East. I have come to warn you – and my friends warn you – that if you do not rapidly succeed in putting the coalition of Great Britain, France and Russia on a firm footing, Hitler will conclude an economic and military alliance with the Soviet Union, and there will be war.'

Kordt left a pause and added: 'I have this information at first hand.'

Vansittart was disturbed. What Erich Kordt told him came as a surprise. He could have put the British cards on the table, but kept them covered instead, making a reply which Kordt afterwards described as a lie.

'Never fear,' he said: 'This time we will not leave Hitler a chance of getting the better of us. This time he will not catch us unawares.'

He added these words, which Erich Kordt reported jubilantly to Canaris and his friends: 'Rest assured. I can tell you that we are on the point of concluding our agreement with the Soviet Union.'

This was entirely wrong. Vansittart knew very well that the British negotiations with Russia were going badly and that it would need a miracle to overcome Chamberlain's ineptitude, obstinacy and prejudices. When Erich Kordt returned to Berlin and reported his conversation with Vansittart, there was relief among the group of conspirators. Canaris himself was taken in. Hitler might rage, he thought, as much as he liked, but he would not in 1939 risk a war on two fronts.

17

But can war be avoided?

Admiral Canaris was about to fly to Salzburg with General Keitel on 9 August when he had another meeting with Erich Kordt. 'Emil is going through a mental crisis and cannot decide what to do', the Admiral confided in Kordt. Hitler was in an insufferable mood. At his Berghof retreat he was cursing the Russians as well as the Czechs, saying that they were exasperatingly slow in making up their minds. He was cursing the Japanese for trying to mediate between the dictators and the democracies and even the Italians for their cautious behaviour.

On 10 August, Canaris lunched with the Ribbentrop family at Castle Fuschl, an Austrian property that Ribbentrop had appropriated. There he heard some more about Hitler's mood. The Foreign Minister, who had seen Hitler on the previous day, gave a survey of the diplomatic position and explained pompously that Hitler had given him a free hand to conclude a commercial agreement and a non-aggression pact with Soviet Russia. He nevertheless stressed that Hitler was in a highly changeable mood and admitted that even he could not see what his master's aims were; especially difficult to understand was his growing antipathy for Italy. Ribbentrop, the architect of the Berlin-Rome axis, rose to the Duce's defence, promising that Mussolini would loyally adhere to the terms of the Pact of Steel. 'I hope', he said, 'that Ciano's visit to Berchtesgaden on 12 August will dispel all misunderstanding'. Ribbentrop, all too confident that Italy would enter a war immediately at Germany's side, explained to a silent but inwardly ironic Canaris what a difference this would make to the British naval position in the Mediterranean; a hundred Italian submarines would close the Straits of Gibraltar to Britain. On hearing this opinion Canaris almost choked on a piece of Viennese pastry. How then was the Atlantic to become German, and the Channel too, and the Mediterranean an Italian lake, he wondered, when the British navy was the most powerful in the world and the French fleet second only to the British in Europe. Canaris repeated

Ribbentrop's views to his *Abwehr* friends: 'Believe me, when the great battle begins in the Mediterranean, we'll sit on a raft and watch the British make short work of the Italians.'

At the meeting with Ciano on 12 and 13 August at Berchtes-gaden Ribbentrop realized that he had been mistaken about the Italians' attitude. While Hitler praised the Pact of Steel, Ciano explained that Italy was not ready by a long way, for war, and that she must gain time. Her chances of victory were still only fifty-fifty, said Ciano, whereas in three years time they would be an eighty-per-cent certainty. Ribbentrop listened with stupefaction and Hitler did not listen at all, giving no weight to the Italian arguments. He had decided to strike and he would strike. He would destroy Poland and everyone else who stood in his path.

Ciano, to whom Hitler said nothing about his negotiations with Stalin, returned to Rome greatly distressed, his self-esteem wounded by the behaviour of Hitler. He reported to the Duce on his mission. 'Apart from the official report', wrote Ciano in his diary, 'I gave him my frank opinion on people and events. I come home disgusted with Germany, with its leaders and their ways. They have deceived us and they have lied to us. Now they are about to drag us into an adventure that we do not relish and which may do harm to the régime and the country. They are traitors and we should have no scruples about abandoning them.'

Mussolini's reactions were variable. At first he was carried away by anti-German feelings and agreed with his son-in-law. A few moments later he declared that honour would oblige him to march beside Germany. A little later he rejected the obligations of the Pact of Steel, saying that Italy was not ready for war and that Hitler would be crushed between Russia and the West. The Duce became still more uncertain of himself a few days later.

On his return from Castle Fuschl, Canaris heard from his friend General Roatta what had taken place between Hitler and Ciano. He lunched with Roatta, who told him that Italy did not want war at that time.

At his office Canaris found a strange piece of news waiting for him. Piekenbrock and Lahousen had been asked by the High Command to obtain 150 Polish army uniforms for an 'Operation Himmler'.

'The name,' said Piekenbrock, 'leads me to suppose that it is not a clean operation.'

'I sent a note,' added Lahousen, 'asking for what purpose the

Abwehr must furnish Heydrich with Polish uniforms. *SS* Colonel Jost repeated the request this morning.'

'Whose is this instruction?' asked Canaris.

'It is from Keitel but it is described as an order from the Führer.'

'I'll speak to Keitel and Heinz Jost,' said Canaris.

Although the major part of the Canaris diary has disappeared, some extracts of it were copied and survive, in which he explains his efforts to convince General Keitel of the mortal peril in which Germany stood. Here is the record of his discussion with Keitel on 17 August 1939:

I report to Keitel on my conversation with Jost, an *SS* officer. Keitel replies that this operation is not his concern since the Führer has not informed him about it, and that he was simply ordered to procure the Polish uniforms for Heydrich. He thinks that I was right to put the General Staff in the picture. He does not himself believe in this sort of operation, but can do nothing since the order comes direct from the Führer. Keitel says to me: 'It is not my place to ask the Führer how he proposes to put his plan into operation.' In Keitel's opinion the best course would be for Mussolini to tell the Führer that he has no intention of making war, but he believes that Italy will take part in the struggle. I reply that there is no question of that, and I repeat to Keitel the substance of the Ciano conversations with Hitler. Keitel objects that Hitler has told him exactly the contrary. I reply that, according to Count Marogna, Chief of the *Abwehr* in Vienna, the King of Italy has told King Alfonso of Spain that if Mussolini brought a mobilization order to him, he would not sign it. Keitel comments that it is interesting to note that even a country governed by a dictator can become fractious when war is in question. The democrats would be even more fractious. He is convinced that the British will not intervene. I attempt to make him revise his opinion and tell him that the British will immediately blockade our ports and destroy our merchant fleet. Keitel replies that the Russians will provide us with petrol. I report that this is not a decisive factor and that we cannot indefinitely withstand a blockade. If we use force against Poland, the British will fight us with all the means in their power. I try to explain to him that an economic war will be disastrous for Germany and that we have only limited resources to protect us against a prolonged blockade. I have just learned that we can deploy only ten submarines in the Atlantic. Keitel replies that it will be easy for us to compel Rumania to provide us with petrol as soon as Poland has been overcome. I tell him that the British have taken precautions in the Balkans and have certainly not overlooked this eventuality.

Events in fact happened more rapidly. The lines between Moscow and Berlin were overloaded with telegrams. Hitler pushed feverishly for an agreement. On 19 August a Russo-German trade pact was signed in Berlin. The Russians proposed that the political agreement should be signed in Moscow on 26 or 27 August. Hitler could not wait until then, having already determined that the date of the attack on Poland would be the 26th, at dawn. He needed the Russo-German agreement beforehand as a paralysing blow to the Western powers.

On 20 August at 4:45 PM Hitler addressed a personal message to Stalin:

I consider it of the utmost importance that we clarify as soon as possible the questions arising from our non-aggression pact. There is no time to be lost. The tension between Germany and Poland has become intolerable. I suggest that you receive my Minister of Foreign Affairs on Tuesday, 22 August or at the latest on Wednesday 23 August. He will have full powers to complete and sign the agreement and the protocol. I should welcome an early reply from you.

Hitler awaited, with growing nervousness, an answer from the master of the Kremlin. He spent the 21st pacing up and down his big study in the Berghof. His intimates and servants became ghost-like, and even his mistress, Eva Braun, avoided being with him. The house was deathly quiet. Yet Hitler was wrong to be agitated; for Stalin wanted the pact as much or more than he did.

On 21 August at 10:50 PM Stalin's reply arrived. One sentence caught Hitler's eye: 'The Soviet Government authorizes me to inform you that it agrees to Herr von Ribbentrop's visit on August 23rd.'

Hitler's jubilation was remarkable. Shouting 'Ho! Ho!' he raised his arms above his head and exclaimed: 'We have won. Now I have the world in my pocket. We can afford to spit in their eye.'

Shortly before midnight the world learned the astonishing news.

On the following morning, Erich Kordt was out riding in the *Tiergarten*. He passed Walther Schellenberg, the Chief of the *SD* Foreign Service, but the two horsemen hardly acknowledged each other. Suddenly Kordt found himself facing Canaris, who reined in and awaited him with a strange look. Kordt had not looked forward to this encounter, and his apprehensions were well founded. Canaris went straight into the attack:

'Good day, Kordt! Have you read the newspapers? According

to you, the British had practically concluded a pact with the Russians in June. What have you got to say?'

Erich Kordt grimaced uncomfortably. Canaris continued: 'My dear friend, how could you let yourself be taken in like that? You must now realize that "Emil" is more cunning than you thought, much more cunning than your friends in London.'

As they trotted on abreast, Canaris said bitterly: 'It has begun. The rot is spreading. The gaudy birds in there [he pointed at the Defence Ministry buildings in the Bendlerstrasse] are extremely impressed with what has just happened.* They have already learned the words of the *Internationale*, ready for the moment when Stalin visits Berlin.'

Two hours later Canaris and several other senior officers were flown to Berchtesgaden, where they arrived before noon. They were driven to Obersalzberg at speed and assembled in the big hall of Hitler's Berghof retreat. There were nearly a hundred of them, all in uniform, the highest-ranking officers of the three services. The meeting was not a secret one, though the proceedings were to remain secret, and there was no official stenographer. Two or three generals, however, stealthily scribbled notes; among these were Admiral Boehm, General Halder, Colonel Warlimont, and particularly Admiral Canaris, who sat in a corner and took extensive notes in shorthand. There are five versions of these proceedings, all differing and some contradictory. I have based this account on Dr Helmut Grainer's version written for the *Wehrmacht* Journal from the notes of Warlimont and Canaris.

I have summoned you [said Hitler], to strengthen your confidence and explain to you the reasons that moved me to take a certain number of decisions. It has been plain to me for some time that sooner or later we would be unable to avoid a show-down with Poland. In the spring I decided that the time had come for action.

These extracts from his long exposé are characteristic of its general tone.

Never has a German head of state embodied to the same degree that I do the will of the whole German people. I possess in consequence an authority that no person in Germany has ever possessed before me. My very existence is therefore most vital. But do not forget that I am in

*Canaris used the words 'gold and silver pheasants', an allusion to the gold and silver braid of staff officers' uniforms.

danger of being eliminated at any moment by a criminal or a madman.

Should there be war now? Hitler declared:

> The powerful personality of the Duce is a guarantee of the Italian alliance . . . We have nothing to lose. In any case we have no choice. Our economic situation is so precarious that we cannot hold out for more than a few years. Marshal Göring will be able to confirm that. Either we strike first or we will soon perish. It is extremely important that the *Wehrmacht*, before confronting the victorious powers of the last war, should prove its strength in a conflict localized in Poland. To begin military operations even against Poland alone is still an act of great audacity. We must take this risk with all our energy. As in the past year and this spring, I remain certain that our action, although daring, will be crowned with success.

The Führer did not ignore the possibility of intervention by France and Great Britain:

> . . . but they have no practicable way of aiding Poland . . . That is why the war will be short . . . The Western powers have always cherished the hope that when we have crushed Poland, we will find ourselves at grips with Russia. This hope is now dashed; for they underestimated my influence. A non-aggression pact has been signed between Germany and Russia . . . The initiative came from the Russian side. Warsaw is now isolated. Any danger of Germany being encircled is removed. I have got Poland where I wanted her. The Russo-German non-aggression pact knocks the cards out of the hands of the Western powers, and that will have considerable bearing on their ultimate behaviour. Now that I have achieved these political preliminaries, it is for the soldiers to go forward!

After an hour's interval to permit the generals to lunch, Hitler resumed his peroration at 3 PM:

> It will naturally be impossible to predict with any certainty what will be the attitude of France and Britain. The situation requires us to have a steely determination. Our leaders must more than ever give an example to others.

Hitler turned from strategy to tactics, and referred to a subject which, though it astounded his audience, threw some light on hitherto unexplained events for Keitel, Halder and Canaris.

> I will find a valid reason for starting this war [he said] which can be

145

exploited by our propaganda. It matters little whether this reason is plausible or not. The victor does not have to account to the vanquished. We won't have to say whether or not we spoke the truth. In time of war, at its beginning and during the course of operations, it is not law that matters, it is victory.

Canaris knew now why he had been asked to provide 150 Polish uniforms for Operation Himmler. The attack launched on 1 September on a German frontier radio station by a company of men dressed in Polish uniform would provide the full explanation.

Hitler defined the task that he was setting the *Wehrmacht*:

It must destroy without mercy the Polish armed forces, even if a war occurs in the West. There must be no sparing of ammunition or equipment. Operations must be carried out with implacable severity and brutality! We need a rapid result ... Our armies must act like lightning. The aim is, I repeat, the destruction of Poland. I have absolute confidence in the courage and ability of the German soldier. I also know that the *Wehrmacht* will be equal to its task and will successfully overcome all obstacles. [A pause, then Hitler said:] I will probably give the order to commence operations on Saturday morning.

He then strode out of the room, signalling to Göring, Halder, Keitel and von Brauchitsch that they should follow him.

Was the war then to begin on Saturday, 26 August 1939? Halder, Canaris and some others did not think so. Despite Hitler's bellicose tones, a peaceful solution was still, to their way of thinking, perfectly possible. They thought that Hitler had made two miscalculations: he was relying on Italy entering the war at Germany's side; and he did not believe that France and Britain would act after he had signed the non-aggression pact with Stalin. Canaris, however, was certain that Italy would not fight, and that France and Great Britain would do so if Poland was attacked. Would this reversal of events deter Hitler from making war? Canaris hoped that it would.

Canaris had another reason for believing that peace could be saved: he learned that after the conference, Hitler had received Admiral Raeder, who told him of his anxiety. Raeder did not underestimate British determination, nor the power of the British and French navies. However, Hitler did not resort to blustering replies; instead he soothed the fears of the naval Commander-in-Chief.

'Rest assured that I will overcome these difficulties through diplomatic channels, without a war. At the moment negotiations with London are still going on. I will give you my definite orders at the right moment.'

On 23 August Hitler received the British Ambassador, Sir Nevile Henderson, at his Berghof retreat, who handed him a letter from Neville Chamberlain, in which the British Prime Minister made a last attempt to prevent Hitler from taking the irrevocable step. Hitler was irritated by the sententious style of the letter and by Chamberlain's manifest desire to act as arbiter between Germany and Poland. When would Britain cease to meddle in affairs that did not concern her? The interview was stormy. In his reply to Chamberlain, Hitler wished it to be understood that Germany would not be intimidated by anybody and that if France and Britain began mobilizing their forces, he also would decide on a general mobilization.

'I am fifty years old,' he explained to Henderson. 'It is better for me to make war now than when I am fifty-five or sixty.'

There were tears in the eyes of the Ambassador, who had so blindly believed in Hitler's good faith and his will for peace. Hitler stunned him with a final threat.

'At the next provocation from Poland, I will act. The moment has come to settle the Danzig question one way or another. Tell them that!'

General von Brauchitsch and the High Command had installed themselves in their war headquarters at Zossen, twenty-five miles from Berlin. The order for attack had been given for 26 August. Was this order irrevocable? Hitler had notified his staff that 'the disposition of troops must be such that movements can always be stopped by a counter-order'. Most of his generals believed that this did not mean an inevitable war but simply intensified pressure on Poland.

By Thursday, 24 August, war fever had risen higher. It seemed that Danzig would be smothered, and the German mechanized divisions rolled eastwards. A partial mobilization was ordered in Belgium and Poland. In Holland mines were laid between Nijmegen and Maestricht. Pope Pius XII and President Roosevelt appealed for peace. Parliament met in London and voted an Emergency Powers Bill by 447 votes to 4. A mysterious person, Birger Dahlerus, in fleeting touch with the highest political circles in London, arrived at Göring's house, Karinhall. This Swedish industrialist had been friendly with Göring since 1934 and was now employed by him in the attempt to keep Britain out of the war, a mission that was doomed to failure.

On the morning of 25 August Hitler heard of an incident at Bielitz on the Polish frontier, in which eight Germans had been killed and several wounded. Hitler fumed with rage and wrote a letter to Mussolini, saying that he would probably not be able to avoid war for much longer. There was chilling news from Moscow too. Hitler had hoped that Stalin was sending an important military mission to Berlin, but Molotov replied that it would not leave at once, though it would be sent soon. The mission did not arrive till 2 September, too late to make an impression on the Western Allies. One more piece of news helped to make Hitler hesitate. Dr von Seltzam, the German Counsellor in London, submitted a report on the political situation in England which disturbed Hitler. 'Honouring the British guarantee to Poland has become a point of principle which is no longer contested in London. The general picture is one of a nation ready for anything and confident in the face of a war that it did not want, but which it considers almost inevitable.' Hitler made a sudden decision that there must be a supreme effort to detach Britain from Poland. He called in Keitel. The Chief of the High Command arrived at the Chancellery at noon.

'I need time', said Hitler, 'can the troops be halted?'

'I believe that they can be stopped, if the order is given right away. We have just enough time.'

'What time would you need the order to attack?'

'Three o'clock, Führer.'

'Hold everything till then, when you will receive my final instructions.'

Hitler summoned the British Ambassador at 1:30 PM. Henderson could hardly believe his ears when, after a grandiloquent preamble about his own generosity, Hitler offered Britain an alliance based on the return to Germany of Danzig and of the Polish Corridor. Germany was to guarantee Poland's remaining frontiers and would ask for guarantees of fair treatment for German minorities remaining inside Poland. In exchange for all this, 'Germany would engage herself to employ the German army in the defence of the British Empire wherever it might be threatened.'

Henderson was amazed. He heard Hitler say: 'I am an artist, not a politician. Once the Polish affair is settled, I would like to live out my life as an artist not as a warrior. I do not want to make

Germany into a gigantic barracks. I will only do so if I am forced to it. When the Polish affair is over, I will retire.'

Sir Nevile heard, as soon as he returned to the British Embassy, that the Anglo-Polish agreement had been signed in London. There was no longer any doubt that when the first German gun was fired into Poland, Britain, like France, would declare war on Germany. Hitler, sitting at a table, read the eight articles of the Anglo-Polish Treaty. His pallor was startling, and he sat for a long time quite still without saying a word. It was three o'clock. At 3:02 PM he rose, walked to the door, opened it and said two words to General von Vormann who was waiting outside:

'Operation White.'

General von Vormann ran to the telephone and transmitted the order. After a pause of three hours, the German war machine rolled on.

All through this decisive day, 25 August, Admiral Canaris did not leave his *Abwehr* office. For a week he had been in a state of extreme agitation. He was not completely in the picture with regard to Hitler's actions, but he could see enough of what went on to be thoroughly alarmed. He took counter-espionage measures to prevent foreign powers from discerning what was going on in the German camp and he urged Section I, Espionage, to obtain maximum information from Warsaw, Paris, London, Rome, Washington and Moscow. His routine work was intensive, and yet even as he dealt with it, the nagging question distracted him: how to overthrow Hitler and save peace?

Generals von Witzleben, Halder and Thomas conferred with the Admiral in his office. They again went over the plan to eliminate the Führer. The conspirators were not of one mind. Gisevius, spokesman for Dr Schacht, explained that Schacht did not want a coup against Hitler but rather the rule of constitutional law. This prescribed that the Council of Ministers should be given a hearing before any declaration of war. Halder inclined to think, with Oster, that Hitler must be assassinated, but that the motivation ought not to come from the *Wehrmacht*. 'But from what other quarter?' asked Oster nervously. Halder could make no reply. Thomas declared a legal coup was a Utopian idea. The mass of the people and the young officers were all for Hitler. There seemed to be no answer to this argument.

At 6 PM the Italian Ambassador, Count Attolico, arrived at the Chancellery, bringing Mussolini's answer. 'At last', said Hitler impatiently. He first read the Duce's personal message and then the official Italian note. Mussolini was emphatic: 'Italy is not ready for war. I am unfortunately obliged to tell you that Italy, lacking raw materials and the necessary arms, cannot take part in a war'.

Hitler dismissed Attolico coldly. Halder heard him saying in a low voice to Ribbentrop a few moments later: 'The Italians are behaving exactly as they did in 1914.'

The Führer appeared to Halder to be deeply worried. Hitler gave him orders, but hardly seemed to look at him. Suddenly, at 7:30 PM, Hitler apparently regained his self-possession, and called for Keitel again, saying to him in a tired voice: 'Cancel the orders to attack! I must reconsider the situation. I must get a complete view of the international scene. I must have time to negotiate. I must see whether I can prevent British intervention.'

When the information reached the *Abwehr* office, Colonel Oster was jubilant: 'The Western powers have not weakened and the Axis is broken,' he cried. 'These orders and counter-orders help our group in that they discredit Hitler in the eyes of the generals. He has dealt himself a blow from which he will never recover. He is finished. Our *Putsch* will succeed on its own.'

Oster was not entirely wrong. All officers, from the highest to the lowest were at that moment furious. Patrols had to be recalled, lorries and artillery brought to a halt and turned round, and aircraft with parachutists loaded for dropping called back to base. Keitel realized that such counter-orders did not only cause confusion. They might also completely dislocate the German war machine.

Early next morning Colonel Oster was in a cheerful mood. The countermanding of operations had been successful. Canaris too looked satisfied with the outcome. He mildly asked his officers why they had been so nervous earlier on, and seemed to think that an historic moment had been reached.

'What do you think?' he asked Gisevius. 'He will never recover from this setback. Peace is safe for twenty years.'

'Yes, but only if we act immediately,' Gisevius records his reply. 'If not, Ribbentrop and Himmler will interfere and within a week we will be back to the same crisis-point.'

'Impossible!' said Canaris.

Gisevius, writing his impressions after the war, paid high tribute to the intuition and prescience of Canaris, but added that although he had seldom seen anyone predict events with such foresight and exactitude, on 26 August Canaris had been completely mistaken. 'He thought that peace had been saved. This was the only error of judgement that I have ever heard him make. . . Hitler was finished, and, so Canaris thought, the only danger was that the civilians among the conspirators would urge the military prematurely to further action against Hitler without letting things ripen in their own way.' Gisevius soon saw his own forecasts justified, on 31 August.

On that date Hitler realized that the Polish fly would never walk into his web and that he would have to wait in vain for a Polish negotiator with full powers to discuss his demands. He would have to resort to force. At 12:40 he summoned Keitel and gave him Directive No. 1, with this preamble: 'Now that all pacific means of putting an end to the intolerable situation on our Eastern frontiers have been exhausted, I have decided to solve the problem by force. The attack on Poland must proceed according to Operation White. Day of attack, 1 September; hour of attack 4:45 AM'.

Speaking to the assembled *Reichstag* on the morning of 1 September, Hitler had discarded his brown uniform for the field-grey of the *Wehrmacht*. He went over the events of August and his demands for Danzig and the Polish Corridor. Then he declared: 'All I desire is to be the first soldier of the *Reich*. I have put on the clothes that mean most to me. I will only take them off when there has been victory. I will not recognize any other conclusion. I do not know the meaning of the word "capitulation". There will never be another November 1918 in the history of Germany'.

Canaris learned in the early afternoon of 31 August that Keitel had received Directive No. 1 to commence operations. It shattered his hopes of avoiding war and catastrophe. Gisevius was on his way to see Oster when he met the Admiral and several high-ranking officers on the stairway of the *Abwehr* office. He tried to avoid an encounter, since Canaris and he did not meet openly; but the Admiral seized him by the arm and pulled him aside, asking: 'What do you say to this?'

Gisevius had no time to reply before Canaris himself in a trembling voice gave the answer: 'It is the end of Germany.'

18
The Polish exterminations

Great Britain at 11 AM and France at 5 PM on 3 September declared war on Germany. The Second World War, which would bring death to fifty million people, had begun. That evening Canaris and his wife were dining with some of the Heads of Section of the *Abwehr* and Dr Werner Best, the liaison officer with the *SD*. Canaris was much depressed by the state of war with the West, believing that it would last for years. His officers were more optimistic, and Colonel von Bentivegni, Chief of Counter-espionage, put it at several months only. Canaris was nervous and silent, and at 10 PM as usual he and his wife took leave of the other guests.

Major Franz Seubert of Section I had been up all night moving marker flags on the huge map in the *Abwehr* office as the positions of German and Polish units changed. The German movements reached him by telephone and Telex machine. At 7:30 AM the door opened quietly and Canaris came in, seating himself on a chair and looking at the map without saying a word. Suddenly he exclaimed:

'Seubert, we have won a great victory.'

'Yes, Admiral,' replied Seubert without emotion.

'Yes, Seubert, a great victory. It *must* be believed.'

The Admiral got up and held out his hand to his junior officer, who gripped it hard and in doing so pressed the crown of his signet ring against the Admiral's fingers so hard that it drew blood. The handshake made Canaris wince and his instantaneous reaction was to slap Seubert lightly on the face, walking immediately out of the room. Seubert stood there astonished, rubbing his cheek. The door re-opened and the Admiral came back and walked up to him, stroked his cheek and asked:

'Did it hurt?'

'No, Admiral,' stammered Seubert.

Canaris showed the blood on his finger, saying: 'It hurt me.'

Seubert never forgot this incident at a critical moment of history and both the tension and human weakness in Canaris's character that it revealed. He continued to move the German flags forward on the map as the war rolled eastwards. Hitler meanwhile was not directing war operations but moving about as Supreme Commander to encourage the troops by his presence.

The world was seeing a *Blitzkrieg* for the first time, with its audacious armoured thrusts and fighter-bomber support. Quick movement and overwhelming fire power made it difficult for any fixed line of defence to survive. At the end of nineteen days only the garrisons of Warsaw, Modlin and Hela were still resisting. Hitler was exultant at the results, believing that victory was due to his military genius rather than to the efficiency of the General Staff. He began to think of taking over the military direction of operations himself. The German generals were equally intoxicated by the rapidity of their success and waited now for the equally rapid peace that ought to follow. For Hitler had assured them on 1 September that Britain and France would not enter the war, and though both were surprised when they did, Hitler maintained his ascendancy over the generals by saying that this was only an Anglo-French gesture of solidarity towards Poland. They would see reason when Poland was defeated. The fact that neither France nor Great Britain attacked in the West seemed also to vindicate the Führer's 'intuition'.

The German generals were not, however, unanimous in their views of the Polish campaign. Some were horrified by the devastation that they had seen and the atrocities that Hitler's *SS* committed. Among the first to discover the terrible truth was Admiral Canaris.

They were unaware that these criminal atrocities were all part of a plan minutely arranged by Hitler himself and imparted to Himmler on the evening of 22 August, the same day that Hitler addressed the generals. Hitler told Himmler: 'Poland will be wiped off the map of nations. What will happen behind the *Wehrmacht* front may not meet with the approbation of the generals. The army is not to take part in the elimination of the Polish cadres and the Jews. This will be the task of the *SS*'. The *SS* mission was to be twofold: to destroy the Polish nobility and intelligentsia so that the Poles could again become the serfs of Germany and to take immediate measures against the three million Jews in Poland. Himmler passed on his orders to Heydrich, who formed five *SD* commandos to follow up the army and liquidate these Polish and

Jewish elements in the rear as the battle moved forward. To disguise from the army the real purpose of these commandos, their rôle was officially defined as being:

To combat our enemies behind the front. Arrest unreliable political elements. Counter-espionage. Confiscation of weapons.

On 12 September Admiral Canaris, accompanied by Colonel Lahousen, arrived at Ilnau in Silesia, where Hitler and Ribbentrop were quartered in their special railway coaches. They entered Keitel's coach and found him sitting there with Ribbentrop. What ensued is recorded in several surviving pages copied from Canaris's vanished diary, which illustrate his terse and guarded method of recording facts, events and opinions.

I The Ukranian problem

Immediately after greeting us, von Ribbentrop gave me his opinion on the possibility of putting an end to the German-Polish war by political means. During the discussion that followed in General Keitel's coach, the Chief of High Command summed up and commented on the possibilities thus:

1st Case – There will be a fourth partition of Poland, Germany renouncing claims to territory east of the Narev-Vistula-San line in favour of the Soviet Union.

2nd Case – With the remaining part, an independent Poland will be formed. The Führer would prefer this solution, as it would enable him to negotiate the establishment of peace in the East with a Polish government.

3rd Case – The rest of Poland disappears
  a) by offering the Vilna area to Lithuania.
  b) Galicia and Polish Ukraine become independent. (If the Soviet Union accepts this arrangement).

In case 3b I am expected to make arrangements with the Ukrainians so that if the plan goes through, the Melnik organization prepares an insurrection aimed at massacring Jews and Poles. It would, however, be absolutely necessary to prevent this movement from spreading to the Soviet Ukraine (the Greater-Ukraine idea). [Here a pencilled note was added to the Canaris diary: 'the conditions do not seem to be justified any more.']

II Propaganda

I then spoke with Keitel about settling propaganda questions. The Minister of Foreign Affairs and Dr Goebbels having reached agreement, representatives of the Foreign Ministry will be sent to propaganda companies to supervise the issue of material and give their advice. (Liaison men with the Foreign Ministry). The responsibility for carrying out propaganda will remain, however, with the propaganda companies.

III Executions

I indicated to Keitel that I was informed of the plans for massive executions in Poland and that the nobility and clergy were to be exterminated. The world would hold the *Wehrmacht* responsible for these acts, since they would be committed in its presence. Keitel replied that the Führer had taken the decision on this point. He had told the Commander-in-Chief of the army that if the army wished to have nothing to do with this business, it would have to accept the presence of its rivals, the *SS* and the *Gestapo*. Each military district would have beside its military commandant a civil commandant. The latter would be in charge of extermination.

IV Bombardment of Warsaw

To the opinion that I expressed to him on the unfavourable consequences of this measure in the foreign political sphere, Keitel replied that the dispositions in this order had been submitted to the supreme decision of the Führer and Marshal Göring. The Führer confers frequently by telephone with Göring. Sometimes he (Keitel) is informed of the subject of their discussions, but not always.

V The Führer's explanations

During this meeting the Führer appeared and asked me immediately what news I had of the West. I replied to him that according to the information and reports that we had in our possession, the French were massing troops and artillery, especially in the Saarbrücken region, to prepare an attack in the grand style. I tell him I have taken steps to inform him rapidly of the area and direction in which this attack takes place.

The Führer then said: 'I find it hard to believe that the French will attack in the region of Saabrücken where our positions are the strongest. That is where we have our best fortifications, and they will find the second and third lines even stronger. I consider the Bienwald sector and the Palatinate Forest as our weakest places, despite the assertion of some that no attack can succeed in an afforested area. I am of a different opinion on this. An adventure across the Rhine is always a possibility. I think it hardly possible that they will attempt an attack through Belgium and Holland, which would be a breach of neutrality. But a grand attack on our West wall would require time.'

Keitel and Jodl expressed agreement with the Führer's opinion, and Jodl said that the artillery preparations for a large attack would last at least three or four weeks. The attack would come in October.

Then the Führer continued: 'In October it is already cold and our

155

troops will be in shelter while the French would be in the open and would have to attack. Even if they were able to seize one of the weaker points in the West Wall we would meanwhile be able to muster enough forces from the East to inflict them a salutary lesson.

'There remains then the way through Belgium and Holland. I don't believe in this, but it is not impossible. There must be vigilance.'

The Führer then turned directly to me, insisting that there must be close surveillance of all that occurred in neutral countries.

The Ukrainian problem. The announcement made by radio to the Ukrainian people, proposed by the *Wehrmacht* propaganda machine, was modified in view of Case 3b. The Ministry of Foreign Affairs agreed to the wording: 'The *Wehrmacht* has no hostile intentions towards the Ukrainian people of Poland.'

A few days later in Vienna, Canaris related his visit to Ilnau to Vice-Admiral Bürkner, Chief of the Foreign Branch of the *Abwehr*, adding: 'a war conducted in contempt of all ethics cannot be won. There is a divine justice even on earth'. Canaris was aware that the extermination of Poles and Jews was more than an accident of the German offensive. With the help of his officers he set about the compilation of evidence on war crimes in Poland. From time to time he would carry specimen documents on these atrocities in his brief-case and show them in confidence to those whose support he was seeking.

Heydrich and his *SD* Commandos were indeed active. They arrested professors, teachers, officials, businessmen, doctors, priests and landowners behind the *Wehrmacht* advance. Of the 690 clergy of the Hulm-Peoplin diocese, 518 were arrested and 214 executed. Political prisoners were sent to a concentration camp at Soldavo. They were put to death by various means on orders from Heydrich. The most frequent was *Sonderhandlung* or special treatment, which could be interpreted as 'killed while attempting to escape'. Within a short time 600 Polish intellectuals perished at Soldavo. On 27 September Heydrich summarized *SD* actions in Poland thus: 'in the territory occupied by us about 3 per cent of the Polish élite has been destroyed.' To these murders must be added those committed by the German minority militia commanded by Gauleiter Forster of Danzig and *SS* General Ludolf von Alvensleben. Another Commando was formed by Himmler and sent into Poland in mid-September 1939, commanded by *SS* General Udo von Woyrsch. It was under orders to exterminate Jews and Poles in the Kattowitz area. Heydrich told the Chief of

General Staff of the German army in Poland, Eduard Wagner, that with the arrival of the Woyrsch Commando, *SS* policy in Poland entered a new phase. Half a million Jews in Danzig, East Prussia, Posen and Upper Silesia were to be 'gathered in Polish ghettos for eventual transport overseas'. Himmler, in a speech to officers of the *SS* Bodyguard to Adolf Hitler on 7 August, 1940, vaunted the severity of this campaign behind the lines:

> You must hear these things and then forget them immediately. We have had to be hard. We have had to shoot thousands of leading Poles to show how hard we can be. I must say to you again, I must proclaim aloud that it is much easier to advance against the enemy in battle than to master an enemy population of inferior race, to shoot, to deport, to hunt down shrieking and weeping women and to gather in German citizens from the Russian occupied zones and give them protection.

The crimes of the Black Brotherhood were such that the army began to grumble about them. General Johannes Blaskowitz drew up a report which was submitted to Hitler: 'This state of affairs undermines order and discipline,' wrote the General. 'It is necessary to forbid summary executions forthwith. The German army is not here to give its support to a band of assassins.' Hitler took no notice. General von Reichenau, Nazi though he was, rebelled too against the Black Brotherhood. The Minister in charge of Poland, also protested and Canaris fanned the flames. General von Rundstedt, Administrator General for the occupied zone of Poland, announced that 'the *Wehrmacht* does not consider the Polish population as its enemy', and that the army 'is there to safeguard the property and civil rights of the people.' Encouraged by Canaris and Oster, the General Staff in Berlin demanded 'the immediate disbanding of the black formations and the calling to order of the *SS* Chiefs, to put an end to a situation that disgraces the German people'.

Hitler reacted in his own fashion. He informed the generals that the *SS* would continue and would in fact intensify its repressions. 'Our struggle cannot be measured in terms of legality or illegality. Our methods must conform to our principles. We must prevent a new Polish intelligentsia taking power and cleanse the Greater Reich of Jewish and Polish riff-raff.' A few days after this ruling, Hitler disclosed to Keitel what Halder afterwards described as 'the diabolical plan for Poland'. He told Keitel that the standard of living must be draconically reduced in Poland to no more than

157

was strictly necessary to prevent people from dying of hunger. It would have to be carried out by methods employed in no other country occupied by Germany. Keitel listened but did not protest!

Towards the end of the German campaign in Poland the American Consul-General in Berlin, Mr Geist, went to see the German State Counsellor, Helmut Wohltat, whom he had known for some years. He wished to discuss with him a delicate matter. He asked for advice and assistance in a case that was causing concern to the State Department in Washington. It was a question of tracing a Rabbi in Warsaw, which the *Wehrmacht* had just entered. This man was known to be one of the spiritual leaders of Judaism in Eastern Europe, both in science and religion. It was hoped in Washington that the Rabbi might be sent to neutral territory.

'I know Ribbentrop's attitude to such matters,' said Geist, 'and I know that I cannot appeal to the Foreign Ministry. I turn to you because I know you and you may be assured of the absolute discretion of the American State Department. I am aware of the considerable risk to any German persons intervening in this matter.'

Herr Wohltat asked for time to reflect on the request. He would see what he could do. On the following day he visited Admiral Canaris in his office and repeated to him, word for word, what Geist had told him. He asked the Chief of Intelligence whether he could and would help. Canaris's reply was immediate and affirmative, recognizing as he did the interest of high political circles in Washington. He said that he would have the Rabbi found by his *Abwehr* officers. Major Johannes Horatzek, Chief of *Abwehr* Counter-espionage in Warsaw, was able to find the Rabbi in the burning capital and to 'arrest' him under the noses of the *Gestapo*. With false identity papers the Rabbi was escorted to Rumania a few weeks later and arrived safely in New York to be welcomed by the Jewish associations there.

Canaris was ready to run considerable risks in helping people in danger, no matter what their nationality. One of his friends in pre-war days was Captain Szymanski, the Polish Military Attaché in Berlin. The two men and their wives often met, and on 23 August 1939, at a quiet dinner in Schlachtensee Canaris warned his friend that Hitler had given orders for an attack on Poland at dawn on the 26th. He advised him to take his family immediately to Warsaw and place them in safety. Szymanski followed this advice before leaving Berlin himself on the 29th. He was killed in battle during the Polish campaign.

Hardly were hostilities against Poland at an end when Canaris made enquiries about Madame Szymanski and her children, who were found to be in Lublin. Knowing the fate in store for the Polish élite at the hands of the *SS*, the Admiral ordered Major Horatzek to go to Lublin and bring back the Szymanski family to Warsaw, where they could live in a house in Ulonska Street under the protection of the *Abwehr*. The Admiral called there early in November during his visit to Warsaw and told Madame Szymanska of his fears for Poland and its people, encouraging her to move to a neutral country. He provided her with travel papers, money and transport and accommodation in a furnished villa in Switzerland. On her arrival at the villa Madame Szymanska found a flower arrangement of red and white roses, the Polish colours, with a message from Canaris and a credit note on a Swiss bank. The Szymanski family moved to England at the end of the war.

19

The German atomic scientists

A secret war was fought between Hitler and the Allies in the field of atomic science, and the question unanswered over the past twenty-five years is why German scientists, among them several of the highest ability, did not succeed in furnishing Hitler with an atomic bomb. When interrogated by the Allies after 1945 these men asserted that they had 'put the brake on' these developments. This was so, but they did not openly explain whose protection and encouragement enabled them to carry on this 'passive resistance' to the Hitler dictatorship. Canaris's role was important in this respect.

At the beginning of October 1939, Baron Ernst von Weizsäcker, Principal Secretary in the German Ministry of Foreign Affairs, received a visit from his old friend Canaris, who brought with him a bulging case of documents. This was the dossier on *SS* atrocities in Poland. His explanations added to the horror of the written and photographic evidence. Weizsäcker was appalled by what he saw. Both men were of the same mind: such deeds done under the eyes of the German army must heavily damage its reputation in the outside world and accused the German people of collective guilt in their blind devotion to Nazi leadership.

The two men shared an anti-Nazi outlook; they had both served in the German Navy; both were discreet and able to dissimulate their actions. They trusted each other sufficiently to be able to discuss problems which might endanger their lives. Weizsäcker learned from his friends in the *Abwehr* what he did not already know from his duties as senior official to Herr von Ribbentrop. He was therefore able, when Canaris showed him that day the frightful dossier from Poland, to proceed to the ultra-secret question of a German atomic weapon.

The Baron was closely informed on atomic developments by his own son, the young scientist, Carl Friedrich von Weizsäcker, a colleague of the celebrated physicist Werner Heisenberg. Speaking of an emotional letter from Einstein to Roosevelt, accusing his father of being a Nazi, his son testified: 'At that time Einstein did not and could not know that my father belonged to the German resistance movement. If that had been widely known, he could not have acted effectively, but it was my own father who advised me not to enter the Nazi party.

Canaris knew next to nothing of atomic theory, apart from Einstein's views on the enormous release of energy that would be obtained from atomic fission. He had heard of the researches of Frédéric Joliot-Curie, the French scientist, and those of the Germans, Otto Hahn and Fritz Strassmann, but he was not closely informed of the progress made by their experiments in 1938 and 1939. Weizsäcker in turn pulled a dossier out of his desk and began to explain rapidly to his friend the meaning of nuclear fission as a source of energy and the fateful military use to which this knowledge could be put. This was a subject being actively considered in the capitals of the world in 1939, and the Nazi government was doing all in its power to activate and accelerate their atomic programme. It was under the shared authority of Abraham Esau, Director of Weights and Measures in the Ministry of Education, responsible for the higher study of physics, and of Erich Schumann a descendant of the famous musician, and a friend of General Keitel, who was Professor in the Scientific Section of the Weapons Office of the *Wehrmacht*. The incompetence of these two men was proving an effective barrier to advances in the field of German atomic science.

In April 1939 there had to be a reorganization. Esau set up the Uranium Association, calling in six scientists, Joos, Hanle, Geiger, Hattauch, Both and Hoffmann and establishing them in Berlin at the Kaiser Wilhelm Institute for Physics, where the greatest German physicist, Werner Heisenberg, was already working with his assistant Carl Friedrich von Weizsäcker. Schumann put a second team of physicists to work on uranium, and from June 1939 the sale of uranium from the Joachimstal mine in Czechoslovakia was restricted to Germany. Anxieties were aroused by this export ban in America, where it was realized that an atomic weapon in the hands of the Nazi régime could be a terrible threat to civilization. The Hungarian physicist, Leo Szilard, a refugee in the United States, succeeded in persuading Albert Einstein to write to President Roosevelt, urging that the American government should proceed with the development of nuclear weapons. Five years later Albert Einstein said: 'If I had known, I would

161

never have signed that letter.' American scientists were entirely mistaken in their estimate of the Nazi atomic threat.

In fact the Germans were far from possessing an atomic programme. Their researches were uncoordinated, muddled, and dependent on limited resources. Heisenberg himself was not certain at that time whether a chain reaction by nuclear fission was feasible. He was appointed director of the Kaiser Wilhelm Institute in August 1939. On being told by Heisenberg of his appointment, the great German scientist Otto Hahn exclaimed:

'Ah, you physicists! You are not going to produce a uranium bomb, I hope. If Hitler ever possesses a weapon of that sort, I will commit suicide'.

Heisenberg replied: 'None of us will take part in any way in developing atomic weapons. What interests us is the study of controlled nuclear reactions.'

At the time of Heisenberg's nomination, the Auxiliary Weapons Office of the War Ministry took over the Kaiser Wilhelm Institute. Was Heisenberg aligning himself with National-Socialism in accepting the directorship? He has commented himself: 'I came back to Germany in August 1939 (after a visit to the United States) in order to salvage a part of German science and to help German physicists to survive the war and face post-war problems. For I have always been convinced that Hitler and Germany would be beaten.' This explanation reflects the thoughts of many anti-Nazis who continued to work for Germany.

There is in the American national archives in Washington part of a manuscript letter written by Himmler to the Head of the *Gestapo*, Heinrich Müller, advising him 'not to kill Professor Heisenberg who is indispensable to the development of German science'. This letter is unfortunately without a date, but was probably written in 1938, the year in which the *SS* weekly *Schwarze Korps* devoted an entire page to a fierce attack on Heisenberg and sought to refute the theories contained in his thesis, *The Physical Principles of the Quantum Theory*. Heisenberg commented afterwards:

In a dictatorship there can be resistance only among those who seem to be the supporters of the régime. He who takes up attitudes against it openly deprives himself of all possibility of effective resistance, or he restricts his activity to occasional protests. If he seeks to encourage a resistance movement among students, he will soon end up in a concentra-

tion camp. He sacrifices his life almost without recognition since nobody
has the right to speak about him.

As for the military resistance that sought to kill Hitler on 20 July
1944, Heisenberg said: 'They put me to shame by the real sacrifice
of their lives. But their example proved that any opposition predi-
cated a feigned sympathy for the existing authority.' This was
precisely Canaris's position.

During the summer of 1939 [related Heisenberg] Flügge published a
study of the process of nuclear fission leading to a chain reaction. It may
be that after the publication of the *Naturwissenschaften* some of our
discussions aroused a certain curiosity in military circles. But there was
never a real examination in depth of our nuclear programme by representatives of the government or members of the Auxiliary Weapons
Office before the month of September 1939 after the outbreak of war.
It was only then that a group of physicists and chemists was assembled
to study the question of chain reaction.

Canaris had listened to a long dissertation by his friend Weizsäcker and finally asked the question:
  'What can be the result of a chain reaction?'
  'According to my son a terribly destructive manifestation, a sort
of bomb at least a million times more powerful than the biggest
bombs now known.'
  Canaris looked appalled at this information.
  'Yes', said the Baron, 'and that is why my son and his friends
are taking care not to work in this direction. They do not want to
give Hitler such a weapon of destruction.'
  The two friends were of one mind on this subject and decided
to do their utmost to retard the development of so dangerous a
weapon. Canaris was informed by the young Weizsäcker of
developments and of the sort of orders likely to emanate from the
Nazi government on this subject. Canaris took care to extend
Abwehr protection to the scientists of the Kaiser Wilhelm Institute
against *SD* and *Gestapo* investigations.
  He had asked Hitler at the outbreak of war for a considerable
increase in his Secret-Service budget, and this had been approved.
Hitler also gave him a free hand in the recruiting of *Abwehr* personnel. Canaris kept a tight control on the very large funds put
at his disposal and insisted on exact accounting by his subordinates. He derived no personal benefit from these funds, and
when in 1936 he bought his small villa in Schlachtensee, he was

able to do so only because his wife, Erika, sold her Stradivarius violin. Karl Heinz Abshagen, who records this, adds what I have also heard from many of the Admiral's former colleagues: 'Canaris avoided all superfluous expenditure in his Service. He never thought of moving it from the old building to a new block, or even of having a presentable carpet put on the floor of his office'.

New faces appeared in the *Abwehr* offices after September 1939 and among them dozens of women secretaries, dressed in the field-grey uniform of army auxiliaries and known as 'the grey mice'. The Intelligence Service began to outgrow its offices on the Tirpitz Quay and in Bendlerstrasse. A confidential telephone directory shows that new offices were acquired by requisitioning a dozen houses in the area round the Bendlerstrasse for the expanding sections of Oster, Piekenbrock, Lahousen and von Bentivegni, as well as for the Brandenburg Division.

Despite this dispersal of its offices, the heart of the organization remained at Tirpitz Quay, and Canaris saw to it that a strong esprit de corps prevailed in the *Abwehr*. He tended more and more to address his staff by their Christian names and to speak in the second personal singular, *Du*, to those whom he knew well. He was constantly aware of the dangers that they ran, and they, for their part, affectionately talked of him as 'the old man', and would have given their lives for him. It was a large family. Dr Werner Best gives this description of the *Abwehr* chief: 'Canaris was obsessed with his work. Although he had a happy family life with his wife and two daughters, he had hardly any time to devote to them. As far as I know he never went on a holiday between 1935 and 1939, though he was always on the move at home and abroad contacting his agents.'

Among the new recruits at the *Abwehr* was one who was going to play an essential rôle in the conspiracies against Hitler, Dr Hans von Dohnanyi. He had already been active in the von Fritsch case as personal representative of Dr Franz Gürtner, the Minister of Justice. At the insistance of Martin Bormann, who expressed surprise that Dohnanyi was not a member of the Nazi Party, he had been removed from the Ministry and in September 1938 appointed a judge in the Reich Court at Leipzig. At a meeting with Canaris on 22 October he was told by the Admiral that in the event of war, he would like to enlist Dohnanyi immediately in the *Abwehr*. On 25 August 1939, Hans von Dohnanyi became head of a special section on Canaris's staff in charge of liaison with the

Central Section, but acting to some extent as private secretary to Canaris. He was thus at the centre of intelligence and conspiracy.

Dietrich Bonhoeffer's biographer, Eberhard Bethge, who was a friend both of Bonhoeffer and of his brother-in-law, Dohnanyi, describes the latter as

a cold intellect, of few words, but always prompt and efficient. His close friends thought him sometimes impulsive; he was of a simple and natural piety. His unusual talents had earned him positions and preferment that sometimes roused the envy of less gifted colleagues. His wife, Christine, sister of Dietrich Bonhoeffer, had been a school-time friend, and during the Nazi struggle against the churches, Dietrich and Hans Dohnanyi had been closely associated. It was Dohnanyi who asked Bonhoeffer suddenly one evening the meaning of the saying of Christ that 'all they that take the sword shall perish with the sword'. Dietrich replied that this saying was true and applicable also to their circle of conspirators. 'We must accept that we fall under that judgement,' he replied, 'but equally there must be men who accept the significance of those words.'

Dohnanyi won the complete confidence of Canaris who shared his fierce hostility for the violent creed of Nazism, 'for the devil and all his works'.

There was another recruit, Theodor Strunck, a former director of an insurance company in Frankfurt, who was taken on by Oster for special missions of non-military character. With his wife Elisabeth, Herr Strunck moved to a small apartment in Berlin which was for security reasons left registered under the name of the proprietor. Here it was that the conspirators gathered, Elisabeth Strunck acting as more than their hostess, joining in their discussions, arranging communications for them and taking various precautions to avoid *Gestapo* attention falling on her visitors and the frequent meetings that they held. H. B. Gisevius praises her work as 'much more important than that of many who vaunt their activity in what is called today "the Resistance". It is a pity that she always refused to keep a visitors book, or she could now show with pride that it was in her house that the real opponents of the régime met.'

The secret opposition had to confront a problem of ethics once war had broken out: they had to consider whether their activity was then harmful to the nation as well as to their Nazi enemies. The senior generals tended to distance themselves from any guilty association and fell back on the oath of loyalty that they had sworn to the Supreme Commander. On the other hand many of the conspirators had entered the army in the lower ranks as officers of the Reserve and some of them were in key positions. Thus the *Abwehr* became at once the field of activity and the sanctuary of the opposition. General von Witzleben took on his staff Peter Yorck von Wartenburg, a cousin of Helmuth von Moltke, head of the Kreisau circle of conspirators, and used him for liaison with General Beck. There was also a group within the High Command of the army, including General Karl Heinrich von Stülpnagel, Lieutenant-Colonel Helmut Groscurth who acted as liaison between Canaris and Halder, and the Quartermaster General, Eduard Wagner, who could arrange for contact with units in the field. The *Abwehr* and the High Command of the army established links with the civil conspirators of the Goerdeler-Popitz group, and these were maintained by such men as Otto John, the Lufthansa official, Klaus Bonhoeffer, brother of Pastor Dietrich and brother-in-law of Dohnanyi, Ludwig von Hammerstein, son of the old Commander-in-Chief of the army who had preceded von Fritsch, Count Ulrich von Schwerin-Schwanenfeld and others. Weizsäcker arranged for contact between the Foreign Ministry and the conspirators through Erich Kordt and Hasso von Etzdorf.

The idea of a coup against Hitler had not been completely discarded. There were, of course, interminable discussions, and the conspirators were aware that they could not hope to get within striking distance of him except through their military members, who had occasional access to the Führer.

Canaris encouraged his Chiefs of Sections, and especially Hans von Dohnanyi, to research and collate the offences of the *SS*. He wanted the evidence kept on their use of Polish uniforms in September 1939 to organize a sham attack, carried out by German convicts, on Gleivitz radio station. By this ruse Himmler had hoped to provide a plausible excuse for attacking Poland. Canaris also wanted full documentation of *SS* and *SD* excesses in occupied Polish territory, believing still with a certain *naiveté* that it might be possible to arrest Hitler, and that publication of this material would open the eyes of the German people. Dohnanyi obtained through Count Helldorf and Arthur Nebe some documents, photographs and films from *SS* archives relating to the massacres in Poland and added these to what Canaris called the infamous dossier.

Canaris's general rule was to keep himself informed but to remain behind the scenes. He emerged, however, in a more active rôle in the case of this dossier and made a series of visits with Erwin Lahousen to the commanding generals, though his intuitive feeling was that the German people was already too closely associated with Hitler's crimes for it to be able to struggle free in time of war.

'The Admiral was inspired by a new ardour, born of his indignation at the hideous behaviour of the *SS*', Lahousen told me:

His eyes shone and his voice was full of fervour. He used to preface his attack by going into the possibilities of a German setback on the Western Front. If his words were attentively heard, he would then open his brief-case and bring out the atrocity documents, aiming his criticisms not at Hitler himself, but at the *SS*. Could the army accept these atrocities in Poland? he would ask. Could it also admit that its authority ceased where the actions of the *SD*, *SS* and *Gestapo* began?

One of the first whom we visited was General von Reichenau, although he was well known for his Nazi sympathies. He had with him General Paulus, the future Field-Marshal who capitulated at Stalingrad. Canaris was agreeably surprised to find Reichenau and his officers very critical of the project that Hitler was then considering for a winter offensive in the West. Reichenau declared himself ready to draw up a memorandum for Hitler on the lines of 'thus far and no further' with a title subtly suggested to him by the Admiral of 'Safeguarding the German victory'. Reichenau wrote his memorandum and was the only army chief who strongly opposed Hitler a few days later on the question of a winter offensive in the West.

When Canaris met von Reichenau, he opened his brief-case and showed the atrocity documents to him. The General was strongly impressed and agreed with him that such actions could only do great harm to the good name of the German army and were indefensible.

Asked whether General Paulus had reacted in the same way as von Reichenau Lahousen told me, after a slight hesitation,

'I am sorry to say that General Paulus, when we had a discussion with him alone, defended the measures decreed by Hitler in Poland. The Admiral did not reveal his own feelings on the spot, but said indignantly to me later that he would never forgive Paulus for his attitude.'

Among the other generals whom he visited Canaris found none willing to oppose the repressions. They turned away their faces, saying: 'it is not my concern'. Canaris went to the headquarters of Field-Marshal von Rundstedt, knowing that when he had drunk a little in the evening von Rundstedt was wont to inveigh violently against Hitler 'and the toadies who surround him and push him into the worst of stupidities'. Von Rundstedt, however, avoided answering the questions put by Canaris, who went away convinced that it was not from von Rundstedt that opposition to Hitler could be expected. He returned disappointed to Berlin, to hear what Helmut Groscurth had to say about General Halder's state of mind. 'Halder has told me that when he is admitted to Hitler's presence, he carries on his person a revolver with the vague intention of shooting him down, but that he can never bring himself to do it. I told this to Ulrich von Hassell, who commented: "These generals who plot Hitler's downfall seem to wait for orders from the Führer himself before they will act".'

'That is also my view,' said Canaris.

Halder at the end of the war gave an explanation of the dilemma in which he found himself and the effect of the oath of loyalty on his will power:

I am the last of a line that for three hundred years has produced nothing but officers from father to son. The words 'treason' and 'conspiracy against the state' are not in a German officer's vocabulary. I had to choose between my duty as an officer and what I conceived to be a higher duty. Numbers of my old comrades found themselves faced with the same alternatives. I chose what I thought to be the higher duty. Most of my fellow officers thought that their duty to the flag came before all others. You may be sure that this is the worst dilemma that a soldier faces. Although I wished for Hitler's downfall I was not satisfied with the political programme of the conspirators. I felt it was for the politicians and not for the generals to rid their country of the Führer, since it was the politicians who had brought him to power.

What Halder omitted to say in this context was that in October 1939 he had used Helmut Groscurth as an intermediary to propose to Canaris that an attempt on Hitler's life should be prepared. Once Hitler was eliminated, he, Halder, would be ready to act. Canaris rejected this idea emphatically, never having wished for Hitler's assassination. He thought that there was a great difference between a military revolt and the arrest of the tyrant, and a murderous ambush. His instinctive aversion to bloodshed, even the blood of such a creature was made stronger by religious scruples. Nevertheless he took an active part in the plans which, one after the other, were formed and abandoned in the winter of 1939 and the spring of 1940, as difficulties arose and the generals remained undecided.

Canaris has been accused of playing a double game, of favouring the opposition against Hitler while serving him faithfully at the same time. We can see from various examples quoted in the course of this book that such a criticism is mistaken. A conference on 20 November 1939, in the Reich Chancellery throws some light on Canaris's attitude towards Hitler and explains why so many people, Hitler among them, were taken in by him.

At the end of October 1939 Canaris received an instruction from Keitel to procure Dutch and Belgian uniforms. After his experience with the Polish uniforms for Operation Himmler and the fake raid on Gleiwitz radio station, the Chief of the *Abwehr* protested strongly at this request, but Keitel told him: 'It is an order from the Führer', adding, 'I cannot yet give you particulars about the use of these uniforms. The Führer will do so himself, but I can tell you that it is not in order to carry out another operation of the Gleiwitz type. In this instance it is not military uniforms that we require but those of the frontier police and customs officers.'

Canaris preferred not to maintain his objections. He gave the necessary orders. Soon after that the uniforms were obtained, but the theft did not escape notice. Belgian and Dutch newspapers published their conjectures about the reasons for it. A Dutch caricaturist hit the nail on the head with a cartoon of Göring in Dutch train-driver's uniform taking a tram-car full of German soldiers through Amsterdam.

Canaris was summoned to the Chancellery on 20 November for a conference on the subject of an offensive in the West by General von Reichenau's 6th Army. Special precautions were required to ensure the seizure of certain bridgeheads on the Meuse inside Belgian and Dutch territory. As men of the *Abwehr*'s Brandenburg Regiment would have an important part to play, Hitler summoned Canaris as well as Göring, von Brauchitsch, Keitel, von Reichenau, Halder and others to discuss the operation.

Hitler was at the outset in the best of tempers. He was keenly interested in the various ruses that would be used to carry out tasks within the main operation. Canaris then heard for the first time what was the purpose of the Belgian and Dutch uniforms. Volunteers of the Brandenburg Regiment would be disguised in these uniforms and sent forward before the attack by von Reichenau's army into the vicinity of the bridges in order to prevent them being demolished by the Belgian and Dutch forces. Hitler invited Canaris to report on what had already been accomplished and what remained to be done. Canaris began by saying that he had obtained the required uniforms, when General Walther Reinhardt, who had nursed a long-standing prejudice against Canaris, since the days of the Kapp *Putsch*, interrupted with the dry remark: 'What you say is already in the Belgian and Dutch newspapers.'

Reinhardt held out cuttings from the newspapers in question. A sudden explosion of anger from Hitler was the immediate result. He cursed the fools who spoiled his best plans. The military shuffled and sat with downcast eyes. Keitel turned pale. Reinhardt turned even paler, realizing that he had gone too far. Only Canaris did not for a moment lose his composure and waited till the storm had passed. Then he began to speak to Hitler in a soft voice, so that the Führer had to pay attention to hear what was being said, and argued that no real damage had been done or surprise lost by this revelation. Hitler was quickly mollified and others at the table commented afterwards on the skill Canaris had shown.

This was in other respects a notable occasion, since the senior officers and Hitler were meeting for the first time since the assassination attempt of 8 November in the Bürgerbrau Cellar in Munich, which had failed to kill Hitler though there were seven dead and sixty-three injured. It was the work of Georg Elser, a Communist, and although some at that early date supposed that Canaris had prior knowledge of the attempt, Canaris was then concerned with quite other matters.

Talks had been opened in Rome that were intended to bring about a compromise peace with the British. They were being conducted by Dr Josef Müller, a Bavarian lawyer and member of the former Bavarian Peoples' Party. Müller was a downright anti-Nazi, a Roman Catholic, friend of Cardinal Faulhaber, and known to Pope Pius XII and many important Vatican officials. Müller was a man of Herculean physique, courageous and indefatigable, who liked his friends to call him by his school nickname, *Ochsensepp* – literally Joe the Ox. The Portuguese consul in Munich, Wilhelm Schmidhuber, had brought together Müller and Oster, who suggested to Canaris in September 1939 that Müller be enlisted in the *Abwehr*. He was attached to the Munich office and sent almost immediately to Rome to refresh his contacts with the Vatican.

Dr Müller fulfilled his mission with the aid of the Roman Catholic hierarchy, notably Father Leiber, personal secretary to the Pope, and Monsignor Kaas, former President of the German Party. Kaas had voted with his party in the *Reichstag* in favour of Hitler on 21 March 1933, had retired from party politics and gone to Rome. There he was given supervision of repair and maintenance work on the fabric of St Peter's and helped von Papen to negotiate the Concordat with Germany signed in July 1933.

Josef Müller of the *Abwehr* was seeking from the British an 'assurance' which would perhaps encourage the German generals to turn their weapons against Hitler. Dr Müller was entrusted with the task of finding out on what terms Great Britain would agree to end the war.

On the slipper terrain of peace talks Canaris moved with the greatest caution. He did not see Müller on his return to Berlin but let Oster and Dohnanyi inform him of what had passed and also what Müller was reporting to General Beck. The following conversation with Hans von Dohnanyi in October 1939 illustrates the position that Canaris took.

'Is there hope', asked Canaris, 'that the Western Allies will make a distinction between Hitler and Germany after the acquiescence of Germans in the invasion of Austria, Czechoslovakia and now Poland?'

'It is necessary', replied Dohnanyi, 'to make it clear to the British that the anti-Nazis have not despaired of removing Hitler from power and of examining conditions for a compromise peace with London and Paris.'

Canaris mused for a moment and then said:

'At the same time there must be acceptable peace conditions if the generals are not to object that the Allies will regard any internal revolt as a sign of weakness which they would then exploit. I have no confidence in the courage of the generals, but ought we not to try everything, even if we know that there can be no possible outcome?'

Father Leiber and Monsignor Kaas sounded Sir Francis D'Arcy Osborne, British Minister to the Vatican, as to his views. They were encouraged in the belief that there was still a chance of Germany obtaining a compromise peace if she rid herself of Hitler, and that there were still people in London with whom it might be possible to talk.

Towards the end of October, these soundings taken in the Pope's entourage impelled Müller to inform his contacts in Berlin that Pope Pius XII seemed surprisingly well disposed towards an

171

equitable settlement of the whole German question and that Lord Halifax, the British Foreign Secretary, while accepting the broad lines of the German argument, was reserved in his attitude towards a decentralization of power in Germany and a possible referendum in Austria. The Pope assured Müller that details of this sort could not really delay the conclusion of a peace if there was agreement on all other points.

The results of Müller's mission were embodied in a report drafted in Rome, reviewed and amended in Berlin by Müller and Dohnanyi, and, with Canaris's assent, shown confidentially to some German generals. Report X, as it came to be known, acknowledged that negotiations with the Allies could only be commenced after the overthrow of the Nazi régime and the establishment of a responsible government, completely unconnected with the old régime and able to honour its own obligations. The report asserted that the Allies would allow Germany to retain the Sudeten territories, that a plebiscite would be organized in Austria and in the Polish Corridor. Report X was completed at the end of February 1940.

General Thomas was asked to take Report X to General Halder, so that it could be submitted to the Commander-in-Chief, General von Brauchitsch. This was done, but it resulted in a resounding setback, as Halder relates:

I asked him to read this document one night so that we could talk about it on the following morning. When I saw General von Brauchitsch next day his expression was grave. He gave me back the document, saying: 'You ought not to have shown this to me. It is a matter of high treason. We cannot under any pretext contemplate that sort of thing. We are at war. It may be permissible to discuss whether we can make contact with a foreign power in time of peace, but in war-time nothing of this kind can be done. Moreover it is less a question of parties now; this is an ideological struggle. The elimination of Hitler would serve no purpose.' He then ordered me to have the author of Report X arrested and to send the document through Service channels to the competent authorities. I replied: 'If someone has to be arrested, I am that man'.

This failure did not discourage the conspirators, who decided to try and persuade Halder to act independently of von Brauchitsch in a supreme effort to prevent the invasion of the Scandinavian countries which the generals knew to be imminent. General Thomas was used as intermediary, but without success. Halder replied: 'Germany's situation is such, especially in view of the non-aggression pact with Soviet Russia, that nothing could justify my breaking my oath to the Führer at the present time.' He added that he could see no sense in a negotiated peace and that there would have to be a military catastrophe before he would act in the way suggested to him.

A last attempt was made by sending Colonel Groscurth to the army Commanders, von Falkenhausen, von Leeb, von List, von Witzleben and von Kluge, to tell them what Report X contained and ask them to make a unanimous demand to von Brauchitsch to arrest Hitler or allow them to do so. Either Groscurth lacked powers of persuasion or the generals were themselves immune against such reasoning – or for both reasons together – this effort too failed absolutely. When Groscurth returned to tell Canaris of the failure of his mission, Canaris spoke a few consoling words which Groscurth noted in his diary*:

'None of these generals knows what he wants. I am not surprised at their reaction. They use the "wait and see" rule of the British, because they are deficient in imagination and courage. But I ask whether they are far wrong. I have myself never believed in Report X. Not that I doubt the sincerity of Pope Pius, Müller and the rest, but because Germany has behaved in such a way since 1934 that it is difficult for a foreigner – and especially difficult for the British – to believe that an opposition to Hitler exists or that it is possible to negotiate to any purpose with Germans. British mistrust is only too easy to understand. I am not certain that even if we did remove Hitler and form a new government, the British would accept the conditions contained in Report X'.

'General von Brauchitsch was perhaps right', said Groscurth, 'when he told Halder that it was less a difference between parties than an ideological struggle.'

'I'm afraid that's so! The crusade of the democracies will go on to the end ... till it has overwhelmed not only National-Socialism but also the German people, accused, not without reason, of having accepted, facilitated and encouraged the crimes of this Black Brotherhood. My dear Helmuth, the German people is at this moment like a drunkard in his cups, joyous, supreme, without a care; but when he is sober tomorrow, it will be too late; he will be at the bottom of the abyss, lower than he has ever been, crushed, torn apart, reduced to long years of servitude. Please God that this servitude is not to be a Communist one as well!'

*Groscurth diary, 1938–40, Munich Institute of Contemporary History.

Canaris modified his attitude considerably in face of these setbacks. He hoped no longer for the rapid downfall of Hitler, but thought it no less urgent to try and limit the extension of hostilities. Such would be his role from April 1940 onwards, and he held to it throughout the war years until his arrest. It is essential to remember this attitude if we are to understand ensuing events.

20
Victories over the West

Standing with his hands in his pockets Canaris stared out of his office window at the rain that had been falling all morning. That 1 April 1940 Berlin did not look at all spring-like and the Admiral's mood reflected the weather. Colonel Oster and Commander Franz Liedig, the source of this part of my narrative, were careful not to interrupt his meditations. They had all three just been looking over Operation Weser, the plan for the occupation of Denmark and Norway. Canaris recalled the origins of this operation.

It was not Hitler's own idea. The German navy had worked out Operation Weser. On 10 October, 1939, Grand Admiral Raeder for the first time drew the Führer's attention to the dangers arising out of a possible British occupation of Norway. If the Germans wished to keep open the Narvik route which brought them essential supplies of Swedish iron ore and to prevent the British from controlling the Baltic, they would have to be the first to land. The British Admiralty and the War Office were well aware of the possibilities of blockading Germany through Norway. *Abwehr* agents in the British Isles were able to report that this was their way of thinking. As a British move was not imminent, Hitler did not allow the case put by Raeder to distract him from his plans for an attack in the West. Occupy Norway as well? No question of that! Apart from the effect on world opinion it would mean another 1,500 miles of coastline to defend.

As the months passed, however, Hitler changed his views. Canaris laid before him a dossier containing numerous *Abwehr* reports on British plans which were beginning to take shape. Hitler admitted that it would be intolerable to see the British violate Norwegian territorial waters and occupy Norwegian soil. He understood that it would be necessary to anticipate this threat. The Russo-Finnish war was being fought at this time and the Western powers were giving military aid to Finland. Aware of the British stratagem of cutting the iron-ore route on the pretext of going to the aid of a country that had suffered aggression, Hitler agreed to Raeder's proposal on 12 December 1939, for a study by the High Command of the *Wehrmacht*. Plans for an invasion of Norway received the code name 'Operation Weser Exercise'. Nobody denied that Norwegian neutrality was the most desirable solution but they knew the importance of preventing Norway falling into British hands and they knew that the Norwegians were ill equipped and only half inclined to oppose a British landing.

On 21 February Hitler gave orders for Operation Weser Exercise to be prepared rapidly, so that by 10 March it could be carried out at four days' notice. The military command was given to General Nikolaus von Falkenhorst, who had seen action with General von der Coltz in Finland in the First World War. Hitler formed a combined force headquarters known as Command XXXII under General Kaupisch of the air force. Neither the High Command of the army, nor even the High Command of the *Wehrmacht* itself were initiated into the secret of these preparations. Falkenhorst and Kaupisch received their orders directly from Hitler.

There was opposition to Operation Weser Exercise from General Jodl of the High Command of the army, and also in the *Abwehr* from Canaris, Oster and Lahousen. They considered it to have been insufficiently prepared and thought out. Jodl and Canaris believed that despite the superiority of the German air force, the German navy would suffer heavy losses when it met the British Home Fleet.

Canaris did not expect to be kept informed on the course of Operation Weser Exercise. Although Command XXXII made every effort to see that the least possible information reached the two High Commands, Canaris nevertheless succeeded in seconding Commander Franz Liedig to the force as *Abwehr* representative. He had known Liedig since the days when he was adjutant to Noske in the Defence Ministry. They had met again in the thirties and Canaris had brought Liedig into the Central Section of the *Abwehr* to work with Oster.

Liedig had on the morning of 1 April given Canaris and Oster the latest details on Operation Weser Exercise which was now in its final planning phase. He was also able to report on a secret visit that he had made to Denmark in the previous week.

Turning away from the window, Canaris went back to sit at his desk. He looked worried. He put to Oster and Liedig the idea that Hitler might not proceed with this plan if he were to be shown in advance the risks that would be run. These risks increased in measure as Operation Weser was extended northwards. Raeder had begun by speaking of Stavanger as his objective, but Hitler looked upon Bergen, Tromso and finally Narvik as indispensable to the success of the campaign. Canaris was convinced that if strong units of the Royal Navy were to patrol off the Norwegian coast in advance of the Weser Operation, that would be enough to deter Hitler. His conviction was based on an objective assessment of the chances of success and also on the opinion that Hitler was a coward at heart and had always recoiled before a superior adversary.

Liedig told him that in his view the British must have long since been informed of German intentions. 'The concentrations of our ships at Stettin and other Baltic ports cannot have remained unnoticed by the Swedish captains who call there. As the agents of the British Secret Service are particularly active in Sweden the British must know by now what is going on.'

Colonel Oster added: 'I have spoken recently about Operation Weser to my friend, Colonel Sas, the Dutch Military Attaché, and he tells me that the Dutch, Danish and Norwegian General Staffs are forewarned and in a state of alert. It is unthinkable that the British are not alerted as well.'

'Let us hope that your optimism is justified,' said Canaris. 'Hitler will make his decision in the next few days. It seems to me important to know whether the British have definite and exact information. If I can prove that Operation Weser is expected it will almost certainly be cancelled.'

Franz Liedig explained to me:

The Admiral sent me immediately to Copenhagen to report to him anything that I could. On 3 or 4 April the Danish press published some sensational news, coming from Stockholm, about camouflaged measures for embarking troops in the German Baltic ports. In view of the general nervousness then prevailing, Danish public opinion interpreted this news as an indication that an operation against Norway was impending. The British Embassy in Copenhagen was intensely interested. In the Danish capital the view was that the operation could no longer be secret and that the British Intelligence Service must have much more exact information than the journalists. I gathered a full report and came back to Berlin to relate my impressions personally to the Admiral. Canaris, who had received similar reports himself, once more expressed his hope that the operation would be cancelled. I told him that in Command Headquarters XXXII there were hesitations about the operation.

Canaris told Liedig:

We can only hope that London is devoting to the situation the attention that it merits, and that the British Admiralty will act as we would
act in their place, by demonstrating to Hitler by appropriate naval
movements what a risk his weak naval forces and troop transports will
run if he persists in this enterprise. I would like to believe that the
British will make their dispositions very rapidly. It will be our duty in
the *Abwehr* to do everything to make Hitler realize the significance of
the British movements when they occur. We must make our reports on
their counter-measures as alarming as possible.

In the next few days all such reports were passed on urgently to
Command Headquarters XXXII and to the Führer. Hitler did
not allow himself to become alarmed and gave orders for Operation
Weser to begin on 9 April. Canaris was soon disenchanted by the
reactions of the British Admiralty to the press alarms and its own
intelligence reports. However he persisted in his illusions as to
the determination of the British to fight, the wisdom of their
political leadership and their real strength. This is shown in a
comment that he made to Liedig in Copenhagen soon after the
Germans entered the Danish capital. There was a rumour of an
important naval engagement between the British and German
fleets. Canaris believed in the first reports and regarded them as
confirmation of his own strategic assessment.

'You see, Liedig,' he said, 'If the British had sailed two days
earlier, all this would not have happened.'

It has often been said that Canaris (or Oster on his orders)
transmitted a warning to the Scandinavian governments a few
days before Operation Weser. This was not the case. Although his
his desire to limit the war became an obsession, he was never
guilty of such treason. Admiral Canaris never imparted to the
enemy information concerning German military plans. Franz
Liedig has affirmed to me most emphatically that Canaris never
suggested to him that he should warn the British or the Scandinavians of the impending operation and that he certainly would
never have revealed to them the day and hour of the attack. Yet
the Scandinavians *were* warned on 4 April that Operation Weser
would begin on 9 April at dawn. By whom? By Colonel Oster. In
a memorandum preserved in the military archives at Freiburg,
Colonel Jacob Sas gives this explanation:

On Wednesday, 3 April in the afternoon, Oster announced to me that the invasion of Denmark and Norway was imminent, and that the offensive in the West would certainly begin soon afterwards. According to a code agreed with Captain Kruls, Secretary to the Minister of War in the Hague, I telephoned him to say that I would be happy to dine with him on 9 April. I also warned the Danish Naval Attaché, Van Kjolsen, and the Norwegian Attaché, Stang. Kjolsen sent this information to his government but Stang did not; for, as was later discovered, he was in contact with Major Quisling and already in the service of Germany.

Oster's treason is established beyond doubt. He acted on his own responsibility without Canaris's knowledge. His action had far-reaching consequences and deserves to be examined closely.

We have already described Hans Oster, an intelligent man, imaginative, sometimes unstable, often imprudent, who was such a dedicated enemy of Hitler that he acted without precautions or scruples. He saw no difference between acts of rebellion and acts of treason such as passing to the enemy intelligence of the sort that might endanger the security of the state. For Oster the end justified the means. He was without illusions, knowing that if his activities were discovered he would be named a traitor. 'I am not a traitor,' he said. 'I am a better patriot than those who fawn upon Hitler. I regard it as my duty to rid Germany and the world of this scourge.' Certain that an offensive in Norway and the West would mean catastrophe for Germany, he decided to do everything possible to forewarn the threatened countries a few days in advance. He calculated that if it was not possible to make Hitler abandon his adventures, a warning of his intentions would result in a setback for German arms which would work to the detriment of National-Socialism. Was this sort of stab in the back justifiable? Oster's friends explain that it was, and Eberhard Bethge, biographer of Dietrich Bonhoeffer, defends Oster in these terms:

Each of these desperate days reduced the chances of putting an end to the crimes planned in the name of Germany. Bonhoeffer considered Oster's action just before the offensive in the West to be perfectly justified. It appeared to him to meet a situation in which a rash German was ruling without scruple while others were afflicted with paralysis of the conscience. A patriot must in such conditions act the role of a villain. Treason had become true patriotism. Having seen what happened in Poland, an officer had taken stock of the devilish aftermath and therefore, unwilling to be an accomplice in further actions of the same sort acted to prevent the same happening in other countries. Pastor Bonhoeffer approved his actions.

At the end of April Colonel Oster sent Dr Joseph Müller and Wilhelm Schmidhuber to Rome, charged to inform the Allies that an offensive in the West was expected in the first days of May – '10 May at the latest'. The concentration of German forces in the West was no secret, being known to the French and British through their intelligence services: nobody, however, knew the exact date of the attack – not even Hitler, who had not yet made up his mind. Two pieces of information were to be passed to the Allies.

My friend, René Dunand, then a Captain in the French army and Assistant Military Attaché in Berne, has told me: 'On 30 April we received at first hand from an authoritative source the following information':

Germany will attack between 8 and 10 May through Holland, Belgium and the Maginot line. Principal point of attack, Sedan. It is expected that Holland, Belgium and France can be overrun in ten days, and the whole of France in one month. We decided to channel this report direct to the Deuxième Bureau in Paris. On 5 May I was at La Ferté-sous-Jouarre, the headquarters of General Georges who commanded the North-east front, and I knew that General Georges and General Gamelin had taken note of this report. I don't know what use they made of it. What I do know is that General Gamelin's reaction was: 'in Berne they allow themselves to be duped by the *Abwehr* men'. Alas, the report was accurate and we know what happened on 10 May. At General Gamelin's headquarters in Vincennes they did not have any supporting intelligence, and so no counter-measures were taken, not even the recall of military personnel on leave.

On 1 May a Czechoslovak married couple, who kept an antique shop in the Hague as the cover for their intelligence activities on behalf of the London Czechs, received from Prague a business telegram containing a pre-arranged code, informing them that 10 May was to be the date of the offensive in the West. It came from Agent A.54, whom we have already seen to have been active at the time of the German march on Prague. The information was passed on from the Hague to the Czechoslovak intelligence centre in London.

Colonel Sas has recorded how his last conversations with Oster went.

On Friday, 3 May, Oster warned me again that the invasion of the Netherlands was imminent. I saw Oster for the last time on Thursday, 9 May at 7 PM. He warned me that all had been prepared for the invasion and that Hitler was on his way to the Western Front, but added:

'A further postponement is still possible. After all we have already been alerted three times, so let us wait a little. The final order to set the offensive in motion will be given at 9:30 PM at the latest, but if it is not countermanded between now and then, it will be definite.' After that we went to dinner together. During this depressing meeting we recalled all that we had done to convey the warning. After dinner I accompanied him back to the High Command and waited outside. He rejoined me twenty minutes later, saying: 'There has been no cancellation. The swine has left for the Western front and the invasion is to begin. Let us hope that we meet again after the war.'

I hurried to the Legation, picked up the telephone, and asked for the Ministry of War at the Hague. I was connected after ten minutes. Fortunately I knew one of the officers on duty, Major Post Uitweer. 'Post', I said, 'you recognize my voice, don't you? This is Sas in Berlin. I have only one thing to tell you. Tomorrow at dawn. Hold firm. Have you understood me? Please repeat.'

He repeated my words and added: 'Letter number 210 received.' This was an agreed code, 200 meaning invasion and the day of the month added to that.

Sas had already, on 5 May, forecast the invasion of his country and of Belgium for 10 May in a telephone conversation with Colonel van Plaasche, Chief of the Foreign Intelligence Service of the Dutch War Ministry, as well as telling the French Naval Attaché in the Hague, who in turn alerted General Giraud.

On 3 May the Vatican informed the Papal Nuncios in the Hague and Brussels that 10 May would be the latest date for a German offensive in the West, and the Belgian Ambassador to the Vatican sent the same intelligence to his government.

M. Charles Roux, French Ambassador to the Vatican, received similar information on 8 May and has recorded that his Belgian and British colleagues were given the same warnings. His own telegram would have reached Paris on 8 May, he thought, and would have been passed to GHQ at Vincennes.

All these messages from the Vatican and Colonel Sas had been detected by German Security, which had taken various foreign codes and was able to decipher each text and transmit it to the *Abwehr*. Piekenbrock and Bürkner guessed at once that Oster was guilty of the leakage; they knew of his friendship with Sas, also of his relations with Dr Joseph Müller and Schmidhuber. They kept silent, but Admiral Canaris was aware and was disturbed by Oster's action.

In fact the *SS* were not inactive. The Chief of the *SD* Foreign

Service, Walther Schellenberg, also received transcripts of the messages intercepted by the *Forschungsamt* and he passed them on to the Chief of the Reich Security, Reinhard Heydrich. Since the beginning of January 1940 Schellenberg and Heydrich had been alerted to the activities of Dr Müller in the Vatican, though over the weeks there was no decisive proof of contact with the enemy. However Heydrich decided at the beginning of May 1940 to rename the existing dossier on Canaris and his colleagues 'the Black Chapel', an allusion to their activities in Rome.

One evening at the end of May Heydrich called in Heinrich Müller, Chief of the *Gestapo*, and Schellenberg for a talk. He motioned to them to sit down and for a long moment there was absolute silence, which made both men nervous. Schellenberg has related to me the conversation that Heydrich then began:

'What progress have you made with the inquiry into the *Abwehr* people in Munich, Josef Müller, Hans von Dohnanyi and the others?' he asked. 'It is evident that these peace feelers started from there'.

'Very little,' replied Heinrich Müller.

'Tell me, Schellenberg,' said Heydrich. 'Hasn't Josef Müller had some contact with your service, something to do with Dr Helmut Knochen, if I remember rightly?' Schellenberg was astonished at Heydrich's memory.

'That is so,' he replied. '*SS* Colonel Helmut Knochen told me that Josef Müller could have access to the highest Vatican circles, that he was most intelligent, although somewhat excitable, and that his information was not without interest for us. Müller was brought into the *Abwehr* by a man called Schmidhuber, who is Portuguese Consul in Munich'.

'Arrange for these *Abwehr* men to be closely watched', said Heydrich to Müller. The Security Chief paused, as if the two subjects were in no way connected. Then he said:

'The Führer and the *Reichsführer SS* have asked me to enquire about a case of treason that seems to be one of the most important ever known in Germany. At the beginning of this month two cipher messages were intercepted by our services on their way from a Belgian representative in the Vatican City to his government, and were deciphered by us. We learned from them that a German, whose name was not given, had revealed the exact date and hour of our attack in the West. Two days before the official order from the Führer! It is unbelievable, but this information was sent by another route to the Netherlands. The Führer is beside himself with fury. He wants the traitors to be discovered at all costs.'

There was another silence. Then Heydrich said:

'Now, this is the point. The Führer has ordered us to hold an enquiry and he has also ordered Canaris to hold one. This is going to put the cat among the pigeons, because we are investigating the Canaris group. I have just had the Admiral on the wire and naturally I have not told him of my suspicions.'

'Is Canaris mixed up in this treason?' asked Heinrich Müller dryly. 'That isn't apparent. I suggest Schellenberg takes over this investigation and tells us what he discovers. The little Admiral suspects him less than anyone else.'

Heydrich stared at Müller, and said quickly:

'Agreed. Schellenberg, you have a talk with Canaris.'

Schellenberg called on Canaris next day but in the course of a general chat did not seem able to bring their conversation round to the question of leakages. It was Canaris himself who mentioned it, just as Schellenberg was about to leave.

'Has Heydrich told you of this unbelievable affair, the date and hour of the Western offensive being revealed?'

'Yes', replied Schellenberg, 'and I think we ought to discuss it.'

Canaris then gave his version of the incident, though without mentioning Rome, the Belgian Ambassador, the Vatican or the intercepted messages:

'My information is that the day before our attack in the West a German diplomat visiting the Dutch Embassy in Brussels saw the Ambassador's wife in a state of extreme agitation. When we occupied Brussels we found a note written by the Belgian Ministry of Foreign Affairs, containing a message from the Dutch Ambassador in Berlin giving notice of our offensive. How did he know this? That is what I would like to know. I have ordered Colonel Rohleder to conduct an urgent inquiry into this leakage.'

Neither Heydrich nor Schellenberg were deceived by this version, but they could find no proof of what they suspected. Canaris with supreme audacity summoned Josef Müller himself from Munich to conduct the investigation in the Vatican, but the concealment of the truth was nearly wrecked by Rohleder himself, an excellent and conscientious Security Chief, who sent an agent of his own to Rome. This man returned with reports that it had indeed been Dr Josef Müller who had revealed the dates to a

Jewish journalist on 30 April and again on 7 May. Rohleder hurried to Oster and Dohnanyi with his findings, and the two two conspirators had some difficulty in damping down his ardour. Finally Canaris used his authority to explain to Rohleder that this allegation was not new, but that it had been proved to his satisfaction to be a calumnious attack on Dr Josef Müller, intended to disrupt his important and influential connections with the Vatican.

The great offensive, as foretold, came on 10 May 1940, and while the Allied armies recoiled under the German hammer-blows towards the Channel coast and then towards the Pyrenees, the *Abwehr* began to install itself in the captured capitals and to extend its network in occupied countries. Canaris himself went to Brussels, the Hague, Luxemburg and Paris to supervise the opening of *Abwehr* offices in these cities. 'He had an extraordinarily rapid grasp of situations and of the capacity of his individual officers to deal with them, as well as a gift for precautionary instructions to those in more senior positions who would have to rectify mistakes not yet committed.' Such was the opinion of one of his officers watching him at this time who heard him exclaim on his way through – 'An *Abwehr* officer must know how to lie. It's part of the trade, and an art into the bargain' – doubtless a reflection of his current difficulties with Heydrich and the *Gestapo*.

There were incidents of comic gravity in these days, as when Major Franz Seubert exclaimed loudly before other German officers after Mussolini's declaration of war when the new Italian liaison officer arrived – 'we'll win all the same'. The Admiral ordered him to go by appointment in full dress uniform and sword to apologize to the Italian for this affront.

As the German army was occupying Paris, Canaris gave his instructions for *Abwehr* activities in occupied French territory. He placed Colonel Friedrich Rudolph at the head of the Central Office in the Lutetia Hotel. Rudolph was one of the most experienced and senior of *Abwehr* officers, extremely competent, brief in speech, serious and given to essentials only. His blond and slightly receding hair lay flat back from a high forehead. His blue eyes, intense gaze and ironic smile gave him an imposing appearance. He left a good deal of initiative to his junior officers. Major Oscar Reile, who arrived on 20 June 1940 as Chief of Section IIIF

(Counter-espionage), was given his first task by Rudolph in a succinct manner.

'We have just seized a train-load of secret documents at La Charité-sur-Loire. Your task, aided by Captain Leyerer, whom you will meet tomorrow, will be to explore this find. Tonight you dine with me.'

The Hotel Lutétia contained Section I Espionage, directed by Major Waag, a nephew of Canaris, a man of experience in this field, and Section II, Counter-espionage, directed by Captain Langendorf. The Central Office consisted of twenty-five officers of the *Abwehr*, twenty female assistants, thirty NCOs and radio officers, drivers and other ancillaries. Colonel Reile in writing his memoirs comments on the arrangements whereby almost the entire *Abwehr* staff ate and lived in the Hotel Lutétia, with an entirely French hotel staff who served them excellently but with a professional detachment and polite reserve. Colonel Rudolph insisted on correct behaviour and appearances, though there were some lapses in private, and maintained a distance between himself and his subordinate officers as well as the French personnel of the Hotel which did much to keep relations balanced in an unusual situation.

Realizing that the *Abwehr* was in France for some time, Canaris set up in Saint Germain-en-Laye, Dijon, Angers and Bordeaux as well as some other Atlantic and Channel ports, branches which were attached to the *Luftwaffe* for the most part. Chief of one of these branches was Dr Kaltenhauser, who was established in Normandy in July 1940 and remained until June 1944, in the course of his duties protecting many Frenchmen from the arbitrary actions of the *Gestapo*.

During a tour of inspection in occupied French territory, accompanied by the eminent Colonel Nicolai, his predecessor in the First World War, and Colonel Friedrich Wilhelm Heinz, Chief of Section II of the *Abwehr*, Canaris voiced his thoughts about the months ahead.

Perhaps a century will go by, [he mused] before the world understands the tragedy of our position. If Hitler wins, it will bring about not only our ruin but that of the Germany we love and would wish to endure. If Hitler is defeated, it will be the end of Germany and the end of us, who failed to frustrate his designs, if we do fail. Even if we succeed in the political war against him, it will be not only his downfall but ours as well, since our enemies abroad will give us no credit for it . . . What-

185

ever we do, our destiny leads us inevitably towards self-destruction. The commonalty evidently cannot understand all this. In other words, even before we have dragged Hitler down, we shall have perished, rejected by the world.

These stoical reflections did not reflect inactivity in the *Abwehr* organization itself. At the Hotel Lutétia the problem was to discover what the French had done with their stock of heavy water and where the French atomic scientists had taken refuge? For in March 1940 Raoul Dautry, French Minister of Armaments, had succeeded in outstripping the Germans, obtaining considerable stocks of this component substance of atomic fission from the Norwegian Azote Company. Twenty-six containers of heavy water had been spirited away from Oslo airport under the noses of the *Abwehr* before the invasion of Norway, flown to Edinburgh and re-routed to Paris for the use of Frédéric Joliot-Curie and the French team of atomic scientists engaged in experiments to develop an atomic weapon for the French armed forces. Before the German invasion of France an experiment with heavy water and uranium had been set on foot by the French physicists but had to be rapidly dismantled.

An *Abwehr* questionnaire that fell into my hands some years ago shows that Major Waag was making enquiries about the laboratories of the Collège de France. Could these be further utilized under German supervision? Where was the material that had been set aside for experimental purposes? What could be found by searching Joliot-Curie's home. What had become of his stocks of radium and heavy water? The *Abwehr* must find and interrogate Joliot-Curie and ten of his scientists. They must also find and interrogate Raoul Dautry himself. The *Abwehr* must obtain the papers on atomic energy written by the Joliot-Curie team.

What was the answer to all these questions? At this stage German scientists, according to Carl Friedrich von Weizsäcker, were at the stage of setting up an atomic reactor in order to separate isotopes. He has denied that the purpose of German experiments was to produce an atomic bomb. However that may be, the *Abwehr*'s interest in French progress in the atomic field was intense.

Lew Kowarsky, one of the French team, relates that the French Government took the decision to evacuate its atomic materials as soon as it heard that the Maginot Line had been pierced. Hans Heinrich von Halban, one of the Joliot-Curie team, was sent south on 17 May with the radium, the heavy water, and important documents. Kowarsky set out on 5 June with several military trucks full of equipment, and joined Halban at Clermont-Ferrand, where the containers were deposited in the vaults of the Banque de France. Kowarsky continued: 'on 16 June we were ordered to proceed to Bordeaux with our material. A British liaison officer, the Earl of Suffolk, who was put at our disposal, requisitioned a collier on which we loaded everything that we could. We were in all fifty French scientists, some with their families, and a quantity of material, including artificial diamonds and our heavy water.' Their orders were as follows:

Messieurs Halban and Kowarsky, accompanied by their wives and children, are to embark on board the steamer *Broompark* at Bassens (Gironde) in the care of the Earl of Suffolk and Berkshire, to continue in England the research begun at the Collège de France in conditions of absolute secrecy. They will report to the French Mission in London (Colonel Mayer), 2 Dean Stanley Street, Westminster House.

Kowarsky related further: 'Joliot-Curie decided to remain in France and to let us leave for England. The crossing had its dangerous moments. A ship close to us blew up on a mine. German aircraft flew over us but they had no bombs left and could do us no harm. We arrived in Britain on 21 June.' The heavy water stocks were placed first in Wormwood Scrubbs prison and then in the library of Windsor Castle. Von Halban and Kowarsky took up their work again in the Cavendish Laboratory.

The Kaiser Wilhelm Institute had meanwhile made considerable advances, and according to Leandro Castellani and Luciano Gigante, 'Carl Friedrich von Weizsäcker had invented an atomic bomb long before the Americans.' It would be correct to say that the Germans had completed the theoretical groundwork which must precede the practical experimental stage in the construction of an atomic bomb. Von Weizsäcker was inclined to disclaim this distinction, though admitting that one of his reports set forth the possibilities of using plutonium as a reactor . . . 'but that does not mean that I invented the atomic bomb . . . You can understand the process of chain reaction, but there are still a thousand steps ahead, and my idea was only one of them . . . The same idea could have occurred to two hundred physicists at that time . . . I alluded with all sorts of reservations to the possibility of producing an explosive in a relatively short period.' But neither the Kaiser

Wilhelm Institute nor Admiral Canaris informed the *Wehrmacht* Weapons Office.

In a private conversation, Canaris asked Baron von Weizsäcker what progress his son and other scientists of the Heisenberg team had made and whether in his view the German scientists could produce a uranium bomb.

'They are building a reactor,' replied Baron von Weizsäcker, 'but none of them to my knowledge, least of all my son, has the intention of producing an atomic bomb. The idea of that sort of bomb is repugnant to them. Besides, let me tell you that there is, according to my information, no probability that they can produce a uranium bomb under the technical and industrial conditions existing in our country in time of war.' Canaris was reassured that Hitler was unlikely to acquire a weapon capable of realizing his bloodthirsty ambitions.

Joliot-Curie on his return home was discovered by Oscar Reile and had to submit to an interrogation by Admiral Canaris himself. Canaris first consulted Werner Heisenberg and then went to Paris, accompanied by an eminent German physicist, Wolfgang Gertner, who translated Joliot-Curie's replies during the interrogation. The Frenchman asserted that the heavy water stocks had to his knowledge been removed to England and claimed that he had so far made no more progress on atomic fission than others in international science.

'I already knew Joliot-Curie,' recalled Gertner, 'and I was embarrassed to see him again in this awkward situation with several German officers present. When they were leaving I stayed behind for a moment and quickly made an appointment with him for that evening in a Montparnasse café. That night we went on to his home and I asked him whether he would agree to my appointment, if I was sent to supervise his future work in the University laboratories and the Collège de France. 'I prefer to have you there, since I know you,' replied Joliot-Curie. I then said to him: 'In that case let us sign an agreement neither of us to work for war and to exchange our information.' Later Gertner intervened several times with the *Gestapo* and *SD* to obtain Joliot-Curie's release, when he was suspected of resistance activities, saying that the French scientist was indispensable to his own researches.

Admiral Canaris approached another of the Joliot-Curie team in September 1940, to ask whether he would transfer to the German team and work in Berlin. This was the Chinese Tchien San-Chiang, who politely declined and remained with Joliot-Curie in Paris till the end of the war, returning afterwards to China to help produce Mao Tse-tung's atomic armoury.

Two more blows were struck at the German advance in the atomic field. An Anglo-Norwegian commando team in February 1943 attacked the Vemork installations in Norway, which had been requisitioned by the *Wehrmacht*, and destroyed 3,000 litres of heavy water stocks. An American heavy-bomber raid in November 1943 destroyed the plant itself. The Germans decided to transfer the remaining 16,000 litres of heavy water to Germany, but four Norwegian resistance men sank the steamship *Hydro*, which was transporting it, as she crossed Lake Tinn. The Germans nevertheless continued their atomic developments. Albert Speer summoned a conference of German nuclear physicists on 6 June at which Abraham Esau emphasized the shortage of uranium and of funds. Speer, to their general surprise, authorized that the programme be continued, though with emphasis on the nuclear reactor and an economy of effort on the atomic bomb. But for their anti-Nazi sentiments, but for protection by Canaris and the ignorance in which Hitler had been kept, German scientists might have had the momentum to produce an atomic weapon before the Allies. In the German magazine *Stern*, in March 1967, Carl Friedrich von Weizsäcker estimated that in April 1945, when the war ended in Germany, German scientists were at a stage when eight more months would have equipped Germany with the atomic bomb.

21

The height of power

In June 1940 Hitler was at the height of his power. After the brilliant victory over France and with hopes of an early peace with Great Britain, the German people were in a state of euphoria. Admiral Canaris was perhaps the only one among the chiefs of the German armed forces who was not infected with the extraordinary optimism of his colleagues. He realized that Hitler since 1933 had passed from one success to another almost like a sleepwalker, until his domination extended from the North Cape of Norway to the Pyrenees, but Canaris believed nevertheless that in a few weeks or months this supremacy could be shaken.

When Piekenbrock questioned him on this pessimism he answered:

The Führer, who possesses an extraordinary knowledge of military detail, knows nothing of the problems of strategy. This ignorance is fundamental, because strategy and policy are closely interwoven. Hitler and certain generals of our High Command are foot-soldiers, provincials, mainlanders. They possess a superficial idea of the world and their ideas of other nations are like a gallery full of caricatures. Hitler lives among the images of *Mein Kampf*.

Piekenbrock was astonished at the force of the Admiral's language and the passionate tones in which he indicted Hitler that day. His blue eyes shone with a strange light.

What is emphatically true, Piki, [he continued] is that Winston Churchill and the British think in terms of the sea and their maritime routes, whereas Hitler thinks in terms of the Continent. Winning against Poland and France with two gigantic blows, Hitler did not finish off the British army at Dunkirk when he could have done so, because he wishes for an Anglo-German settlement. He put all his strength into the upper-cut against France in the hope that the obstinate British would return home and, having meditated on the downfall of their ally, would make a compromise peace. Nor does he realize that in leaving France her fleet and her empire, he has left her the trump cards. He cannot visualize the British Empire, its capital strongly protected against

190

war in the air, secure in its sea routes and linked to the East by a sea route as well as the chain of countries between Gibraltar and East Africa which Great Britain dominates. Hitler remains convinced that Britain will negotiate simply because he regards acceptance of his terms as a wise move. He is completely mistaken. Britain can only be moved to negotiate if she feels her Empire is in danger. We ought not to be making efforts to land in the British Isles, but in Gibraltar and Suez. If we succeeded in that, peace would be possible.

A few days after the conversation, about 10 July, Keitel instructed Canaris to examine the possibility of an operation against Gibraltar. A Minute of 30 June 1940, written by General Jodl for the Führer, declared that: 'The final victory of Germany over Britain is only a question of time. The enemy is no longer able to undertake large-scale offensive operations. If political means do not attain peace, the British resistance must be broken (a) by an attack against the British Isles or (b) by carrying the war against her into other regions.'

Marshal von Brauchitsch and General Jodl since the beginning of July had been studying simultaneous operations against Gibraltar and Suez. They were convinced that if it was impossible to strike directly at the British Isles, it was essential to expel the British from their Mediterranean bases. Admiral Raeder shared this view. Like all sailors who think in terms of continents and seas, his first requirement was that control of the Mediterranean should be wrested from the British. Hitler was not opposed to this plan, which he called Operation Felix, but he still believed in a rapid peace with Britain and thought that in France he had bases enough already while the Mediterranean was a secondary consideration. As days passed without sign of the British coming to terms, Hitler was won over to the idea of Operation Felix.

Vice-Admiral Leopold Bürkner, Chief of the Foreign Section of the *Abwehr*, was a witness to Canaris's reactions when instructions came from Keitel. Bürkner wrote: 'Just after the campaign in France, Canaris was of the opinion that a surprise attack on the fortress of Gibraltar was feasible. The time was propitious since the British were still suffering from the shock of Dunkirk and were immobilized on their island by the threat of invasion and by *Luftwaffe* attacks.' Canaris did not at this stage think that an attack on Gibraltar by Germany would automatically involve Spain in war. He had, we may recall, a deep affection for Spain, was a close friend of Franco, and knew only too well the wretched condition of the country after its civil war. He did not wish Spain to take up arms on Germany's side. He was glad to make a visit to Spain, but it had to be postponed until after the investiture of 19 July when Hitler showered decorations and honours on the victors of the campaign against France and made an immense speech threatening and cajoling the British in the same breath.

Canaris left for Spain on the following day, taking with him Colonel Hans Piekenbrock, Lieutenant-Colonel Mikosch, and Captain Hans-Jochen Rudloff. At the Madrid office of the *Abwehr*, directed by Captain Leissner, Canaris went meticulously over the intelligence material about Gibraltar. At first sight he thought that the Rock could be taken, not by seizure, but by completely annihilating the place. The group went on to La Linea and Algeciras to look across at Gibraltar.

The Felix plan required the use of Special Regiment 800 and the 51st battalion of Engineers. On further examination Canaris came to the conclusion that the operation would be impossible without heavy artillery and strong air support. He made the following report on 2 August 1940 to Field-Marshal Keitel:

1) That a battalion of the Brandenburg Regiment would have to be moved from France to the Algeciras region, camouflaged so that it did not appear to be a German unit. Canaris suggested plain clothes or at least civilian overcoats over their uniforms, and that the military trucks should travel with closed flaps. The route taken would avoid towns. Meals would be prepared in uninhabited spots along minor roads. The movement would take three days.

2) Another battalion must be moved by sea to a small Spanish port within a short distance of Gibraltar.

3) Heavy artillery and ammunition would be sent to Ceuta, so that Gibraltar could be shelled across the Straits before the infantry went into action. He remarked that Ceuta possessed no equipment capable of lifting and transporting heavy artillery. He suggested the use of the *Luftwaffe*'s long-range bombers to saturate Gibraltar and sink the warships anchored there.

On 24 July while Canaris was at Algeciras, Hitler received Air-General Wolfram von Richthofen, who had commanded the Condor Legion in Spain. Hitler sent him to join Canaris in staff talks with the Spanish Defence Ministry. The first of these talks was a disappointment to General von Richthofen. He commented to Canaris: 'In principle Spain is greatly interested in our plan to attack Gibraltar, but she fears that she would not have the resolution to go through with it herself.'

The Canaris group returned from Algeciras to Madrid where Canaris met one of his nephews. The young man, Joachim Canaris had just become engaged and asked his uncle whether he ought not to delay his marriage until victory brought peace, which could not be far distant. As Joachim Canaris mentioned the word 'victory' he noticed his uncle's sombre expression and was astonished to hear him say in a hollow voice: 'On the contrary, marry as soon as you can so that you can both enjoy your youth while the sun shines. There are many clouds on the horizon and the wind is against us. The storm that will soon break on everything that is German will be a terrible one.'

On 28 July Canaris and his staff paused at Biarritz on their way to Germany. They were joined in Biarritz by General Juan Vigon, Chief of the Spanish General Staff, and General Martinez Campos, Chief of the Spanish Military Intelligence, General von Richthofen caught up with them a few hours later. Before Richthofen arrived Canaris was able to speak freely with his two old Spanish friends, and he put his cards on the table, not concealing the difficulties that he foresaw in Operation Felix or the dire consequences of involving Spain in it.

He questioned his companions: would Franco maintain Spain's neutrality? Was he considering entering the war on the side of the Axis? How would Franco react if Hitler, without first asking for Spanish collaboration, were to seize Gibraltar?

The two Spanish generals replied as best they could, emphasizing that although they knew him well, the Caudillo was secretive, and that they were not aware of his intentions. General Vigon said to Canaris:

'Admiral, you know the Caudillo more intimately than we do. He is very fond of you. Why not return to Madrid and have a talk with him?'

The Admiral made a mock grimace of horror:

'You don't know Ribbentrop,' he replied. 'He will howl if I intrude on his territory. If I see the Caudillo without being sent by Hitler, Ribbentrop will have a fit and Himmler will set the *Gestapo* on me.'

'However', Canaris resumed in a more serious vein, 'I hope soon to be able to make a private visit to my great friend Francisco

Franco. I think that I will be able to take a holiday if . . . Great Britain accepts our great Führer's offer of peace'.

The Spaniards smiled at his change of tone, seeing that it occurred just as General von Richthofen joined the group.

They then discussed together the condition of Spain. German victories had strengthened the Spanish faction that wished to join the Axis and take military action to regain Gibraltar but Franco was a realist and there was famine in Madrid. In his New Year message of 1940 he had not ignored the hardships that Spain suffered, short of food and the primary necessities of life, wheat, petrol, meat and sugar, with industry at a standstill. Franco remained cold to the clamour for Gibraltar and watched with anxious attention the bellicose gestures of Hitler and Mussolini. He did not wish to be dragged into their war, but he had to take account of the invincible German armies beyond the Pyrenees.

In this situation, on 12 June 1940, Franco made the gesture of renouncing neutrality in favour of 'non-belligerency', borrowing the equivocal expression from Mussolini. He thus showed that since the war had spread to the Mediterranean with the declaration of war by Italy on 10 June Spain was 'directly interested in what happens in this area and holds herself ready for any eventuality'. On 14 June Franco sent Spanish troops into the international zone of Tangiers. His propaganda proclaimed this to be 'a manifestation of the independent strength of Spain'. In fact the military occupation had been agreed with the British and French governments to forestall any Italian coup. Hitler was duped by this event.

To make known Spanish wishes about the future of her territorial possessions in North Africa, Franco sent General Vigon to meet Hitler at the 'Wolf's Lair', his field headquarters near Brussels. There in the Château Azoz on 16 June Vigon met Herr von Ribbentrop and was then received by Hitler with Ribbentrop present. Vigon informed Canaris afterwards of these proceedings.

Hitler exclaimed that he had learned 'with joy' that the Caudillo had occupied Tangiers, and 'above all that Spain had gone over to action instead of discussion'. Vigon said that he had with difficu`ty refrained from smiling at this remark. He had proceeded to explain to Hitler the reasons why Spain could not immediately align herself beside Germany in the War. Spain had always felt a perfect sympathy for Germany, he said, not out of self-interest but because the two countries shared common enemies. After about forty-five minutes Vigon touched on the problem of Gibraltar. Hitler said:

'The ideal solution, desired by Germany, is that Gibraltar should be united to Spain. Just as I rejoice at your occupation of Tangiers, I wish Gibraltar to fall to a power that is not in the main area of the present war.'

Vigon expressed Spain's desire to take over the whole of Morocco as a Spanish protectorate and Hitler replied that clearly Germany had no economic interest in Morocco. Ribbentrop found a formula: 'If the Führer, the Duce and the Caudillo will form an alliance, a solution for Morocco can be found that will satisfy Spain as well as Italy and Germany.'

Germany's tactics were clear. Hitler was ready at that moment to say anything that would satisfy Spain, but would examine the problems with more attention when he had won the war.

On 18 July Franco made a bellicose speech in which he laid claim to Gibraltar and spoke of 'two million Spanish soldiers reliving their glorious past'. In reality the Spanish army was deficient in equipment not just for war but even for the defence of her frontiers. This did not matter. Hitler was impressed by the speech and it produced a remarkable effect on Sir Samuel Hoare, the British Ambassador in Madrid, who never succeeded in understanding the delicate game that Franco was playing.

What would Franco do next? In fact he signed a triple agreement with Portugal – and Britain – on commercial exchanges within the sterling area. He authorized the British to open an institute in Madrid. He also dismissed General Lopez Pinto who had demanded that Hitler and the Duce should be acclaimed at a reception on the Spanish frontier when the first German armoured formations arrived there: words on one side, but actions on the other.

Canaris returned to Berlin and made his report to Keitel, taking stock himself of the flow of ideas and opinions at headquarters. He could discern that Hitler's enthusiasm for an operation against Gibraltar and Suez had cooled since early July. He also formed the opinion that Hitler would never succeed in making a landing in Britain. The Italians, even with the Germans helping them, would never seize Egypt and the Suez Canal. If Spain and Germany took Gibraltar, the British would land in Morocco and in French West Africa with the probable assent of Marshal Pétain and the certain agreement of General Weygand – perhaps that of Admiral Darlan as well. He was more than ever certain that Spain had everything to lose and nothing to gain by entering the conflict on the side of Hitler and Mussolini and he calculated that Franco must be equally aware of the chances.

Indeed, having consolidated his position with the Allies and affirmed his independence, as we have seen, Franco summoned the German Ambassador, von Stohrer, on 8 August, to tell him on what conditions he would agree to enter the war on the German side. Thus began the blackmail by Spain that lasted for the entire duration of the war. Von Stohrer reported to Berlin that 'Franco is effectively ready to make war' but wanted first 'to be reassured that Spain will obtain Gibraltar, French Morocco, and the Oran region of Algeria'. He had also 'need of military and other assistance to play his part in the war'. He expected wheat and petrol from Germany. Even if all these conditions were fulfilled, reported von Stohrer, 'the Caudillo thought that Spain could not move until Germany had landed on the British coast, in order to avoid entering the war prematurely and being unable to continue it or running into certain danger.'

Knowing of the friendship between Franco and Canaris, Hitler, who was convinced that a rapid operation against Gibraltar was necessary, asked the *Abwehr* Chief to return to Madrid, to meet Franco and explain the German position to him. He was to urge Franco 'to enter the war quickly on the side of the Axis' and 'to abate for the time being his *legitimate* claims'.

The exact course of the interview between Franco and Canaris is not known, but it is certain that the Caudillo multiplied his reservations, showed himself unwilling to be overcome by pressure from Hitler and succeeded with some difficulty in extricating his country from the corner into which it was being manoeuvred.

It may be supposed that Canaris suggested to Franco that Spain ought only to take sides with the victor and that it was in no way certain which power would be victorious. Canaris repeated his misgivings to Piekenbrock and to Lahousen, who told me after the war: 'Canaris was in 1940 very pessimistic about the general trend for Germany. He would have considered it a crime to have urged Franco to bring Spain into a war which he considered Germany already to have lost'.

A shorthand report of the meeting on the Brenner Pass between Hitler and Mussolini on 4 October 1940, shows that Hitler said: 'a declaration of war by Spain has no strategic significance other

196

than the conquest of Gibraltar. The military assistance that we
can give Spain is negligible, especially if we realize the fact reported by Admiral Canaris very precisely after his interview with
the Caudillo – internal conditions in Spain are bad, very bad, and
the economy completely stagnant.'

At the end of the month of August 1940 Piekenbrock was present
when a young *Luftwaffe* General, wearing the highest grade of the
Iron Cross, forecast to Canaris that the British would crumple
under the *Luftwaffe*'s blows within six weeks.

'Not at all,' said Canaris gravely, 'the Führer is said to give them
only fifteen days and the Führer is always right.' This show of
confidence disconcerted the younger man who murmured his
agreement with the improbable estimate.

'An ass with the Iron Cross and Oak Leaves,' commented
Canaris to Piekenbrock.

Hitler told Count Ciano in Berlin on 7 July that he did not
think a political compact between Great Britain and Russia in the
Balkans was impossible. Russia had just seized Bessarabia and
Bukovina from Rumania, and if war spread to the region of the
Ploesti oil fields and these changed hands, Hitler thought it would
be 'very harmful' to Italy and Germany. The ceding of these two
provinces to Russia on 28 June 1940, disquieted Hitler. Rumania
was delivering to Germany an increasing amount of petrol. Now
Soviet Russia was supporting the territorial claims of Hungary
and Bulgaria against Rumania.

Abwehr Section II (Sabotage and Security) had before the war
received orders to 'protect' the Rumanian oil industry and the
navigational channels of the river Danube, notably the 'Iron
Gates'. The *Abwehr* feared sabotage of the oil wells by the British
Secret Service and the French Deuxième Bureau. Admiral
Canaris had therefore visited Bucharest, accompanied by Colonel
von Bentivegni and Colonel Lahousen, to negotiate a security
agreement with Colonel Morusov, the Rumanian Chief of Security.
The intention was that in those Rumanian petroleum companies
in which German capital had been heavily invested, there should
be an infiltration of security guards, chosen by the German
Abwehr. After the outbreak of war, Canaris, Lahousen and
Morusov had with the consent of King Carol set up a special
security network of men from the Brandenburg Regiment to
watch the Ploesti oil fields.

On 28 June, 1940, there was a panic exodus from Bessarabia and

Bukovina as the tanks and lorries of the Soviet Red Army moved in. 'Where would the Russians halt?', the German Embassy and the *Abwehr* in Bucharest asked anxiously. Might they have an agreement with the British to seize the Ploesti oil fields? The Russians in fact halted on the Sereth river. Hitler reacted quickly by a direct proposition to Stalin defining their respective limits of interest in Rumania after which he demanded 90 per cent of Rumanian petroleum production for Germany. The Rumanian Government accepted this ultimatum.

The British took the only possible decision, that this 90 per cent flow of oil to Germany must be stopped. The oil companies brought new personnel from Britain, and Rumanian officials were astonished at the numbers that these reached. The Head of *Abwehr* in Bucharest was not hoodwinked; he thought that the new arrivals looked more like British officers in plain clothes than oil technicians. Their free use of money in Bucharest gave him the impression that these men belonged to the Secret Service.

A German lieutenant of the Brandenburg Regiment, seconded to the Ploesti oil fields, reported in July 1940 to his *Abwehr* Chief in Bucharest that the British were sending to their Middle East headquarters plans of all the oil installations in Rumania. On the following day the heads of the oil companies were asked to take part in a secret conference organized by the British Intelligence Service. A code word had been agreed for a simultaneous sabotage action in which the wells would be blocked with quick-setting concrete and steel plates.

The *Abwehr* passed on this information to the Rumanian Security Service. On the following morning on board a steamer in the port of Constanza Colonel Morusov's men seized the Astra-Romana Company's consignment of maps and plans of the oil fields consigned to Alexandria. Lahousen and the Head of the *Abwehr* group in Bucharest meanwhile mustered and armed their agents from the Brandenburg Regiment and infiltrated them into the oil fields. They were carrying explosives bearing British marks of manufacture.

The British secret conference was being held in the Transylvanian foothills not far from Ploesti at the guest-house of the Astra Romana company. The British Intelligence Service had taken every precaution and had brought in men specially from London, co-opting the managers and technical directors of the oil companies on the spot. The plan was to increase deliveries of petrol in the immediate future, so that the suspicions of the *Abwehr* and the Rumanians would be allayed. The sabotage operation itself would be synchronized to the minute, but about three days would be needed before the concrete set hard in the wells. Businessmen who had worked for twenty years in Rumania on oil production found themselves in the sad position of planning to destroy their life's work. There was a tense atmosphere in the oil-company guest-house.

The British Colonel in charge of the operation told the meeting that ships were ready to embark all British personnel, but that evacuation orders were only to be issued at the last minute. He added:

'The operation begins at 9 AM tomorrow.' At this moment a watchman entered, breathless, and said:

'The Rumanians are here.'

For the first time the Rumanian police were taking action inside the Astra-Romana concession. Captain Stefanescu and half a dozen Rumanian officers burst in on the bewildered British. Stevanescu bowed and said:

'I am sorry, but Colonel Morusov orders me to make a search here.'

'Here?' exclaimed Page, the technical director of Astra-Romana. 'What for?'

'We are looking for contraband explosives.'

The British burst out laughing, but Stefanescu and his men remained serious and began a room-by-room search of the guest-house. In every room there were packages of explosives and crates of revolvers, rifles and sub-machine guns of British manufacture.

'These damned Germans!' exclaimed Miller, the Director-General of Astra-Romana, who had guessed at the conspiracy between the *Abwehr* and the Rumanian Security Service. Despite an energetic protest from Sir Reginald Hoare, the British Ambassador in Bucharest, the Rumanians did not relent, expelling all British oil personnel from the country. The *Abwehr* men meanwhile occupied the oil fields to await the arrival of German technicians.

On 26 July Ion Gigurtu, the Rumanian Prime Minister, discussed with Hitler at the Berghof the future of the Rumanian oil industry and the possibility that Rumanian would nationalize it. Germany would succeed to the British and French shareholding in the oil companies and precautions would be taken to ensure

199

against sabotage of the wells. Germany would provide a military mission to assist in training and equipping the Rumanian army. As to Hungary's claims on Transylvania, Hitler decided that these would best be submitted to arbitration, which took place on 30 August when a German-Italian tribunal decided in favour of Hungary. In October 1940, on information from the *Abwehr* that there were concentrations of Soviet troops in Bukovina, Hitler sent into Rumania his first allocation of German military assistance, to the strength of one armoured division commanded by General Erik Hansen. He also ordered Canaris to intensify his security measures for the protection of the oil fields.

Canaris did not go to Bucharest after receiving these instructions but to Vienna instead. Colonel Morusov was in Vienna at the end of the arbitration hearing when Canaris succeeded in making contact with him and the two men decided to meet at the Hotel Danieli in Venice. Their meeting place was a hundred yards from the Doge's Palace, looking out on the island of San Giorgio. It took place on 3 September, first anniversary of the British and French declaration of war on Germany.

They discussed the serious discontent that was evident in Rumania after the Vienna tribunal had awarded a large part of Transylvania to Hungary. King Carol II felt that his throne was insecure and on 4 September he dismissed Gigurtu and named General Ion Antonescu as Prime Minister.

On hearing this news Canaris asked Morusov what he thought of General Antonescu. Morusov replied:

The King may think he has saved the situation. I cannot think of a more unhappy choice. Antonescu represents nobody, neither a party nor a political idea. The army refer to him as the red dog. He was no more than a bandit chief in 1919. He hates the King and holds him responsible for everything that has gone wrong in Rumania. The King asked me to arrest him early this year and shut him up. I would have liked to have eliminated him altogether.

'Can there be a compromise between the generals and the Iron Guard?' asked Canaris.

'King Carol is making use of the Iron Guard with the idea that the compromise cannot last for long and that he will emerge as the arbiter of power.'

Events went even more swiftly than Morusov had predicted. Antonescu held a conference of the three main parties: Julian

Maniu of the National Peasant Party, Dinu Bratiano of the Liberal Party and Horia Sima of the Iron Guard. The three Party leaders refused him their co-operation as long as King Carol retained power. The walls of Bucharest were plastered with posters accusing King Carol of murder and every imaginable crime against his country. When Antonescu informed the King of their views, Carol realized that he must abdicate. The terms that he made included safe passage to the West for himself and his mistress Magda Lupescu, and permission to take with him the collection of pictures in Sinaia Palace as well as the royal treasure. Fearing a *coup* by the Iron Guard, Antonescu accepted all these conditions and the King declared in favour of his heir Prince Michael, aged nineteen. The royal train loaded with treasure left Bucharest on 6 September and arrived in Yugoslavia scarred by the parting shots of the Iron Guard.

On the evening of 7 September Canaris and Morusov emerged from the Hotel Danieli and walked along the St Mark canal, pondering over the dramatic events in Rumania. They made their way along the crowded pavements, sunset colouring the domes and spires of Venice, and sat down for a drink at the Café Florian. Morusov was still talking about General Antonescu.

'He's not what you would call a Germanophile. He was a military cadet at Saint-Cyr, don't forget. He was one of the group of Rumanians who worked with General Berthelot and the French mission in Bucharest. He was Military Attaché in London for years and a close friend of Nicolas Titulescu when Titulescu was Ambassador there. He is no friend of Germany, but he will have to work within the framework that King Carol left behind him'.

Canaris came out of his reverie and asked:

'Do you believe that the arrival of the German military mission can upset him?'

'We are dealing with a man whose power has no basis and who imagines that his own will power can suffice to keep the country on the path that he has chosen. This is one reason why I am going back tomorrow to Bucharest.'

'From what you tell me, I have some fears for your personal safety.'

'Do not worry. Antonescu needs me. I am the only one who knows what precautionary measures you and I have taken for the oil fields. I am the only one who knows how to run the Security

Service and works in collaboration with the *Abwehr*. No, I must go home.'

Canaris, who did not find Morusov entirely congenial, hesitated and then said: 'Well, Morusov, if you change your mind and decide not to go home you may be assured of my protection.'

'My sincere thanks, Admiral. I will go home tomorrow as I have already decided. We have a lot to do together in Bucharest.'

They walked back towards the Hotel Danieli and dined at the Taverna dei Dogi on seafood with a Verona wine that Canaris especially liked, their last dinner together. For on his return to Berlin, Canaris found a message awaiting him from the *Abwehr* in Bucharest. Morusov had been arrested on his return to Rumania by the Chief of the Gendarmerie, Aurel Tobescu. He was in Jilava prison, and Colonel Eugene Christescu had been appointed as his successor. The Admiral reacted in a characteristic way: he set out at once for Bucharest with the idea of speaking to Antonescu on Morusov's behalf. He felt under an obligation to the prisoner, who had worked closely with the *Abwehr*, though Canaris knew that he had also worked closely with the Soviet Intelligence Service.

Canaris was received by General Antonescu and explained to him Germany's interest in Morusov as a man who could help further to foil British sabotage attempts in Rumania. He even added that Hitler had shown an interest in his welfare. Antonescu assured Canaris that nothing disagreeable would happen to Morusov, whose arrest had been an exceptional measure, and that he would soon be released. Canaris was reassured, and after some routine work at the *Abwehr* office in Bucharest and with the German military aid mission, he returned home.

Shortly after this visit Canaris heard that Morusov had been brutally murdered in Jilava prison with a score of other prisoners, apparently by legionaries of the Iron Guard. He expressed a harsh opinion to his staff about Antonescu, whose assurances he had accepted in good faith, saying: 'I wish to have nothing further do do with a man of that sort.'

22
Meetings with Franco and Pétain

Canaris was hardly back from Venice when Field-Marshal Keitel summoned him to the High Command Headquarters to be acquainted with the conclusions of a meeting on 6 September at which Hitler, with Göring, Raeder and Jodl present, had laid down the strategic lines for the autumn and winter of 1940-41. Hitler had directed at the end of this meeting that Admiral Canaris should be kept informed, so that the necessary measures following on the decisions made could be taken in the intelligence field.

At the Hitler meeting Admiral Raeder had explained his conception of the new strategy that ought to be adopted by Germany. 'Gibraltar and Suez are the essential objectives for the next stage of war. It is absolutely necessary to drive the British out of the Mediterranean before the United States intervenes in the war. This is the chance to deal a decisive blow against Britain.' Jodl agreed, but added that 'in the Western Mediterranean we must have the support either of the Vichy Government or of the Madrid Government or both.' Göring was in agreement with both Raeder and Jodl, visualizing that three columns would advance, one on Gibraltar through Spain with Franco's consent, a second through Morocco with Pétain's consent, and a third through the Balkans with Antonescu's consent, to seize the Dardanelles and Ankara and march on Suez, while the Italians advanced into Egypt from Libya.

Göring's plan was not without its drawbacks, as Hitler pointed out, since it put Turkey in the Western camp. Hitler went on to say that the Italians could very well carry out the attack on Suez on their own. In the Western Mediterranean the collaboration of the Vichy Government would have to be sought either by pressure or by some spectacular concessions, such as releasing the French prisoners-of-war; and General Franco would have to be persuaded to enter the war on the Axis side. He added, 'the Duce must accept the idea of collaboration with France'.

Canaris listened and said nothing, apart from agreeing with Keitel what the *Abwehr* rôle was to be. So he now knew that Hitler realized that he could not succeed in a direct attack on the British Isles. Hitler also appeared not to believe that air attacks could bring the British to the point of surrender in spite of Göring's claims. His thoughts were turning once more to Operation Felix, and Canaris realized that he must fight hard to prevent Spain being dragged into a war that could end only in an Axis defeat. The French would also have to be warned. In wishing to limit the operation to the seizure of Gibraltar and to allow the Italians to attempt alone the attack on Suez, Hitler was wrecking the idea of Operation Felix, which had a purpose only as part of a strategic move on Suez and the Middle East. Confirmed in his view of Hitler's inability to grasp the art of strategy, Canaris doubted whether he would show himself more adept in diplomacy. He decided to use his influence to prevent the war spreading in the direction of Spain.

General Franco knew nothing about the conference of 6 September. Canaris therefore made a quick visit to Madrid and explained to the Caudillo what pressures Hitler was about to exert on him. Franco thereupon took a grave decision to replace his Minister of Foreign Affairs, Colonel Juan Beigbeder Atienz, who was pro-British, with his brother-in-law Serrano Suñer, who was considered to be an Axis man. This would be seen by Hitler as a positive step, but the change was not made quickly and Suñer was sent first to Berlin to take stock of German intentions.

He was accompanied by the German Ambassador in Madrid, von Stohrer, and took with him a retinue of prominent Falangists. Suñer had meetings with Ribbentrop and Hitler on 17 and 25 September about which Canaris was told by his friend von Stohrer.

These exchanges produced a mood of evident dissatisfaction, since both Ribbentrop and Hitler discovered that Spanish foreign policy was 'somewhat equivocal'. Suñer expected this reaction and so did Canaris. Suñer noted that the German Government wished to assume no definite attitude to Spain's Moroccan pretensions, and he was disturbed to hear Ribbentrop talk of setting up a German base on the Canary Islands. He flatly rejected this suggestion and sent a messenger to warn Franco what was afoot. Franco replied in a letter of 21 September praising Suñer for I° obstinacy in face of a demand 'which my pen refuses even t°

copy'. Suñer described German reluctance to agree to Spanish claims on Morocco as being 'due to their obligations to Pétain or to ambitions of their own in Morocco'.

Suñer returned to Madrid via Rome, where he talked with Mussolini and Ciano. He could clearly see the points of difference between Spain and Germany. He did not hesitate to warn Franco of the danger that Germany might occupy Spain if Spain refused Hitler's demands. Canaris had told Franco exactly that. Spain faced the choice between a war on the side of Germany, a war against Germany or a neutrality that became even harder to maintain. Two men, however, enabled the Caudillo to continue in the third and most beneficial course, of neutrality, and these were Canaris and Pétain.

If Franco had cares, so did Pétain. Three months previously he had been called to the leadership of a nation by a kind of unanimity at a tragic moment when the entire French army, parts of it courageous and well commanded, had retreated in an extraordinary and shameful manner from Belgium to the Pyrenees and an entire people fled in mass fear along roads that were continuously bombed and machine-gunned. Two million men of the French army had been made prisoners-of-war. France had perhaps lost a battle and not a war, but she had suffered a blow in the stomach that left her gasping, in chaos and without initiative or leadership. With millions of refugees, her supplies and communications in an impossible condition, hundreds of thousands of soldiers without arms or commanders, and similar numbers of unemployed, France was on the edge of an abyss and the German horde was in occupation of half her territory. A little flame of resistance flickered in London, lit by a man who was practically alone. Who cared about London? For the French it was a question of survival in the autumn of 1940.

Marshal Pétain did what was most necessary at that time, restoring order and arranging for the refugees to return home, getting men back to work, trains moving again, and repairs and reconstruction begun. Life started again and people set about their work with a will. France retained sovereignty over half her territory and all her empire, but two wounds remained that would not heal: the German-occupied zone of France and two million prisoners-of-war behind barbed wire. The victor was insistent, the occupation costs heavy, and winter on the way.

There were some like Weygand and Paul Baudouin who favoured

strict adherence to the terms of the armistice and an eventual re-entry into the war beside Britain and the United States. This attitude did not exclude some contact with Germany, to obtain alleviation of the harsh armistice terms, while keeping a free hand in the French overseas territories, thanks to the fact that the French navy remained intact. Marshal Pétain did not quite share this point of view; his policy was more practical and more subtle. He was inclined to finesse, to temporize and to be strictly neutral, negotiating at the same time with both the British and the Germans, but allying himself with neither; he sought to safeguard France's future against any imaginable contingency. This passivity appeared to some to be harmful, and Pierre Laval particularly was convinced that Great Britain had lost the war and that Germany had won the whole of Europe. He wanted to obtain for France a place, honourable if subordinate, in this new Europe. Laval was the protagonist of a change of alliances, and an *entente* with the victor. He was doing everything he could to bring such a policy into being. Pétain knew this and was not happy about it. He did not much like the manners of 'l'Auvergnat' as he called Laval, or his way of establishing close links with the German Ambassador in Paris, Otto Abetz, to whom Laval had sent the pro-German Fernand de Brinon as his special envoy.

Since Laval was pursuing a policy that Pétain did not like, Pétain would pursue a policy of his own, making overtures to Hitler, but to Britain as well, sending Louis Rougier to London to make a secret agreement with the British. He also went to Montoire on 24 October for the celebrated interview with Hitler. He made use of Colonel Fonck, the French flying ace of the First World War, who had maintained friendly relations with his old enemy Göring, confiding in Fonck that he wished to meet Hitler. Fonck took soundings in Paris in the second half of September and returned to report to the Marshal. Canaris learned that the Vichy Government was trying to make contact, but did not know about the Fonck mission. He sought to offer a line of contact through his old friend General Hirosho Oshima, the Japanese Ambassador in Berlin, with whom he had a private interview, telling him of Hitler's plans.

Colonel Fonck learned from René Sawada, Japanese Ambassador in Paris, whom he had known in the days of the Versailles Treaty negotiations in 1919, that Hitler planned to seize Gibraltar and certain strategic points in North Africa.

At once I realized the gravity of the situation, all the more so as Sawada also had information that Hitler would visit Franco in October. That would be the beginning of the execution of his plan. It was clear that Hitler would demand passage through Spain for the twenty German divisions stationed in the South-west of France ... I reported all my information to Marshal Pétain, and we decided to anticipate Hitler's action and so frustrate it. Pétain had, of course, been French Ambassador in Madrid and enjoyed great prestige there.

Hitler would play a separate hand with each of them, hoping that neither Franco nor Pétain would know of his propositions to the other. The message that went from Pétain to Franco through the Spanish Ambassador, Señor de Lequerica, contained my information on Hitler's intentions and continued that in no circumstances would Marshal Pétain lend himself to the occupation of North African territory by German troops; nor would he open the way through the Pyrenees to them. The Pétain message ended with these vital words: 'Under no circumstances or pressures, will I depart from the terms of the armistice.'

Colonel Fonck relates further that in order to elicit the timing of Hitler's plans, he suggested to Marshal Pétain that they should ask for an interview with Hitler, calculating that Hitler would arrange a meeting with Pétain to fit in conveniently with his visit to Franco. Meanwhile Señor de Lequerica made his visit to Madrid and returned with a message from Franco that in view of Pétain's firm attitude, he would not associate Spain with the projects of the German dictator.

'We breathed again,' concluded Colonel Fonck. 'A great peril had been averted, and probably from that moment Hitler had lost the game.'

Admiral Fernet has told the author that Pétain did not inform Laval or any other minister of his exchanges with Franco. Canaris's subtle manoeuvring thus led to success.

The next scene in this battle of wits was set on 22 October 1940, when Pierre Laval found himself suddenly invited by Otto Abetz to meet Hitler and Ribbentrop on board the Führer's train at Montoire-sur-Loire. The interpreter Paul Schmidt has left no very extensive account of this meeting, at which Hitler expressed the wish to meet Marshal Pétain as soon as possible – 'even the day after tomorrow', and declared to Laval that 'I do not seek a vindictive peace'.

Wednesday, 23 October was the day fixed for a meeting between Hitler and Franco at Hendaye. Upon this meeting would depend the entire strategic direction of the Third Reich in the autumn of 1940, a turning point in the war.

Arriving a little after midday at Hendaye, Hitler and Ribbentrop strolled along the station platform in splendid sunshine. Hitler explained to Ribbentrop:

'We can give the Spaniards nothing in writing about their claims to French colonial territory. If they have even a scrap of paper on this subject, the French will certainly get to hear of it. Moreover I want to get the French during my interview with Pétain to take an active part in the war against Britain.'

He went on:

'So I can't demand this kind of surrender of territory. In any case an agreement with the Spaniards would start the rumour that we were selling the French empire, which would send the French into de Gaulle's camp. To help Franco make a decision, we can suggest to him some parts of the French colonial territories, for example Morocco and the Oran district, provided that France can be compensated with British territory when we have defeated Britain.' Hitler was playing a very close game, imagining that he could bring both Franco and Pétain to agree with his proposals. Before going to meet the Duce on 4 October at the Brenner Pass, he had confided in his entourage that to reconcile Italian, French and Spanish interests in Africa would only be possible through a gigantic confidence trick, but Hitler was not aware that the French and Spanish Heads of State were acting in concert to frustrate him.

One hour behind schedule General Franco's special train crossed the Bidassoa bridge and drew up at the Spanish station. Conforming with protocol it was Hitler who took the last few steps across the frontier onto Spanish soil. The hour's delay had not improved his temper, but he smiled as he shook the Caudillo's hand. Together they inspected the guard of honour and then entered the Führer's railway carriage where the conversations were to take place.

Hitler from the start sought to intimidate Franco by asserting that 'Germany will emerge victorious from this war', but Franco did not flinch. Hitler suggested that Spain should enter the war in January 1941, in which event German shock troops would assault Gibraltar on 10 January sure of success. As a reward Germany would offer Gibraltar to Spain as well as 'certain increases in Spanish colonial territory'.

Franco did not blink. His tanned face and dark eyes remained so immovable that the interpreter, Paul Schmidt, could not discern whether he was disconcerted or simply preparing to reply with the utmost calm. Canaris would have known the real answer. Franco's reply in his highly pitched tones, came in the form of a refusal. He referred to the bad conditions in Spain, lack of petrol and raw materials. He listed the shortage of all essential commodities, as Canaris had advised him to do at their last meeting in September. It was a long list. He spoke of the risk to the Canary Islands, too remote to be securely defended. Finally he claimed for Spain, 'the honour of retaking Gibraltar . . . which the Spanish will do . . . when they are ready'. He mentioned also the sort of resistance of which Britain, backed by supplies from the United States, was now capable. The wily Canaris had been over all this ground with him, knowing full well how Hitler could be most easily thrown off balance.

As Franco's list of objections went on, so Hitler's nervous agitation increased. His fingers drummed on the arm of his chair. Once he got up and said that it was useless to continue the discussion. Franco persisted, however, with his calm dissertation, as if he had not even noticed the Führer's exasperation, until Hitler, not wishing for a complete breakdown of their talk, resumed his seat. He tried to make Franco change his mind, but without success. At the end of seven hours a draft agreement was drawn up, setting forth the conditions under which Spain would feel able to enter the war. Even then, such differences of view emerged that Ribbentrop and Suñer had to be asked to work over the agreement again. There was then a dinner in the Führer's restaurant car, followed by another two hours of talking, during which the atmosphere grew perceptibly cooler. Nine hours without any result for Hitler – a complete set-back. He could not count on Spain.

The Führer and the Caudillo thus parted, each in his special train, leaving further dialogue to their Foreign Ministers. During the night any vestiges of the day's agreement crumbled away as Ribbentrop went over the ground again with the cautious Suñer. Finally Ribbentrop demanded agreed minutes of their discussion by 8 AM, as he had to leave for the meeting with Marshal Pétain at Montoire. The Spanish Under-Secretary Espinosa de los Monteros put up a draft, but to any suggested insertions at that late hour he returned the elusive answer that he would refer these matters. Ribbentrop, furious and cursing the 'Jesuit Suñer' and

209

the 'ungrateful Franco', left by air for Tours to rejoin Hitler at Montoire.

Coming by road from Vichy, Pétain arrived at Montoire about nightfall on 24 October to be saluted by a German guard of honour and the strains of the *Marseillaise* played, as he noticed, at a rather slower pace than usual. The towering German Chief of Protocol, Herr von Dörnberg, received him, and Pétain returned the salutes, of Marshal Keitel and Herr von Ribbentrop without handshakes, passing down the ranks of the Adolf Hitler Bodyguard battalion to meet the Führer. Hitler was surrounded by his General Staff on the central platform, draped for the occasion with the German and French colours. When the grave-faced Marshal was still a few paces away, Hitler, in the brown jacket and black trousers of the Party uniform, wearing his Iron Cross, advanced to meet him with a stern expression. Suddenly the victor of Verdun came face to face with the victor of Sédan. 'In the indistinct lights of the station,' wrote the interpreter Schmidt, 'it was difficult to distinguish victor from vanquished. France and Germany personified seemed to confront one another. Everybody there, including the sentries standing at the salute, felt at that moment the breath of history.'

After a few words of welcome, Hitler at his most engaging, Marshal Pétain reserved, both parties climbed into the Führer's carriage, where Pétain and Laval sat on Hitler's right and Ribbentrop on his left.

Hitler began by saying that France had not wanted war, which she had entered on the orders of Great Britain. He then began a long diatribe against the British, ending in this way.

I cherish the sincere hope, however, of putting an end as quickly as possible to this war, as it is not an enviable or desirable situation nor can it become permanent. I am convinced that there is no business less profitable than war and I am resolved to use every military, political and economic means to put an end to it. I am aware that to prolong it will weigh heavily not only on Germany but on Europe too, and raise the final bill to be paid. It is evident that this bill must be paid, having due regard to the vital demands of certain European peoples and to the war costs. Someone must pay. It can only be France or Britain. As Britain bears most responsibility for starting it, I personally think that Britain must pay most. . . .

In hastening Britain's collapse the war will be shortened and the people of Europe freed from their anxieties and sacrifices. Each month that passes diminishes this chance and increases Europe's sacrifice, retarding the return to normal and decent conditions. All countries that wish to stop the war should form a Continental community. For my part I want to organize it against the common enemy, Britain. Is France inclined to join this community? It would be in her interest.

The Marshal, who had followed Hitler's declarations with keen interest, Schmidt thought, beneath his cold and almost detached manner, did not reply to this proposition. Hitler rattled on about his generosity over the armistice conditions and then came to the main problem – French participation in the struggle against Britain. 'Will France continue to defend her colonial empire against British attacks, as at Dakar? Is she ready to reconquer those territories that have been taken over by dissident forces?'

The Marshal may not have understood the translation. He did not reply. Hitler repeated: 'What will France do if Britain attacks again?'

This time the Marshal did understand and he replied that France had suffered too much, morally and materially, to be able to engage in a new conflict.

Hitler was plainly irritated by this. 'If France does not wish to defend herself and harbours sympathies for the British,' he cried in menacing tones, 'she will lose her colonial empire at the end of the war and will be subject to peace terms as hard as those imposed on Britain.'

'No vindictive peace settlement in history has ever lasted,' replied Pétain coldly.

'I don't want a vindictive peace and I am, on the contrary, ready to give France favoured treatment,' exclaimed Hitler. 'What I want is a peace based on *entente* that will last for centuries, but this is only possible if France resolves to help me to defeat the British. Blood spilt in a common cause will bind us more closely than treaties.'

Marshal Pétain skilfully ignored this overture. 'It would be useful for the French Government to know what sort of final peace treaty Germany envisages,' he said. 'France must know what her fate is to be, and the two million prisoners-of-war must return as soon as possible to their families.'

It was Hitler's turn to be evasive. 'The final peace treaty can only be determined after the defeat of Britain,' he replied.

Each man repeated his question. Dr Schmidt expected Hitler, in view of Pétain's negative attitude to reject all his demands, but he did not do so. At this juncture the word 'collaboration' was heard for the first time. If the two countries could find a way of agreeing, France could hope for concessions on all the points raised by the Marshal, averred Hitler. Pétain made an intervention on behalf of the *Départements du Nord*, which had been attached to the German military government of Belgium, an administrative arrangement which the French viewed with concern. He claimed their return to France and he also alluded to Alsace and Lorraine. Hitler replied that he would consider these questions and write to him in reply.

'Marshal, we can perhaps end our meeting,' said Hitler. 'I believe that it has been useful.'

The meeting had lasted two hours. It ended with the same ceremonial salutes and national anthems. Pétain shook Hitler's hand as he entered his car, taking leave of Keitel and Ribbentrop with a salute only. The French motorcade drove off into the night. Pétain stayed the night at Tours and declared himself satisfied with the outcome of the meeting, in that as he he had entered into no engagements.

The Germans stayed overnight at Montoire station. Ribbentrop's train, *Heinrich*, left at 5 AM and that of Hitler, *Erika*, an hour later. Morale was not high in either train as it returned to Germany, and a disagreeable letter from Mussolini, dated 19 October and announcing his intention to attack Greece, was delivered to the Führer's train at Yvoir. An accompanying report from Prince Bismarck, the German Ambassador in Rome, gave the date of the Italian attack as 28 October. Hitler was beside himself:

'The Italians can achieve nothing against the Greeks in the Balkans in winter,' he told Ribbentrop. 'This stupid war must be prevented. Telephone Rome and propose a meeting on the Brenner Pass, and I will redirect our trains to Italy.'

Mussolini had long been preparing a war of his own against Greece, hoping to achieve there the military successes that he had missed over France and Britain. He was not sorry to have disconcerted Hitler, after so many occasions on which the Germans had told him of military operations at the last minute. The Duce offered Florence as a meeting place on 28 October. When *Erika* and *Heinrich* had reached Verona on the way there, Hitler learned that the Italian attack had already begun at 3 AM that morning. There was nothing for it but to smile amiably when Mussolini on his arrival at Florence announced to him 'the victorious advance'.

They then discussed the balance-sheet of Europe at the Vecchio Palace, and Hitler began by relating the course of his Montoire conference.

'Say what you like. France will never be a friend of the Axis and one day she will go back to Britain. However I am convinced that although Pétain considers a declaration of war against Britain to be inopportune, he will vigorously defend French positions in Africa against any aggressor.' As to the Hendaye meeting, Hitler spoke angrily about 'that arrogant Spaniard', 'pig of a Jesuit', with his preposterous conditions for entering the war. 'Rather than face another meeting like the one at Hendaye with Franco, I'd prefer to have three or four teeth pulled out.'

Count Ciano was pleased that the Germans and the French had not come closer together. Mussolini was pleased with his prospects of victory in Greece, and seemed only half attentive to what Hitler had to tell him. They parted at 6 PM after the usual civilities, but Hitler reflected on the way home that his long European tour had won him nothing.

Canaris, from bits and pieces of conversation with those present, worked out the pattern of the talks with Franco, Pétain and Mussolini, and was able to say to Piekenbrock, with a smile of satisfaction:

'The wind is changing, Piki. For the first time since 1933 "Emil" has suffered a total defeat. He has been obliged to surrender quite openly. Pétain and Franco have been stronger than he. Mussolini has played a swinish trick on him, it won't stop there. We can expect some other blood-bath. After this check in the West will he turn East? I wonder how all this will end.'

23

Relations with Russia and with Spain

Canaris appeared anxious and depressed in November 1940. He knew that Hitler was making preparations for yet another adventure, and as he told Piekenbrock, the Führer was refusing to admit the self-evident truth that with her limited war potential Germany must concentrate on victory in one theatre of war only, either in the West or in the Mediterranean.

But no, he wants to extend the conflict to the South-west, though he was checked at Hendaye and Montoire, or he wants to turn East and attack the USSR. It is madness. As long as Britain continues the struggle against him he ought not to think of a second front ... If our forces are tied up in the East, the British can easily muster their strength and, who knows, deal us a decisive blow! ... The parallel with Napoleon in 1812 is clear, and in each case the decision stems from disappointment at having failed to invade the British Isles. Our generals and marshals with their dreams of encircling enemy armies in vast battles have lost all sense of reality. They are even excited at the prospect of a war on two fronts and want to go and win laurels for themselves on the Russian steppes. I bombard them with warnings but my warnings go into the waste-paper-basket. We have already virtually lost the war, and with the Russians on our hands, our suicidal end will come even sooner.

Walther Schellenberg has emphasized in his memoirs the deep pessimism Admiral Canaris felt in November 1940. He wrote that:

although Canaris under-estimated Russia's technological progress in technique, my conversations with him revealed his fears that Germany would imperil herself by engaging in a war on two fronts. The opinion of the General Staff was that with our overwhelming superiority in arms, men and military formations, a war with Russia would be over in a few weeks. Heydrich and Himmler put forward the view, shared by Hitler, that a military defeat would weaken Stalin's position to such an extent that by sending in agents on a large scale Germany could bring down the Soviet régime. Canaris and I thought that the military's opinions were far too optimistic and Canaris thought the ideas put forward by Himmler and Heydrich extremely unsound.

214

Schellenberg found the Admiral, in these circumstances of disagreement with the leadership, nervous, erratic and sometimes obscure to the point of evasiveness. 'One day I told him jokingly during a telephone conversation that I would feel it my duty to acquaint the *Gestapo* with his defeatist opinions. "Oh, dear", rejoined Canaris, "I had forgotten we were on the telephone".'

When a prisoner-of-war in Moscow in 1945 General von Bentivegni revealed that Canaris had known of Hitler's intention to attack Russia since August 1940.

'The Admiral told me this during a private conversation in his office', declared Bentivegni, 'and that Hitler had first alluded to this plan during a Gauleiters' conference in Berlin in 1938. Canaris also told me that the plan was already beginning to take a perceptible shape in August 1940 and that a large number of German divisions would be transferred from the Western to the Eastern front, to positions of attack against Russia.'

It has been suggested that Canaris provided Hitler with false information on Russia, so that the Führer would gain the impression that Stalin was preparing to attack in the West and would therefore decide on a pre-emptive strike against him. Nothing could be further from the truth. Hitler knew very well that Stalin had no aggressive intentions against Germany, but as he recorded in *Mein Kampf*, Germany needed space in the East for the 'German *Herrenvolk*' at the expense of the 'sub-human Slavs'. Canaris knew this only too well, and any other explanation of Hitler's decision to attack Russia is quite fictitious.

Von Bentivegni, as Head of Section III (Counter-espionage), received a sealed envelope from Hitler's Headquarters on 7 September 1940, containing a directive marked 'Most Secret' and signed by General Jodl. This directive concerned the *Abwehr* alone.

Our Eastern territories will be occupied by stronger military effectives in the next four weeks. At the end of October the dispositions shown on the attached map will have been made. These dispositions must not give Russia the impression that we intend to attack in the East. On the other hand Russia will realize that strong and well-trained German formations in Poland and Bohemia-Moravia indicate that we are able, at any moment and with strong forces, to defend our interests against a Russian attack, especially in the Balkans.

To facilitate the work of our Intelligence and to be able to reply to any questions that the Russian Intelligence Service may put to us, the following instructions are issued:

1) The total of German effectives in the East must be distorted as far as possible by reports suggesting frequent changes of unit location. These movements can be explained as part of the training programme and as regroupings.

2) The impression must be given that the main concentration is in the south of the Bohemian protectorate and in Austria, and that effectives in the north are relatively unimportant.

3) In the matter of troop equipment, especially in the case of the armoured divisions, there can be exaggerations if need be.

4) Reports must suggest that anti-aircraft defences in the East have been considerably strengthened since the end of the war in the West, and that this process is continuing, thanks to equipment captured in France.

5) As for improvements in communications, by rail, road and air, it should be indicated that these are normal activities, made necessary for economic reasons in the recently conquered territories.

The High Command has decided that exact details of military dispositions will be made available for the purposes of the Counter-espionage Section.

(signed)
Jodl

Before the International Tribunal at Nuremberg on 5 June 1946, General Jodl sought to give credence to the idea of 'a Russian threat weighing on Germany'. He explained that the directive quoted above:

was one of the sort that I used to give Canaris every six weeks as a basis for counter-espionage work. I need not go further into that here, but in this case the intention was to make our forces in the East seem much stronger than they were in reality. This is shown by the permission to exaggerate the strength of the armoured divisions and our anti-aircraft defences, if need be. The purpose was to make the Russians recoil from an attack on Rumania which was feared at that time. Had I known on 6 September, 1940, that the Führer harboured aggressive intentions against Russia, my instructions would have been different. For those orders that I actually gave would have indicated to the Soviets our intention to attack.

Jodl said that he first heard Hitler speak of his fears of Russian hostility towards Germany, on 29 July 1940, at the Berghof. Hitler had kept him back after the daily conference and told him that he feared a Russian attack on the Rumanian oil fields before the winter was out, and that the oil fields were absolutely vital to the German war effort. On 9 and 27 August Hitler had made out two orders for the movement of ten infantry divisions and two armoured divisions into Poland for the contingency of protecting the Rumanian oil fields.

In fact Hitler was hesitating, sometimes looking towards Gibraltar, sometimes hoping that the Italians would reach Suez and sometimes looking east at Moscow, but neither Russia nor the United Kingdom was at the forefront of his mind. He imagined the British to be staggering under the concerted blows of his *Luftwaffe* bombers and U-boats. His conclusion was simple: when Stalin had been defeated, Churchill would capitulate.

Stalin coolly sized up the military picture in the autumn of 1940. He was certainly not going to take on the *Wehrmacht* just to relieve the pressure on Britain at a time when the German armies were no longer tied down in the West. Ribbentrop sensed the cooling of Russo-German relations and, because he too feared a war on two fronts, suggested to Hitler a meeting with Stalin.

'You must be dreaming', replied Hitler. 'You know that Stalin will never come to Berlin. Are you suggesting that I should go to Moscow?' He allowed Ribbentrop to invite Molotov to Berlin, and Stalin agreed, settling on 10 November as the date for Molotov's visit.

Molotov had a long conference with Ribbentrop and then on the thirteenth with Hitler. Relations between the two countries were in public regarded as being close; in fact they were not so. Molotov made cautious soundings about Finland. Germany refused to accept the annexation of the whole country by Russia, but declared that there could be concessions. Molotov was informed that Germany was planning military action against Greece to rescue Italy from defeat. He expressed approval and asked Germany to recognize a Russian interest in Bulgaria like that of Germany in Rumania. The Germans did not reject this suggestion, going as far as to say that they did not want Turkish domination of the Dardanelles to be perpetuated. Finally the Germans stated that they had no special interest in Iran and the Russians expressed readiness to settle their differences with Japan.

It was practically a statement of agreement, but Hitler did not regard it as such. On the following day Keitel said to Canaris:

'The demands advanced by the Russians have alarmed the Führer. The Russians intend resuming their war with Finland and taking the whole country. They want to extend their influence in the Balkans and the Dardanelles. The Führer sees these projects as the beginnings of a grand plan to encircle Germany. He has decided to continue with Directive Number 18 of 12 November, which you have seen.'

This directive stated that 'Political conversations with Russia are now taking place in order to determine what is Russia's policy for the near future. Whatever may be the outcome of these talks, all preparations ordered by word of mouth for the East must continue. Further instructions will be issued after the army's outline plans have been submitted to me and approved by me.'

Canaris asked the question burning his tongue: 'In this case, is Operation Felix postponed?'

'No,' replied Keitel. 'Your instructions are precise and must be followed.'

The Admiral was dismayed. All his intrigues of the summer of 1940 to keep the war out of Spain seemed to have failed.

Keitel added: 'The Italian position in Albania is catastrophic, as you know.'

What had happened was that Hitler had been strongly impressed by the resounding British victory over the Italian fleet off Taranto. He was expecting a Greek counter-offensive which took place on 14 November driving the Italians north over the frontier that they had invaded. Keitel explained to Canaris that Hitler wanted to force Spain to enter the war as soon as possible, and that he had decided to invite the Spanish Foreign Minister, Serrano Suñer, to visit him at the Berghof in the next few days.

'He will have to give way,' affirmed Keitel, leaving Canaris to wonder whether the almost comic Spanish affair might not turn out to be a tragedy in the third act. He read over again Directive Number 18 of 12 November, with its provisions for the conduct of war and for consequent events, and came to the conclusion that, with Italy failing in the Balkans and Egypt, and the invasion of Britain being postponed from week to week, Hitler could not adhere to a cohesive strategy and was falling back on Operation Felix. Canaris called in Oster, Piekenbrock, Lahousen and Bentivegni to brief them on the latest possibilities. He read out to them a new set of instructions that had just reached him from Hitler.

Political measures are in motion to bring Spain into the war in the

near future. The aim of a German intervention on the Iberian peninsula (code name Felix) will be to throw the British out of the Western Mediterranean. For this purpose:

a) Gibraltar must be taken and the Straits closed.
b) The British must be prevented from installing themselves elsewhere on the Iberian peninsula or the Atlantic islands.

Certain preparations were expected of the *Abwehr* before the Operation. Hitler had given to Canaris the following instructions which he now read out to his heads of section:

'Special agents (officers in civilian dress) will make the necessary preparations for the attack on Gibraltar, and the capture of air fields. They will be subject, with regard to disguise and to collaboration with Spanish nationals, to security measures laid down by the Chief of the *Abwehr*.'

Colonel Piekenbrock smiled, because the Admiral had stopped reading and was looking at him.

'Piki', he said, 'this means that you must go to Madrid.'

'Yes, Admiral.'

'You may be fond of Spain, but it can be cold in November and December in Madrid.'

'It will be warmer in Algeciras, Admiral.'

The Admiral read on: 'This passage will interest our friend Lahousen: "Special *Abwehr* units will work with the Spaniards to forestall the British if they seek to extend their perimeter or to uncover and disrupt our preparations".'

Lahousen nodded.

'Now I will read the following paragraph for your information only: "Units selected for the attack will be stationed at a distance from France's frontier with Spain and kept on instant alert. There will be three weeks notice of the operation, which will take place only after preparations have been made concerning the Atlantic islands." It is a question, gentlemen, of ensuring the defence of the Canary Islands, but that is another kettle of fish and is not our business for the moment.'

Colonel Oster drew nervously at his cigarette and asked:

'Admiral, you have just briefed us on the preparative phase, but how does "Emil" expect to plant the swastika flag on the Rock of Gibraltar?'

'In the second phase, and after some work by Piekenbrock, *Abwehr* observers placed in Algeciras will call up at the proper moment a *Luftwaffe* strike force based on French soil, which will make a surprise attack on British naval units in the Gibraltar anchorages and will land after the attack at Spanish air fields. At the same time our troops will cross the Spanish frontiers by land and by air. The third phase will be an assault on the Rock itself. This directive gives us some interesting details. It says that the units taking part must be strong enough to capture the Rock without Spanish assistance. Also the *Wehrmacht* must be strong enough to repel what Hitler calls "a most improbable attempt at a landing by the British". Hitler says furthermore that "for an entry into Portugal light formations would be used". To conclude all this, gentlemen, I have to inform you that our dear Führer says that "Italian participation is not expected." Gentlemen, long live the Axis!'

The four colonels smiled. Canaris looked at them and then said in a voice that was scarcely audible:

'It is understood that we shall adhere point by point to this new directive from the Führer and put everything in hand so as to be quickly prepared. . . .'

Piekenbrock interrupted him:

'But Admiral, do *you* believe in this Operation Felix?'

'No, Piki, I don't believe in it, but Hitler believes in it, at least he believes in it at this moment. If he postpones for a time his attack on the USSR, he is capable of striking at Gibraltar. He needs a fresh crack of the whip and is disappointed with the results achieved by his victory over France.'

'Do you really believe', asked Oster 'that General Franco will accept Operation Felix?'

'I don't know. I would have thought that the Caudillo will hold fast as he did at Hendaye, but I don't know his mood at this moment and I don't know what influence Suñer may have on him.'

'But if Franco does not march, will Hitler do so regardless?'

'Certainly, if he has decided to attack Gibraltar, he will do so with or without Franco. Only without Franco means against Franco. The Spaniards have just emerged from a civil war which has bled them white, and if the *Wehrmacht* crosses the Spanish frontier, it will be a case of guerilla war. Inevitably Hitler is putting on Napoleon's boots. If he attacks Spain it is almost certain that the *Wehrmacht* will suffer the fate of the *Grande Armée*; if he attacks Russia it will be exactly the same.'

'We are in a fine position,' exclaimed Oster. 'When can we rid ourselves of Emil?'

'Gentlemen, don't dream of that,' said Canaris. 'It is realities that matter. We have a job to do. Let us do it. I hope I shall succeed once more in checking Hitler on this Gibraltar business. We shall see!'

On 15 November Hitler invited Suñer to visit him. Franco held a meeting next day with Suñer and his military advisors, Generals Vigon and Varela and Admiral Moreno. The conclusion reached by these five men was clear: Spain could not and should not in any way take part in the war. The situation would be difficult in any circumstances because a violent German reaction was to be expected. Admiral Moreno ended by saying that because the situation was so serious, it would perhaps be best to avoid accepting Hitler's invitation. Suñer commented:

'If we don't go to Berchtesgaden we risk having the Germans come to Vittoria.'

Suñer arrived at Berchtesgaden on the evening of 18 November, to be met by Ribbentrop and the protocol officials. Next day Ribbentrop entertained the Spaniards and Ciano at Castle Fuschl, east of Salzburg, to a light lunch of spaghetti and pancakes, which the guests did not appear to relish. They then set out by car to the Berghof to meet Hitler.

The conversation between Hitler and Serrano Suñer, with Ribbentrop attending, lasted four hours. Hitler explained the need to attack again before the enemy could recuperate their powers of resistance, saying with his usual gestures of excitement:

the absolute closure of the Mediterranean is a necessity. In the West this can be achieved quickly and easily by the Gibraltar operation. At the same time we will act in the East by blocking the Suez Canal. Blocking the Straits of Gibraltar is an honour that falls to Spain, just as Spain must guard the Canary Islands ... Regarding the economic difficulties which you instance to defer the question, I must tell you that Spain has nothing to gain by postponing her entry into this war. A rapid end to the war will, on the contrary, bring improvements sooner.

Then Hitler unmasked his big guns, with some menacing but exaggerated statistics: 'Of 230 German divisions, 186 are inactive at this moment and are able to move in any direction at any time ... I have decided to attack Gibraltar and my operation is prepared in detail. It only remains to undertake the enterprise, and this must be done.'

Suñer spoke again of economic difficulties, but Hitler asked him in sarcastic tones whether the Caudillo believed he could improve the situation in Spain by staying out of the war. Suñer changed his tactics, saying 'taking Gibraltar only has a meaning for the Spanish people if we take the whole of Morocco and Oran in Algeria as well'. Hitler declined to be drawn, but Suñer insisted, and Hitler finally replied that these claims by Spain would lead to endless disputes and could not be discussed at that time. For they might lead to the loss of North Africa to the Axis influence and rather than that, he would prefer to leave Gibraltar in British hands and have Pétain in North Africa. 'Spain must have confidence in the Führer's word and not expect written pledges.'

'Spain, of course, has confidence in the Führer's word,' objected Suñer, 'but . . .'

'Don't forget that Germany will treat her friends with generosity but will destroy those whose conduct is disloyal to her.'

Having said that, Hitler's expression softened and he declared that he wanted to speak as Spain's best friend . . . He would leave Spain another month for preparation and decision. The months of December, January and February would be easiest for the Spanish operation, but later the heat would trouble German troops . . . 'and in March, April or May, they will perhaps have to be committed elsewhere'. The *Stuka* bombers that Hitler required for his campaign in Greece in March and April could not at the same time be available in Spain. There were in fact technical and military reasons for disposing of Gibraltar by February 1941 at the latest, or postponing the operation until after the war with Russia.

A series of telegrams from the German Ambassador in Madrid, von Stohrer, beginning on 28 November 1940, reported first that Franco had 'assented to preparatory measures'. Canaris was told about this by Keitel and said nothing, though it astonished him. A second telegram from von Stohrer next day spoke of the Spanish preparations taking 'long to accomplish, therefore no precise date can be fixed for the beginning of operations against Gibraltar'. According to the Ambassador, the Caudillo would welcome a German mission of military experts, including 'an officer who enjoys the Führer's personal confidence'.

Hitler had just had a long and disappointing interview with the Yugoslav Foreign Minister, Alexander Cincar-Markovitch, and was in no mood for more double talk. On his return from the Berghof to Berlin, he summoned Canaris to the Chancellery and put this question to him about the Caudillo's attitude. 'Duplicity or understandable caution?' Hitler stared at the little Admiral with a trace of anxiety in his large blue eyes, standing there stiffly though with his shoulders slightly bent. Canaris, who was not susceptible to the famous magnetism of those eyes, made a wry face and replied so softly that Hitler stepped forward and bent his head to hear what he was saying:

'General Franco is a man of great wisdom and he is extremely cautious. If he tells us that he will enter the war on the Axis side, we must believe him; if he says that the preparations for war necessitate some delay, that too must be believed; but I don't know how far his preparations have gone or why he is asking for a group of military experts.'

'But von Stohrer tells us on the 28th that Franco agrees to 10 January as the date for the *Wehrmacht* to cross the frontier, and then a day later he tells us that Franco seems to have gone back to his previous tactics. It is not at all clear what is happening.'

'Well, it may be that our Ambassador was a victim of his own wishful thinking.'

'That would not surprise me in the case of your friend von Stohrer. Never mind! I am asking you, Admiral, to go to Madrid and oblige Franco to fulfil his promises as quickly as possible. You must tell him that my decision is taken: the *Wehrmacht* will cross the Spanish frontier on 10 January 1941, and will attack Gibraltar on 4 February.'

'Very good, Führer.'

Back at the *Abwehr* office, Canaris rehearsed the scene in the Chancellery for Piekenbrock:

Hitler is playing a double game again. I know he has no high opinion of von Stohrer and that he expects a lot from my friendly relations with the Caudillo, but is this a reason for again making me an ambassador extraordinary? However, I am quite happy to go back to Madrid for a frank talk with the Spanish Head of State – he must not give in to Hitler's blackmail. [A pause . . .] It's amazing. Hitler is really convinced that all Germans think as he does. It appears not to have entered his head for a moment that I could have a different opinion from his on the usefulness of getting Spain to enter the war.

Ribbentrop told von Stohrer on 1 December that in response to the Caudillo's request for 'an officer enjoying the Führer's personal confidence', General Jodl, Chief of the Operational Staff of the *Wehrmacht*, would be made available. In another telegram dated 4 December to von Stohrer, Ribbentrop said that Franco should be informed of Admiral Canaris' arrival in Madrid on 8 December.

Before this telegram reached him von Stohrer reported to Ribbentrop in a telegram of the same date that Spain was willing to allow German destroyers to refuel in certain sheltered bays on the Spanish coast – good news for Berlin. It was interesting that Franco had chosen that exact movement to make one of his rare conciliatory gestures towards Germany. This permission had been sought by the Germans on 31 October and the reply had been outstanding for a month. Franco's reasoning may have been that his concession would be evidence of good will and might help to avoid more heavy obligations during the visit of Canaris to Spain.

The mission with which Hitler entrusted Canaris was curt. The Admiral was to brush aside all Spanish prevarications and obtain from Franco a firm commitment and a date on which operations could commence.

The Admiral arrived a day early, on 7 December, in freezing weather with the streets of Madrid covered in snow. He went to the *Abwehr* office and consulted the files there on the strength of the Spanish armed forces. Then he had a brief conversation with his friend, General Vigon, the Spanish Air Minister, with whom he called on General Franco at 7:30 PM.

The US Government produced a white book on Spain in the Second World War. It contains one version of this critical interview and there exist others. All of them describe Canaris as presenting Franco with an ultimatum from Hitler to enter the war on 10 January 1941. They are all entirely misleading and I am able to provide evidence from *Abwehr* sources of what really happened. All three men were close friends, and Canaris had no need to disguise his true thoughts. Having discharged his mission he asked Franco to describe his reactions, so that together they could 'find a way out of this wasp's nest without being stung too much'. He then unfolded Hitler's proposition that the *Wehrmacht* should enter Spain on 10 January and attack Gibraltar on 4 February. He added that 'when the first German troops have crossed the frontier, German economic aid to Spain will commence'. Franco gave his official reply that 'for reasons that have been presented already it is impossible for Spain to enter the war on that date'. Canaris commented that Hitler thought these reasons very slender, whereupon Franco became more precise and quoted details of the reasons for his decision. Gibraltar could naturally be captured, he said, but Spanish Guinea and one of the Canary Islands would fall to the British. Britain and America would then have a pretext to occupy the Azores, Madeira and the Cape Verde Islands. Spain needed a million tons of wheat and lacked rolling stock. The war would inflict great hardship on the Spanish provinces. Wheat was being bought in South America and Canada, and rolling stock as well; many locomotives were being repaired and oil refineries constructed but all this would take time. Franco threw out his arms in a gesture of welcome, inviting Canaris to travel anywhere in Spain and 'see what the famine is like, the shortcomings of the railways, the lack of coal and shipping'. He said that he was thinking not only of Spain but of Germany; for 'if the war was prolonged Spain would be a heavy burden to her ally'.

Canaris beamed with approval: 'Bravo, that is exactly what I am going to tell the Führer. After that sort of talk, he will cool off. But since the date of 10 January is not acceptable to you, can you propose another? Perhaps in April or May?'

'Impossible,' replied Franco. 'You know that one should never be too exact with your Führer. The solving of our economic difficulties is not a matter solely for Spain. It would be useful to have a German economic adviser here, and for the studies already begun to continue as discreetly as they were started. As for General Jodl who is waiting in Berlin to come and see me, between ourselves he can stay there. You may give my cordial regards to the Führer.'

Franco, Vigon and Canaris then set about an appraisal of the war situation. They agreed that Britain's war capacity was certainly larger than some people thought and that the possibility of Germany bringing the war to a rapid and victorious close was becoming less and less probable. The Spanish motto must therefore be 'to win time'. The Axis was far from winning the war, whatever Hitler, Ribbentrop and Goebbels might say. Spain could not hope to sustain a war against Britain without assistance greater than Germany was able to afford. All three men realized the weaknesses of Hitler's strategy. The *Abwehr* Chief could see clearly why Franco had no desire to commit the Spanish people to an adventure that might one day be rewarded with no more than the Rock and vague promises of French Morocco. They agreed that it would take at least six weeks after the first German troops

225

had crossed the Spanish frontier before the operational force would be ready and in position to attack Gibraltar. These movements would be immediately detected by the British intelligence service, and British counter-measures could lead to a bloody struggle on Spanish soil.

These risks that they depicted to each other were in fact not so great as they made them out to be. For a hundred tried German divisions could have easily thrown a British expeditionary force out of the Spanish peninsula, and British lines of communication would have been strafed by the *Luftwaffe* from Atlantic and Mediterranean air fields.

On 9 December Canaris was back in Berlin, where he was received by Hitler in the presence of Marshal Keitel and Ribbentrop. He expounded very clearly and at length everything that he and Franco had agreed between themselves to say. Despite Franco's categorical refusal, Hitler did not lose his temper. Canaris had an art in presenting such matters. Ribbentrop, who disliked him, did not dare to say anything with Hitler present, but suspected the rôle that Canaris might have played. He sent a furious telegram to von Stohrer, asking the German Ambassador to discover why the interview between Franco and Canaris had been 'in flagrant contradiction with the Hendaye conference and with the proposals made by Suñer at the Berghof on 19 November.' He also instructed the Ambassador to remain aloof for the time being from the Spanish leadership. Von Stohrer reported back that there was a split in the Spanish military, isolating Franco and making difficulties for Suñer. He added in a later telegram that acute famine among the Spanish people had helped to strengthen Franco in his present decision. Von Stohrer evidently did not advance the view that Franco had never had any intention of taking part in the war.

On 11 December Canaris was in the best of humours. For a brief intimation had just reached him from Keitel that 'Operation Felix as defined in Directive 18 of 12 November will not be proceeded with, since the political basis that would have been necessary no longer exists. All measures and preparations already begun must be stopped immediately'. He was, however, no sooner rid of Operation Felix than Operation Attila landed on his table. One of the twelve copies of Directive 19 reached him from the Führer's Headquarters on 11 December, an outline plan for a German occupation of the rest of France and seizure of the French fleet and air force if General Weygand's command of the French colonial empire went over to the enemy. Operation Attila required much secret and detailed preparatory work by the *Abwehr*, so that, in the event of Weygand's defection, French military and naval bases with their warships, installations and aircraft could be seized intact. Just above Hitler's signature on the Directive Canaris read:

'Preparations for Operation Attila require the greatest secrecy. In no circumstances must the Italians be aware of our preparations and intentions.' Hitler was not intent, however, on violating the armistice agreement with France, for he added: 'I retain the final decision on the method of carrying out this operation. The order to attack will not be given unless the French army offers resistance or unless French warships attempt to escape in disregard of German orders.'

Canaris was all the more surprised by this Directive because he had been told by Colonel Friedrich Rudolph of the *Abwehr's* Paris office about a military conference between the Germans and French, held on 10 December in Paris, with the German Ambassador, Otto Abetz, and General Warlimont on the German side and General Huntziger, Admiral Darlan and Pierre Laval present from France. According to Colonel Rudolph, the French leaders agreed to a German suggestion for a French offensive in Africa in the spring of 1941, with Nigeria as one of its targets. While accepting the idea, the French responded with extensive demands for the reduction of occupation costs and release of French prisoners-of-war. Warlimont was satisfied and intended to report to Hitler that there was 'no longer any need to doubt the goodwill and sincerity of the Pétain Government'.

Canaris could not quite grasp Hitler's reactions, not realizing that he was under growing pressure from Mussolini, who had always viewed askance any collaboration between France and Germany. Marshal Badoglio had been sowing seeds of mistrust against General Weygand and General Nogués, French Resident-General in Morocco, saying that unless France were carefully handled, there would be serious difficulties in North Africa. He had even suggested 'the elimination of Weygand and Nogués.' Directive Number 19 thus corresponded to certain suspicions that Hitler had readily assimilated.

On the morning of 12 December Canaris was able to throw some light on this subject in a two hour discussion with Keitel about Operation Attila and about Weygand. Back in his office by noon, he called in Piekenbrock, Lahousen, Oster, Bentivegni and Vice-Admiral Bürkner, all of whom saw immediately from his expression that something had gone wrong.

The *Abwehr* Chief began by explaining Operation Attila in outline and in detail, and then touched on the precautions that he had been asked to take to prevent the French navy from leaving Toulon, if necessary by acts of sabotage. He exclaimed:

These are the ideas of a layman. Imagine dozens of warships anchored, some in the naval port closely guarded by French troops and fenced in between the town and the commercial harbour, and some in the roads off Toulon. To get to the spot sufficient explosives to immobilize all these vessels at a given time is an operation that could not be carried out without detection. It would be obvious to anybody, but not apparently to Hitler or Keitel! As it is no use pointing out the stupidity of such orders to Keitel, and still less to Hitler, I showed no sign of disagreement. Once more we will have to approach these orders in a dilatory fashion. I will tell Keitel that Lahousen is getting on with the job, but that he has to surmount considerable difficulties. I will give him the impression that something is being done, while in fact we will do nothing. Are we agreed?

His officers smiled and nodded, but Canaris did not smile, because he had something still more serious to divulge. He turned to Colonel Lahousen.

'You must know General Weygand?'

'I know who he is, Admiral.'

'Well, the Führer has charged us with a mission that he considers of capital importance. Marshal Keitel requires us in the Führer's name to proceed with the elimination of the French Generalissimo. That is a task for your section.'

'What does Marshal Keitel mean by elimination?'

'That we should kill him. Herr Hitler fears that Weygand, with the undefeated part of the French army, will form a centre of resistance in North Africa and join the British.'

The *Abwehr* officers present were indignant and forcible in protesting against this demand.

' "Emil" thinks that we are no better than his *Gestapo* soldiery,' cried Oster, red with anger.

Bentivegni, usually equable, was furious.

'He's the one we should be eliminating,' he exclaimed.

Lahousen said curtly:

'I have no intention of carrying out this order. My section and my officers are combatants and not a band of assassins.'

'You are quite right,' agreed Canaris, 'but keep calm and we will talk it over together in a moment.'

Before the Nuremberg Tribunal, Marshal Keitel denied ever having passed on such an order from Hitler, and General Jodl supported him in this assertion, but it was noticed that from that day in the Nuremberg proceedings, 30 November 1945, the other military prisoners ceased to eat at table with Keitel and Jodl.

Canaris kept Lahousen behind after other routine matters had been dealt with, and when they were alone, looked up at him and said:

'I repeat that you are perfectly right not to obey such an order. Article 14 of the Military Code reads: "It is a crime to execute orders given for criminal reasons" . . . I recollect that Goebbels once said in one of his speeches: "there is no excuse for carrying out a criminal order, contrary to public morality." Not only will this order not be carried out, but it will not be repeated to any other person.'

Keitel raised the matter on 23 December when Canaris and Lahousen were at his office in the High Command, but Lahousen gave such a convincing account of his difficulties in penetrating the French security net round General Weygand that no doubt can have remained in the minds of Keitel and Hitler as to the *Abwehr*'s willing obedience. As for Operation Attila it remained in Hitler's drawer for another two years.

At Vichy on 13 December 1940 there was a coup that led to the downfall of Pierre Laval, and this struck a mortal blow at Franco-German collaboration, if it ever really existed. Canaris, who was well served in Vichy, was not surprised, and Hitler, though it came as a surprise to him, remained indifferent to the outcome. Hitler had a meeting with Darlan on 25 December but it was a hollow encounter and left the German Ambassador in Paris, Otto Abetz, in despair of ever building on the Montoire meeting between Hitler and Pétain. A High Command directive of 8 February 1941, to the German Armistice Commission in Paris declared that 'the Laval affair has destroyed the confidence that was beginning to be established between Germany and France. It falls to the French Government to re-establish that confidence. Until that happens, relations with France will continue on the basis of the armistice convention.'

Hitler realized that the Montoire *entente* had been stillborn. His thoughts turned back to Operation Felix, with or without Spanish aid, with or without crossing Spanish territory. Von Stohrer was told to extract a date from the elusive Caudillo, but reported on 20 January that Franco had replied with a long catalogue of Spain's economic difficulties. Ribbentrop responded on the 21st that von Stohrer must not accept a negative reply and sent him the text of a stern message to be read to the Caudillo, recalling his indebtedness to the Axis powers from the time of the Civil War, expressing the Führer's deep dissatisfaction, and warning Franco that unless there was an immediate resolution to declare war on the Axis side, he 'foresaw the rapid collapse of the Franco régime'. Von Stohrer was stunned. He asked Ribbentrop to couch his message in less offensive language, but the Foreign Minister refused and so obliged his Ambassador to pass on the note as it had first been drafted. On 23 January Franco listened to this ultimatum and reacted with an indignation unusual to a man of his temperament. He told the Ambassador that 'Spain will indeed enter the war, but it is my responsibility that she does not do so in the disastrous economic circumstances of today.'

Ribbentrop's reply was to insist on immediate action, with an offer of 100,000 tonnes of wheat when the date of war was fixed, but this time Franco refused to receive von Stohrer, keeping him waiting for three days till 27 January when the outcome was again an obstinate refusal. Ribbentrop sent von Stohrer a severe reprimand for the setback that was rather more his own fault than that of the Ambassador.

Hitler meanwhile sought to enlist Mussolini's support for the Gibraltar operation, and at a meeting in the Berghof on 20 January the Duce accepted the idea. Von Stohrer's failure drew a furious letter from Hitler to Franco on 6 February, full of reproaches, in which he warned him that 'the Caudillo will never be forgiven for having won his victory in the Civil War with German and Italian aid', and that it would be false to assume that 'the Franco régime can be maintained except if the Axis is victorious.'

General Franco did not reply to Hitler until after a meeting with Mussolini at Bordighera on 12 February and with Pétain at Montpellier on the 13th. He wrote calmly that in his view an attack on Gibraltar must coincide with an attack on the Suez Canal; one without the other was of no use; moreover he had complaints to make about the small amount of German economic aid reading Spain. He still avoided any precise commitments but declared his 'full agreement to be totally and resolutely at your side in a common destiny'.

Ribbentrop, in an instruction to von Stohrer on 22 February seems to have accepted that the Caudillo had 'no intention at all of bringing Spain into the war', and that 'it is totally useless to try and convince the Spaniards'. Thus at the end of seven months of diplomatic battle, the persistent Spanish policy of procastination defeated Hitler. Both Franco and Pétain were following strictly the interests of their own countries with a determined egoism. The outcome was in fact beneficial to the Western Allies. These two men, aided by Canaris, succeeded, first, in deflecting Hitler from his projects in the Western Mediterranean, which left North Africa open to an Anglo-American landing, the turning-point of the Second World War; and, second, in channelling his activities in the direction of the Balkans and the USSR.

On 13 December 1940 Hitler signed Directive 20 for Operation Marita, to establish a German front in the Balkans. On 18 December he signed Directive 21 for Operation Barbarossa, the grand attack on Russia. Pétain and Franco, when they met in Montpellier, could be satisfied with the measure of success that had crowned their common diplomacy, a dangerous game in which curiously they had been supported by the German Chief of Intelligence. They had worked, despite certain divergences of interest in North Africa, on approximately parallel lines, Franco professing friendship, Pétain deferring to Hitler, the former possessed of some freedom of action, the latter pinioned by German occupation of half his country.

World opinion was surprised by a public tribute paid to General Franco in 1944 by Roosevelt and Churchill. In his war memoirs, Churchill recorded 'the inestimable advantages' to Great Britain that resulted from the policy pursued by General Franco. Churchill and Roosevelt might have added a tribute to Pétain, who had helped to inflict on Hitler in the West a kind of diplomatic Stalingrad. As to Canaris's dual rôle, that lay in the shadows, where statesmen in office are not meant to look, and thus could make no appraisal.

24
Operation Barbarossa

Paul Thümmel, confidential agent of the *Abwehr* since 1934, had worked for Canaris first in Dresden and then in Prague before his war-time transfer to the Balkans and Turkey. He was an unusual recruit to have been acceptable to the *Abwehr*, as he was National-Socialist Party Member 61,574, a veteran who wore the golden party badge and was on friendly terms with *Reichsführer SS* Heinrich Himmler. On 19 December 1940, having just returned from Prague, Thümmel happened to be reporting to Canaris on the activity of his men in the Balkans and Turkey; but he found that the Admiral was only half listening to what he had to say, muttering to himself and making notes.

'I am going to Turkey and I will take you with me,' he said suddenly, 'the date is not yet fixed.'

'Very good, Admiral.'

'Goodbye!' Canaris rose from his desk and shook his hand.

On the way out Thümmel met Oster and said:

'The old man seems preoccupied with something.'

Oster replied:

'There is something in the air, but I do not know what.'

Coming out of the Bendlerstrasse, Thümmel thought he would drop in on Heinrich Himmler, whose long friendship had enabled Thümmel occasionally to provide Canaris with classified *SS* documents. This friendship was close enough for Thümmel to walk into Himmler's office without an appointment, and he was greeted by the Reichsführer with these remarks:

'Sit down. How is the family? Does your father still make those wonderful cakes?'

Thümmel's father was a master-baker at Neuhausen and Thümmel took the opportunity to answer: 'the flour is not of the same quality now. Things will get better when we have good flour. We are importing some, but the French don't grow good wheat.'

Himmler grinned and the little eyes behind his thick-lensed pince-nez narrowed as he answered:

'Don't worry, my dear Paul, soon we will have a vast new wheat granary.'

Thümmel did not dare to question him further, and as the telephone rang, he rose to take his leave, with the customary 'Heil, Hitler!'

As he walked out into the street, Paul Thümmel thought hard what these things might mean. What he could not know was that on the previous day Hitler had signed a secret order, Directive Number 21, for Operation Barbarossa, the plan for the invasion of Russia, of which there were only nine copies, one of which was in Canaris's hands and another in Himmler's safe-keeping.

And yet this 'Secret Matter for the Command Only' would be known to the British Intelligence Service no more than a week later! There was amazement in London as this extract from the Barbarossa Plan was read:

'The most far-reaching preparations must be commenced now and completed by 15 May 1941, if not before.' We know that Winston Churchill was immediately informed and wrote personally to Stalin to warn him of the danger. The Twentieth Congress of the Russian Communist Party was told by Nikita Khruschev on 25 February 1956, that 'Churchill emphatically foretold the coming attack on the USSR by the Third Reich. Stalin, however, paid no attention to these warnings. Moreover he issued orders that no credence was to be given to warnings of this kind, so as not to precipitate military operations.'

It was Hitler who was preparing 'to precipitate military operations'. On 3 January 1941, in the course of a conference with Marshal Göring, Keitel, Halder, Warlimont, Jodl, von Brauchitsch, Wagner, Grand Admiral Raeder and Joachim von Ribbentrop, the Führer declared:

Stalin is shrewd; he won't act directly against Germany. At the same time he will pile up difficulties whenever the occasion offers. What he wants to do is to inherit an exhausted Europe. To deal with Russia the time factor is of extreme importance. The Russian army is a giant with feet of clay and no head, and it is unpredictable. Best to attack it immediately while it lacks leaders and equipment. We must not underestimate Russia, and when we attack, we must concentrate all our forces ... With the immeasurable wealth of Russian raw materials, Germany will have the means to wage an inter-continental war, and the world will then hold its breath and be silent.

Yet Hitler hesitated, though the date for the completion of preparations had been fixed at 15 May 1941. This was, as he said, 'the most difficult of all his decisions'.

Jodl in Nuremberg denied that Hitler's intention to attack Russia was settled in February 1941, adding that he was influenced by events in Yugoslavia. It was on 1 April 1941, according to Jodl, that Hitler made the decision to attack Russia on 22 June 1941. The fourteen armoured divisions and twelve mobile infantry divisions that led the attack were moved on 1 June and final clearance for the campaign came as late as 17 June. These arrangements, argued Jodl, proved that it was a preventive rather than an aggressive war, but he was ignoring Hitler's method of masking his true intentions and in the military stages concealing those projects that he had formed for mass extermination of the Russian people.

Jodl recalled Hitler's military and strategic reasoning, that Britain was pinning her faith on Russia entering the war, 'without which she would have given up after Dunkirk. There must certainly have been secret agreements and there are definite Russian preparations ... The *Abwehr* gives us this approximate picture: in the summer of 1940 there were about 100 Russian divisions along the frontier. By January 1941 there were already 150 divisions.' But this talk of a preventive war was no more than an argument with which Hitler could brush aside objections and whip up propaganda. For on 3 March, in explanation of Directive Number 21, he described Operation Barbarossa as more than a military campaign: 'an ideological struggle as well, with the pressing aim of eliminating the Jewish-Bolshevik intelligentsia ... But we won't replace Bolshevik Russia with nationalist Russia, which has always been the traditional enemy of Germany'. He envisaged a socialist state, tied to Greater Germany, its vast territories divided up and administered by Reich commissioners. He added that the use of the *SS* would be necessary behind the lines to reduce the Bolshevik leadership to impotence.

The *Abwehr* was caught up in these intensive preparations for Operation Barbarossa. Admiral Canaris gave Colonel von Bentivegni, his Chief of Section III (Counter-espionage) the following orders:

a) Prepare all branches of Section III for intensive activity against the USSR through counter-espionage units attached to the armies that will operate in the East and through general activities to combat the Soviet Intelligence Service.

b) In order to deceive foreign intelligence services it should be suggested that Russo-German relations have improved and that an invasion of Great Britain is being mounted.

c) Counter-espionage measures must be taken to cover our present preparations with regard to Soviet Russia and the transfer of German troops eastwards.

Colonel Piekenbrock and Colonel Kienzel, Chief of Eastern Service, brought up to date German intelligence documentation on the Red Army. Together with General von Tippelskirch, of the Quartermaster-General's Department, they worked out staffing arrangements for forward intelligence units for the Russian campaign. They paid particular attention to the existing Soviet order of battle. Section I was ordered to increase the numbers of its agents working inside Soviet Russia, and Canaris set up a special intelligence headquarters near Warsaw, known under the code name Walli I, to organize all these additions to the *Abwehr* service. Wilhelm Baun, former Press Attaché in the German Embassy in Moscow, was put in charge of Walli I. Similar headquarters were later established by Sections II and III of the *Abwehr* to assist, direct and co-ordinate the expansion of sabotage and counter-espionage services for the Russian front. These were known as Walli II and Walli III. The whole organization was placed under the direction of Colonel Heinz Schmalschläger.

Colonel Lahousen meanwhile held a series of conferences with General Warlimont, deputy to General Jodl at the Führer's Headquarters, to discuss subversive operations and sabotage in the rear of the Soviet armies. Colonel Erwin Stolze gave evidence on this subject while a prisoner-of-war in Russian hands after the war. A High Command directive exhorted 'agents to promote rivalries and hatred between the various peoples of the Soviet Union'. Stolze made contact with Ukraine nationalists in the *Abwehr* service and directed them to prepare disruptive activities in the immediate rear of the Red Army.

As the winter of 1941 turned to spring, Canaris and Schellenberg, under the strain of preparing their two Foreign Intelligence Services for this gigantic new task, were nervous and disturbed. They felt that these events were of such enormous importance that no outside influence should be allowed to interfere with their work. There were also considerable divergencies between them on their common task, the *Abwehr* possessing a less efficient Russian network than the Foreign Intelligence Service, according to Schellenberg, and tending to under-estimate the production of Russian heavy industry and the number of Russian divisions. He also considered the *Abwehr* to be less well informed on the Soviet railway system. Schellenberg recorded in his memoirs:

These differences with Canaris showed how difficult it was for the military chiefs responsible for planning to appreciate the real value of the information that was provided. If that information did not fit in with their own fundamental ideas, they simply discarded it. As for the big men at the top, they were even worse. Until the end of 1944 Hitler systematically rejected any unfavourable reports, whether they were based on real facts or on sound argument.

Whatever their differences of perspective, Canaris and Schellenberg agreed on the view that it was very dangerous for Germany to engage in a war on two fronts. They were both worried about the attitude of the United States, with its vast war potential. Canaris said to Schellenberg:

The attitude of the United States is of prime importance to us. If the Americans enter the war this year, we won't be able to finish off Russia for a long time. And if Great Britain feels that she has behind her the great industrial potential of the United States and American capacity for manpower mobilization, there will soon be an invasion of the Continent, either in Southern Europe through the Balkans or Italy, or in the West through France or Belgium.

Schellenberg foresaw that any such invasion would be preceded by an intensive air offensive against Germany, which would seriously affect her industrial production. The prophecies of Canaris and Schellenberg were accurate, but neither they nor the intuitive Hitler foresaw what would happen meanwhile in the Balkans.

In November 1940 General Wavell, the British Commander-in-Chief in the Middle East, emphatically expressed the view that Germany would not be content to see Italy defeated or even held in check in Greece. Hitler did indeed mention in the same month the idea of occupying Northern Greece when he composed Directive Number 18. In Directive Number 20, Operation Marita of 13 December 1940, he visualized the capture of Salonika and the Aegean coast. He gave orders on 9 January 1941 to cease work on Operations Felix and Sealion, the invasions of Gibraltar and the British Isles, in order to accelerate Operation Marita. Operation Barbarossa continued to be developed, but Hitler's immediate objective was to rescue his friend Mussolini by chasing the British out of Greece.

Canaris had a sentimental attachment to Greece, hardly less strong than his love for Spain. That was why he received the Greek Ambassador in Berlin in a friendly fashion when the Ambassador sought his aid in a matter of diplomacy. General Metaxas, the Greek Prime Minister, had addressed a long memorandum to the German Government in an attempt to avert the threat of German intervention in Greece, but Herr von Ribbentrop had flatly refused to acknowledge it. Thereupon the Greek Ambassador went to Canaris and asked him to submit the memorandum to Hitler.

Canaris, with some courage, resolved to take it to Keitel, asking him to show it to Hitler. Keitel finally accepted the importunate memorandum, but to no purpose; for Hitler had it returned to Canaris through Ribbentrop, who attached a note to it asking the Chief of Intelligence not to intervene in future in matters which did not concern him. Canaris did not reply to this rebuke. He was grieved at the prospect of the Hellenic world being overrun by war. General Metaxas died on 30 January and was replaced by Alexander Koryzis, a man of integrity and patriotism but lacking the iron determination that such a situation demanded.

After the British had taken Tobruk on 21 January, Churchill considered Egypt secure enough to permit a British force from the Middle East to be sent to Greece. The Greeks accepted the proposal on 24 February, and the British Prime Minister sought at the same time to get the Turks and especially the Yugoslavs to join him, which would have made the Italian position in the Balkans perilous in the extreme. Turkey remained hesitant and the Yugoslav Government, under strong German pressure, decided instead to join the Tripartite Pact, of Germany, Italy and Japan, which left the way open for Operation Marita. At the last moment, after demonstrations in the streets of Belgrade and Zagreb against the Axis, a group of young Serbian officers overthrew Prince Paul's Regency on 27 March and with young King Peter at their head set up a Yugoslav Government of anti-German sympathies.

Hitler received the news at first with incredulity and then with fury. He summoned Göring, Keitel, Jodl and Ribbentrop to a meeting which resulted in Directive Number 25 for a blitz on Yugoslavia, without any diplomatic prelude or ultimatum. Hitler ordered that 'as soon as sufficient forces are concentrated and the weather conditions are favourable, the Yugoslav air force on the ground and Belgrade itself must be destroyed by incessant air attacks day and night'. Operation Marita was to commence at the same time. In the haste of his preparations Hitler put pressure on Hungary to permit German troops to march through, and although Count Teleki, the Hungarian Prime Minister, committed suicide rather than accede to this request, the Hungarian General Staff yielded. Hitler ordered that the operation should commence on the night of 5-6 April. The offensive began with a three-day bombardment of the city of Belgrade, which was left in ruins with 17,000 corpses in the debris.

Canaris had no special liking for the Yugoslavs, whether Serbs, Slovenes or Croats, but he was horrified by the brutal and pitiless attack on that country. On 12 April he arrived in Belgrade, accompanied by Piekenbrock and Lahousen. The ruins were still smoking and the air was heavy with the smell of burning and putrefaction. Hundreds of corpses lay about the streets, and the three *Abwehr* officers, wherever they went, met people with bandaged wounds and others who were physically unscathed but nearly demented as a result of their recent ordeal. Animals that had broken out of the Belgrade zoological gardens were straying in the rubble. After wandering all day in this shambles, Canaris returned with his two companions to their lodging in Semlin, north of the Danube, where their small hotel had escaped serious damage by the *Luftwaffe*. He flung himself in a chair and burst into tears.

'I can stand no more of this,' he said. 'We will leave tomorrow.'

'Where do we go?' asked Lahousen.

'To Spain, to Madrid.'

Hans Piekenbrock, in telling me of this visit to Belgrade, recalled that this was the predictable answer. Every time that the Admiral felt in need of recuperating his energies and spirits, it was Spain that he wished to visit, the country that was able to make him smile again. 'The Admiral recovered his equilibrium and even his sense of humour. One day as we were driving along a road on the plateau of Old Castile, we met a large herd of sheep. Sitting in our open car the Admiral stiffly gave the Nazi salute and cried "*Heil* Hitler!" "Why did you do that, Excellency?" I asked him. This was the form of address that I used when we were in a light-hearted mood. "Because we never know whether one of our superiors is not among them", replied the Admiral.'

Another day, as he was driving with Piekenbrock and Captain Leissner, Head of the Madrid office of the *Abwehr*, he saw from the road a charming little property and asked Leissner what its price might be, as he intended to buy a villa in Spain when the war was over. Leissner replied that he would enquire in Madrid and make a purchase for him if that was what he wanted, adding:

'So, Admiral, you will be able to settle down here after the war.' A grim thought occurred to Piekenbrock which he spoke aloud without thinking:

'Your Excellency wishes to live here in Spain after the war? Your Excellency must be mistaken. After the war we will all . . .': he made the gesture of putting a rope round his neck. Their carefree mood suddenly gone, each of them sat silent with his own thoughts.

Hitler stayed in his headquarters at Semmering throughout the Balkan campaign, while Marshal List, General von Kleist and General von Weichs carried out operations with skill and precision. The remnants of the Yugoslav army surrendered on 17 April, and three days later the Germans pierced the Metaxas line and reached Thermopylae while the British were still disembarking. Four days later the Greek army laid down its arms at Epirus. On 27 and 28 April mobile units of the German army reached Athens, the Corinth canal, Nauplia and Kalamata, with quite negligible losses, 67 officers and men killed, and 4,800 of all ranks wounded. Then General Student attacked the British in Crete, which was captured at a cost of 3,250 killed and 3,400 wounded out of 20,000 engaged, while the British left behind 12,000 prisoners and suffered heavy losses as the Royal Navy evacuated the rest of the land forces.

Canaris made a rapid visit to Greece to assess the situation. During this visit he was able to give some assistance to friends, in particular to a Greek family of Jewish origin who might have been victimized by the *SS*. There was little time, however, to spend in Greece as the day for Operation Barbarossa was approaching.

Yosuke Matsuoka, the Japanese Foreign Minister, had meanwhile made a visit to Europe to discuss with Mussolini and Hitler the possibility of a war with the United States and a Japanese attack on Singapore, but at no time during his talk with Hitler was the possibility mentioned of a German war with Russia. On his way home Matsuoka made a stop in Moscow and met Stalin and Ribbentrop. Canaris was impressed by the report that reached him of Matsuoka's departure from Moscow on 13 April, the same day that the German army entered Belgrade. Stalin himself went with Molotov to the railway station to see their guest leave Moscow and lavished attentions on the Japanese. He then called for the German Ambassador and when Count von der Schulenburg came forward, embraced him, saying: 'We must remain friends. You must do everything to make sure of that'. Stalin then remarked to Colonel Krebs, the acting German Military Attaché: 'We will remain your friends, whatever happens'. Canaris did not consider this mere propaganda but an indication of Russian policy. He told Piekenbrock that:

'Stalin and the men of the Kremlin are greatly impressed by the *Wehrmacht*'s rapid advance through the difficult mountain passes of Greece and Yugoslavia. They think that with our formidable military instrument, we could even win a total victory over the Red Army. Fear that the German war machine will overrun Russia exceeds every other fear in their minds. They may well be fearful. Our German armour will ravage their country. I am disturbed by this new line of Russian policy and it is so obvious that it seems impossible that Hitler won't draw the logical conclusion'.

'Yet Russian troop movements on their Western frontiers must appear to you aggressive in character', ventured Piekenbrock.

'No, Piki, you don't understand. These movements are no more than a puny manifestation of their anxiety. Far from thinking of an attack on Germany, Stalin wants closer co-operation and economic concessions. Hitler has everything in his favour. When he strikes at Russia, his attack will be a total surprise, and the *Panzer* will get as far as Moscow. What will happen then, God knows! I may be mistaken about the Red Army's powers of resistance, but if Hitler wavers and doesn't take either Leningrad or Moscow, that will be the beginning of the end for Germany.'

'But Admiral, we could perhaps be held up for a few days or weeks without that altering the margin of superiority of the *Wehrmacht* over the Red Army.'

'You forget that if Hitler cannot reach his objectives before the winter, he must wait till spring to recommence his offensives. Don't you think that something will happen during the winter?'

'But . . .'

'I don't believe in a lightning victory against Russia,' continued Canaris. 'I am convinced that this campaign against Russia, which the Führer sees as the answer to all his difficulties, will only over-burden Germany and destroy the few remaining chances of peace. Far from proving to Great Britain the futility of fighting on, the invasion of Russia will cement an alliance between London and Moscow. Hitler has also made a grave mistake in not taking Matsuoka into his confidence about the attack on Russia. The Japanese do not like to lose face. They will not attack Russia. They will attack America and that will make America our enemy. This Operation Barbarossa will commit Germany and Italy to a war on several fronts, for which neither is prepared. Anything that I have been able to say along these lines to Keitel, Jodl and Halder has been to no purpose. They accuse me of being a pessimist. As for Hitler, he thinks that he is already in the Caucasus.'

A few weeks after this conversation, on 21 June, Canaris was host to three uniformed colleagues at a dinner in Horcher's restaurant. He sat at a corner table, out of earshot of other guests, with Reinhard Heydrich, Heinrich Müller, the *Gestapo* Chief, and Walther Schellenberg. This was a last attempt on his part to warn the Nazi leadership that it was being over-optimistic about the outcome of a war with Russia, which was to begin at dawn on the 22nd.

He was dining with his deadliest enemies, he knew, but he had chosen this informal way of trying to get Heydrich's support for his views after Keitel had rebuked him in a condescending manner: 'My dear Canaris. You may know your way about the field of intelligence, but you are a sailor. Don't try to give the army lessons in military strategy'.

During the course of this dinner, however, he was disappointed to find that Heydrich was not apprehensive about the next day. The *SD* Chief told him that Himmler knew the Führer to be in a serious mood about the venture against Russia. Hitler had replied to some flattering words by Martin Bormann with a cautious appraisal, merely remarking that future events would show to what extent Bormann's confidence was justified, since in an operation of this immense size nobody could claim to have foreseen and provided for all contingencies. It was necessary to be optimistic and to invoke providence to give the German people victory. Heydrich added:

'The Führer's words show that he himself is much less optimistic than his military advisers. Halder assures the Führer that the Russian armies will be destroyed in six weeks. Keitel and Jodl calculate that it will take eight weeks, but the Führer has told Himmler that he himself reckons on ten to twelve weeks.'

'The Führer is right', echoed Müller.

'I believe it will take two to three months,' said Heydrich. 'What do you think, Admiral?'

The Admiral shrugged his shoulders and was silent, but when Heydrich insisted on an answer, he replied in a solemn tone:

'Firstly, I am worried about seeing us engaged on two war fronts at once, which is very dangerous. I do not share the General Staff's view that with our overwhelming superiority in men and material, the war will be over in a few weeks. It is just possible that a military defeat rather than an annihilation of the Red Army, (I make this distinction) will have the contrary effect of enabling Stalin to fortify his Party and Government by appealing to the ancient patriotism of the Russian people. A war of this kind on Russia may prove a source of strength to Stalin'. Heydrich remarked coldly:

'It is curious, Admiral, that our friend Schellenberg has been talking to me in more or less the same language. You both sound to me as if you exchange some pretty defeatist views during your morning rides in the *Tiergarten*'.

Schellenberg knew how fundamentally Canaris and Heydrich differed in their appraisal of the political strength of the Russian Government and he sought to turn the conversation a little:

'Marshal Göring is more optimistic than any of us. He says the *Luftwaffe* will crush the Russian air force, flatten Moscow and pick off Soviet tanks like sitting ducks'.

'Göring!' exclaimed Heydrich, 'he said the same about England in 1940'.

All along a thousand miles of the Russian frontier from the Baltic to the Black Sea, men with synchronized watches listened in the early hours of 22 June to the ticking of destiny. Three million German soldiers waited to go into the attack, hearts beating faster and shoulders taut in the emotion of the hour. It was 3:14 AM and the faint red light of dawn was seen in the east. The second hands now took over from the minute hands and when together they showed 3:15, it was as if they had made an electric contact with a million detonators. Gigantic flashes broke the darkness, as all weapons opened up and star-shells lit up the night.

The shriek of mortars and the roar of heavy artillery produced an instant cloud of flame and smoke in the target areas. The officers shouted *Vorwärts*, and the three million surged eastwards. The Second World War was entering a new, gigantic and most bloody phase. As the event became known, to use Hitler's words, the world held its breath.

25
The duel with Heydrich

Canaris was in a sombre mood after 22 June. He was a convinced enemy of Bolshevism and glad to think that Germany was dealing the system some resounding blows, but at the same time he knew that the *Wehrmacht*'s victories in the East would enhance Hitler's prestige, and his humanity made him feel uneasy at the exterminations that were the secret policy of the *SS* Special Commandos of Himmler and Heydrich. Neither the successes of his own Brandenburg Regiment, nor the achievements of Major Oscar Reile of Section III in the field of counter-espionage in France, nor Major Seubert's excellent reports on Egypt and Libya, consoled him or effaced his lasting obsession with the Decree for the Commissioners and Marshal Keitel's orders of 13 May.

On 31 March 1941 Hitler had drawn up a decree providing for the administration of conquered Eastern territories after the invasion of Russia, not by the military forces but by 'Reich Commissioners', giving Heinrich Himmler and his *SS* Commandos special powers over those vast territories.

Knowing the *Gestapo*'s methods, Canaris was horrified, the more so when Marshal Keitel backed up this decree by his orders of 13 May, that all Communist leaders and Russian political commissars were to be 'physically liquidated'. When captured in places from which it was not easy to transfer them to *Gestapo* custody, execution must be carried out on the spot by army units. Canaris was indignant that Keitel should so violate the Hague and Geneva Conventions with such a lack of Christian principle. He was well aware that the honour of the German soldier was thus besmirched and that it was being made impossible for limits to be set to the Russo-German war. He saw that it was the definite policy of Himmler and Heydrich to involve the *Wehrmacht* in these crimes against humanity. He explained himself in these terms to his Heads of Section, who supported his views.

It was therefore, he reasoned, up to army commanders to refuse to obey such orders, or else they would become Hitler's creatures, on a level with Himmler and Heydrich. Canaris tried to explain their dilemma to the generals and field-marshals whom he met, but he was once more sadly disillusioned by their reaction. The only one who protested energetically against the extermination orders was the Commander-in-Chief of the Central Army Group, Field-Marshal von Bock. The others just ignored Hitler's orders and did not pass them on. The *SS* Special Commandos would do the dirty work, but the honour of the *Wehrmacht* was nevertheless gravely affected.

General Hermann Reinecke, Chief of General Services of the army, organized in the summer of 1941 a conference with the *SS* on matters concerning prisoners-of-war. His purpose was to settle divergences and difficulties created by the administrative Decree and by Keitel's orders on the treatment of commissars. Although he was in Berlin at the time, Canaris refused to attend, disliking Reinecke and considering him to be a lackey of the *SS*: he called him 'a little Keitel'. Instead he sent Colonel Lahousen to represent him.

Canaris had long since realized [Lahousen told me] the futility of raising in his instructions arguments of humanity or law. Only if an order could be shown to be a direct hindrance to the conduct of war was there a chance of objections being considered. That is why Canaris directed me to found my opposition to the decree on the difficulties that it would make for my Section II in its security work, its sabotage operations and its counter-guerilla activities. In consequence I made observations about the adverse effect that mass executions would have on army morale and even on the morale of the *SS*. The troops were opposed to massacres of prisoners-of-war. Clearly they would be disturbed by the thought that the Russians could respond by massacring their German prisoners. I also objected emphatically to the idea of applying the decree to the minority peoples of Russia, such as the Ukrainians, whose support we as liberators had sought. Our task would be impossible if they saw themselves treated with the same severity as the Russians themselves. In any case, I asked, how could a prisoner of-war be said to be 'contaminated by Bolshevism'? I drew attention to the appalling ignorance of the *SS* Commandos. There was the example of certain Moslem communities in Southern Russia who were mistaken for Jews because they practised circumcision. Finally, in Canaris's name I declared that executions of large numbers of prisoners would certainly become known, and would deter Russian troops from deserting to us and induce them to fight with more determination. So the *Wehrmacht* would be the loser in the end. My arguments had no effect whatsoever.

The formidable Heinrich Müller, Chief of the *Gestapo*, listened to Lahousen with a contemptuous smile, while his eyes showed his plain dislike of the speaker. Reinecke himself opposed any withdrawal of Keitel's orders, saying that Russian troops must not be regarded as human beings but simply treated as ideological enemies who must be exterminated. Reinecke probably stood in fear of Müller, who ended by saying that he was prepared in future to order that executions should take place outside camps where the troops could no longer see them. He remarked: 'These gentlemen of the *Abwehr* are very tender-hearted on the soldier's account'. These words, spoken in a broad Bavarian accent, were loaded with menace, and Lahousen did not return to the subject, but Admiral Canaris and his Chiefs of Section did not cease to address warnings and protests to Marshal Keitel in cases of inhuman treatment contrary to the rules of war.

On 8 September General Reinecke issued the following instructions resulting from the conference:

The Bolshevik soldier has lost all right to be treated as an honourable adversary in accordance with the Geneva Convention. Orders must be given to react pitilessly and energetically to the least sign of insubordination, especially in the case of fanatical Bolsheviks. Insubordination, passive or active resistance, must immediately be broken by force of arms, bayonets, rifle-butts or fire-arms. Whoever carries out these orders without use of arms or with insufficient energy is liable to punishment. Prisoners attempting to escape must be fired on without warning, and warning shots must never be fired. Generally speaking the use of arms against prisoners-of-war is legal.

Canaris thought it necessary to contest these regulations, grounding himself on international law, if only to register his protest. With Count Helmuth von Moltke, legal adviser to the *Abwehr*, assisted by Dr Wilhelm Wengler and Admiral Bürkner, he drew up a memorandum refuting the idea that Russian soldiers were not protected by international law and submitted it to Marshal Keitel.

In this memorandum Canaris wrote:

The provisions of the Geneva Convention concerning prisoners-of-war do not apply between Germany and the USSR. That is why only the fundamental provisions of international law on prisoners-of-war come into question. These customary rules have evolved since the eighteenth century, so that captivity is neither an act of vengeance nor a punishment, but simply a security measure, of which the sole aim is to prevent prisoners again taking part in the war. This principle has developed in conformity with the universally accepted idea that from the military standpoint it is inadmissible to kill or maim prisoners. Every belligerent has, besides, the interest of ensuring that his own troops are protected from bad treatment if they are made prisoners-of-war. The instructions embodied in Appendix 1, relating to our treatment of Soviet prisoners-of-war, are based on a different conception.

Canaris went on to say that Reinecke's instructions

reject a certain number of things which, as a result of long experience, have been considered not only useful from the military point of view but also essential for the maintenance of the morale and the keenness of troops. These instructions are drawn up in very general terms, but they could give rise to an orgy of unpunished crimes. This is apparent in the orders to camp guards in the case of unco-operative prisoners who may not speak the same language. It is often impossible to know whether disobedience arises from obstinacy or from badly interpreted orders. In justifying the use of arms against Soviet prisoners-of-war, these orders dispense with the need for guards to account for their conduct. Camp guards armed with clubs, whips and other arms of this kind contravene the military code, even if selected prisoners are themselves supplied with these weapons. In fact, the military authorities have entrusted the administration of punishment to others without retaining any control over the methods employed.

Keitel read this memorandum and reported on it to Hitler, who shrugged his shoulders. Keitel minuted the report on the last page:

'These objections are the result of a chivalrous idea of war. We are concerned here with the destruction of an ideology. In consequence I approve these instructions and give them my authorization. Signed: Keitel.'

The Field-Marshal handed the memorandum back to Canaris, saying: 'Poor fellow, you think you are still in the eighteenth century. We are faced in the East with a horde of savages. We must treat them as such if we do not want to suffer a setback.'

Canaris raised his eyes to the Marshal's face and his lips began to form a reply, but he realized that it was useless to reason with this tin soldier. He took back his memorandum and returned to his Tirpitz Embankment offices, a little more bowed and depressed than before.

Interventions of this sort, of course, provided additional material for the file that Heydrich in 'the house across the way' was piecing together on 'the Black Chapel'. The Admiral was cunning, but so was his enemy, a real hound following the scent, prowling to and fro around these difficult men in the *Abwehr*. He had no proof of treason yet but suspected strongly that the man who had been his former chief in the navy was personally acting against the *SS*, if not against Hitler himself. Heydrich had been informed about the various conspiracies among the generals between 1938 and 1940, but these men no longer appeared dangerous, and he was much more concerned to know exactly what rôle Canaris had played in these affairs.

In February 1941 Heydrich spoke to Schellenberg about the need to strengthen counter-espionage against the Soviet Union, saying that Hitler was closely interested in this, and added:

'Canaris is in danger. The other day the Führer said to Himmler: "The *Abwehr* pours in personal and undigested reports to me. Of course they are all of great importance, coming from the best sources, but it is left to me to draw conclusions from them. This is impossible. Tell your men to revise their methods." '

'It's a bad sign for Canaris,' added Heydrich. 'We must recognize that his work as Chief of Intelligence is open to criticism. We can go even further than that: I am more or less certain that it was Canaris who betrayed to the British and French the date of our attack in the West in May 1940. Do you remember the leakages through the Vatican? You may say that this did not make any difference and that we crushed the French army and drove the British off the Continent. It still remains an obvious case of treason.'

'Why don't you act, then?' asked Schellenberg.

'Not now. I prefer to wait and collect more evidence. The day will come when Canaris will be punished for all the wrongs that he has committed against the Reich.'

We may ask whether Heydrich was telling all that he knew. Himmler, Heydrich and Schellenberg knew more about the *Abwehr*'s activities against the Government than they spoke of even among themselves. They were no longer completely open with each other, and this is what kept Canaris and his friends safe for a long time yet. Each one of them had his own dossier on the *Abwehr*, and Heydrich already felt that he was himself Himmler's rival in the succession to Hitler. Karl Heinz Abshagen believes that they may even have been prepared to see the plots against Hitler explode so that the *SS* could then intervene and take over power while restoring the Government's authority. Schellenberg, shortly before his death in Italy, gave me this opinion:

I believe that at some time or other Canaris had learned something very serious about Himmler and that Himmler knew it, or he would never have remained inactive after I had laid before him my dossier on the *Abwehr* in 1943. It may be that Canaris had kept evidence of the contacts that Himmler had himself taken up with Germany's enemies through the lawyer, Carl Langhehn, (who was executed in October 1944 because he knew too much). As for Heydrich, Canaris himself admitted to me, on one of our morning rides soon after the Security Chief's death, that he had, or had once had, – I don't remember altogether – in his possession formal proof of Heydrich's Jewish parentage. I believed him all the more readily as I recalled my own conversation with Heydrich alone together at his hunting lodge, in the summer of 1941. Heydrich said to me: 'The way we are behaving, things are certain to come to a bad end. It was complete madness to have taken up this Jewish question'. This remark seemed to make it likely that Heydrich was thinking of his own Jewish parentage.

The parentage of Heydrich in Halle-an-der-Saale had long been the subject of rumours and he had himself three times gone to law in 1935 and 1937 to disprove allegations of his Jewish origin. In one of these cases the defendant disappeared without trace. A family tombstone inscribed Sarah Heydrich also disappeared and was replaced with one bearing the inscription S. Heydrich. Canaris had inherited the Heydrich dossier from his own predecessor Patzig in 1935, and Piekenbrock told me that he had seen a part of it. The dossier contained the complete verbatim records of all three court cases, as well as the bill from a Leipzig stonemason who had altered Sarah Heydrich's tombstone. This dossier may have been among those papers that Canaris in 1943 took personally to Spain for safe-keeping in four suitcases and which are said also to have contained his diaries.

Despite all that they may have known about each other, Canaris, Heydrich and Schellenberg still met frequently, though Heydrich and Canaris seemed to dislike meeting alone without the third of the trio, and Schellenberg acted as a kind of buffer between them.

After the invasion of Russia in June 1941, relations between Canaris and Heydrich appeared to deteriorate. Heydrich's cold bearing seemed to have inspired in Canaris a morbid physical dread and Heydrich incessantly put Schellenberg on his guard against 'the tricks of the *Abwehr* Chief'. He was no longer so ready to compromise. 'Don't let Canaris fool you', he warned Schellenberg. 'You two look like intimate friends, but you'll gain nothing by handling him with a velvet-glove ... Canaris is a fatalist and you have to be firm with him, even more so with his gossiping subordinates. Remember that, and take this as an order from me – act as a mediator between him and me. The Admiral must end up by coming to the mountain – to us, that is. If not ...'

Canaris said to Schellenberg a few days later:

Our victories in the East are intoxicating everybody. The Führer expected to crush the Red Army, but surely he must now see that he won't finish the war this year? Haven't we told him again and again that things wouldn't go the way he and his advisers imagined? They will never face the truth. I am older than you, Schellenberg, I know, but I beg of you, let us hold closely together. If the men at the top see that we are of the same mind, maybe they will pay some attention.

Canaris now felt that Heydrich was closer on his heels, and his disquiet manifested itself in repeated journeys abroad. While in Berlin he listened with only half an ear to the talk of a conspiracy against Hitler which Oster repeated to him, but which never took any positive shape.

During this period in August 1941, Canaris made a working visit to Paris and assembled his *Abwehr* officers to tell them that Marshal von Rundstedt, Commander-in-Chief in the West, and General Otto von Stülpnagel, Military Governor of the occupied zone of France, were well satisfied with their intelligence and security operations. It was on this occasion that Commander Langendorf suggested that groups of Spanish refugees were a menace to the security of some *Départements* of the French occupied zone and would be 'best rounded up and put in detention camps'. Canaris interrupted him and stated in moderate terms that this recommendation did not confirm to his own outlook. Colonel Oscar Reile, who was present, noted that Commander Langendorf did not long remain with the *Abwehr* after this incident. 'His exhortations to the *Abwehr* to adhere to respectable methods and standards of treatment,' said Reile, 'remained an inspiration to us long after he had ceased to direct the intelligence services.'

One night at his Headquarters, the Wolf's Lair, at Rastenburg in East Prussia, the Führer made a speech at dinner; Canaris was among those at table.

'In 1914 I went to the Front in a mood of pure idealism. Then

I saw men fall in thousands all round me. It was a lesson to me that life is nothing but a cruel struggle for the survival of the species. The individual may disappear, provided that there are other men to replace him.'

Those present listened with profound deference, and nobody spoke. Canaris sat between Colonel Scherff of the Historical Section of the *Wehrmacht* and the *SS* General Karl Wolff, Chief of Staff on Himmler's General Staff. He did not talk to either and managed to finish his cauliflower soup, followed by white cheese and bread with twenty grams of butter.

Canaris listened while Hitler's voice wandered on about the fate of St Petersburg in war . . . how he would prefer not to see people suffer . . . or do harm to anybody . . . 'but when I see my race in danger, cold reason takes over from sentiment. I weigh the sacrifices that the future will exact in payment for sacrifices that we hesitate to make today'.

Canaris did not enjoy these occasions, but he had been obliged to keep an appointment with Keitel who wanted to talk about intelligence work on the Eastern front. There were twenty at dinner in the upright waxed oak chairs round the waxed oak table. Apart from Hitler and Keitel, Jodl was there, Dr Dietrich, Martin Bormann, Admiral Krancke and others. On the wall hung wood engravings representing Götz von Berlichingen, Henry the Fowler (a compliment to Heinrich Himmler), Ulrich von Hutten and other Nordic heroes. Opposite the Führer hung a large map of Europe. Canaris hoped that the meal would not be prolonged; he had at first intended to return to his own *Abwehr* field headquarters at Nikolaiken immediately after his exchanges with Jodl and Warlimont. He particularly tried to avoid the officers' mess at General Headquarters, though many senior officers liked to linger there in the hope of a chat with Hitler's ADCs about his views and intentions. On this occasion, having finished his review of intelligence with Keitel, Canaris had been making his exit when he found himself face to face with Hitler – hence the invitation to dinner. 'Stay, and General Karl Wolff will explain to you certain decisions that I have just taken and that Reichsleiter Bormann has just given to him in detail. It will certainly be of interest to you.'

So Canaris had stayed for dinner, ruminating on a remark from General Wolff as they sat down to table:

'It is all fixed, Admiral. Your friend Heydrich will be Protector.'

Canaris wondered at first whether Heydrich was giving up his position as Chief of Reich Security to take up the protectorship of Bohemia and Moravia, but General Wolff soon undeceived him. He explained to Canaris, after the Führer had withdrawn at the end of dinner, that Heydrich would retain his security functions while assuming those of Protector in Prague. That same day, 27 September a telegram from Heydrich had arrived at the Führer's headquarters:

Mein Führer
I have the honour to report that in conformity with your decree of today I have taken over the duties of acting Protector in Bohemia and Moravia. The inauguration ceremony will be at the Hradschin Palace tomorrow at 11 am.
All reports and political despatches will reach you through Reichsleiter Bormann.

Heil mein Führer

Reinhard Heydrich was thus, at the age of thirty-seven, transferred to an active post with direct access to the Führer and promoted to the rank of *SS* General. His position now made him the equivalent of a minister and brought him to the highest point of power that he was to attain. It is not known exactly when Hitler made the decision to appoint him, but it was at Bormann's insistence, so Walther Schellenberg affirms, with Himmler's support. The purpose of the change was clearly to remove from Prague the former Protector, Baron von Neurath, who was ill and said to be surrounded by anti-Nazis. Bormann promised Heydrich even higher promotion, if he dealt effectively with the economic and social problems of the former Czech state. It may be that Bormann, who in fact detested Heydrich, was simply manoeuvring to detach him from Himmler and strengthen his own position in relation to the *SS*. Heydrich was eager for a more active rôle, as he was beginning to find tedious his police duties in the Central Office of Reich Security. He gladly took the plane from Berlin to Prague, arriving there on 27 September with a small staff recruited from his Berlin office.

Heydrich lost no time. Within hours of installing himself in the sumptuous apartments of the Hradschin, he had given the all clear to the *Gestapo* and it went into action. The Czech Prime Minister, General Alois Elias, had long been in contact with the Benes Government exiled in London. Now he found himself in the hands of *Gestapo* thugs who, by all too notorious methods sought to squeeze out of him the secrets of these Prague-London contacts. They left Alois Elias like a rag doll, but on the first day they did not manage to make him talk. There was another session on the second day and this time the former general could no longer withstand *Gestapo* methods. He told them all that he knew. Four days after his arrest when a German court martial tried him and condemned him to death, Alois Elias was no more than a bloodstained caricature of the man that he had been.

Heydrich's task was twofold. It was known in Berlin that the great majority of Czechs were resolutely opposed to National Socialism and that President Hacha's régime was feeble. The Protectorate hummed with subversive activities directed by the Benes Government in London. The Protectorate also assumed a growing importance to Germany as the war continued. The eight million Czechs possessed excellent industries and they were clever technicians, while German industry suffered increasingly from Allied bombing and lack of manpower. Heydrich's double mission was therefore to crush the secret resistance movement and to obtain a bigger Czech contribution to the German war effort.

He was convinced that massive intimidation would achieve these ends. On arrival in Prague he ordered a series of preventive executions, which he described as 'educational'. Selected persons were rushed through a summary trial for political offences and immediately executed. The victims included intellectuals, politicians, resistance workers, factory workers suspected of sabotage, farmers who were behind with their deliveries of produce. Heydrich was named 'the butcher of Prague', but this did not worry him.

On 4 October he declared in the Hradschin Palace: 'that in the history of Germany, Bohemia and Moravia have always been the heart of the Reich. This area must one day become German, and the Czechs will have no place here. We will try, using the old methods, to germanize these Czech vermin. It is useless to try and win them over to us. We don't need them . . . We know what we will do with them, but certain tactical considerations must be observed . . . It will be possible to have agreeable social relations with them . . . but we must always remember that they are vile Czechs.'

By the end of October Heydrich had 'cleaned up' Bohemia and Moravia. Thousands of Czechs had gone to the concentration camps of Mauthausen and Theresienstadt. Hundreds of others had simply been liquidated by the *Gestapo* after summary courts martial. His adjutant, K. H. Frank, expressed his admiration for 'the sure political instinct with which Heydrich first destroyed the chiefs of the resistance – the Prime Minister, the generals and the high officials – before getting down to the trouble-makers, the black-marketeers and the Jews.'

By 1 November Heydrich felt sure enough of success to lay down the bludgeon and try persuasion. At the same time he was fighting another battle in the shadows, not against the Czechs, but against the *Abwehr*. Since his arrival in Prague he had reopened the dossier on the 'Black Chapel', under the ironic name of 'Black Orchestra'.

On the night of 3 October, raiding the home of a customs officer in Prague-Jinovice, where the *Gestapo* had discovered a wireless transmitter, they made a valuable haul of documents which the radio operator, Jindrich Klecka, had failed to destroy before committing suicide in the lavatory. Having deciphered some of these coded messages, the *Gestapo* found that their contents revived old suspicions of a high German functionary, alleged to be working for the Czech resistance under the pseudonyms 'Franta' or 'René'. Since 1939 they had been on the trail of this mysterious person, who had betrayed some of the closest secrets of the Third Reich. The general theory, shared by Heydrich, was that this unknown person must be someone with an important position in the National-Socialist system, but that he must be a subtle operator, as no trace of his identity could be found. In December 1939 a special *Gestapo* group had been formed, headed by the Criminal Inspector Willi Abendschön, to mark down the traitor. The group searched through all possible clues and indications that might lead them to 'Franta' or 'René'.

Fortune now served the *Gestapo*. For a friend of Jindrich Klecka, the dead radio operator, admitted that his circle had been in touch with a man called René, a *Wehrmacht* official. The Abendschön group thereupon made a close inquiry into the *Wehrmacht* personnel stationed in Prague. An official of the NSDAP propaganda services in Liberec was first arrested and then released, as it became clear that it could not be him. A Captain Bernhard Leidl of the *Abwehr* was arrested next and released after long interrogation, with profuse apologies. Canaris had protested at this treatment of his subordinate officer and to good effect.

The *Gestapo* was back to its first position, but Abendschön now had an inkling that it was in the *Abwehr* that the search must be made. This conviction was intensified when he read the statements of three *Abwehr* agents in Prague, who had been working in and out of Allied territory. None of these three had ever heard of 'René', but they knew of a Dr Holm who was the *Abwehr* officer in charge of their activities within the Balkans and Turkey. Abendschön already knew that this Dr Holm was in fact Paul Thümmel, in whom the *Gestapo* was already interested. Abendschön pulled out the Thümmel dossier.

In the month of April 1941, when Yugoslavia had been crushed and occupied, Walther Schellenberg's counter-espionage agents had followed the German army into Belgrade and rummaged around in the abandoned diplomatic missions of the Allied powers. In the British Military Attaché's office they had found a copy of a recent dispatch: '. . . The German air force will begin the attack with a terrible bombardment of the capital, as our faithful friend Franz-Joseph tells us. Inform the Yugoslav Government'. The dispatch had come from London, but the origin of the information that it contained seemed to have originated in Prague. Schellenberg's Service made enquiries in Berlin, from which it appeared that the information that the British had circulated had been drawn from secret operational instructions deposited in the safe of the *Abwehr* office in Prague. Three persons only had access to these secret instructions, Colonel von Kornatzki, the *Abwehr* Chief in Prague; Colonel von Engelmann, his assistant, and the Officer in charge of confidential agents, Paul Thümmel. Both the senior officers had been absent from Prague at the time of the leakage, so that suspicion fell squarely on Thümmel, but the *Gestapo* were put off the scent by a telegram from Schellenberg: 'Paul Thümmel, veteran member of the NSDAP, holder of the Party's golden badge, serving with the *Abwehr* for many years and friend of the Reichsführer *SS* Heinrich Himmler enjoys the complete confidence of the Party, the *SS* and the High Command of the *Wehrmacht*.'

Abendschön, during his interrogation by the Czechoslovak Intelligence Service after the war recalled that he had never discovered the real identity of the Franz-Joseph mentioned in the British secret dispatch captured in Belgrade. The *Gestapo* man told his interrogators how he had come to suspect Paul Thümmel. During the raid on the secret transmitter station on 3 October 1941, his men had found a number of dispatches still uncoded which were to have been sent to London.

These contained such phrases as 'René states . . . René confirms . . . According to René . . .' The information attributed to René appeared to me of such particular secrecy that it could only be known to a very few people in Prague, such as K. H. Frank, the Protector's adjutant, Dr Oscar Geschek, Chief of the *Gestapo*, and Dr Holm, alias Paul Thümmel of the *Abwehr*. My chief, Dr Geschek, decided to refer the matter to Heydrich, as Thümmel was a senior officer of the *Abwehr*. Heydrich gave his assent, and we arrested Thümmel in his office on 13 October.

At first Thümmel seemed surprised and then protested vigorously. He denied flatly that he was René. We could find no direct proof against him. During the interrogation he was clever in arousing suspicion against other people. After several days he obtained permission to inform his superiors of these accusations. The result was a cascade of protests from Bormann for the Party, Himmler for the *SS* and Admiral Canaris for the *Abwehr*. The *Gestapo* Commissioner Oscar Fleischer protested as well. I had to defer to my chief Dr Geschek.

Canaris said to Lahousen on 15 October two days after Thümmel's arrest:

'Heydrich must be damnably sure of his ground to risk an open attack of this kind on an *Abwehr* special officer, a Party veteran and into the bargain such a close friend of Himmler.'

With Thümmel as his trump card, Heydrich went over to the attack. As was his custom he used Walther Schellenberg.

On 25 October Canaris and Schellenberg were riding in the *Tiergarten* when Schellenberg explained that Heydrich, though entirely committed to his new duties as Protector, continued to show interest in security matters, remaining more than ever Chief of the Security Service.

'Heydrich is anxious to have a conference with you, Admiral. You know of the great tension existing between our services. Heydrich wants to do away with it.'

'Heydrich wants to do away with the *Abwehr* itself', retorted Canaris. 'I know what his intentions are.'

'Believe me, Admiral, I know of Heydrich's ambitions', said Schellenberg. 'I myself consider that we must work more closely. What do you think?'

The Admiral did not reply, but set his horse in a gallop along one of the broad sandy rides of the *Tiergarten*. Schellenberg urged his own mount into pursuit. As they rode, Canaris reflected on Heydrich's tactics. Was his influence with Hitler strong enough to obtain from him a decision to merge the *SS* intelligence service with that of the *Wehrmacht?* Canaris did not think so. The Admiral still had a few cards in his own hand. The *Abwehr* citadel was difficult to assail and his military chiefs, mostly anti-*SS*, if not anti-Nazi, formed a solid bloc, fiercely defensive of their relative independence. Heydrich would bruise himself on this obstacle. All the same the Admiral was worried and he sensed that Thümmel's arrest might have something to do with Heydrich's newly aggressive attitude to the *Abwehr*. As Canaris brought his horse to a walking pace, Schellenberg caught up with him.

'What exactly does Heydrich want?' asked the Admiral.

'He wants you to visit Prague in the near future and discuss with him some recent problems that have created tension between our two services.'

'Is that really all, Schellenberg?'

'Yes, Admiral, I can assure you.'

Returning at a trot to the stables the Admiral was thoughtful and silent. His dachshund ran up to greet him, wagging her tail.

'You see how superior animals are,' said Canaris. 'My dog is discreet and will never betray me. I can't say the same of humans. Tell Heydrich it is agreed. I will come to Prague shortly for a discussion with him. Bentivegni and Piki will accompany me. You will come to this meeting?'

'Certainly, Admiral.'

A few days later in Prague, Heydrich unmasked his guns in the presence of Heinrich Müller, Chief of the *Gestapo*, and Walther Schellenberg.

'In proposing negotiations to you, Admiral, I knew very well that I would be wasting my time. If I persist in seeking compromise solutions with you, it is not in order to cajole you but solely because of the military situation. At the same time I will not conceal from you that after the war the *SS* will take over everything still in the *Abwehr*'s field.'

'After the war, my dear Heydrich?' said Canaris, smiling.

'Perhaps even before the end of the war.'

Canaris looked hard at his opponent and said:

'My dear Heydrich, I have never doubted your intentions nor your ambition. I have known you for a long time, since our days in the navy. But you know me too and you know very well that nobody will touch the *Abwehr* as long as I am alive.'

'Nobody will touch the *Abwehr*, Admiral? Not even the Führer?'

'Do not imply what I have not said. The Führer is not concerned in this, as you know very well. It is you and I. That is very different and very clear.'

Heydrich played his strong card.

'Do you think, Admiral, that the Führer will not have questions to ask when he hears that one of the important men in your Prague outfit is accused of treason, and dealings with the Czech resistance and with the British Intelligence Service? What do you think? Do you agree?'

'You are referring to Paul Thümmel, I suppose?'

'Exactly.'

'Allow me to draw your attention to the fact that Paul Thümmel, before becoming a member of the *Abwehr*, was a Party member and a veteran Party member at that.'

'True, but he is not *SS*. He is directly responsible to you. If I send to the Führer through Reichsleiter Bormann the dossier that I possess on the Thümmel affair, I know very well what his reactions will be.'

'You would be wrong, my dear Heydrich. I am not so sure that the Führer's reactions would be as you wish.'

Then, as if to ease the tension a little, he added:

'That said, my dear fellow, who says that I am not ready to examine certain questions concerning both the *Abwehr* and the *SD* loyally and in depth?'

Heydrich too gave way a little:

'I have not tried to harm you, Admiral. Our friendship, which goes back many years, proves this. Schellenberg here is a witness that when the *Abwehr* has been attacked, I have defended you.'

Schellenberg appeared ill at ease.

'If those are your feelings,' said Canaris placidly, 'we can reach an understanding, but release Paul Thümmel for a start. He is an excellent *Abwehr* agent who has done wonderful work. Even if he may have committed some indiscretions in his contacts with the resistance, he has certainly not committed treason. I am certain of that, and I know that the Reichsführer Heinrich Himmler thinks as I do.'

Heydrich's face hardened. Canaris's last words had gone home. The Admiral did not give Heydrich an opportunity to recover, making the final point.

'At least, that is what the *Reichsführer* told me last night in Berlin. He added that *Reichsleiter* Bormann too, did not wish the

Führer to be troubled with this affair. The accusations made against an old Party comrade, Paul Thümmel, appeared to him, to say the least, unsubstantial and hastily drafted. Our Führer has at this moment enough anxieties about the military situation. Don't let us ask him to arbitrate. A release, under observation if you wish, would be the right way. What do you think?'

Schellenberg, who described this scene to me, noticed that Heydrich went very pale, sensing that the Admiral had outwitted him by combining on the *Abwehr*'s side the two most powerful men of the régime, Himmler and Bormann.

His cold anger did not show. He knew how to control himself and play by the rules.

'Admiral, we will release Paul Thümmel, but we will keep him under surveillance. Do you agree?'

'Absolutely!'

'But if we find irrefutable proof against him, I will inform the Führer.'

'I am in entire agreement with you. As for friction between the *Abwehr* and the *SD*, our friend Schellenberg here can make contact with my Heads of Section. They are ready to work out with him a *modus vivendi*.'

Canaris had skilfully defused the Heydrich bomb. He had won so far, but the *SD* Security Chief would seek his revenge. Meanwhile, on 25 November 1941, Dr Holm, alias Paul Thümmel, was set at liberty.

Willi Abendschön did not like this at all and continued to cast doubts on Thümmel's innocence. Heydrich too was impatient, and almost daily enquired about the investigations, feeling sure that the evidence pointed to the *Abwehr*. He greatly desired to break down Thümmel's defence and so gain another weapon against Canaris and his *Abwehr*, but Thümmel was proving tough.

Abendschön travelled around, busily enquiring in Berlin and Dresden, perusing registers, and noting statements made in the past. Thümmel, however, ignored the *Gestapo* and got on with his own work. Before his arrest he had formed, at the *Abwehr* offices in Prague, a special group which he named 'the house group', concerned to track down the three leaders of Czech resistance, Lieutenant-Colonel Balaban, Lieutenant-Colonel Masin and Captain Vaclav Moravek, not in order to arrest them, as Thümmel told the *Gestapo*, but in order to enable the *Abwehr* to

Canaris

establish precisely what were the activities and ramifications of the Czech military resistance.

Colonel Balaban was arrested by the *Gestapo* on 22 April 1941, and executed. Colonel Masin, in *Gestapo* hands since 13 May 1941, awaited execution. Captain Vaclav Moravek was still at liberty, and Abendschön found evidence that Thümmel not only knew Moravek but also where he was hiding.

On 22 February 1942, Dr Holm-Thümmel was invited to an important meeting with Police Superintendent Schultz of the Criminal Branch of the *Gestapo*. Abendschön was waiting there for him and again put him under arrest. He was taken immediately to Kladno prison, far from the turmoil of Prague, for lengthy interrogations. Finally, when documents were put before him that he could not explain away, Thümmel staked all on one throw:

'Yes, I am René,' he said, but explained that if he had collaborated with Moravek, it was for the purpose of discovering the ramifications of Czech resistance. Abendschön seemed to accept this explanation; in fact he thought that Thümmel could put him on the trail of Moravek, who had been hunted by the *Gestapo* since 1939. Abendschön obtained permission from Heydrich to give Thümmel enough freedom to enable him to assist in the search for Vaclav Moravek. On 2 March 1942, Thümmel was again provisionally released.

The co-operation between Thümmel and Abendschön could not be described as felicitous; for two or three traps were laid and each time Moravek cunningly eluded them. It was evident that Thümmel was not really trying to assist the *Gestapo*. Abendschön lost his nerve and arrested Thümmel for the third time on Friday, 20 March.

Coincidence or a tip to the *Gestapo* brought Abendschön the opportunity that he had been seeking for so long. Captain Moravek was known to have made a rendezvous at the Orechovce tram depot for the following day, the 21st. Otto Geschek was witness of the final encounter between Abendschön and Moravek.

At approximately 7 : 15 PM my men were leading away their prisoner, Rehak, one of the Moravek bodyguards. At that moment Moravek emerged from a side street. When he saw that his aide was under arrest, he opened fire. Our men returned his fire. Moravek, hit in the ankle and thigh, tried to escape. At 7 :19 PM, seeing that he was surrounded, Moravek committed suicide before my men could seize him. Moravek had fired fifty shots in this short space of time. He himself had been hit

260

by ten bullets. We found two nine-millimetre pistols in his possession with seven empty clips of ammunition.

In Thümmel, the *Gestapo* had in their hands a man suspected of treason, but also an eminent Nazi and a wearer of the Party's golden badge. It seemed necessary to obtain his discreet expulsion from the *NSDAP* before his trial could begin. On 27 March 1942, Dr Otto Geschek presented a report to Heydrich to the effect that other treasonable activities committed by Paul Thümmel, during his previous service with the *Abwehr* in Dresden, were under investigation. He recommended Thümmel's exclusion from the Party and that his arrest should not generally be made known for the time being. Heydrich approved Dr Geschek's recommendations, marking the report with his green pencil, but it was not sent on to Bormann until 23 May, a delay of eight weeks. During this time Heydrich exploited the undisclosed incident to increase his pressure on Canaris, urging him to accept his general proposals for the *Abwehr*. In this form of blackmail, Heydrich succeeded, but it was to be his last triumph.

Thus Thümmel was unmasked, but his precise activities as a spy remained unknown to the *Gestapo*, to Heydrich and to Canaris alike. Dr Holm, Paul Thümmel, and 'René' they knew to be one person, but there were also 'Franta' and Paul Steinberg, as well as A.54, agent of the Czechoslovak Intelligence Service since 1938, and Thümmel was all these people as well. What were the motives that brought him into such desperate conflict with Hitler's Germany? According to my German sources he began by being a convinced and active Nazi, but had numerous difficulties with the *SS* after the 1934 purge of the brown-shirts. Only Himmler's friendship protected him, and this intensified the jealousy of certain high Party men, among them Heydrich and Müller of the *Gestapo*. This did not in the least retard his promotion, so that his behaviour cannot be ascribed to disappointed ambition. Nor was Thümmel greedy for money. After 1938 A.54 very quickly ceased to demand payment from the Czechoslovak Intelligence Service, as if his first demands had the sole motive of establishing that his activities were genuine.

As to the reasons for his significant aid to the Czech resistance movement, nothing is positively known; but it may be that he needed a channel of communication to London and so made use of the secret Czech organization. It appears that a kind of common cause against the *Gestapo* had grown out of this system of collaboration, an indestructible fraternity of spirit.

Was Thümmel a double agent? He had as A.54 given immense help to the Czechoslovak resistance and provided information of considerable importance to the British. It is no less true that as an *Abwehr* officer in Prague his espionage work had been effective. He was under the orders of Canaris, who saw him often. This is perhaps the explanation. I have already described the mental conflict in which Germans stood when it came to choosing between state and country. Paul Thümmel was never sent for trial, but instead to a concentration camp, where he was shot on 27 April 1945. He takes his place, an heroic if enigmatic figure, in the foremost ranks of those who fought on the secret front in the Second World War.

26

Crushing the serpent

At 9 PM on 28 December 1941, a Halifax bomber of the RAF, flown by Flight-Lieutenant R. C. Hockey, took off from an air field near London carrying seven Czech parachutists, who had received special training in a commando camp at Mallaig. They were formed into three groups: the first, named *Anthropoid*, consisted of Joseph Gabcik and Jan Kubis; the second, *Silver A* and consisted of Lieutenant Alfred Bartos, Joseph Valcik, and Jiri Potucek as radio operator; *Silver B* consisted of Jan Zemek and Vladimir Skacha. Each man had been given an operational pseudonym. At 2:15 AM the aircraft was over Pilsen and at 2:24 AM it released the three groups of parachutists.

Theirs was a perilous mission and it would take them exactly five months to accomplish it. They needed several weeks to collect the essential information, upon which *Anthropoid* group would proceed to strike a memorable blow at the Nazi police system by attempting to assassinate the man at the top, Reinhard Heydrich.

Several plans were examined and in turn rejected. They thought of firing a bazooka at his special train; of blowing up a wing of the Hradschin; of ambushing Heydrich in the Panenske Brezany forest by stretching a steel wire across the road. Finally in May 1942 they decided upon an attack in a Prague suburb, through which Heydrich regularly drove on his way to Panenske Brezany where the Protector had requisitioned as his residence the archbishop's palace.

Death prowled close to Heydrich. He did not care and was not worried by plots against him, despising 'these Czechs bourgeois who haven't the guts to try anything like that'. His staff warned him of the risks, but he continued to behave more like a film star than a high German official who was the focus of all the hatred of an oppressed nation. Weather permitting, he would drive through Prague sitting in the front seat of his open grey Mercedes with no more protection than his own revolver and his trusted driver, Sergeant Klein, a giant of a man, quick and intelligent.

According to Schellenberg it was during the winter and spring of 1942 that Heydrich decided to finish off the *Abwehr*. He knew that Hitler had complained to Himmler of the inefficiency of Canaris and his Service; the occasion of this complaint was after a surprise raid by the British on the French coast near Le Havre on 27 February 1942. He thought that Canaris's position had weakened and he saw the possibility of exploiting the situation, if not to take over the entire *Abwehr* service, at least to annexe important parts of it.

Numerous factors had strengthened Heydrich's position. The *Gestapo* had, at the beginning of 1942, arrested a former magistrate, Dr Strassmann, suspected of organizing an internal information network for obscure purposes. When Strassmann alleged that he was acting at the instigation of two members of Colonel Oster's Central Section of the *Abwehr*, Heydrich suspended any further action, taking the opposite cause and directing that for the moment the whole inquiry was to be dropped. The *SD* in Madrid supplied him with another lever. Canaris had arrived in Madrid with four large leather suitcases and had left Madrid without them, it was reported. The *SD* report suggested that he had deposited large sums in a Spanish bank. There was also the arrest of Paul Thümmel, a trump card. Schellenberg, though I have found it advisable to treat his evidence with great care, adds that at this time Heydrich was also aware of Oster's conspiratorial activities inside the *Abwehr*.

In April 1942 relations between the *Abwehr* and the *SD* were dangerously strained, and Heydrich proposed to Canaris on a form of agreement the respective duties of the two services. Canaris responded with counter-proposals of the concessions that he was prepared to make. Heydrich reacted violently, saying that in such circumstances it was useless to negotiate with Canaris and threatening to call in Himmler. The estrangement reached such a pitch that when Canaris called at the Central Security Office to reason with him, Heydrich refused to receive his former chief. Realizing the dangers, Canaris asked Keitel to intervene, and after Keitel had spoken to Heydrich on the telephone, Canaris was received and drew up in writing a series of points of agreement with the *SD* Chief. This time Canaris was not the winner. The finalized document was to be tabled at a joint meeting of senior *SS* and *Abwehr* officers in Prague on 18 May. Heydrich meanwhile visited Paris to ensure greater activity in the occupied zone of France by *SS* General Oberg and his formations.

The conference in Prague began at 10:30 AM in the Hradschin, in a vast Baroque gallery, flanking the third courtyard, called the Hall of the Germans. This had been built in the reign of Rudolph II (1552-1612) to house a superb collection of Rubens, Van Dyck and Breughel pictures.

The agenda of this meeting was:

Re-organization of co-operation between the *Abwehr*, the *Gestapo* and the *SD*. The following will speak: the Chief of Security Police and the Security Service, *SS* Chief Group Leader and Police General Reinhard Heydrich. The Chief of the *Abwehr* Foreign Service of the *Wehrmacht*, Admiral Wilhelm Canaris. Participants: the Chief of Secret Police, *SS* Group Leader Heinrich Müller, the Chief of Criminal Police, *SS* Group Leader Arthur Nebe, the Chief of *SD* Foreign Service, *SS* Group Leader, Walther Schellenberg.

Those invited to attend were the Heads of Section of the *Abwehr*, the Bureau Chiefs of the *Gestapo*, the Chiefs of Section of the Reich Security Service and senior officers of the Criminal Police.

Heydrich opened the conference with a speech in a fairly low key, after which Admiral Canaris unfolded his ideas for closer collaboration between the *Abwehr* and the *SS*. Then Müller spoke and launched a ferocious attack on Canaris, asserting that the *Abwehr* was working on obsolete lines, that its personnel were 'not professionally up to standard' and that 'some of them are politically questionable'. Walther Schellenberg spoke in more moderate terms, offering a basis for compromise. Heydrich took up the subject again and proposed a *modus vivendi* based on the ten-point programme previously drafted with Canaris extending the existing system of co-operation between the services.

'The internal and external situation requires changes in the organization and personnel of the *Abwehr*', concluded Heydrich. 'Its present members have displayed their incapacity and must be replaced by new men trained in *SS* centres. The security of the Reich demands a reorganization of the secret services on a centralized basis. They must be able to act and give instructions throughout all departments and to all agents. Each will be responsible to his own minister, to the minister of state and to myself.'

This proposal amounted to evicting Canaris and installing Heydrich in his place, a triumph for the *SS*. The Admiral did not react during the conference, but that afternoon at a smaller meeting with Heydrich, Müller and Schellenberg, he contested the accusations levelled against the *Abwehr* in the course of the morning. Heydrich then referred to the treason case of Paul Thümmel, to the activities of Dr Strassmann, to Admiral Canaris's recent journey to Spain and also to the leakages through the Vatican in 1940. When Canaris objected, Heydrich cut him short by describing the Thümmel affair as 'the worst case of treason in the history of the Third Reich'. However Canaris, probably because Heydrich did not feel entirely sure of his ground, did obtain the concession that he might keep his present senior staff officers, though he must 'work out a scheme of reforms in the structure of the *Abwehr* services with a view to unifying the secret services'.

Heydrich appeared to have won the contest. Two days earlier he had forwarded to Bormann a long report on the Thümmel case and on his own policy in the Protectorate. He would now prepare a second report on the Prague conference, he said, but he was first awaiting a reply to the letter to Bormann that was attached to his report on the Thümmel case. He had dispatched these on 16 May and the reply did not leave the Führer's Headquarters until 27 May arriving in Prague too late for Heydrich to read its contents.

On 27 May at 10 AM it was a sunny spring morning in Bohemia, with a light warm breeze blowing round Panenske Brezany. Heydrich's field-grey Mercedes stood at the palace steps, with Klein beside it ready to drive his master into town. Heydrich came out of the door, leading by the hand his fair-haired daughter, Silke, his favourite child. The boys, Klaus and Heider, walked beside their mother. Lena was already five months pregnant with a fourth child. Heydrich embraced and kissed them all, leapt into the Mercedes and drove off to Prague.

The Mercedes drove rapidly along a tarmac road for ten miles in the direction of Prague, between rows of chestnuts in early leaf. It travelled at more than seventy miles an hour. Heydrich had received a summons to Hitler's Headquarters on the Eastern Front and wondered what was the reason for it. He drove on through Libenice with its cobbled streets and church spire and saw Prague on the right, the mists rising from the river, and the little suburb of Holesovice. Tram-lines led up the big Troja bridge across the Vltava, and from time to time the squat little red tram-cars rattled and lurched up and down the hard curves of the Liben road leading to the bridge.

At 10:20 AM one of these tram-cars was slowly climbing the hill, coming from Prague, when the long low Mercedes breasted the hill-top half a mile away. Driver Klein slowed down at the end of the straight before coming to the Liben turning. It was by then 10:27 AM, and suddenly there was a bright flash – sunlight reflected by a pocket mirror. Another minute passed and the car slowed down at the corner. A man standing on the kerb flung back the raincoat folded over his arm, and sprang forward, his sub-machine gun aimed, pressing the trigger. Nothing happened. The gun had jammed. As the Mercedes passed, he remained rooted to the ground by the shock of the moment. Heydrich turned in his seat and tried to draw his revolver. The tyres screeched on the road as the car slowed down in front of a young man who seemed to want to board the slow-moving tram. He passed behind the Mercedes. A grey ball rolled towards the car's rear off-side wheel and changed suddenly into a ball of blinding orange flame. After the explosion there was a cloud of black smoke. The tram windows were shattered. Two field-grey tunics, apparently folded on the back seat of the Mercedes, sailed into the air, hung for a moment on the overhead wires of the tram-way and then flopped to the ground. The car swerved violently several times, the off-side rear tyre collapsed on its rim. There was a large hole in its rear bodywork.

As it came to a standstill Heydrich and Klein flung open the doors, brandishing their revolvers. The man who had thrown the grenade, Jan Kubis, heard the first bullet whistle past him and rushed to his bicycle, leaning against the railings. Ten yards away the other parachutist, Joseph Gabcik, still stood motionless, but seeing Jan jump on his bicycle he ran for his life. A bullet whizzed past his ear. Looking back he saw that it was Heydrich himself who was firing. So Jan's grenade had done him no harm! His revolver in his hand, Gabcik ran for the far side of the tram-cars, which would shield him from some of Heydrich's bullets. He brushed past the astonished spectators, with Heydrich still firing at him, and reached the far side of the street, when a very near miss instinctively made him turn and, crouching behind a lamp standard, he began firing back. He and Heydrich were thirty paces apart, the by-standers by now flat on their stomachs and unable to believe their eyes at this scene from the Wild West.

Suddenly Joseph Gabcik saw Heydrich's revolver hand shake convulsively and realized that he had fired all his shots. At that precise moment the gigantic Klein, red and breathless from the pursuit of Jan Kubis, returned to his master. Gabcik seized the opportunity to leave his shelter and run up the hill at top speed. Klein dashed after him, firing as he ran. Not wanting a bullet in his back, Gabcik halted behind a telegraph post and fired at Klein. Klein took similar cover and the pistol duel began again, but Gabcik realized that both time and his ammunition were running out and that the police must be on the way. He fired at Klein twice in rapid succession and again ran with Klein in pursuit. Gabcik dashed into a butcher's shop, looking for a way out of the back, but there was none. So, facing the advancing Klein as if on pistol drill, his right arm fully extended, he fired carefully at twenty paces. The bullet hit Klein in the thigh, and he fell to the ground with a yell. Joseph Gabcik darted out of the shop like an arrow, firing again at Klein as he passed him, less than ten yards away. This time Klein was hit in the ankle and yelled again. Gabcik ran flat out for the top of the hill, where a tram was just moving. The conductor, unaware of all that had happened a quarter of a mile away, left the door open and Gabcik jumped into the moving vehicle after slipping his revolver into his pocket. There were not many other passengers. He dropped like a dead-weight onto a seat and when the tram reached Wenceslas Square changed into a second tram that took him past the home of friends, the Fafka family, in the suburbs.

The explosion had blown thin fragments of metal and upholstery into Heydrich's lumbar regions and spleen, but at the time he had felt nothing and had begun to shoot at Gabcik, firing up to the moment when Klein rejoined him. Then he began to feel pain and, doubled up, found his way to a stone balustrade and sat down. After a short rest he staggered over to the Mercedes and leaned on the bonnet like a man who had run an exhausting race. His face was grey. The passengers from the tram-car stood round him at a distance, still afraid of his German uniform. Two Czech policemen arrived on the scene and recognized the *Reichsprotektor*. They stopped a passing baker's van, arranged Heydrich among the sacks of flour at the back and ordered the driver 'to the Bulov hospital'.

Two of the best surgeons in Prague, Professor Hohlbaum and Dr Dick, operated on Heydrich an hour later. The X-ray revealed internal lesions five inches in length caused by the splinters of metal. One rib was broken, the thorax fractured and the diaphragm punctured in two places. The doctors removed the splinters and the operation was apparently successful.

There was at first incredulity and then fierce indignation when news of the attempted assassination reached the ruling circle in Germany. There was also anxiety over Heydrich's fate. Himmler ordered Inspector Nebe, Heinrich Müller and Schellenberg to Prague, as well as the two most eminent doctors in the Third Reich, Professor Karl Gebhardt and Ferdinand Sauerbruch.

At the Bulov hospital the doctors fought for five days with blood transfusions and anti-gangrene injections to save Heydrich. He soon began to take food again and his temperature dropped, so that he seemed to be no longer in danger. On 3 June, however, his condition took a turn for the worse, his complexion becoming greyer, his features sunken and his pulse weak. His lips were pallid and he could no longer open his eyes. Septicaemia had set in, and against this the Germans had no penicillin. The poison spread through his blood-stream. His death agony lasted throughout that night, and he died in the early hours of Thursday, 4 June.

When his death was announced, Heinrich Himmler took a plane for Prague. He drove from the airport to the Bulov hospital. There he asked: 'Where are the clothes that the late Protector was wearing?' A nurse led him to the cupboard where Heydrich's personal effects had been placed. Himmler rummaged in the tunic and removed a small bunch of keys, which he put in his pocket. These were the keys of the safe in Heydrich's Berlin office, which nobody else had ever opened, and in which he kept his most secret files. Himmler then asked to be taken to the mortuary where the body of Heydrich had been laid out.

A catafalque was erected in the main courtyard of the Hradschin for the funeral ceremony, with a huge backcloth bearing the silver *SS* insignia on a black ground. An *SS* guard of honour in dress uniform and steel helmets kept watch over the coffin. Two days later a funeral cortège took the coffin from the Hradschin to the railway station with muffled drums and the thud of boots in the slow march. In Berlin the coffin lay for two days in the Wilhelmstrasse palace. At 3 PM on 8 June Hitler arrived by air from his Winnitza headquarters to take part in the obsequies. The Führer looked pale and drawn. He was flanked by ministers, generals and admirals. Among them Canaris stood next to *SS* General Sepp

Dietrich, Commander of the Hitler Bodyguard. Dietrich, when he had first heard that Heydrich was dead had used these words: 'Thank God that bastard has gone at last'. The widow, Lena Heydrich, because of her pregnancy, remained at Panenske Brezany, but the two boys were present, hand in hand with Heinrich Himmler, who later made a long funeral oration at the Invalides cemetery.

Schellenberg was surprised to notice that Admiral Canaris sobbed as the coffin was lowered into the grave. He did not realize what a relief it was to Canaris to see the last of his arch enemy. The Admiral had lived through days and nights of extreme tension since the Prague conference three weeks earlier and this was the moment when his nerves gave way. He covered up his reasons for breaking down, by saying to Schellenberg in the car as they drove away:

'After all, he was a big man. I have lost a friend in him'.

The *Gestapo* was now in a quandary. The assassination had taken place in broad daylight, but at the time of the burial the Prague police investigators were still groping in the dark. Hitler was in a towering rage, demanding that the assassins and their supporters should expiate their crime in the most pitiless way. Heinrich Müller directed operations and 60,000 auxiliary police were drafted to the Protectorate. A reward of ten million Czech crowns offered for information leading to the discovery of the assassins brought no results whatsoever.

Ballistic experts could tell from fragments of the bomb that it was of foreign origin and an ingenious design hitherto unknown in Germany. They proceeded to the conjecture that the deed had been done by parachutists from England, with the assistance of the Czech resistance, but there was still no trace of them. So a campaign of terror and reprisals began, to force the secret out of the hostile population and to persuade all other occupied countries that it was inadvisable to imitate the Czechs. At length a clue led them to the village of Lidice, which was destroyed with all its inhabitants and among them the parachutists from London who put up a desperate resistance to the last. Under the direction of Karl Hermann Frank, the campaign of reprisals led to the killing of thousands of others in *Gestapo* cellars or in the concentration camps of Theresienstadt and Mauthausen. The spring of 1942 in Bohemia had ended in a holocaust.

Why was Heydrich assassinated? The only certainty was that

two Czechs from London did the deed, but why, I asked myself, should the operation have been directed from London with all the problems of transport and security thereby entailed, when a strong and efficient Czechoslovak resistance had existed in Prague since 1939? Colonel Frantisek Moravets, former Chief of Czechoslovak Intelligence, whose acquaintance I first made in Paris after the war and renewed later in the United States, gave me the answer to this question. Colonel Moravets had himself briefed the parachutists on 3 October 1941, in the presence of four senior officers of the Czechoslovak forces in Britain. Colonel Moravets reminded them of the killings in Czechoslovakia for which Heydrich and Karl Hermann Frank were responsible and exhorted them to the utmost determination and presence of mind in discharging their difficult and dangerous mission. He explained that the group would work on a self-contained system. 'This will be necessary for reasons that will become clear to you; for you must carry out your task without the co-operation of your compatriots who have remained in Czechoslovakia ... I mean by this that no assistance will be forthcoming until the operation has been completed.'

Colonel Moravets then told me why he had decided upon this operation, at the request of President Benes and the British Intelligence Service.

At that time there were patriotic reasons enough to justify such an action, but I will be frank and say that political considerations did predominate. President Benes and his provisional Government in London, were hardly recognized by the Foreign Office, which did not admit his jurisdiction, for instance, over the Sudeten-Germans living in the United Kingdom during the war, at least until Benes had come to some agreement with them over the best form for a united state of Czechoslovakia in the future.

It should be added that President Benes was at that time the victim of two conflicting ideas. As a European he wished to reach an understanding with the Sudeten-Germans. At the same time he was attracted by the Pan-Slav idea, which necessitated collaboration with the Czech Communists. However the crux of the matter, in my opinion, did not lie there. It lay in the unwillingness of the British Foreign Office to furnish him with a formal declaration that the Munich Agreement was no longer valid. Benes had sought an understanding with the Polish government in exile which had resulted in an agreement signed on 11 November 1940, but the Poles were the favourites of the Foreign Office and treated us Czechs as poor relations.

The British and the Poles never ceased to reproach us with passivity under the German occupation. It was, alas, partly true. The Germans had not behaved in Czechoslovakia with the same ferocity and cruelty as in Poland, in Greece and in Soviet Russia. We had excellent intelligence agents inside Czechoslovakia, but a solid resistance movement was yet to be created and when Heydrich was appointed Protector, Benes hoped that a hardening of the German attitude could be met with a stiffening of Czechoslovak resistance. The opposite happened at the beginning of the Protectorship. Heydrich was a ruthless butcher, but he displayed a spectacular personality and seemed an acceptable figure to the workers and the peasants at the same time as he increased the severity of his treatment of the intellectual and ruling classes.

It was out of this lack of reaction to Heydrich's methods that the idea of assassination was born:

an abominable calculation without a doubt, but we weighed up for a long time the immense propaganda advantages abroad of such an action against the obvious suffering that would ensue for the Czech population . . . So you see that there was a fairly close connection between the operation against Heydrich and the political needs of the Benes government in London . . . Alas . . . I must say that at that time we had not imagined the tragedy of Lidice!

I asked Colonel Moravets whether it was true that the resistance movement inside Czechoslovakia registered its disapproval before the assassination:

Yes, that is correct. There was a meeting in Prague on 21 March 1942 at the home of Ludmilla Persinova at which the leader of the parachutist group, Alfred Bartos, with the two volunteers Gabcik and Kubis, met Captain Vaclaw Moravek, the last surviving leader of the army resistance movement. As a result of this meeting I was asked to forego the whole project. On 3 May 1942 I received in London this very explicit message from Bartos in Prague: 'From the preparations made by Ota and Zdenek* and the location in which they make these preparations, we conclude, despite their obstinate silence, that they intend to attempt assassination of H. This action will not really serve the Allied cause and it will have tragic consequences for our nation. It will not only constitute a threat to the lives of hostages and political prisoners but it will also cost the lives of thousands of others. It will lead to appalling reprisals and sweep away all that remains of the anti-German movement. After that it will be impossible to do anything further to help the Allies. That is why we entreat you to give orders through *Silver A* not to carry out the attempt. It is dangerous to delay. Send orders by return.

*The code names of Gabcik and Kubis.

If an attack is necessary from the point of view of foreign opinion, choose some other target.'

Colonel Moravets' hand trembled as he read out this message to me and recalled those dramatic hours. His eyes were moist and he read it in a hollow voice, ceasing to look me in the face. He added:

'I showed this communication to President Benes and the Chief of the British Secret Service. The former ordered me not to reply. The second said nothing, but I learned after the war that the British not only did not cancel the operation, but continued to insist on it being carried out, though without telling me.'

'Why?'

'I really cannot say. I have been told that the reason was that Heydrich was on the track of important British agents and that to protect them it was necessary that he should die. It is possible.'

Some historians have suggested that the killing of Heydrich was motivated by the British Secret Service. A few have pointed at Himmler and Bormann as the instigators. Among those who advance the latter theory is Schellenberg in his somewhat dubious memoirs. Other historians have suggested that the assassination was inspired by Canaris, who used the British as his instruments: a fantastic theory, though at first sight their arguments may appear plausible.

At this time, in fact, Canaris had just suffered the grave setback of the Prague conference. The *Abwehr* was threatened with rapid absorption by the *SS*, a reason that could explain action against Heydrich. And how would Canaris have been able to exert influence on the British? Through A.54, alias Paul Thümmel, is maybe the answer.

Let us add straightaway that none of the documents available in London, Germany or Czechoslovakia supports this hypothesis. Such a hypothesis would conform with the possibility examined by Ian Colvin in his book *Chief of the Intelligence*, that Canaris might have been a a British agent, a theory which everybody who has read the present book so far will discard, sharing my conviction that Canaris never worked for the Allied Secret Services. What about Oster? one might ask. That possibility indeed cannot be entirely excluded, but a connection between Oster's past activities and the decision to arrange Heydrich's assassination does not yet seem to have been established, though it might be if the British War Office were to lay open its secret intelligence files for this period.

Even if the sort of rôle that Oster played in relation to Paul Thümmel in providing the Allies with information was extended, it is out of the question that Canaris would have known about it. He would have disapproved, as he did of the idea of killing Hitler or of the plan to kill General Giraud after his escape on 17 April 1942, from the German fortress of Königstein.

This feat infuriated Hitler, who offered 100,000 Marks for recapture of his most prestigious prisoner-of-war. Later, when it was known that Giraud had safely reached Switzerland and had passed on into unoccupied France, Hitler wanted him brought back 'dead or alive' to Germany. He then directed that a plan to murder Giraud, known as Operation Gustav, should be put into execution, just as he had demanded two years earlier that Weygand should be liquidated. Canaris took the decision that he would tell Keitel that the *Abwehr* wished to be exempted from any such task. As Colonel Piekenbrock exclaimed:

'Herr Keitel should be told once and for all to inform his Herr Hitler that we of the *Abwehr* are not an organization of assassins like the *SD* or the *SS*.'

General Lahousen related in his testimony to the Nuremberg International Tribunal certain recollections in detail of the ruses by which Canaris avoided carrying out Operation Gustav, or indeed making any attempt to organize such an action. His final stratagem was to tell Keitel that the whole operation had been handed over to the defunct Heydrich and so was no longer on the *Abwehr*'s books.

Other examples can be quoted to show that the *Abwehr* avoided criminal actions during the war, such as omitting to place a time-bomb in a British airliner on the London-Stockholm route, and neglecting to do the same when directed to blow up an airliner on the Allied route between Lisbon and New York.

All this duplicity cost Canaris much nervous strain as he had to cover his traces, cleverly using his personal relations with Hitler to suggest to third parties that the Führer and himself were really of one mind on many matters. He used to drop into his conversation phrases such as: 'the Führer tells me' or 'as the Führer says'. This gift for acting a part was all in character with his unusual working methods and his unorthodox outlook. Canaris was now climbing alone a narrow path between chasms, as Dr K. H. Abshagen aptly describes it, the only path to the fulfilment of the task that he had set himself, but a path from which there was no safe escape. The Admiral went ahead and the mortal danger in which he stood seemed to stabilize and keep him on balance.

27
The *Gestapo* closes in

Canaris seemed to breathe more freely after Heydrich's death, though he remained haunted by the idea of inevitable defeat and pessimism became the dominant trait in his character. One evening in Paris during a dinner at which he had preserved a brooding silence although his *Abwehr* officers were in a gay mood, he suddenly came out with everything that was on his mind, his words striking a chill in the hearts of those at table. After the Admiral had left them Major Oscar Reile asked:

'What meaning is there any longer in our activities? Look at the kind of leaders for whom our soldiers are dying so bravely! They are worth a better and a juster cause! What our Chief has just said shows clearly the direction in which we are being led. Behind Goebbels's propaganda machinery defenceless people are being exterminated. Military defeat is inevitable, and after the collapse, the whole world will be against us. What is the sense in what we are doing now?'

Captain Pfeiffer tried to answer Reile:

'What Canaris has told us he must have said to Keitel and even, though perhaps more guardedly, to Hitler and he will probably go on telling them. We must leave it to him and carry on with our own duties.'

'But', asked Reile, 'how can a man as intelligent and far-sighted as Canaris continue to serve Hitler faithfully? When all is said and done, that remains a mystery.'

'I have asked myself the same thing. The Admiral listens to God and to his own conscience, but he has told us a dozen times that we must continue to carry out our duties to the best of our ability.'

So the officers of the various *Abwehr* Sections continued their work, as is witnessed by the number of cases of espionage and counter-espionage with which they were concerned during the Second World War. Among the espionage cases were, to give them their code names, Harmisch, Pastorius, George Owens,

Johnny, Vera, Jacques Berg and Olaf Klausen. These were memorable counter-espionage cases like Operation North Pole, the Red Orchestra, Porto I and Porto II, the Cat and the Interallied Network. There were also some extraordinary exploits by the Brandenburg Division on the battle fronts. It would require a large volume to describe all these cases, in which the *Abwehr* men bore in mind the Admiral's words that 'the intelligence service is the domain of gentlemen. When others are put in charge of it, then it will collapse.'

Contrary to Schellenberg's assertions, Canaris did not neglect his duties and travelled indefatigably from one *Abwehr* centre to another to keep alive 'the *Abwehr* spirit'.

The conspiracies against Hitler annoyed him increasingly, as he himself had no illusions as to the effectiveness of 'these talkers who split hairs forty times over.' He spoke some sharp words to Oster and Dohnanyi and then was reconciled with them, but he no longer had any hopes of conspiracy, as he had done in 1938 and even as late as 1941. Canaris sensed or knew that the *Gestapo* was watching all these subversive movements and that he no longer had the power to fend off the blow when the *Gestapo* struck.

In February 1942 Dohnanyi and his brother-in-law Pastor Bonhoeffer received a warning that their telephones and their mail were being watched by the *Gestapo*. Bonhoeffer nevertheless increased the number of his foreign contacts, visiting Norway in April and Switzerland in May. While he was in Geneva he learned that his friend George Bell, Bishop of Chichester, was in Sweden on a three-week visit. Bonhoeffer cut short his stay in Switzerland and returned to Berlin, where he discussed with General Beck, Oster and Dohnanyi the idea of a visit to Sweden and a meeting with the Bishop. He thought it would be useful to acquaint the British of the workings of the German resistance, to inform them of the names of its leaders and to seek to arouse British sympathies and understanding for their cause.

On the morning of 30 May 1942, Canaris arranged clearance for Bonhoeffer as a diplomatic messenger of the Foreign Ministry, and the Pastor flew to Stockholm, where he met Dr Bell. The Bishop left him in no doubt that the German resistance could not hope for encouragement from London. Bonhoeffer nevertheless told him what he knew, and the names of the principal conspirators: Beck, Hammerstein, Goerdeler, Leuschner, Kaiser and Schacht. Among the generals he mentioned Marshals von Kluge and von

Bock, who commanded the army groups on the Eastern front, and General von Witzleben. The two men agreed on methods of communication and forms of code that would permit them to correspond through neutral countries.

Bonhoeffer returned to Berlin on 2 June and Dr Bell was back in London on the 10th. The Bishop wrote to the Foreign Secretary, Anthony Eden, on the 18th to inform him of his meeting in Sweden and asked for an interview. They met on 30 June and Dr Bell handed Eden a detailed memorandum. Eden appeared very interested in the report from Sweden and promised his comments which reached Dr Bell on 17 July. The reply was negative: 'Without wishing to cast doubt on the good faith of the informers, I am convinced that it is not in the national interest to send them a reply of any kind. I realize that this answer will cause you some disappointment, but in view of the delicacy of these questions I am obliged to ask you to accept it.'

Bell went to see the American Ambassador, George Winant, on 30 July with the documents that he had collected on the German resistance. The Ambassador promised to inform Washington, but no reply came back. On 23 July the Bishop had sent to the Secretary General of the Ecumenical Council of Churches in Geneva a message intended to be passed on to Bonhoeffer. It read: 'Undoubted interest. Extreme regret. No reply possible. Bell.'

When Bonhoeffer, Oster and Dohnanyi heard of this negative British response, it was a desperate moment. Canaris who had hoped for nothing from these exchanges, said to Oster in Piekenbrock's presence:

'As long as our generals will not decide to act, the British will remain true to their attitude of wait and see.'

A short time before, as if to give credence to the activities of Bonhoeffer and Bell, the conspirators in Berlin tried again to activate the Commanders-in-Chief. General Henning von Tresckow, Chief of Staff to Marshal von Kluge, tried to draw the latter into the conspiracy. 'Day after day,' wrote Fabian von Schlabrendorff, 'von Tresckow hoped that he had convinced the Field-Marshal, only to find that he had again lapsed into indecision. Tresckow did not relent and eventually von Kluge responded to his influence.'

The outlines of the conspiracy that led to the attempted assassination of Hitler on 20 July 1944 were laid in the autumn of 1942. The plan was for the assassination to be followed immediately by a coup d'état by the Army Reserve in Germany, com-manded by General Fromm.

Canaris, whom General von Tresckow consulted, was still sceptical but for the first time did not entirely reject the idea of assassination. He would have preferred Hitler to be arrested and tried, but von Tresckow argued that it was not a matter of choice. They must act swiftly if they wanted to succeed. Once Hitler was dead, the army commanders would be released from their oath of allegiance. Canaris was won over by this argument.

After Heydrich's death, Himmler did not replace him with another man but himself took over the duties of Chief of the Reich Central Security Office. Every time Heinrich Müller of the *Gestapo* came to report to him on the conspiracy against Hitler, he gave him the same answer: 'Leave them at liberty so that you can watch their movements and discover the numbers involved. When we have discovered enough and have proof, we will strike like lightning without regard for persons or rank.' Müller passed on these orders to his subordinates, but excess of zeal in the *SD* or the *Gestapo* led them to take premature action.

In the autumn of 1942 a business man named David was arrested when preparing to leave Germany with a considerable sum in dollars. When questioned he replied that he was holding this sum on account for Dr Wilhelm Schmidhuber, the Portuguese Consul in Munich, who was attached to the *Abwehr* with the rank of a Wing-Commander of the *Luftwaffe*. The *Gestapo* informed the *SD*, and Schellenberg opened an inquiry on Schmidhuber, who was at that time in Italy. The result was that the Italian police arrested Schmidhuber at Merano and handed him over to the *Gestapo* at the German frontier. During his interrogation in Munich Schmidhuber gave confused and contradictory answers concerning his currency transfers and his relations with the *Abwehr*. The *Gestapo* threatened him and Schmidhuber collapsed, admit-ting enough for Müller to be able to report the affair back to the *Wehrmacht*. Schmidhuber was transferred to the Tegel prison in Berlin. The second part of his examination was entrusted to Dr Manfred Röder of the Air Ministry legal department, a skilful interrogator, who felt that he was on the verge of a significant discovery. For meanwhile Dr Josef Müller of the *Abwehr*'s Munich office had been interrogated by the *Gestapo* in connection with the Schmidhuber affair.

Josef Müller told after the war how a brief-case had been left in his care by Schmidhuber when he departed for Merano, containing notes on various money transactions, which gave scope for further interrogation. Müller was questioned and gave answers that appeared more truthful than Schmidhuber's obviously confused account of his money affairs. One day during his interrogation Müller heard Schmidhuber in the next room of the *Gestapo* offices making some political criticisms of Bonhoeffer and Dohnanyi. He realized that this man could easily betray the activities of their resistance group. Canaris turned up in Munich to find out about the case. Karl Süss, one of the Munich conspirators, knew that there were in the *Abwehr*'s Munich files papers which were politically compromising for Admiral Canaris and which also showed what assistance the *Abwehr* had been giving to Jews going abroad. Süss was able to arrange for Josef Müller to weed out the files before War Ministry officials arrived from Berlin to take up the *Gestapo* inquiries.

Canaris and Oster were appalled to hear that Schmidhuber had been talking to the *Gestapo* about 'a clique of generals' and had indicated that Herr von Dohnanyi had been responsible for certain discussions at the Vatican. Dr Manfred Röder, when himself on trial after the war, declared that Oster came to him at this point and asked for the *Abwehr* to be told what judicial proceedings might follow the Munich enquiry. While Oster was still with him, Röder was able to ascertain that no proceedings were intended at that time. He undertook to keep Admiral Canaris informed and learned that the papers on the inquiry would be forwarded from Munich to Berlin. Röder testified that:

when the dossiers arrived from Munich the record consisted of sixty-five to seventy pages of typewritten notes. I looked through them and passed them on to Hammerstein of the *Luftwaffe* legal branch, as it was his duty to appoint a judge to investigate further. As far as I can remember, the report from Munich dealt with currency offences and contained certain admissions by those involved. It also contained evidence according to which Admiral Canaris was alleged to have organized a *Putsch* against the Government in 1939–40 and to have worked for the secession of East Prussia. Whatever the truth of this, the dossier was very compromising for Canaris and I was relieved to hear that the case was not being left with the *Luftwaffe* legal branch and would not become my responsibility. Until 4 April that was my sole connection with this affair.

Did Canaris know at this stage what dangers to himself lay in the allegations made by Schmidhuber during interrogation in Munich? It does not seem probable. He was not informed of the details of Schmidhuber's statements and he was anyway too preoccupied between September and December 1942 with the Allied landings in North Africa to have much time or inclination to reflect on his own fate.

After the Allied landings in North Africa on 8 November 1942, the *Abwehr* was criticized for having failed to foretell what had happened. Canaris defended himself vigorously against this accusation and had good grounds for doing so. Colonel Franz Seubert, whom I met in March 1970 has supplied me with dozens of anecdotes about Admiral Canaris, under whom he was serving in Western Armies Section of the *Abwehr* in 1942. His evidence has helped me considerably on this subject. During our conversation, Colonel Seubert said something which would have intrigued any historian:

I am going to tell to you something that for various reasons I have kept secret for twenty-eight years – how I learned of the Allied landings in North Africa twenty days before they happened, and who told me.

In October 1942 I was in Libya. Admiral Canaris had sent me there because the *Gestapo* in Berlin was taking too close an interest in my actions and attitudes. One day I received a telegram from Rome signed by the Grand Mufti of Jerusalem, Hadi Amin al Husseini, asking me to come immediately to the Italian capital and meet him.

I had known this strange and picturesque character for a long time. He had fled from Baghdad to Teheran in 1941 after the failure of Rashid Ali's rebellion in April and May of that year. Before the end of 1941 he arrived in Berlin, but since Mussolini was affecting to be the sword of Islam, Hitler advised the Grand Mufti that he ought to go to Rome and negotiate with Mussolini on the basis of aligning the Arabs with the Axis forces. Admiral Canaris had known the Mufti much longer than I, since 1938 when he had made a journey to Baghdad with Major Groscurth. The Admiral found him an attractive personality, though he regarded the Mufti's political outlook as unrealistic and sterile. He knew also that the Mufti hoped to profit from divergences of view between the *Abwehr* and the German Foreign Ministry. Canaris liked to converse with intelligent people and the Mufti was certainly such a one. He was able to learn many things from him about the tortuous politics of the Middle East. They talked either in English or French, both of which languages the Mufti spoke perfectly. I often took part in these conversations.

I understood that this invitation by telegram was important and I flew at once to Rome and called on al Husseini. He thanked me for my promptness, telling me that he had some important information for me 'from a completely reliable source'. He showed me a long letter, hiding the letter-head with his hand and saying: 'I cannot disclose to you the name of the author of this letter, but read it.' It forecast an Anglo-American landing 'in the first days of November, probably between the 5th and the 10th'. It stated that the objectives were Casablanca, Fort Lyautey, Oran and Algiers, and that the invasion force was, 'nine American divisions coming from the East Coast of the United States across the Atlantic and four British divisions coming from ports in the United Kingdom'. The letter continued: 'it is an operation on a grand scale, its first objective being to penetrate the Central Mediterranean, then to destroy the Axis forces in North Africa and finally to prepare bases essential for the subsequent elimination of Italy.'

This was not the first time that I had heard of the possibility of an Allied landing in Morocco and Algiers and I had already warned my chiefs. However, in view of the number of possible objectives, it had been hitherto difficult to discern the exact enemy's intentions. The letter shown to me by the Grand Mufti was amazingly precise and should have removed from our minds all doubts about the intended operation and enabled us quickly to take the appropriate counter-measures. Unfortunately in order to carry out such measures, it would be necessary first to convince Hitler that the information was true, and I knew that Admiral Canaris would ask me: 'who is the author of this letter?' I told the Grand Mufti that his letter was of the first importance. I then explained to him that its anonymity prevented me from imparting its contents to my Chief.

The Grand Mufti began by refusing to disclose any name to me but at last he gave way. Asking me on my word of honour as an officer not to reveal it to anyone but Admiral Canaris, with the proviso that he should not reveal it to the Führer, the Grand Mufti handed me the letter so that I could read the letter-head. The mysterious author was none other than Mohammed V, Sultan of Morocco. In writing to his friend, he must have known that the Grand Mufti would warn us. Thus the Sultan made common cause with the Moroccan nationalists who were working with the *Abwehr* and Schellenberg's *SD* Service, believing that a German victory would mean the liberation of their country. Leaders of the Istiglal Party were collaborating with the *Abwehr*, as were some Algerian nationalists. Mahamedi Said, trained by Lahousen's Section II and parachuted into Algeria, was one of them. He was to become a leader of the National Liberation Front and after independence one of the Ministers of Colonel Boumédienne, the Algerian President.

I commented to Colonel Seubert that Sultan Mohammed Sidi ben Youssef had been decorated after the war by General de Gaulle as a Companion of the Liberation and had moreover been supported for years in his struggle for independence by the governments in London and Washington, whose secrets he was thus betraying.

Colonel Seubert pursued his narrative of the events of October 1942, saying that he had decided that he must fly immediately to Berlin and report to Admiral Canaris. The Admiral's face shone when he heard from Seubert the contents of the Sultan's letter to the Grand Mufti of Jerusalem.

'This is exact confirmation of the information that I have received from Algeciras and Tangiers', he exclaimed. 'They have just reported to me a strong British naval force at anchor off Gibraltar, consisting of a battleship, two aircraft carriers, five cruisers and twenty destroyers. This points to immediate operations on a grand scale in the Western Mediterranean.'

The little Admiral was in high spirits on receiving proof that his *Abwehr* men were equal to their task; but then a shadow came over his face, his shoulders sagged and he said in the saddest of voices:

'But they won't believe me at General Headquarters, Seubert. Even if I revealed your source to "Emil" he would not believe it. He is convinced that if there is an Allied operation in the Mediterranean, it will be against Tripolitania, or more probably the Balkans, but certainly not North Africa. Never mind! I must go and warn them all the same.'

On the following day Canaris was received by Keitel, who laughed in his face at the report of an operation in the Western Mediterranean. Thereupon Canaris sought an interview with Hitler but did not succeed in arranging it. He asked Keitel to ensure that his report was forwarded to the Führer and obtained his consent to this with some difficulty. That night Keitel informed Canaris in the presence of Jodl, who had just come out of Hitler's room with him, that the Führer did not attach any importance to his report.

'But my views on this must be accepted', insisted Canaris. 'If the Führer doubts my word and my information, he must be more stupid than I imagined him to be.'

General Jodl nervously snapped back:

'I know the Führer better than you do. He is a great chief of the rarest quality. His knowledge, his intelligence, his rhetoric, his will-power bring him out on top in all discussions. He combines the gift of logic with clarity, and his intuitive gifts often permit him to foresee events . . .'

'But mislead him, sometimes,' interrupted the Admiral calmly. 'That is so,' conceded Jodl. 'He is sometimes mistaken. But believe me, I really admired him during last winter when he put his faith in the Eastern Front and bent all his energy to stabilizing it. For don't you remember, Admiral, you yourself said then that a catastrophe was imminent, as with Napoleon in 1812.'

'And now? If you don't withdraw the Paulus army behind the Don before winter and so shorten the front and permit the troops to pass the winter in endurable quarters, the 6th Army is destined to certain destruction.'

'What you say about the Eastern Front is right,' replied Jodl. 'The Quartermaster General, Eduard Wagner, shares this view, but we cannot convince the Führer. I don't understand him. Two days ago he spoke to me of Stalingrad, using odd phrases like "supply centre", "holy city of our civilization, sullied by Bolshevism". I could not follow his train of thought, but on the strategic plane I know that he is making a mistake.'

'I agree,' rejoined Canaris, 'though I have not your experience in strategic matters. Also I think that you are committing a grave error – you, he and Marshal Keitel – in not taking seriously the report that I have just made to you. You talk of the Führer's military genius, but this time, once again, he falls far short of genius. You are about to have a powerful Allied second front open in North Africa, which will be an excellent springboard for an assault on Italy.'

Marshal Keitel replied:

'A landing in Africa is less suitable for an Anglo-American attack on Italy than a landing in Sardinia and Siciliy.'

General Jodl, who appeared to find this conversation tedious, interrupted them brusquely.

'Admiral, it is no use pressing the matter. The Führer has said to Marshal Keitel in my presence: "Canaris is a fool. He swallows everything that the Americans feed him. Give me a rest from *Abwehr* reports which are always defeatist and always wrong. When I make a plan, Canaris always smells disaster, but our victories prove that my intuition is much better than his." The Führer is right. Remember, Admiral, how you warned us of disaster before the *Anschluss*, before we marched into the Sudetenland, when we attacked Poland, before we attacked France and Britain, before our Balkans war and our attack on Russia, and what happened? The opposite of what you expected! No, Admiral, you see everything in too sombre a light.'

'Maybe, maybe', said Canaris wearily. 'What will be will be! I have at least warned you all.'

Canaris saluted the two military chiefs and withdrew. He was met in the officers' mess by Colonel Heinz Schmalschläger, head of the *Abwehr* at General Headquarters, who saw Canaris's downcast expression and realized what had happened. They had a cup of tea without saying more than a few words. Then Canaris got up, saying: 'Let's go. There's nothing more for us to do in this mad-house.'

As they came out of the mess, they saw Hitler no more than twenty yards away, pacing up and down with an ADC.

'A pretty pair for your sights at that distance', mused Schmalschläger.

'Have a go then,' rejoined Canaris.

Neither of them was armed, and this was no more than an instinctive reaction without serious meaning, but it showed what they thought of the man who was leading Germany towards destruction. Canaris knew that Hitler obsessively resisted all advice against risks and dangers. Canaris's own fatalism inclined him to await the dénouement, but his humane instincts were outraged by the suffering and misery that would precede and follow the collapse of Germany's military power.

When it became known on 8 November that the British and Americans had landed on the North African coast, there was lively reaction in Berlin. There was amazement in Foreign Ministry circles and in the army. Canaris was away at the time in Copenhagen with Piekenbrock, but was recalled urgently to Berlin.

His agents in Morocco had fallen back on the international zone of Tangiers where they continued to be supplied with information by the Moroccan nationalists. On 11 November 1942 Canaris received from them the following telegram:

Prince Mohammed, brother of the Caliph of Tetuan, has asked, on instructions from the Caliph, for a declaration from Berlin concerning the independence of Morocco like that made in the case of the other Arab countries. At this moment there need be no fear of offending France, or injuring Spanish interests. Moroccans who have long hoped for German support are embittered by Roosevelt's declaration guaranteeing the existence of French Morocco. The people are reserved in their attitude towards the disembarking American troops, and so is the Pasha of Marrakesh with whom the Caliph is in touch and who has more influence than the Sultan.

Other *Abwehr* reports followed from Tangiers, suggesting that the Americans were beginning to appreciate the case for an independent Morocco, while the British favoured the idea of a Protectorate. The Sultan dined with Roosevelt at Anfa on 23 January 1943, accompanied by his son Hassan, who was to succeed him. They came loaded with gifts, a gold-hilted dagger for President Roosevelt and a tiara and golden bracelets for Mrs Roosevelt. After dinner the President offered his guest a photograph of himself in a fine silver frame. At table the Sultan sat on the right of the President, on whose left sat Mr Winston Churchill. An animated conversation, in French, developed between Roosevelt and Mohammed Sidi Youssef, about Morocco's resources and the future prospects of the Cherifian lands.

Mohammed V spoke of his desire to modernize his country and Roosevelt responded by offering American technical assistance, to the visible annoyance of Churchill who found himself out of this conversation. The President went on to discuss the war and the operations to take place in Tunisia. What the Moroccans discovered from the American President in the course of this dinner will never be known for certain, but what we do know is that the Sultan drew up a long memorandum about the dinner at Anfa, which was sent through the German Consul in Tetuan (Spanish Morocco) to Admiral Canaris. The Admiral presented it personally to Hitler in Keitel's presence. Colonel Lahousen noted in the *Abwehr* diary that 'Hitler gave orders to classify the letter from the Sultan of Morocco as "Most Secret". It contains information of the highest strategic and political importance.'

What remains unknown is how much of what Sultan Mohammed heard at the dinner party was transmitted to the Germans and how much he kept to himself. 'Do not accuse the Sultan of treason', Colonel Seubert concluded with a smile. 'He had been giving information to the *Abwehr* for a long time past, but in the case of sovereigns and heads of state, contact with intelligence services is not espionage or treason – it is high politics'.

The same could be said about the Grand Mufti of Jerusalem, who in exchange for the support of the Arab world for the Nazi cause, claimed from Hitler that those Arab countries still under British and French protection should be liberated. On 9 December

1942 the Grand Mufti had a conversation with Canaris, who had just arrived from Madrid. Colonel Lahousen and Franz Seubert were also present. He proposed to the Germans that he should use his influence with the Moslem countries of North Africa to win their support for the Axis 'in exchange for the kind of liberty that Egypt obtained from Britain in the Treaty of 1936. Germany could have bases in these countries'. He suggested going to Tunis and seeing the Bey, to set in motion 'a large-scale revolt in Algeria and French Morocco'. He asked Canaris to accompany him to the Tunisian capital and also asked that the Arab Legion, formerly stationed in Greece, and moved from there to the Caucasus, should be transferred by the Germans to Tunisia. The Grand Mufti spoke of Arab leaders who would work with him, 'among them Habib Bourguiba, who is in prison in Marseilles and has much sympathy for the Axis cause'.

When being informed of these proposals, Hitler drew his portrait of the Grand Mufti:

He does not mix sentiment with politics. With his fair hair and blue eyes he gives the impression, in spite of his sly face, of having more than one Aryan ancestor. It is possible that there is the best blood of the Romans somewhere in his distant lineage. During our conversations he showed himself to be a real fox: to gain time for reflection he had some statements translated not only into French but in Arabic as well. He is so cautious that he immediately commits to paper any proposal that he considers important. When he speaks he appears literally to weigh every word he utters. His superior intelligence puts him on a level with the Japanese.

Despite this qualified praise, Hitler rejected the Grand Mufti's plans on Ribbentrop's advice who thought them untimely. It was fortunate for the Allies that Hitler did not seize this opportunity. As for Bourguiba, whom the Germans released from imprisonment in France, he went first to Rome to regain favour with the Italian régime, and then to Tunis where his activities had only a minimal influence on the course of events. When the German and Italian forces were routed, Bourguiba did not linger in Tunis for the arrival of the Allies, but moved to Cairo to await better days. Bourguiba left in the company of other *Abwehr* contact men, among them Anwar el Sadat, an intimate friend of Gamal Abdu Nasser and Aly Sabry, who rose subsequently to the positions of President and Vice-President in the United Arab Republic.

The first message that reached Canaris when he returned from

Copenhagen on 8 November 1942, after the Allied landings in North Africa was from Marshal Keitel. He was to come at once to the Führer's Headquarters at Winnitsa in the Ukraine. When Keitel saw him, he fired his question:

'The power in the Mediterranean depends today, as it did in 1940, on the behaviour of the French navy. Admiral Darlan is now in Algiers. The Toulon fleet is commanded by Admiral de Laborde. What will that fleet do?'

'If it joined ours, the Anglo-Americans would not be able to hold out for long in North Africa, but . . .'

'But what will happen?'

'The Toulon fleet will not join us. Laborde will scuttle his ships rather than work with us. Not that he is in principle opposed to such military co-operation, but he is unconditionally loyal to Marshal Pétain, and as long as Pétain gives him no orders he will remain at anchor'.

'Can we not force him to join our side?'

'Certainly not! If we did he would scuttle his ships'.

'The Duce, Ciano and Pierre Laval have to come here for a conference with the Führer and I wanted your opinion first. For once it agrees with what the Führer has told me. He has no illusions about the rôle of the Vichy Government and he has decided to apply the "Attila Plan" which we drew up in December 1940 and which is now named Operation Anton – the occupation of southern France and seizure of the fleet in Toulon'.

As far as Spain was concerned, Canaris had warned Franco of German preparations in July 1942, when Hitler had returned to the idea of capturing Gibraltar. Franco had thereupon set up concrete defence positions on all roads leading through the Pyrenees to prevent or hamper a German advance into Spain. This activity was reported by Schellenberg's secret service, and in consequence Operation Felix was revised, becoming an advance into Spain in the face of opposition by the Spanish forces and was renamed Operation Ilona or Isabella. Keitel now referred to this plan.

'Perhaps the Führer will also consider Operation Ilona.'

'Against Spain? Why?'

'Because your friend Franco is not trustworthy. He could very easily go over to the Allies.'

'I don't believe it,' replied Canaris emphatically. 'The Spaniards fear that they will be dragged into a war against their will is not based only on any position of strength that the Anglo-Americans may soon possess, but also on the possibility that Germany could find it in her interest to take our enemies in the flank in Africa by crossing Spain and closing the Straits of Gibraltar.'

'The Führer is not thinking of that for the moment. He even said to me this morning that it would be better for the conduct of the war if Spain remained neutral. In fact it would be a very heavy military and economic burden to us to invade Spain. Nevertheless, I can tell you that Operation Felix, renamed Operation Ilona, has been taken out of the files again. In the meantime I will ask you to do everything possible to extend the *Abwehr*'s control of the southern zone of France and to infiltrate the fleet at Toulon. We must find out what Admiral de Laborde is thinking.'

By 11 November the twenty-fourth anniversary of the 1918 armistice, the remainder of France was entirely occupied by the *Wehrmacht*, with the exception of the naval base at Toulon, Hitler having himself asked the two French Admirals, Marquis and de Laborde, to give him their word of honour 'not to take any action against the Axis powers and to defend Toulon with all their strength against the Anglo-Saxons and the French forces opposed to the Government of France.' However, on the night of 19 November Hitler signed an order 'to take possession of the French fleet of Toulon intact'. On 27 November at 4:30 AM General Hausser's 1st *SS* Armoured Corps began the assault on Toulon. At 4:57 AM Admiral de Laborde was alerted and gave the order to clear the decks for action. At 5:20 AM the first German armoured vehicles forced the gates of the Toulon arsenal. At 5:29 AM Admiral de Laborde gave the order 'Carry out scuttling immediately.' At 5:45 AM scuttling operations were put into effect on all ships, thus denying the Germans the use of the French fleet.

The battle for Stalingrad was turning into a disaster for the Germans. In North Africa the British and Americans were pausing for breath, settling in and discussing the future with Admiral Darlan, General Giraud and General Nogués, while preparing their offensive against Tunisia. Hitler did not believe that the offensive would be in that direction, but against Spain instead. It was therefore 'of the greatest strategic importance to occupy the entire Iberian peninsula, including Portugal'. He considered this the only way to intensify the U-boat war and 'neutralize' the Allied move into North Africa.

Canaris went to Nice where he spent two days with his close

friend General Cesare Amé, Chief of the Italian Intelligence
Service. On his return he was once more summoned to General
Headquarters, where Hitler, in the presence of Keitel and Ribbentrop, directed him to return to Spain. He was to engage his friends
the Spanish military chiefs in talks and Franco as well, to discover
'the Caudillo's intentions in the event of Spain being invaded by
Anglo-American forces'. Hitler did not mention Operation Ilona
to Canaris and Canaris did not betray that he knew all about it.

An incident then took place that might have had immediate
and serious consequences for Admiral Canaris. Whether it was
Hitler's tone or the form of order given to him, or for some other
reason relating to their differing views on Spain, Canaris faced
the Führer and boiled with a fury that was difficult to conceal.
Moreover when Hitler invited him to dinner, Canaris im-
pulsively declined on the pretext of service duties. Hitler looked
surprised but did not insist or make the invitation mandatory. It
was the only time that a serving military officer had been known to
refuse an invitation from the Führer of the Third Reich. Canaris
then took leave of Hitler and the petrified Keitel, nodded goodbye to Dr Picker and, at his short, quick pace, quietly left Headquarters for the car that would take him to the air field.

Accompanied by Colonel Lahousen the Admiral crossed the
Pyrenees to Madrid. He was aware that Germany's setbacks
would change the character of the war. Peace and war had until
then been directed, even dictated, by the Reich; now the course
of the war would be set by the Allies. There was fierce German
resistance still in Stalingrad, but Paulus was on the defensive and
encircled; he would not hold out for long. In North Africa
Rommel could not work miracles without reinforcements. All he
could do was to delay the evacuation of the *Afrika Korps* and the
Italians. In view of all this Canaris felt that he was going to
Madrid less to sound out his Spanish friends on their intentions
than to examine with them how Spain, without enraging the
Führer, could avoid being drawn into the war on the Axis side.

They arrived in Madrid on 7 December, a bitterly cold evening
with the snow crackling under-foot, and went immediately to a
meeting with General Martinez Campos and General Vigon.
The two generals advised him, in view of the political nature of the
discussion, to seek an appointment either with Franco himself or
with Count Gomez Jordana, who had preceded Colonel Beigbeder

as Foreign Minister and now succeeded Serrano Suñer to that post. General Campos confided:

'With regard to our national territory, the Caudillo will only, I think, make one concession. If the Allies attack Spain, he will permit German troops to cross – I repeat cross – the country to enter Morocco. I am quite certain that he would refuse to have German troops fight in the defence of Spain itself; his reason is that none but Spaniards have the right to die for Spain. And if the Germans attacked Spain, we would resist to the last man.'

Canaris explained to his friends that he had really no desire to go to the Santa Cruz Palace for a talk with Count Jordana. He feared that there would be fresh difficulties with Ribbentrop, who always reacted strongly to other organizations encroaching on his diplomatic field, especially the *Abwehr*, which he detested. Canaris was all the more cautious since his good friend von Stohrer had been replaced as Ambassador by Helmuth von Moltke, a conforming Nazi with whom he was not on good terms. General Campos therefore arranged an unobtrusive meeting with Jordana by inviting the Foreign Minister to tea at his home, when Canaris and his staff were there.

On the following day Colonel Lahousen was astonished to be called in by the Admiral after lunch and asked to help draft a telegram to Berlin which the Admiral dictated to him. It was a report on a second interview with Jordana, the official one, which was not to take place until three hours later. According to this text Jordana stated to Canaris that Spain would defend herself against any powers that attempted to violate her frontiers and would fight to the last man to maintain her independence. Canaris added that the Spanish might make war on the Axis side if the Eastern Front were stabilized, Tunisia successfully defended and several other conditions met, such as a reconciliation of the Reich with the Christian churches and some assurance that National Socialism would not develop into a kind of Western Bolshevism.

There were seven such conditions in all, which Lahousen found hardly credible as he wrote them out, but when Count Jordana arrived, Lahousen noticed that Canaris showed him the draft telegram and explained it to him in Spanish. When Jordana left, Canaris called Lahousen over and said:

'You can now put that telegram into cipher and send it off.'

'Without changing a word?'

'Without changing a word.'

This kind of tactic may appear questionable, but it was characteristic of the way Canaris worked. He had not the slightest doubt what the Spanish Minister's answer would be. His own sympathies for Spain led him to regard such an answer as the most natural. Canaris was anxious that Jordana's reply should be a plain warning to Berlin against a German invasion. He could not tell Jordana exactly what the German position was, but he could furnish him with a ready-made reply to the German questions that was in the right sense and most likely to serve the Caudillo's purpose.

There was a predictable explosion of indignation at Hitler's Headquarters and the Foreign Ministry at Berlin, which Canaris allowed to subside while he effaced himself on a tour of the Eastern Front. During this time he visited his friend General Munos Grandes, in command of the Spanish volunteer legion on the Russian front, the Blue Division, to whom he told the story of the telegram. He returned from Russia not to Berlin but to Madrid and then called his home in Berlin. The German and Spanish monitoring services were both dumbfounded that this long telephone conversation between Madrid and Schlachtensee consisted entirely of enquiries about the health, behaviour and diet of his two dachshunds. What an odd Chief of Intelligence, the monitoring officers thought, as they read over the transcript. There are numerous such stories about Canaris and his pets, and about his general affection for animals. The *Abwehr* drivers had orders to avoid running over animals, and at least once the Admiral risked overturning his own car to avoid a stray dog crossing the road.

On 31 December 1942 Canaris was in Algeciras in the company of Piekenbrock and Lahousen, not living in the Hotel Reina Cristina, but in the villa of the *Abwehr* chief for the area, situated above the port with a magnificent view from its garden of the Rock of Gibraltar. With the best optical instruments that Germany could produce, a day-and-night watch was kept from this spot on the movements of Allied ships to and from Gibraltar through the Straits.

That New Year's Eve, the Chief of the *Abwehr* put on a cook's apron and a chef's cap, taking part in the roasting of the turkey and the preparation of all kinds of Spanish dishes. He had not enjoyed himself so much for a long time. Over the meal he could relax and engage in good-humoured conversation, shaking off his heavy responsibilities and forgetting the latent threat of *Gestapo* action against himself and his Services. He was jovial and paternal in his manner and, to the surprise of his staff, even produced a few conjuring tricks before retiring to bed at his regular hour of 10 PM. The younger officers went on to a ball at the Reina Cristina Hotel, noticing but mutually ignoring the officers of the Royal Navy and the RAF who had come over from Gibraltar and vying with them for Spanish partners on the dance floor.

Hitler continued to believe that the Allies would land in Spain, and despite the rebuff from Franco that was so distinct in the last telegram sent by Canaris, he pushed ahead with preparations for military operations in Spain. Meanwhile January, February and March went by without the least indication that the Allies were about to invade Spain or Portugal. At the beginning of April, under the impact of defeat in Tunisia and Paulus' catastrophic surrender at Stalingrad, Hitler suddenly lost interest in Spain. Admiral Doenitz emphasized strongly to Hitler on 11 April the need to occupy the Iberian Peninsula and close the Straits of Gibraltar. Doenitz admitted, however, that the German plan could only succeed with Spanish consent, and Hitler retorted that the Spaniards did not consent. He gave the Canaris telegram of December 1942 to read and a long report sent on 22 January amplifying it.

Doenitz returned to the subject on 14 May, urging that an occupation of Spain and Portugal would break the net that the Royal Navy had cast round the German U-boat fleet, which at that time could only operate from bases as far south as Gascony. Hitler silenced him, shouting:

'There can be no question of occupying Spain without the consent of the Spaniards. They are the one really stubborn Latin people and they would harass the *Wehrmacht* in the rear with guerilla warfare, as they did to Napoleon I. All the reports from Admiral Canaris, who has known them well for the past twenty-five years, are firm on this point, and for once I believe him, because there is no better authority on this subject. It might have been possible in 1940 to have persuaded the Spanish to accept a German presence, but it is quite certain that the Italian invasion of Greece in the autumn of that year was a severe shock to Spain. It was proved impossible since then to get them on our side, except in the sending of General Muños Grandes and the Spanish Azul Legion to the Eastern Front. No, there can be no further question of occupying Spain and taking Gibraltar.'

That was the end of Operation Felix-Ilona-Isabella, though the plan was not officially abandoned till 14 June 1943. In his biography of the Caudillo, Brian Crozier describes Franco as having won the day in his last confrontation with the Nazi dictator by his unyielding attitude. It may be added that without the constant and effective aid of his friend Admiral Canaris, Franco would perhaps not have succeeded in finally checking Hitler. A grateful Spain might have erected a memorial to 'the little Admiral'.

28
The *Gestapo* strikes

The *Gestapo* inquiry into the case of Schmidhuber, the *Abwehr* man in Munich, was meanwhile being pursued. Manfred Röder, the *Luftwaffe* legal officer and Franz Sonderegger of the *Gestapo* were jointly in charge of it. The *Gestapo* dossier on 'the Black Chapel' grew steadily thicker. Canaris felt that Röder, Göring's man, hard and intolerant, was more of a menace than the *Gestapo*. How could he be rid of him?

The respite given to the *Abwehr* since Heydrich's death seemed to run out at the beginning of 1943. The Reichsführer *SS* had by then decided that it was time to appoint a successor to 'the man with the iron heart'. His choice fell on Ernst Kaltenbrunner, who had been a lawyer in Linz, had entered the clandestine Austrian *SS* and had become Chief of Police in the so-called East Mark. Kaltenbrunner was not so deep a villain as his predecessor, but he was a fanatical Nazi, an enthusiastic admirer of Hitler, devoted to him personally and utterly convinced that Hitler's star was in the ascendant. In February 1943 Kaltenbrunner demanded a meeting with Canaris, whom he did not know personally, and this was arranged for 22 February at the Hotel Regina in Munich. Erwin Lahousen, who already knew and detested Kaltenbrunner, accompanied the Admiral to this meeting and has given me an interesting account of it.

The Admiral was nervous, almost intimidated, during the first part of their meeting by this big rough-looking man with duel scars on his cheeks. He did not get on well with tall men and seemed ill at ease. Kaltenbrunner's slow and heavy speech was indicative of an inferior intelligence and affected Canaris's nerves. Matters were not improved when Canaris referred to the case of Hans and Sophie Scholl, two young Munich students beheaded that day for having distributed at Munich University leaflets attacking the régime. This incident aroused much feeling in the city, Canaris remarked, but Kaltenbrunner's brutal rejoinder was that 'these vermin deserved nothing else, and their three accomplices will suffer the same fate, but my *Gestapo* men will work on them first to discover the names of the others involved.' Canaris was horrified; Heydrich, he thought, had at least kept up appearances. He found it more and more difficult to continue the conversation, and confined himself to banal remarks about the need for close co-operation. However, this subject led Kaltenbrunner to criticize sharply the *Abwehr* chief in Vienna, Count Rudolf von Marogna-Redwitz, a personal friend of the Admiral.

Kaltenbrunner alleged that according to his information the Count maintained contacts with the Conservative opposition in Austria, and was closely in touch with the Hungarian Intelligence Service, which was pro-British in outlook. Both Canaris and Lahousen knew that these accusations were well founded and that they implied a threat to the *Abwehr* itself. Lahousen saw a sudden change come over his Chief, who began quickly and easily to allay Kaltenbrunner's suspicions with a series of well-presented explanations. Lahousen felt himself sweating slightly at the risks that this discussion entailed, but he noticed that Kaltenbrunner appeared to be satisfied about Marogna-Redwitz's activities though not accepting that everything was quite so harmless as Canaris made it appear. The Admiral, as they left the Hotel Regina, turned to Lahousen with an appalled look and asked:

'Did you see his hands? The paws of a murderer!'

Canaris breathed a little more easily after this meeting. He would force himself, despite his physical revulsion, to maintain direct contact with Kaltenbrunner and observe his opponent's activities. These tactics were, however, of little avail. The web already woven around Canaris and the *Abwehr* by Heydrich, now taken over by Kaltenbrunner, would steadily tighten.

A few days before meeting Kaltenbrunner, Admiral Canaris went to the Eastern Front and called at the Headquarters of the Central Army Group, commanded by Marshal von Kluge, to take part in a conference of General Staff officers. He brought with him an important delegation from Berlin, consisting of Hans Piekenbrock, Erwin Lahousen, Egbert von Bentivegni, Hans von Dohnanyi and Fabian von Schlabrendorff. Schlabrendorff had emphatically expressed his point of view to Canaris before they left Berlin:

'Only Hitler's death will put an end to this mad slaughter of people in the concentration camps and in the armies fighting this criminal war. It is either Hitler's life or the lives of hundreds of thousands. If ever assassination was justified, it is now.'

Canaris, still tied by his Christian convictions and high moral standards, had never been entirely reconciled to the idea of assassination, although he had recently found it difficult to reject the arguments for it. At last he was coming round to the same way of thinking as Beck, Olbricht and Henning von Tresckow, Kluge's Chief of Staff, though without wishing to participate in the preparations being made within the *Abwehr*.

The official conference at Smolensk was followed by a secret conference, with two purposes: firstly to sound out Marshal von Kluge on his attitude to a coup d'état; secondly to make arrangements for an attempt on Hitler's life in the next few weeks.

Canaris had a long conversation with Hans von Kluge in the presence of General Henning von Tresckow. The Field-Marshal, nicknamed the 'clever (*Kluge*) Hans', was a disappointment to the conspirators. On the return journey Canaris remarked to Lahousen and Dohnanyi:

'Our generals have cold feet.'

But Dohnanyi himself was much more satisfied, having spoken with Tresckow, Schlabrendorff and Gersdorff far into the night. Tresckow's plan to lure Hitler to Marshal von Kluge's headquarters and place a time-bomb in the plane that would take him back to his own headquarters at Rastenburg. When the bomb exploded in mid-air it would be easy to attribute Hitler's death to an accident.

The choice of a particular time-bomb had to be considered, and in his Section II Lahousen possessed specimens of Allied sabotage material parachuted into occupied territories by the RAF. The *Abwehr* had a certain number of British time-fuses of a silent type. To set them going a capsule had to be broken, after which a corrosive acid worked on the release mechanism of a detonator. The time factor depended on the thickness of a wire retaining the striker pin. Lahousen took with him to the Smolensk conference three such time-bombs, with ten-minute, half-hour and two-hour fuses.

After many hesitations the Führer agreed to visit Marshal von Kluge on 13 March. Kluge had not been let into the conspiracy. Von Tresckow and Schlabrendorff prepared the attempt, though neither of them had a specialized knowledge of the use of explosives. They tested the equipment that Lahousen had left with them and found it remarkably efficient, though the intense cold of the Russian winter was apt to have a delaying action on the acid fuses. Von Tresckow placed in a brief-case two bombs disguised to look like bottles of brandy.

Hitler arrived on 13 March, accompanied by his staff and his personal physician, Dr Morell. After an inspection of the troops and a meeting between Hitler and Kluge, there was a lunch in the officers' mess at Smolensk. Before it began, General von Tresckow asked Colonel Heinz Brandt to take back with him to Rastenburg two bottles of special brandy for General Helmuth Stieff. Brandt agreed to do this, and Schlabrendorff thereupon informed Dohnanyi in Berlin that Operation Flash was about to begin, so that Oster and his friends could be ready to seize strategic points in the capital.

After the lunch Schlabrendorff picked up the brief-case containing the two bottles and followed Hitler to the airport. The flight from Smolensk to Rastenburg would last two hours. The two bombs were set to explode after half an hour. While the Führer was saying farewell to the assembled officers, Schlabrendorff at a sign from Tresckow compressed the acid capsules, setting the time-fuses in motion. He then handed the brief-case to Colonel Brandt as he embarked. Escorted by a flight of fighter aircraft, Hitler's plane took off three minutes later.

There was nothing more to do but wait for the news. Schlabrendorff put through a call to Berlin to say that the first phase of Operation Flash had begun. The 'accident' would occur when the aircraft was over Minsk. The conspirators believed that one of the escorting fighters would report the destruction of the Führer's aircraft. 'One hour gone already,' exclaimed von Tresckow, 'and no message!' After two hours he telephoned Rastenburg and was told that the Führer's aircraft had landed safely.

Von Tresckow and Schlabrendorff were overwhelmed by this setback, which they were at a loss to understand. They were able to inform their group in Berlin that the operation had miscarried. Now it was vital to recover the ill-fated brief-case. Tresckow telephoned Brandt and asked him as naturally as he could to keep the brief-case, as there had been a mistake. He explained that he would be sending Schlabrendorff with the regular courier to Rastenburg on the following day and that he would retrieve it. Brandt appeared to suspect nothing, and when next day Schlabrendorff entered Brandt's office, he broke into a cold sweat when the

Colonel carelessly picked up the brief-case and swung it over the desk to him. Schlabrendorff took the next train to Berlin and defused the bombs in the solitude of his sleeping compartment. He discovered that the striking pin had been released by the acid eating through the wire but that the detonator (affected by the intense cold of the Russian winter) had not reacted. Hitler had the luck of the devil on his side.

While Schlabrendorff was travelling to Berlin on the night sleeper, the persistent Röder was continuing to interrogate Schmidhuber. Arthur Nebe knew that the *Gestapo* was preparing for a blow against the *Abwehr*. He informed Canaris himself, though he emphasized that Himmler had not yet decided to act, as 'he is afraid of you'. Canaris smiled, as if to say, 'I know why', but he did not comment, simply replying:

'Clearly an attack on the *Abwehr* at this moment could have considerable repercussions, and Himmler must question whether the already strained relations between the *SS* military formations and the army could survive such a test. I know that Schellenberg and Kaltenbrunner would like to speed things up, but Himmler is keeping the brake on. We must redouble our precautions.'

Canaris's analysis was correct, but he was unlucky with his precautions. After Nebe had left he gave an order that Colonel Oster was to destroy all compromising papers. Oster and Dohnanyi knew that General Beck was not in favour of destroying records which might be useful after a coup d'état. Neither did they imagine that the *Gestapo* would one day officially search the *Abwehr* offices. Canaris too did not seriously believe that it would come to that. To a large extent his authority shielded his subordinate officers, but the final decision on the right of the Reich Security Service to search a military establishment lay with Keitel.

Dohnanyi, a serious and conscientious man, nevertheless removed to the headquarters of the Army Command at Zossen the most important and most compromising documents in the *Abwehr* Central Office, the bulk of the evidence against the Nazi régime. They were locked in a large box provided by Colonel Groscurth and consigned to a disused cellar. Dohnanyi, however, kept the key to the Zossen box in his own box in ZB Section of the *Abwehr* Central Office in Berlin. The key was attached to a file containing the reference numbers of current papers in the registry and code names of official documents. This reference file also contained the code names of the papers in the Zossen box.

When Röder had completed the dossier on Schmidhuber, he submitted the case to the military court. A few days later the head of the Army legal division, Dr Lehmann, having studied the charges preferred against Dr Müller, Dohnanyi and Pastor Bonhoeffer, reassured Admiral Canaris that the consequences should not be unduly serious. He wished to withdraw the case from the *Gestapo*, although the inquiry was not yet terminated. On Sunday 4 April Canaris informed Dohnanyi and Bonhoeffer of this by telephone.

On that same Sunday there was a meeting between Kaltenbrunner, Müller of the *Gestapo*, Schellenberg and the *Gestapo* investigator, Franz Sondereggar, at which it was decided to go into action. The *Gestapo*'s plan was extraordinarily clever. They created deliberate confusion between the case of Schmidhuber, who was alleged to have trafficked in foreign currency for his own profit, and another case of Jews being smuggled out of Germany disguised as *Abwehr* agents who received the equivalent of their German property from Reich funds abroad. It would be easy, once the proceedings began, to move from a criminal to a political inquiry.

Keitel authorized the arrest of those *Abwehr* members who had been compromised over currency offences. He later denied this to the Nuremberg International Tribunal, but Kaltenbrunner contradicted him. What happened was that on Sunday 5 April Röder telephoned Canaris and informed him that he was going to search Dohnanyi's office with Sonderegger. When he arrived at the *Abwehr* offices Röder produced a search warrant. Although appalled at this intrusion into the inner precincts of his service, Canaris did not lose his *sang-froid*. He also felt that after his warnings about compromising papers to Oster and Dohnanyi, they would have taken the necessary precautions. He therefore conducted Röder and Sonderegger to Group ZB and General Oster came out of his office and followed them.

Dohnanyi rose to meet the four of them as they entered his room. Röder displayed his search warrant and asked Dohnanyi to open his desk drawers and unlock his safe. Dohnanyi hesitated and seemed to be searching for his keys, which he at length pulled out of his trouser pocket. While Sonderegger stood guard, Röder examined the papers and the dossiers. The *Gestapo* men noticed that Dohnanyi was trying to draw Oster's attention to some papers on the top of his desk. Oster understood and made a clumsy move to take them away, but Sonderegger intervened and Oster had no choice but to hand them over.

These were notes made out for General Beck, informing him that on 9 April Pastor Bonhoeffer would be accompanying Dr Josef Müller to Rome. There was another note about a meeting with a Jesuit official in the Vatican to discuss Pope Pius XIII's peace message. All these notes were marked with an O in coloured pencil. Röder at once impounded all the pencils on Oster's desk.

The search lasted two hours, but Röder, despite his zeal, had missed what would have been the most important discovery. For a moment he held in his hand the file of papers to which was attached the key of the strong box in Zossen. He replaced it, thinking that they were normal service documents. However, the search had been productive enough for Röder to put Dohnanyi under arrest and have him committed to the Tegel military prison, where he was soon joined by his brother-in-law, Bonhoeffer, and Dr Josef Müller, while Christine Dohnanyi, *née* Bonhoeffer, and Marie, Dr Müller's wife, were committed to the Charlottenburg prison for women. Oster was placed under house arrest and forbidden to return to the *Abwehr* offices or to have any contact with officers of his service. He was for a time allowed to remain at liberty, but was closely watched, so that he was unable to continue to take part in the conspiracy against Hitler.

Far from being cowed by the *Gestapo*'s coup, made cunningly by using Röder as a front man, Canaris was spurred into activity. Röder, sensing that he was onto something big, gave himself airs, bullied the witnesses and boasted of his personal relations with Göring. His behaviour was odious, but his inquiry did not make any progress. Canaris, aware of the danger, became extremely active and was helped in frustrating the inquiry by Röder's own clumsiness.

Dr Josef Müller, who survived these perils and gave evidence in 1948 during the course of an inquiry into Röder's rôle, described the method of interrogation in the *SS* prisons.

'I was arrested on 5 April 1943', he related, 'at the *Abwehr*'s Munich offices in the presence of the Chief of the office, Lieutenant-Colonel Ficht. I learned that at the same time my wife had been arrested at home. I gained time by asking Colonel Ficht to telephone Admiral Canaris to inform him of my arrest. I also insisted that as a member of a military organization I had the right to a military investigation. In this way I avoided a *Gestapo* prison and was confined in the Ludwigstrasse military prison, where I was at first well treated. After several days things changed and I was continuously disturbed in the night by warders flashing bright lights at me.

Müller was taken under close military escort to Tegel prison in Berlin, one of his escort directing the prison authorities in his presence 'to see that the execution chamber is in working order'. His first interrogation by Röder was brief and related to Müller's work in Munich and his relations with Dohnanyi, but 160 hours of interrogation followed, with Röder threatening, shouting and bluffing in turn, though the *Gestapo* officer Sonderegger behaved better, giving Müller time to reflect on his questions, and even permitted him to destroy one document of a highly compromising character. Sonderegger explained to him that Röder's annoyance arose from not being able to get Müller to admit the existence of a military opposition, directed by a clique of generals.

Röder arranged for Müller to be confronted with Oster in circumstances that suggested that Oster too was under arrest, but this trick did not really help the inquiry.

I admitted that I had taken soundings in Rome [declared Müller] but added that I had seen the impossibility of engaging in peace negotiations. I tried to explain that these conversations in Rome had been part of my work as an *Abwehr* official. Röder missed no occasion of criticizing the *Abwehr*, especially Admiral Canaris and of course Oster. One day Röder shouted at me: 'a trial for high treason is what you will get. Nobody will shield you. As for General Oster, I will deal with him.' I retorted that the fact that Admiral Canaris was still in charge must disprove all these wild stories of alleged negotiations and conspiracies.

Röder's threats were also directed against Frau Müller and the secretary who had taken dictation and typed for the accused. He gave instructions that Müller should be treated like a prisoner under sentence of death. His aim was to discover documents relating to Müller's visits to the Vatican in 1939 and 1940 and to extract from him statements that he could use for a political prosecution.

Canaris succeeded in obtaining the release of Müller, his wife and Christine Dohnanyi. Bonhoeffer and Hans Dohnanyi remained in prison, but their friends in the *Abwehr* continued to work for them. They had on their side the head of the legal division, Dr Lehmann and Dr Karl Sack, the Judge Advocate

General, for whom Canaris and Dohnanyi had formed a high regard at the time of the Blomberg-Fritsch affair. He gave advice to the arrested men and had regular discussions with Canaris on their cases.

Röder took the view that the notes that he had seized on Dohnanyi's desk when arresting him were clear evidence and proof of high treason. Dohnanyi remained unshaken in his declarations that these were ordinary and official *Abwehr* notes. Oster admitted that the pencilled O on the papers was his initial, but he argued that this merely confirmed the official character of the papers. Canaris supported Oster's affirmation, declaring that the papers relating to visits to Rome and conversations with leading figures in the Churches were all part of regular *Abwehr* work. The ferment then died down, though mistrust and suspicion persisted. By the end of July 1943 the worst of Röder's attacks were over and Dr Sack had meanwhile convinced Marshal Keitel that Röder had been much less interested in Dohnanyi's offence than in discrediting Canaris and the *Abwehr*, an attack indeed on the High Command itself, he said. Keitel thereupon instructed Dr Lehmann to report to him personally on the Dohnanyi dossier. As Lehmann was in secret sympathy with the conspirators, the result was a favourable report, whereupon Keitel directed, on 23 July that political aspects of the inquiries, including the investigation of high treason, were to be dropped. It was an immense success for Canaris. Keitel presided over a meeting at which Canaris, Sack, Piekenbrock, Bentivegni, Klamroth and Duesterberg of the *Abwehr* were present. Most of them spoke critically of Röder, and Duesterberg recalled that Röder had referred to the *Abwehr* field unit, the Brandenburg Division, as 'a band of shirkers'. Canaris memorized this remark and soon made use of it.

He called in General Alexander von Pfuhlstein, Commander of the Brandenburg Division, and told him that Manfred Röder had been insulting the Brandenburgers by calling them 'a band of shirkers'. Pfuhlstein, an upright and courageous soldier, was furious and offered to make a complaint to Keitel. Canaris persuaded him that this would not help, but Pfuhlstein left in a state of high indignation, saying that he would 'punch the nose of this *Luftwaffe* bird who has rigged himself up as a Military Prosecutor'. Pfuhlstein has described to me how he arrived at Röder's office on 14 January strode up to his desk and said:

'Just one short question. Have you in fact said that the Brandenburg Division was a band of shirkers?'

'Yes,' stammered Röder uneasily, as the big fellow towered over him.

General von Pfuhlstein stepped forward two paces and gave him a heavy smack in the face; then clicked his heels, turned about and stamped out of the room.

This incident was widely talked about in Berlin. Canaris was full of glee. The upshot was that Pfuhlstein was sentenced to eight days' close arrest and Röder was promoted to another job. The investigation against Dohnanyi, the *Abwehr* and Canaris was less grimly pursued after that, though this respite did not diminish the ultimate threat to the Admiral and his Intelligence Service.

29
The end of the *Abwehr*

Hitler had made it a rule that no intelligence or espionage work was to be undertaken by German organizations within the territory of his 'faithful friend and ally', the Italian Duce. In fact the Foreign Intelligence Service of the *SD*, the Foreign Ministry and the *Abwehr* all possessed agents in Italy, unbeknown to the Führer. Colonel Helfferich was the *Abwehr*'s efficient agent in Rome, but Admiral Canaris had no need of him or any other well-placed German in Italy to be well informed. He himself had a close personal relationship with General Mario Roatta and General Cesare Amé, Chiefs of the Italian Intelligence Service.

Canaris confided in Piekenbrock his estimate of the value of these contacts, saying that: 'I like the Italians, just as I like the Greeks and the Spaniards. However, while having complete faith in a Spaniard's word of honour, I am more cautious with the Greeks and especially with the Italians. Sincerity is sometimes lacking in Italy and changes colour like a Neapolitan ice-cream. I ought not to say all this since my own ancestors were Italians, as my excellent friend General Amé has told me. As for Amé and Roatta, they are the two Italians in whom I have most confidence. Amé never conceals his thoughts from me and nor does Roatta.'

Canaris had the best possible information on the intentions of the Italian Government and the morale of the Italian people. He was able to make surprising estimates of the Italian position and had not many illusions about Mussolini's real authority. He was well informed of the spread of discontent in the Italian army after the autumn of 1941 and even discontent in Fascist Party circles. He could see the strange game that Count Ciano, the Duce's son-in-law was playing in seeking a basis for peace, parallel to the efforts being made by the *Abwehr*. He was well informed on the rôle of Dino Grandi, former Italian Ambassador in London, for whom he had a high regard. He knew that Grandi's *Fronde* aimed at breaking up the Axis, overthrowing Mussolini and taking Italy out of the war. Canaris calculated that such a withdrawal by

Italy would hasten the end of the war on other fronts too, while the overthrow of Mussolini would shake the faith of both the German people and the *Wehrmacht* in Hitler.

Developments in Italy went much more slowly than Canaris at first hoped. However he became convinced in the winter of 1942-3 and the spring of 1943 that the Italian monarchy would rapidly become the focus of resistance by the army to Mussolini and Fascism.

'If Hitler is wondering about Mussolini's intentions,' Canaris told Lahousen in the spring of 1943, 'he is probably right to do so, but he may not be aware that the Duce is not the man that he was and that the Fascist régime has been undermined. The acute crisis in Italy could lead to serious upheavals.'

Canaris was right, but Ribbentrop and Himmler's agents were greatly misled. *SS* General Gottlab Berger of Himmler's staff returned from a special mission to Rome and reported on 23 June 1943 that 'all depends on the Duce, and his loyalty (to us) cannot be doubted. The royal family is loyal to him and therefore the army too . . . The Prince of Piedmont is neither anti-German nor anti-Fascist. A split between the officers and the Duce need not be feared, although the latter has overestimated the fighting spirit of the people.'

Canaris, who accompanied Joachim von Ribbentrop to Rome on 25 February 1943, for a four-day visit, and went back there in April and May, formed a quite different opinion. He told Ribbentrop on 3 June that his organization had intercepted a cable from the American Embassy in Berne, reporting the amount of military aid that Hitler had promised to the Duce. 'This proves that high officials of the Italian Foreign Ministry, close to Bastianini, are in secret communication with the enemy,' said Canaris. 'This leakage proves that the subversive organization in which Ciano is included is spreading.' On 25 June Canaris submitted a list of members of the Italian Foreign Ministry and their wives (some of foreign birth) who could be in contact with the enemy. Vittetti, head of the Western Department, was especially suspect.

Why did Canaris act in this way when Ciano's aims were identical to his own? Once more it is necessary to affirm that despite his anti-Nazism Canaris remained a German patriot. He considered it his duty to warn against the possibility of German troops being stabbed in the back by an Italian clique disengaging itself from the collapse of Fascism.

On 24 July at the Fascist Grand Council a majority led by Count Grandi and Ciano declared against the Duce and his policy. Mussolini went naïvely to an interview with King Victor-Emmanuel and was arrested outside the Palace. Marshal Badoglio formed a government on the evening of 25 July. This came as a bomb-shell to the leaders of the Third Reich, and they were amazed and indignant at these events. Canaris was the least surprised, though he had not expected the overthrow of Mussolini to be achieved so easily, without a hand being raised to restore the Dictator when he was abandoned by his King.

'The Fascist structure has collapsed because it is rotten,' Canaris told Lahousen. 'These events cannot be reversed. I don't think the new government will continue the war for very long. I place no reliance in the assurances of Badoglio, who will go over to the Western camp as soon as he can.'

Hitler assembled all his principal advisers and military chiefs on the evening of 26 July. There was an atmosphere of confusion, with generals coming and going. Canaris was called in but not asked to give his advice. Göring, Kesselring, Keitel, Jodl and Doenitz were there. Doenitz was strongly for holding fast in Italy but uncertain whether a coup against Badoglio could succeed.

'There might be regrettable consequences if we replaced the present Italian leaders,' he remarked. 'The operation would have to be cleverly organized. I wonder whether Fascism still exists. We cannot impose our own conditions on the Italian people. Everything depends on the way in which the operation against the present Italian government is carried out. I calculate that we still have time: that time must be used to strengthen our position. We need several more divisions in Italy.'

Canaris did not react when Kesselring told the meeting that he regarded the Badoglio Government as 'worthy of confidence' and that there should be no interference in the internal affairs of another country. Hitler, as usual, cut across all other proposals made, exclaiming:

'We must act at once; if not the enemy will occupy Italian air fields ahead of us. The Fascist Party is only confused. It will regroup behind our lines. We must restore its confidence. Those are things that a soldier cannot understand. Only a man with political instincts can discern clearly the direction to take.'

Next day Keitel told Canaris to go at once to Italy and bring back a clear picture of trends under the Badoglio Government.

This was 'an order from the Führer,' but perhaps the devious Admiral had himself set the order in motion, wishing as he did to see what was happening. He made contact with General Cesare Amé and arranged to meet him on 2 and 3 August in Venice. During the Nuremberg Tribunal this meeting in Venice was mentioned and has since been referred to in vague or inaccurate terms. I have therefore questioned General Amé himself on what happened there. We met on 25 August 1970, at Cortina d'Ampezzo, and the General described to me over lunch his last meeting with Canaris in Venice twenty-seven years previously.

Admiral Canaris asked me to meet him urgently and we arranged that Venice should be the rendezvous. Our ally, Hitler, already made suspicious by the collapse of Fascism, which he had always feared, wished to know our exact situation so as to be able to intervene before being surprised by another eventuality, the withdrawal of Italy from the conflict. Hitler had therefore sent Canaris, a skilful observer well versed in Italian affairs, who would be able to size up the situation, which had until then been reported by numerous German observers in a variety of ways. It is true that the situation was complicated and difficult even for us, the Italians, to understand. I was therefore well aware of the delicacy and the extreme importance of the task that I had to discharge on this occasion. In what direction was the Italian Government to move during the near future? What developments could be foreseen? How was I to behave towards the Admiral? I asked for directives from my superior officers, but they left me without any guidance and I therefore arrived in Venice understandably perplexed.

Admiral Canaris and his officers, among whom was Colonel Lahousen arrived in Venice during the afternoon of 2 August. I arrived with my officers in the early evening. Informed of our arrival, the Admiral came to meet me in the hall of the Hotel Danieli and after greeting me led me aside, so that our conversation could not be overheard by anyone. The Admiral then said: 'My warmest congratulations. We also hope that our 25 July will come quickly.'

This put me at my ease. The official conference took place on the morning of the 3rd in a private drawing-room of the hotel. It was brief and overshadowed by the presentiment of serious events threatening both countries. After a few words about the reasons for his visit, the Admiral asked me to explain the Italian situation and to define our intentions.

I spoke briefly, bringing up in face of an obviously rooted German mistrust some persuasive arguments in favour of keeping to the alliance and continuing to the end the struggle against the common enemy. Then, after an exchange of ideas, the Germans drew up an official account of the proceedings on lines dictated with great emphasis by the Admiral, basing himself on the case that I had just put. The conclusion was that Italy wished and had resolved to continue the war beside her ally.

Our meeting ended more serenely in a walk on the Lido. On the deserted beach with nearly a mile between ourselves and our officers, who had been instructed to keep at a distance, Canaris and I spoke for an hour and a half quite alone.

Admiral Canaris revealed to me that he was informed of the real situation in Italy and was convinced that Italy would withdraw from the war before long. I could only share his opinion. He then spoke to me of the situation in Germany and the need to eliminate the Führer and his political system, indispensable in his opinion to bringing the whole cruel tragedy to an end. Canaris repeated his previously expressed conviction that any event that could lead to the collapse of Nazism and the end of the war would be of benefit to Germany. In his view the defection of Italy was desirable. I told him that removing Italy from the war would have such an effect on events that Germany would suffer unforeseen consequences in both the military and the political field. I explained to him that Italy needed time to prepare for such a step without running the risk of being paralysed by a German military occupation. I asked him to give his support to the version contained in the report of the conference that morning, in which he had expressed his conviction that the interests of the two countries coincided. He promised me his backing in this respect and he kept his word.

As we took leave of each other that evening, Admiral Canaris said to me confidentially: 'Take my advice and allow as few German troops into Italy as possible. Otherwise you will regret it.'

I commented to General Amé that in thus misleading the German High Command and the Führer himself, Canaris was playing a very dangerous game. Amé agreed, saying: 'It is evident that at this time Canaris had abandoned every precaution. According to the penal code of the Hitlerian system this was "high treason", ... "a crime committed against the government in Germany or abroad".' I asked the former Chief of Italian Intelligence what were his impressions and recollections of the Admiral. He gave the following assessment:

My personal exchanges with Admiral Canaris on the war were lively, continuous and honest in character, and we nearly always agreed in our appreciation of a situation. We had frequently to discuss personnel and service matters. We met several times in Germany and in Italy; we were together in France, in Yugoslavia and in North Africa, and each meeting increased our mutual confidence and esteem for one another.

I recall the day when I showed him records relating to his own family, which he thought until then to be of Greek origin but which was quite evidently Italian. He looked at the papers and his hands were trembling. He seemed to be very moved and there were tears in his eyes: 'Thank you, Amé, thank you!' he said.

Canaris was not a great talker, sober and austere in his habits, versatile and cultured, incisive and sometimes severe in his judgements. He had a profound knowledge of the working of intelligence services. His sensitive mind and quick intuition were characteristics of his Mediterranean origins. He possessed a wide knowledge of European countries and was a fund of secret information, both military and political, which was a source of professional strength to him.

He loved Germany deeply and seemed convinced after the events of 1943 that every event that could hasten the downfall of the Nazi régime would be of benefit to his country in tending to avoid a total catastrophe. He used to say when we met that the blood and tears shed through the actions of Hitler's régime would one day be repaid by Germany.

His information and forecasts were exact, honest and profound when he told me about Germany in the decisive phases of the war. His reports on trends and future possibilities were numerous and valuable to me.

The Duce, to whom I put these views and reports with some reserve – for they were often pessimistically in conflict with his own information – was sometimes visibly annoyed by them.

On 21 August 1943, Amé was replaced as Chief of Intelligence by General Carboni. On 3 September Marshal Badoglio had an interview with the German Ambassador, Rudolf Rahn, in which he reaffirmed his Government's intention to remain faithful to its Axis ally. Badoglio exclaimed: 'The German Government's mistrust of me is impossible to understand. I have given my word and I will keep it. Have confidence in me.' At that very hour at Cassibile in Sicily, General Castellano was signing on Badoglio's behalf an armistice with General Walter Bedell Smith and General Kenneth Anderson. It was not until 5:45 PM on 8 September that Allied broadcasts revealed Marshal Badoglio's defection.

On 9 September at 5 AM King Victor Emanuel, Badoglio and their entourage left the capital for the port of Ortona and slipped away to Brindisi. Within a few hours the Italian army disappeared, disarmed by the Germans. Crowded into livestock trucks marked 'Badoglio Troops', 700,000 Italian soldiers and officers were deported to the Reich to share the unenviable fate of the Poles and Russians in German camps and factories. On 12 September Mussolini, prisoner in the Grand Sasso, was set free by an *SS* Commando led by Otto Skorzeny. On 15 September urged on by Hitler, Mussolini proclaimed an Italian Republic, with his seat of government on the shores of Lake Garda.

Canaris took every precaution after 9 September to prevent the *SD* discovering the real facts of his past relations with Roatta and Amé. Roatta had gone to Brindisi with the King and Amé had gone into hiding somewhere on the coast near Venice. Canaris set up a 'liquidating branch for Italy', intended to study the military files and official documents captured by the German armed forces after Badoglio's defection. He gave orders for anything that concerned himself and the *Abwehr* to be sent to him personally and he had to act quickly. He did not know that Kaltenbrunner and Schellenberg had sent their own agents to Italy precisely to take charge of dossiers that might relate to the contacts between the two military intelligence services. Thanks to the co-operation of the Italian military intelligence officers, the *Abwehr* men were able to find a large number of compromising documents in time. However the *SD* and the *Gestapo* made several discoveries that were to have dire consequences.

Badoglio's defection surprised Hitler and his entourage. He raged against 'these Italian scoundrels' and recalled the confident report that Canaris had made to him after his conference with Amé in Venice. At the time Hitler had only with difficulty been persuaded by Keitel that there was 'really nothing to fear on the Italian side' and had long delayed his decision on pre-emptive intervention. He bitterly regretted having listened to Keitel and on 8 September fiercely rebuked him. On the same evening Schellenberg received an order from Himmler 'to inquire into the reason for Admiral Canaris's error of judgement.' Schellenberg and Müller were hot on the trail, sending their best *SD* and *Gestapo* investigators to Italy. The results were soon forthcoming. Schellenberg gave the following account of his investigation.

The facts were brought to light in the following manner. One of the *Abwehr* officers in Italy, Colonel Helfferich, was attached to the staff of the German Military Attaché in Rome, General Enno von Rintelen. The *Abwehr* Colonel had engaged two Italian homosexuals as drivers without knowing that they were both in the service of General Cesare Amé's Military Intelligence. I had warned Canaris of the risks that this entailed, but Helferrich was a personality of such high standing that

311

Canaris derided my fears. 'Ah, Schellenberg,' he said, 'before very long in your profession you begin to see monsters everywhere.' One of these drivers was in fact a valuable source of information for my political intelligence service, as he related all General Amé's conversations and movements to a friend who was in our pay. We were thus able to reconstruct, bit by bit, a fairly clear picture of the rigging of the Venice conference by General Amé and the way in which the Admiral was compromised in the affair. I remember having minuted the file sent to Himmler as follows: 'It would have been better if Admiral Canaris had carried out his proper duties in Italy instead of taking parts in these sessions with General Amé.'

When I presented to Himmler the dossier covering the various treasonable activities of Canaris, Himmler bit nervously at his thumb, and his reponse was: 'Leave that here! I will show it to Hitler at an opportune moment.' I came back to the subject several times, insisting that this was of national importance and concerned the war effort, but Himmler was plainly not willing to take upon himself this responsibility. Like Heydrich he appeared incapable of action in matters relating to the Admiral. I am fairly certain that at one time or another Canaris had discovered something compromising about Himmler, or the Reichsführer *SS* would never have hesitated to act on the dossier that I submitted to him.*

This caution on Himmler's part was due to some concealed factor that the historian may seek in vain. Perhaps Canaris in turn possessed dossiers on Heydrich and Himmler containing definite proof of some subversive activity against Hitler. This evidence may have been contained in the mysterious suitcases that Canaris took with him to Spain. Perhaps, as some of the old *Abwehr* hands assert, part of the Canaris papers are in the hands of the British Secret Service which has never been communicative about *Abwehr* documents found after the occupation. Whatever his hold on Himmler may have been, the Admiral must have felt very sure of himself to have dared to use his authority, as he was still doing in the autumn of 1943 to protect certain activities on the part of his staff after they had been shown by the *Gestapo* and the *SD* to have been of a more or less seditious character.

The war raging on all fronts in the autumn of 1943 went on through a severe winter. Admiral Canaris increasingly felt the weight of his lonely and exposed position, watched as he was ever more closely by the *Gestapo*.

*The *SD* dossier on Canaris related to Dr Müller's 1940 peace soundings in the Vatican, the relations of Canaris with General Franco, and the activities of Dohnanyi and Bonhoeffer.

The ranks of his friends were being thinned out. Helmuth Groscurth was reported missing in the Stalingrad disaster. Dohnanyi had been in prison since April. Oster was under house arrest. Piekenbrock had gone to the Eastern Front in command of a regiment. At the end of the summer of 1943 it was Lahousen's turn to go also to the Eastern Front. Neither of these two changes of appointment were for political reasons and should in the ordinary course of events have happened sooner. To each he said at the moment of parting:

'Why can't I go to the Front like you?'

He could not console himself at losing these two; Piekenbrock told me after the war: 'I felt an acute sense of loss when I said goodbye to the Admiral, feeling that I would never again see this dear friend and senior officer who had almost been a father to me.' Lahousen added: 'I seemed to be losing everything when I shook his hand for the last time. There were tears in our eyes. I fought the last months of the war with an empty heart and when I heard of his atrocious death, I felt like an orphan.'

Some excellent and loyal staff officers still remained with him, like Colonel Egbert von Bentivegni, Chief of Section III, Colonel Georg Hansen, who took over from Piekenbrock in Section I, and Colonel Wessel von Freytag-Loringhoven who succeeded Lahousen in Section II. Vice-Admiral Leopold Bürkner remained in charge of the *Abwehr* Foreign Section. During these months Canaris saw a lot of the pianist Helmuth Maurer, who, when his conscription for active service was imminent, had been taken by the Admiral into the *Abwehr* in a civil capacity. He confided a good deal in this musician, who was a frequent visitor at the Schlachtensee and enlivened the family evenings by his talented and sensitive playing. The Admiral used to call him Uncle Mau and relied much on his presence and his sympathy during his last months of freedom. When I met Maurer at an *Abwehr* reunion in Wurzburg in April 1970, he told me how great the temptation had been for Canaris in the autumn of 1943 to abandon the struggle against the *SS*, but the Admiral had been sustained by the thought that there was still much that could be saved, as long as he was in charge.

'He was borne up by his resolve to prevent Kaltenbrunner, Müller and Schellenberg from taking over the *Abwehr*,' Maurer told me. 'He knew that it was a desperate cause, and that the *SS* would triumph and that Germany would go under in the ensuing chaos.'

Indeed, the end was near at hand for the *Abwehr*. Storm signals were increasing, though the *Gestapo* was amazingly patient in stalking its prey. For this was big game, and more evidence of a conspiracy against Hitler was coming in to Schellenberg and Heinrich Müller.

Schellenberg scored a point when one day in September 1943 an agent of his, a Swiss medical student named Reckzeh who posed as a convinced opponent of the Third Reich, succeeded in working his way into the fringe of the conspiracy by penetrating the Solf Circle. This was a group referred to with some contempt by the *Gestapo* as a 'drawing-room *Fronde*,' which had formed round the widow of the last Foreign Minister of Imperial Germany, Dr Wilhelm Solf. Frau Solf met her political friends occasionally in the drawing-room of Elisabeth von Thadden headmistress of a well-known girls' school at Weiblingen near Heidelberg. In this circle there were a number of convinced anti-Nazis who since 1933 had devoted themselves to the care and assistance of Jewish and Christian victims of Nazism.

The *Gestapo* waited for four months before acting, and one afternoon in January 1944 arrested everyone to be found at the home of Elisabeth von Thadden. These included Otto Kiep, a former Ambassador, since employed in the *Abwehr*, and two former diplomats, Count Albrecht von Bernstorff and Richard Künzer. They also arrested the lawyer Count Helmuth von Moltke, of the *Abwehr* Foreign Section who led the Kreisau Circle, another group of conspirators. With the exception of Frau Hanna Solf and her daughter Countess Ballestrem, all those arrested were later executed. In February 1944 Captain Ludwig Gehre of Section III of the *Abwehr*, was arrested for having warned members of the Solf Circle that their telephones were being tapped by the *Gestapo*. In all the *Gestapo* arrested seventy-six people in Berlin society, among whom were too many members of the *Abwehr* for Canaris to doubt that there would be repercussions for him.

One disaster led to another, the arrest of Otto Kiep arousing suspicions about his friend, Erich Vermehren, who was working for the *Abwehr* in Turkey. Recalled to Berlin for questioning, Erich and Elisabeth Vermehren preferred to seek British protection in Cairo. The *SS* accused the fugitives of having taken with them the German Embassy code books, though the Vermehrens denied this after the war. Another married couple of Austrian origin named von Kletchkowsky, who had worked for the *Abwehr* in Turkey for years, defected in the same manner. The secretary to the *Gestapo* Chief in the German Embassy in Ankara took refuge in the American Embassy rather than face recall to Germany.

The defection of the Vermehrens infuriated Hitler, who remembered *Gestapo* suspicions that Vermehren's chief, Dr Paul Leverkühn, had been in contact with the American Intelligence Service, though factual proof had been lacking. Himmler had spoken to Hitler about this and about a speech by the German Ambassador in Ankara, Herr von Papen, which had seemed to hint at peace soundings. Hitler raved against the *Abwehr*, encouraged by Martin Bormann, despite Keitel's timid objections.

A few days later Marshal Keitel ordered the *Abwehr* Chief to prepare and present personally to Hitler a report on the situation on the Russian Front. This report was frankly pessimistic. Hitler listened for a while, controlling his anger, but suddenly sprang at Canaris, seizing him by the lapel and demanding whether this was an insinuation that Germany would lose the war! The Admiral was not intimidated, replying gently that he had offered no such opinion, but was simply basing his report on the facts of the situation given in communiqués and reports from the Front. Hitler thereupon changed the subject to the case of the Vermehrens, for which he vehemently blamed Canaris. The Admiral left General Headquarters with the premonition that he would never see Hitler again and that the *Abwehr* was doomed.

Although Himmler continued to stand aside from attacks on Canaris and the *Abwehr*, Kaltenbrunner and Schellenberg saw that now was their chance to act. These two younger men, ambitious for more power, possessed enough compromising material to destroy Canaris's empire and build up their own on its ruins. They urged Himmler to demand the dissolution of the *Abwehr* and proposed that its members should be absorbed into their own *SS* Services. Hitler accepted their arguments and on 18 February 1944 signed a decree setting up a unified German Intelligence Service under the supreme direction of Himmler, with Kaltenbrunner taking direct charge. Contrary to what might have been expected, Canaris was neither arrested nor accused of treason. He was simply placed in retirement.

Negotiations began between the *Wehrmacht* and the *SS* to implement the Führer's decree. General Winter, Chief of the

Central Office of the *Wehrmacht*, presided over a joint co-ordination committee. Rear-Admiral Bürkner and General von Bentivegni represented the *Abwehr* at these meetings. Section I and II were unified in a Military Office (*Militäramt*) and taken over by the *SS* but put in charge of Colonel Hansen, who had until then been Chief of Section I (Espionage) and whom the *SS* considered (quite wrongly) to be loyal to National Socialism. Section III passed into Schellenberg's control, and the Central Section which had been Oster's domain was abolished.

With bitterness and grief Admiral Canaris saw his service destroyed after defending the organization so steadfastly and with such determination over nine years. The last ditch in the struggle against the *SS* had been overrun. The policy of terror could now take its course and the *Gestapo* could operate without a rival in the field. The *Gestapo* chiefs, however, were not satisfied with victory and pressed their advantage, intent on having the heads of Canaris and his accomplices. That would be the last and most atrocious act of the tragedy.

30
Hanged at dawn

No other blow struck by the *Gestapo* and the *SD* at the political opposition to Hitler was as decisive as the dissolution of the *Abwehr*. After this had taken place, contacts between the conspirators and their friends abroad could only be partially maintained with the assistance of Colonel Hansen. But the retirement of Admiral Canaris, who was asked to reside in Lauenstein Castle in Franconia where he was watched by the *Gestapo*, did not bring to the *SS* the advantages that Schellenberg, Kaltenbrunner and Himmler at first hoped. The *Abwehr* was difficult to digest. Schellenberg had been especially naive in supposing that it sufficed to supplant Canaris and that the *Abwehr* with its network of thousands of agents would continue to work as in the past, if not better. He had not reckoned that the Admiral would exert a greater influence after his removal than during the time when he directed the *Abwehr*.

The reaction of *Abwehr* officers to the decree dissolving and merging their service was immediate. Captain Richard Protze, Chief of the *Abwehr* office in Amsterdam, said that 'when the Admiral was no longer there, I ceased to send my reports to Berlin. Without him we no longer had confidence in the Intelligence Service.' Major Paul Leverkühn, *Abwehr* head in Istanbul, wrote: 'Canaris was the *Abwehr*. When they dismissed him the *Abwehr* began to disintegrate'. Colonel Oscar Reile, Head of Section III F in France, wrote: 'These changes in the Intelligence Service caused inestimable damage, especially to military intelligence against Great Britain and the United States. Canaris's work was suddenly and stupidly destroyed. The subordinating of *Abwehr* members to the Reich Security Office, where nobody had the least idea of the methods and aims of military intelligence, produced some startling consequences.'

Hundreds of *Abwehr* officers offered their resignations with requests to be transferred to the Eastern Front, from which many did not return. On the Western Front there was an astute reorganization within the *Wehrmacht*, which kept the Counter-espionage Sections in being as mobile commando units directly dependent on the armies in the field, on the pretext that an Allied invasion was so imminent that close co-operation between the army and the Intelligence Service was indispensable.

From his office in the Brussels Hotel Metropole [wrote Gilles Perrault] Colonel Hermann Giskes directed 'Commando Number 307' and received orders only from the *Wehrmacht*. Like so many others, Giskes was prepared to resign rather than take his orders from the Himmler-Schellenberg-Kaltenbrunner trio. His work and outlook were un-mistakably formed by the personality of Canaris who was to his men an example, a chief and a symbol. Even if the Admiral sometimes exasper-ated them by his excessive scruples, they knew that it was him they had to thank for being able to keep their hands clean from the mire and blood in which Germany was foundering. Thanks to him the *Abwehr* was not contaminated. After he went it was impossible to work with the men in black uniform. In April 1944 Brigade-Leader Walther Schellenberg realized that his victory had been in vain. He had himself taken over from the Admiral on the bridge of the vessel, but part of the crew had deserted the *Abwehr* ship and the remainder refused to serve her any longer. When the intelligence war in the West attained its climax, the *Abwehr* was no longer battle-worthy.

Canaris, even in his guarded residence, realized that Schellen-berg's operations were a fiasco. The Admiral, aware that he him-self was doomed sooner or later, took pleasure in the discomfiture of 'little Schellenberg', but his enjoyment was mixed with appre-hension. The *Gestapo* was pursuing its inquiries into his own activities and God alone knew what they would discover.

In fact the *SS* inquirers had found out very little. One case was interesting them particularly, without their being able to throw full light on it: Operation 7, one of the most daring instances of giving protection to Jewish victims of Nazism. It originated in September 1941 when a decree was published making it com-pulsory for all Jews to wear a yellow star of David sewn on to their clothes. Forcible change of domicile and regrouping in ghettos were just beginning in Germany, having been in effect since 1939 in Poland. Canaris had given instruction for some twelve to fifteen Jews to be given clearance to enter Switzerland under the cover of service in the *Abwehr*. The case was called Operation 7, because it was first concerned with the transfer of seven people only. It was organized by Dohnanyi and required some considerable acts of camouflage. Unforeseen difficulties arose both on the Swiss and German sides. To be able to employ Jews in the *Abwehr*, financial clearances were necessary which entailed delays and obstruction at a low level, and it was also necessary to have the agreement of the Reich Central Security Office. To overcome these obstacles Canaris used a ruse that was characteristic of him.

In July 1942 Operation Pastorious had just failed. This was a landing from U-boats on the North American coast of ten young German saboteurs, all of whom had been arrested by the FBI within a fortnight and six of them later executed. Hitler had summoned Canaris and Lahousen on hearing of this fiasco and accused them of incompetence in the matter. Canaris listened quietly while Hitler raged that they had chosen men who were not qualified for such a difficult exercise. The Admiral then offered the excuse that the unfortunate agents were in fact not *Abwehr* men but untrained young Nazis selected by the *SS*. Hitler, his fury unabated had shouted back: 'why not use ordinary criminals or Jews?' The interview ended on a stormy note, but Canaris was not dissatisfied, since this scene took place in the presence of Keitel and Himmler. Later Canaris was able to quote these words as 'an order from the Führer', when obtaining clearance from Heinrich Müller of the *Gestapo* for certain Jews to leave Germany under the cover of service in the *Abwehr*.

The Reich Central Security Office continued to regard Operation 7 as highly suspect, and Müller felt that he had been tricked by Canaris. He brought up the subject in 1943 during the interrogations of Dohnanyi and Bonhoeffer. Kaltenbrunner sent an inspector to Switzerland to report on the financial aspects of the affair, suspecting that Dohnanyi and his colleagues in the *Abwehr* had themselves made money out of this traffic. The *SD* inspector discovered nothing, but the *SS* remained suspicious, not being able to imagine any other motive for such a complicated operation. At first Canaris was able to cover the actions of his subordinates, but after his fall from power he feared that the inquiries might be resumed, since there had been other cases after Operation 7.

At the end of June 1944 Canaris left Lauenstein Castle and returned to Berlin. He had just been nominated Chief of the Special Office for Economic Warfare attached to the High Command of the *Wehrmacht* and situated at Eiche near Potsdam. It was a fairly static form of employment, but it was surprising that Canaris, after falling from favour, should receive any new appointment at all. That he was considered for this sinecure may be due to a certain confidence that Hitler still felt in him, despite all the arrests of *Abwehr* men and accusations against the organization. It may also have been intended to avoid the impression abroad that there was a severe internal crisis in the Reich. In fact it was not possible to keep secret the reorganization of the *Abwehr*, for the news travelled along its own tentacles abroad.

In his new position Canaris was still closely watched by the *Gestapo*. He knew this, but it was not his main reason for distancing himself from the conspiracy against Hitler that was being reactivated by the young Colonel Claus von Stauffenberg. Canaris had always been opposed in principle to an attempt on Hitler's life; he was also mistrustful of the political capacity of Stauffenberg and his friends. He had been informed about the preparations for the coup and had misgivings that these were not comprehensive enough. He disapproved of the contacts made by the conspirators in the spring of 1944 with the secret Communist movement in Germany. It may be added that Canaris was tired, worn out by nine years of conflict with the *SS* and that his pessimism was increasing. He believed with some reason that it was already too late for Hitler's overthrow to produce positive results.

Karl Heinz Abshagen describes very well the Admiral's state of mind at the beginning of the summer of 1944.

Yes, Canaris was tired. After years of unbelievable tension, mental and moral, years of perpetual movement and overwork, this abrupt and forced inactivity . . . was to lead to a violent reaction. This man who for years had never rested, who had not even taken a break from work on Sundays, was suddenly in a situation in which he had practically nothing to do. At home in Schlachtensee the house was still and empty, as he had evacuated his family under the threat of Allied bombing and sent them to Bavaria. When not in his Eiche office he sat and read in the garden at Schlachtensee, studied Russian with a Baltic friend, Baron Kaulbars, or chatted with the pianist, 'Uncle Mau' who brought him news of the working day under the *Abwehr*'s new *SS* masters.

Hitler pulled back his battle headquarters on 14 July to Rastenburg in East Prussia. The simultaneous offensives against Germany on the Western and Eastern Fronts were on 17 July marked by another fateful blow to those who opposed Hitler inside Germany. Marshal Rommel's car was attacked in Normandy with cannon shell by an allied fighter aircraft and the Marshal, who had quite recently been drawn into the conspiracy against Hitler, suffered severe head wounds. Carl Goerdeler, former Lord Mayor of Leipzig, another leading figure, was informed on 18 July that the *Gestapo* were after him and was obliged to go into hiding. On 19 July Von Stauffenberg was summoned to Rastenburg for the following day and he resolved to act. He hid in his brief-case a bomb made of British components and flew north shortly after dawn on 20 July accompanied by his adjutant, Werner von Häften, who was carrying a second time-bomb of identical pattern. The sequel in Hitler's headquarters, where the bomb was placed under the map table during the daily situation report is well known. Soon after von Stauffenberg had left the blast killed four of those present and wounded several others, but Hitler was not seriously injured.

Stauffenberg, waiting outside, was certain from the force of the explosion that he had killed Hitler. He at once flew on to Berlin to set the coup d'état in motion. Towards the end of that afternoon Canaris was at home in Schlachtensee with Helmuth Maurer when the telephone rang. He lifted the receiver and recognized Stauffenberg's voice.

'The Führer is dead,' said the voice. 'A bomb has ended his days.'

Canaris's reaction was instant and admirably controlled for he knew that his telephone was connected to a recording instrument.

'Dead?' he exclaimed. 'My God! Who did it? The Russians?' Stauffenberg, though rash and impulsive, did not reply that he himself was responsible.

The Admiral went back to Uncle Mau and told him the news, adding:

'Even if Hitler is dead, and I have no reason to doubt it after Stauffenberg's precise explanation, that does not mean that the *SS* and the *Gestapo* have been removed as well. Himmler, Göring and Goebbels have not been killed with the Führer. Stauffenberg says nothing about them. And who is going to clean up *Gestapo* Headquarters in the Prinz Albrechtstrasse?'*

Uncle Mau nodded. The affair was by no means over. Canaris asked:

'Do I go to Eiche or the Bendlerstrasse?'

This question needed no reply. There was nothing for him to do at the War Ministry. He decided to wait at home and see what would happen.

*Helmut Maurer's narrative.

About 5 PM the telephone rang again and Canaris was this time told that the attempt on Hitler's life had failed. Hitler was still alive. Canaris thereupon decided to go to his office at Eiche, where he arrived at about 6 PM. His ADC was already preparing a congratulatory telegram from his office and staff to 'the beloved Führer'. Canaris could not do otherwise than approve and sign it with a grimace. The *Gestapo* was about to exact vengeance. Any precaution that tended to reduce that risk was worth-while. Those who saw Canaris between 20 July 1944 and 23 July found him physically and intellectually on his mettle, without a trace of fatigue or depression. Danger stimulated him and he was ready for the supreme conflict.

On 23 July he was at his Schlachtensee villa and the weather was fine. After lunch Uncle Mau was on his way home and Canaris sat in the garden with a relative, Erwin Delbrück, and Baron Kaulbars. The Admiral was playing with his two dachshunds, and his valet-cook, the Algerian Mohammed, was handing round glasses of iced water with slices of lemon.

Suddenly a black Mercedes drew up in front of the house and two SS men sprang out. They were Schellenberg himself with Baron Völkersam, an SS flying ace who had previously served under Canaris. The Admiral was not surprised by these visitors. He asked them into the house but only Schellenberg came into the drawing-room. Völkersam remained discreetly in the next room. Canaris said calmly to Schellenberg:

'I was expecting it to be you who would call. Before anything else, tell me whether they found anything in writing by that imbecile Colonel Hansen with his obsession for putting everything on paper!'

Schellenberg replied:

'Yes, when he was arrested the *Gestapo* found a notebook containing, among other things, a list of those who were to be executed after the success of the *coup*. But nothing about you, Admiral, not a hint of any participation by you in the plot against the Führer.'

'These brass hats on the General Staff are compulsive scribblers,' grumbled Canaris.

Schellenberg then explained the situation and what his mission was.

'I have to arrest you, Admiral. It is an order from Kaltenbrunner through SS Group Leader Müller. I have to accompany you to

Fürstenberg and not return to Berlin with you until everything has been cleared up.'

The Admiral wondered exactly what game Schellenberg was playing and why he spoke of an order from Kaltenbrunner without mentioning Himmler's name.

'It is a great pity that we have to meet under these circumstances,' he said to Schellenberg, 'but things will come right in the end. Only promise me that in the next three days you will arrange for me to have a personal interview with Himmler. The others, Kaltenbrunner and Müller, are no more than butchers who are after my blood.'

Schellenberg realized that the former *Abwehr* Chief still had some powerful weapons in his armoury and would use them against Himmler to defend himself. This future contest between Canaris and Himmler was not his concern, and he promised to arrange the meeting. Then he said:

'If, Admiral, you wish to settle any personal affairs, I am entirely in agreement. I will wait here in this room for an hour, during which time you may do what you want. In my report I will say that you went to your room to change . . .'

The Admiral interrupted him.

'No, no, my dear Schellenberg. Flight is out of the question for me, and I have no intention of killing myself. I am sure of my own case and will rely on your promise.'

After washing and changing his clothes, the Admiral packed a small suit-case, put on a fur-lined overcoat and followed Schellenberg to the car. Canaris did not talk as they drove away, sitting deep in thought. Brigade-Leader Trümmler received his new prisoner at Fürstenberg with military courtesy and showed him the mess where he could dine with Schellenberg. A score of generals and senior officers, all arrested in consequence of the plot against Hitler, were finishing their dinner. After numerous greetings from those already seated, Canaris and Schellenberg dined alone together at a small table. Schellenberg tried to get Himmler on the telephone after dinner but without success. He left Canaris at 11 PM and as they shook hands the Admiral said:

'You are my only hope. Farewell, my friend. Do not forget your promise to arrange an interview for me with Himmler.'

It is not known whether Canaris ever succeeded in obtaining a last interview with Himmler. Schellenberg wrote in his memoirs:

I had a long telephone conversation with Himmler next day. He assured me that he would see Canaris, and the meeting must have taken place, for how else can we explain the fact that Canaris was not condemned to death until the last days before the collapse of the Third Reich. Proof of his guilt was easily enough to have satisfied the Peoples' Court and its bloodthirsty president, Judge Roland Freisler.

On 22 September 1944, Commissioner Sonderegger of the Criminal Police was pursuing enquiries in the army headquarters at Zossen when he came across a metal box in the cellar in which the *Abwehr*'s most secret documents had been hidden. Sonderegger was amazed. A glance sufficed to show him the importance of this find. He impounded them without a moment's delay, returned with them to Berlin and placed them before *Gestapo* Commissioner Walther Huppenkothen who was in charge of the enquiries. Huppenkothen studied them in detail and then devoted three weeks to making out a 160-page report, which he entitled 'Discovery of Documents at Zossen'.

After the war, appearing before courts trying war crimes, Huppenkothen made a number of statements about the contents of the Zossen box.

Among the papers were notes concerning preparations for a coup d'état, dating from 1938, some in Oster's handwriting; reports on the talks with the British Government through the Vatican, conducted by Dr Joseph Müller; reports on Bonhoeffer's conversations in Sweden and Switzerland; a record of the talks conducted by Herr von Hassell at Arosa; a letter involving General Halder in the conspiracy; a review of the situation after the Polish campaign in 1939, written by General Beck; an outline plan written in pencil by Oster for an attempt on the Führer's life; and suggestions for making use of various members of the German resistance, whose names were indicated by their initials. There were also memoranda by General Beck and Dr Karl Goerdeler on the military situation, initialled by Oster and Dohnanyi. There was Dohnanyi's notorious X Report. Some extracts from Admiral Canaris's diary were also there, with notes on the activities of the resistance movement and on journeys undertaken to the various army commands with the idea of winning them for the rebellion.

In one of his statements during questioning, Huppenkothen said:

It took me three weeks to make out my report on this material. One copy was sent to Hitler, another to Himmler through Martin Bormann, a third to Kaltenbrunner who gave it to Heinrich Müller to read, and the fourth remained in my office. According to the Führer's instructions, the Reichsführer *SS* Heinrich Himmler and the Chief of the Gestapo,

Müller, the discovery of the Zossen documents had to remain a Most Secret matter. We were obliged to preserve absolute silence about them. None of the functionaries of the Peoples' Court was to learn of them. Hitler reserved the right to decide what the sequel to this affair would be.

For this reason the Führer altered his orders about the liquidation of the conspirators and directed instead that there should be a special inquiry 'restricted to those conspirators who had some kind of relationship with the *Abwehr*.' Some of those whose death sentences had already been passed by the Peoples' Court then had their sentences suspended for weeks and even months, contrary to the general treatment of prisoners, many of whom had been summarily executed.

Huppenkothen's report has never been found, and his own explanation is that all four copies were destroyed before the end of the war.

The prisons of Berlin in September 1944 contained thousands of suspects waiting to be tried. The principal men accused were kept in the cellars of the *Gestapo* Headquarters in the Prinz Albrechtstrasse, or in Lehrterstrasse prison. The cells of the Prinz Albrechtstrasse were a bare five feet by eight feet with a bed that folded back during the daytime, a table and a stool. Among the inmates with Admiral Canaris were Generals Halder, Thomas and Oster, Pastor Bonhoeffer, the former Ministers Popitz, Schacht and Planck, the former Lord Mayor, Dr Goerdeler, Judge Sack, Dr Josef Müller, Liedig, Strünck, Gehre, Herbert Göring, cousin of Marshal Göring, the Reverend Hans Böhm, Dr von Schlabrendorff, and a son of General Lindemann, to name only the most important.

Twice daily the prisoners received a bowl of *ersatz* coffee, two slices of bread and lard, and some sort of jam. At midday there was also a thin soup. Food packages were sometimes allowed to be sent in to prisoners, according to the whim of the jailers, whose methods varied from sadism to studious correctitude. A washroom at the end of the corridor alongside the cells gave a welcome opportunity for prisoners to exchange views while taking showers. Outside exercise was not permitted, but during the frequent Allied air raids the prisoners were escorted to a concrete bunker in the courtyard, which they named 'the Himmler shelter'. Discipline was not so strict as to prevent all human contact.

Canaris, like Oster and Müller, was among those prisoners put

325

under an especially severe régime. They were made to wear a painful sort of manacle; they were entitled to only a third of the normal food rations; sometimes they were forced to carry out the most menial duties, such as scrubbing out the corridors. One day when Canaris was kneeling down at this work, an *SS* guard shouted at him:

'Well, sailor, you never expected to come back to scrubbing the deck!'

Canaris's morale was nevertheless high. He seemed to have been transformed since he arrived in prison, fiercely determined to maintain his identity in the moral and intellectual conflict with the *Gestapo*. He was not tortured during interrogations and fought with the interrogators a relentless war of wits in which he was usually the victor. He had also developed a technique of his own for inducing his jailers to impart information. Schlabrendorff heard him one day say to an *SS* guard: 'I suppose we are pushing the Russians back over the Vistula at the moment.' 'Don't be ridiculous!' retorted the *SS* guard. 'The Russians are advancing on the Oder.'

After the discovery of the Zossen documents, Canaris attempted, in Dr Goerdeler's fashion, to swamp the investigation with a quantity of contradictory evidence. 'For months Canaris duped them,' related Schlabrendorff, 'inventing new pitfalls day after day. His talents as an actor, his shrewdness, his imagination, and the ease with which he affected stupidity and suddenly abandoned it for the most subtle arguments, confused the *SD* interrogators.' Lahousen thought that 'by an artistic deformation of the truth' Canaris succeeded in admitting nothing. The statements taken by the *Gestapo*, which have been found and shown to me, display Canaris's extraordinary and vivid imagination. By half-admissions followed by a show of contrition, carefully measured doses of truth and falsehood, he himself took charge of the interrogation, emphasizing facts that were already known or were undeniable, making mistakes and constantly correcting himself. He also built up secondary incidents to distract the attention of the interrogators until, weary of the struggle, they lost patience, revealing the extent to which they had been distracted from the truth. This showed great cleverness on Canaris's part, and although it required enormous energy and resourcefulness, he did not divulge the most important secrets, knowing how to camouflage them and mislead his inquisitors. It is certain that his success saved the lives of many people.

Other prisoners did not possess the same moral, intellectual and nervous strength. Many gave way under interrogation and collapsed. Some were confounded by irrefutable evidence, as was General Hans Oster, while others were subjected to such mental and physical torture that the *Gestapo* extracted from them everything that they knew. It was the subordinates in the conspiracy who were physically tortured, a sign perhaps that Kaltenbrunner and Müller's henchmen sensed that they had not much time left to complete their enquiries, before retribution overtook the inquisitors themselves.

On 2 February 1945 Dr Josef Müller heard the familiar voice of the executioner shouting to Goerdeler, 'Come along, come along, hurry up!' The former mayor of Leipzig was hanged in Berlin on the same day as the former Minister of Finance, Johannes Popitz. Several hours later Freisler sentenced to death Klaus Bonhoeffer, brother of Pastor Dietrich Bonhoeffer, Rüdiger Schleicher, Friedrich Justus Perels and Hans John, brother of Otto John, the *Lufthansa* official who had fled to Spain and taken refuge with the British.

The Peoples' Court was in session in its buildings near the Potsdamer Platz. In the late morning of 3 February, began the most formidable daylight attack that the Allies had yet made on the German capital. For more than two hours successive waves of bombers could be seen in the blue sky of that freezing winter day. They made an inferno of the heart of the city, with buildings collapsing everywhere, while delayed-action bombs and incendiaries added to the chaos, the flaming phosphorus running along the gutters and penetrating cellars where thousands of Berliners were hiding, men, women and children who were buried or burnt alive. It was the day of the apocalypse. For one man it was also the day of judgement. Judge Roland Freisler, President of the Peoples' Court, was struck by a nearby explosion as he left the Peoples' Court to enter the air raid-shelter. Dr Rolf Schleicher, brother of Rüdiger whom Freisler had condemned to death on the previous day, was called in to examine the body and muttered between his teeth:

'The brute is dead.'

The terrible air raid of 3 February had far-reaching results. Several of the Reich Security offices were destroyed. Some departments of the *SS* had to be evacuated from Berlin into parts of the Reich not yet occupied and less exposed to bombing, moves which had to be made with communications in a state of complete disorganization. Sachsenhausen concentration camp was being evacuated because the front was too close. The Prinz Albrechtstrasse prison could only be partly used, owing to bomb damage, and it was decided to evacuate the prisoners.

On 7 February 1945, came a summons for twenty prisoners. Into a van with seats at the most for eight persons, the *SS* crowded twelve men, General von Falkenhausen, Gottfried von Bismarck, Werner von Alvensleben, Josef Müller, Franz Liedig, Ludwig Cehre and Dietrich Bonhoeffer among them. The latter said to Dr Müller as he got into the van: 'Let us go as Christians with courage to the gallows.'

The van drove to Buchenwald concentration camp in Thüringia.

Another van contained Admiral Canaris, General Oster, Judge Sack, General Thomas, General Halder, Dr Schacht, Theodore Strünck and Dr von Schuschnigg, former Chancellor of Austria. This second van drove to Flössenburg concentration camp in the Palatinate.

Eberhard Bethge, who has given me the details of these dispositions, found it difficult to discover any guiding principle in these removals and in the composition of the two groups. Some prisoners may have been thought valuable as hostages with whom to bargain with the Allies. Others may have been thought to possess useful and unconfessed information.

The drive from Berlin to Flössenburg lasted fifteen hours. When they arrived at the camp, the prisoners were escorted to cells in the central bunker, that was a solid brick building unlike the wooden barrack hut of the camp itself. Canaris was put in cell 22. His neighbour in cell 21, he was to learn later, was Lieutenant-Colonel H. M. Lunding of the Danish army General Staff, former Chief of the Danish Intelligence Service, who had for eight months been an inmate of Flössenburg. Lunding at once recognized the Admiral and noted that if his face was pale his movements were lively and that he had kept his confident bearing. The Admiral was not in prison dress, nor was he in naval uniform. He wore his own clothes, a grey suit and a grey overcoat, fur-lined, which he put on each time that he went for interrogation. Lunding saw that Canaris was tidily dressed and wore a white collar and a tie.

In his valuable recollections of Admiral Canaris's last days, Lunding noted that the Admiral was obliged to wear fetters on his wrists and ankles day and night. He heard them dragging on the ground as the Admiral moved up and down his cell. The *SS* only removed these when he was allowed to walk inside the narrow yard of the bunker and when he was taken in for interrogation.

Lunding and Canaris repeatedly tapped messages from one cell to the other, not using Morse code, but a simpler system known widely to prisoners. It consisted of splitting the alphabet into five groups, omitting 'j', which produced the following pattern:

	1	2	3	4	5
1	A	F	L	Q	V
2	B	G	M	R	W
3	C	H	N	S	X
4	D	I	O	T	Y
5	E	K	P	U	Z

The first tap in each call indicated the group and the second gave the letter of the alphabet.

In the course of these tapped conversations Lunding gained the impression that his neighbour had not lost hope of escaping from the *Gestapo* noose. Canaris repeated several times that they had no conclusive proof against him and he knew well that the National-Socialist régime was rapidly approaching its end.

The interrogations continued and the *Gestapo* harassed Canaris in the hope of obtaining an admission of complicity in the plot against Hitler. Lunding noticed that he was still not treated as a condemned man.

In the second fortnight of March Ernst Kaltenbrunner came to Flössenburg to interrogate his old adversary personally. Lunding could see the two men in conversation in the courtyard of the bunker: the huge Kaltenbrunner, loud-mouthed and making menacing gestures at Canaris with his 'murderer's paws'; Canaris, a slender, distinguished figure, gesticulating as he spoke, with expressive gestures. 'He is not yet at the end of his resources,' thought Lunding as he peered out at the confrontation. The end was, however, not far off now.

After Kaltenbrunner had left Flössenburg the camp interrogators added physical torture to their other methods and between 1 and 2 April Admiral Canaris tapped messages to Lunding about this, though without complaining.

On 5 April with Berlin encircled by Russian troops and a hail of artillery shells falling on the capital, the Führer in his bunker with the ruins of his Chancellery all round him, took the decision to have Canaris hanged, with Oster, Dohnanyi, Bonhoeffer, Gehre, Strünck and Sack.

What was the motive for these death sentences? The German historian, Gert Buchheit, wrote:

> It was not until early in 1945 that General Buhle, quartered by chance at Zossen, found in a safe Canaris's diaries volumes I–V, and six notebooks of travel reports and forwarded them to the Chief of Hitler's Bodyguard, *SS Standführer* Rattenhuber. He turned them over to Kaltenbrunner on 6 April. Rattenhuber, on his return from a prisoner-of-war camp in Russia, visited Dr Josef Müller in Munich, whom he had known previously, and told him what had happened next. After receiving the Canaris diaries Kaltenbrunner gave him the order to proceed with the immediate liquidation of the conspirators.

My own researches convince me that it was in the afternoon of 5 April that Hitler, having glanced through the diaries and notebooks, decided on a furious impulse to have the conspirators hanged. Himmler and Schellenberg were not in Berlin at that date, and it was Kaltenbrunner and Müller who passed on the Führer's orders to Huppenkothen.

On the morning of 6 April *SS Standführer* Huppenkothen arrived at Buchenwald and arranged for a summary court to meet, which condemned Hans von Dohnanyi to death. He was brought before the court on a stretcher semi-conscious. The hanging took place on 9 April at dawn.

Pastor Dietrich Bonhoeffer had been transferred from Buchenwald to Flössenburg, where Huppenkothen arrived on 7 April, accompanied by Commissioner Stawitzky of the *Gestapo*. A summary court was organized, with *SS* Judge Otto Thorbeck of Nuremberg on the bench. Huppenkothen acted as prosecutor and the Camp Commandant, Kögl, as counsel for the defence.

The first hearing was on Sunday, 8 April. Oster, who appeared first, admitted his complicity in the conspiracy but denied having plotted to assassinate Hitler. Then it was the turn of Canaris, Bonhoeffer, Sack, Gehre and Strünck. Huppenkothen, who must have had their death warrants in his pocket, made a last attempt to obtain confessions. He ordered new and 'pressing' interrogations before the execution of all six at dawn.

At about midnight on the night of 8-9 April, when Canaris returned to his cell from one of these 'pressing' interrogations, he tapped out a signal to his neighbour Lunding: 'I believe this is the end.'

He went on to transmit that he had been brutally treated and he thought that they had broken his nose. His fate was determined, he thought, and he would die with his five companions. The Admiral then tapped on the wall:

I am dying for my country. I have a clear conscience. As an officer you will understand that I did no more than my patriotic duty in trying to oppose the criminal madness of Hitler, who was leading Germany to its ruin. It was in vain, as I know now that my country will go under, as I knew already in 1942.

The conversation went on, Canaris asking Lunding to give a last message to his wife Erika. It was well after 2 AM before the taps on the wall ceased.

Shortly after 5:30 AM on Monday, 9 April 1945, under the harsh light of arc lamps, the *SS* put a noose of piano wire round the Admiral's neck and hanged him slowly. He was a witness who knew too much about them and could have confronted them with their criminal guilt before a world tribunal, and so they, the agents of death, eliminated him.

Sources

Official sources and unprinted papers
In the Document Centre of the Military and Historical Research Office, Freiburg in Breisgau

The Service papers of Admiral Wilhelm Canaris.

High Command and Führer Headquarters papers in the same office.

In the Institute for Contemporary History, Munich

Personal papers and documents relating to the *Abwehr*.

Papers in the above institute relating to General Hans Oster, Lieutenant-Colonel Groscurth, Colonel Wilhelm Heinz, the War Diary of Section II of the *Abwehr*. Papers relating to the trials of Röder, Huppenkothen and Sonderegger. Extracts of the Lahousen Diary.

Evidence of Otto Abetz, Achenbach and others.

In the State and Military Archives at Koblenz

The Reichs Chancellery Papers.

Various personal memoirs.

Luftwaffe Archive papers.

Papers of the German Military Command in France.

Reichsführer *SS* and Reich Central Security Office papers.

Papers of the Reich Ministry of the Interior.

In the Political Archives of the German Foreign Ministry at Bonn

The records of the official interpreter, Dr P. Schmidt.

Reports of German Ambassadors.

Secret archives relating to Paris.

Canaris

In the Institute for Occupation Matters, Tübingen

Papers of the High Command of the German Army.

The papers of Werner Best on occupied France.

Printed Records

Records of the International Military Tribunal at Nuremberg (42 volumes)

Nazi Conspiracy and Aggression (10 volumes).

International Military Tribunal: The trial of the German Major War Criminals (22 volumes).

Documents on German Foreign Policy 1918-1945 (10 volumes).

Trials of War Criminals Before the Nuremberg Military Tribunals (15 volumes).

Index

Abendschön, Criminal Inspector Willi, 254–6, 259–61
Abetz, Otto (German Ambassador to France), 206, 207, 227, 229
Abshagen, Dr Karl Heinz, xiv, 27, 89, 113–14, 248, 275, 320
Abwehr (German Military Intelligence), ix, xii, xiii; Canaris takes over as Chief, 19–20, 21; '10 Commandments' agreed with SD, 23, 72; reorganization, 26–33; Foreign Section, 29; Espionage, 29–30; use of women, 30–1, 164; Sabotage and Subversion, 31–2; Counter-espionage, 32–3; intelligence network in America, 44–7; and Aubert's spying activities, 47–9; fire in Russian Affairs section 52; internal politics section set up, 72; Viennese branch established, 88; Lahousen transfers to, 102–3; Canaris and Oster groups, 104–5; generals' conspiracy centered in, 114, 164, 165; secret report on Czech crisis, 118–19; special army units destroy Czech defences, 120; Czech intelligence informed of invasion by Agent 54, 127–8; Operation Himmler, 141–2; Canaris's tight control of budget, 163–4; acquisition of new offices, 164; *esprit de corps*, 164; Dohnanyi and Strunck recruited, 164–5; Müller attached to Munich office, 170; Heydrich's 'Black Chapel' dossier, 182–4, 247–8; operations and administration in France, 184–5, 250; and inquiries into French atomic research, 186, 188–9; in Romania, 197–9; Jodl's directive on military effectives in Eastern territories, 215–16; Operation Felix, 218–21; and Operation Attila, 226–9; preparations for Operation Barbarossa, 234–6; Heydrich's 'Black Orchestra' dossier, 254; and Thümmel affair, 255–62; Prague conference on co-operation with SD, 264–6; criminal activities avoided

by, 274; espionage and counter-espionage cases, 276–7; Schmidhuber affair, 279–81, 295, 299; information on Allied landings in North Africa obtained by, 281–6; Kaltenbrunner's suspicions, 296; Zossen box of secret documents, 299, 301, 324–5; offices searched and members arrested by *Gestapo*, 299, 300–3; agents in Italy, 305, 311; arrests and defections, 314–15, 320; dissolution of, 315–16, 317; reaction of officers, 317–18; and Operation 7, 318–19; *see also* Canaris
Adam, General, 111, 112
Agent 54 (alias Thümmel), 128, 261, 262
Algeria, Algiers, 196, 222, 282, 287, 288; *see also* North Africa
Alsace and Lorraine, 212
Amé, Cesare (Chief of Italian Intelligence), 25, 290, 305, 311; Venice meeting with Canaris, 308–10, 312; replaced by Carboni, 310
Anschluss, see Austria
Anthropoid (Czech commando group), 263
Anti-Comintern Pact, 101
Antonescu, General Ion, 200–2, 203
Arranz, Captain Francisco, 36, 38
Astra-Romana Oil Company, Rumania, 198–9
atomic scientists, research, 160–3, 186–9
Attolico, Count (Italian Ambassador in Berlin), 149–50
Aubert, Henri, espionage activities, 47–9
Austria, 54, 61, 62, 91, 124, 172, 216, 296; *Anschluss*, 79, 80, 81–9, 102, 108, 109–10, 131, 171, 284

Badoglio, Marshal, 227; forms government after Mussolini's downfall, 307; and signs armistice with Allies, 310–11
Balaban, Lieut-Col, 259–60

335

investigated, 318–19; discovery of Zossen Box, 324–5; prisoners held in Prinz Albrechtstrasse prison by, 325–7; and Allied air raid on Berlin, 327–8; Canaris interrogated by, 326, 329; *see also* SD; SS

Gibraltar, 292, 293, 294; Operation Felix planned against, 191–7, 203–4, 206–7, 208, 209, 217, 218–26, 230–1, 236, 288

Gibhardt, Dr Fritz Unterberg, 47–8

Gigurtu, Ion (Rumanian Prime Minister), 199–200

Giraud, General, 32, 181, 289; Operation Gustav planned against, 274

Gisevius, Hans Bernd, 50, 68, 105, 107, 133, 165; friction with Heydrich, 22–3; his view of Oster, 28–9; von Blomberg scandal, 68, 70, 72; tribute to Count Redwitz by, 88; involvement in conspiracies, 149, 150; his view of Canaris, 150–1

Gleiwitz radio station, attack on, 146, 166, 169

Goebbels, Dr Joseph, 26, 154, 276, 321; Austrian *Anschluss*, 81–2; and Czech crisis, 119–20

Göltz, Count Rüdiger von der, 77, 78

Goerdeler, Dr Carl, 112, 126, 138, 166, 277, 321, 324, 325, 326, 327

Goring, Field-Marshal Herman, x, 14, 65, 135, 136, 145, 146, 169, 295, 301, 307, 321; Research Office created by, 24; Spanish Civil War, 36, 37, 38, 39, 41, 94, 137; attends 1937 secret conference, 59, 60, 62; role in Blomberg and Fritsch scandals, 66–7, 68, 69, 70, 74, 75–6, 79, 80; promoted to Field-Marshal, 77; *Anschluss*, 83, 86; failure of Dahlerus mission, 147–8; bombardment of Warsaw, 155; attends Hitler's meeting on 1940–41 strategy, 203; Operation Barbarossa, 233, 242; and *blitzkrieg* on Yugoslavia, 237

Grainer, Dr Helmut, 144–6

Greece, 287; attacked by Italy, 212, 213; Germany plans military action, 217, 222, 236–7; and German occupation, 239, 240, 272, 293

Groscurth, Col Helmut (Chief of Section II, *Abwehr*), xii, xiii, 32, 45, 82, 102, 105, 134, 168; involvement in conspiracies, 115, 166; his views on Nazi occupation of Sudetanland, 120–2; and on Hitler, 124–6; Report X, 173; Zossen box left with, 299; reported missing at Stalingrad, 313

Guderian, General, 84, 87

Gürtner, Dr Franz, 77, 164

Hacha, President (of Czechoslovakia), 130, 253

Hahn, Otto, 161, 162

Halder, General Franz, x, xi, xii, 28, 77, 118, 126, 136, 137, 138, 150, 157, 169; succeeds Beck as Chief of General Staff, 113; involvement in conspiracies, 113–14, 117, 149, 166, 168, 324; talks with Canaris and Kordt in *Tiergarten*, 132–3; attends Hitler's Berghof meeting on Poland, 144, 145, 146; Report X, 172–3; Operation Barbarossa, 233, 241, 242; imprisonment, 325, 328

Halifax, Lord, 116, 117, 172

Hammerstein, Ludwig von, 166, 277, 280

Hansen, Colonel George (*Abwehr*), 313, 316, 317, 322

Hassell, Ulrich von, 105, 112, 168, 324

Heinz, Colonel Wilhelm Friedrich (*Abwehr*), xii, 115, 185

Heisenberg, Werner, 160, 161, 162–3, 188

Helfferich, Col (*Abwehr* agent in Rome), 305, 311–12

Helldorf, Count Wolf Heinrich von, 50, 67, 68, 69, 105, 112, 114, 138, 166

Henderson, Sir Nevile, 147, 148–9

Henke Service (attached to Foreign Ministry), 24

Henlein, Konrad, 120, 121, 123–4

Heydrich, Lena Mathilde (*née* von Osten: wife), 17, 50–1, 266, 270

Heydrich, Reinhard Tristam Eugen (Head of SD), ix, xi, xiii, 3, 28, 32, 100; early friendship with Canaris, 12–13, 20; his rapid promotion in SS, 16–17; and appointed head of SD, 17–18; rivalry between Patzig and, 18–19; his view of Canaris, 21–2; friction between Gisevius and, 22–3; '10 Commandments' agreed with Canaris, 23, 72; and renewed friendship with Canaris family, 50; his jealousy of Schellenberg, 50–1; Tuchachevsky affair, 51–2, 55–7, 106; Nebe mistrusted by, 69; rôle in Blomberg and Fritsch scandals, 70, 71, 72, 75–6, 80; and Austrian *Anschluss*, 86; as likely successor to Canaris as head of *Abwehr*, 106, 107; his jealousy of Henlein, 121; 'Operation Himmler', 142; extermination policy, 153–4, 156–7, 244–5; 'Black Chapel' dossier, 182–4, 247–8; his attitude to war¹ with Russia, 214, 241–2; rivalry with

Canaris

Schmalschläger, Colonel Heinz, 235, 285

Schmidhuber, Dr Wilhelm, 170, 180, 181, 182; *Gestapo* inquiry into activities, 279–81, 295, 299, 300

Schmidt, Hans (alleged blackmailer of Fritsch), 73, 78–9, 80

Schmidt, Dr Paul (Hitler's interpreter), 207, 209, 210, 211

Schmundt, Major-General, 75, 110, 111

Schulenburg, Count von der, 114, 240

Schuschnigg, Dr von (Austrian Chancellor), 81, 83, 84, 85, 87, 328

SD (*Sicherheitsdienst*: SS Security Service), xi, xiii, 56, 57, 114, 129, 258, 259; Heydrich appointed Chief of, 17–18; rivalry between *Abwehr* and, 18–20, 21, 46; and '10 Commandments' agreed, 23; Tuchachevsky affair, 56–8; *Anschluss*, 86–7, 88; extermination policy, 153–4, 156–7, 166–7; inquiry into *Abwehr* secret activities, 182–4, 264; Operation Barbarossa, 235–6; Prague meeting on co-operation with *Abwehr*, 264–6; Himmler takes over as head, 279; and Kaltenbrunner appointed head of, 295–6; agents' activities in Italy, 305, 307, 311–12; *Abwehr* taken over by, 315–16, 317; Canaris interrogated by, 326; *see also* Gestapo; Heydrich; SS

Seeckt, General von, 27, 64

Seubert, Colonel Franz, xii, 30–1, 152–3, 184, 244, 281–3, 286, 287

Seyss-Inquart, Dr, 84, 124

Sicherheitsdients see SD

Skoblin, General Nicolas, 55, 58

Skubl, Dr, 86, 87

Sonderegger, Franz (*Gestapo*), 295, 300–1, 324

South America, 6–7, 9, 225

Soviet Union, 61, 64, 110; Spanish Republicans supported by, 37, 39–40; Tuchachevsky affair, 51–8; Polish crisis, 133, 142; negotiations with Nazi Germany, 138–9, 140, 141; and Russo-German non-aggression pact, 143–4, 145, 146, 173; partition of Poland, 154; Russo-Finnish war, 175–6; Bessarabia and Bukovina ceded to, 197–8, 200; Hitler's plans for war against, 214–18; Molotov-Hitler talks, 217; Operation Barbarossa (attack on), 231, 232–6, 239–43, 284; and Nazi extermination policy, 244–7, 272; Battle of Stalingrad, 289, 290, 293; Canaris's pessimistic

report on war with, 316; bombardment of Berlin by, 329

Spain, x, 12, 13, 30, 64; Canaris's service as agent during 1st World War in, 8–9, 20, 25; Civil War, 34–43, 62, 66; and Franco's victory over Republicans, 90–101, 137; neutrality agreement with France, 97–8; atrocities in, 99–100; joint Anti-Comintern Pact, 101; neutralist attitude towards Operation Felix, 191–7, 203–5, 207, 208, 209, 218–26, 230–1; secret agreement with Pétain, 207; Hitler-Franco meeting at Hendaye, 207–10; Canaris's love of, 238–9; SD report on Canaris's activities in, 264, 266; Operation Ilona planned against, 288–9, 290–4

SS (*Schutz-Staffel*: military police), ix, xvi, 1–2, 22, 63, 75, 78, 80, 102, 105, 106, 112, 114, 248, 319, 321; reorganization of (1934), 16; Heydrich's rapid promotion, 16–17; Tuchachevsky affair, 51, 53, 55–8; Austrian *Anschluss*, 86–7, 88–9; commandos' behaviour in Sudetanland, 120–1; Operation Himmler in Poland, 141–2, 146, 166; extermination policy in conquered Eastern territories, 153–4, 155, 156–7, 244–7; Canaris compiles evidence of atrocities, 156 160, 166–7; Heisenberg criticized by, 162; Operation Barbarossa, 234; Prague conference on co-operation with *Abwehr*, 264–6; guard of honour at Heydrich's funeral, 269; methods of interrogation by, 301–2; Skorzeny commandos free Mussolini, 311; *Abwehr* dissolved by, 313–16, 317; *see also* SD; Gestapo; *Waffen SS*

Stalin, Josef, 37, 51, 148; Tuchachevsky conspiracy, 53–8, 77; Russo-German non-aggression pact, 141, 143–4; Hitler plans 2nd front against Russia, 214–17; and Operation Barbarossa, 233, 240, 242; *see also* Soviet Union

Stalingrad, battle of, 284, 289, 290, 293, 313

Stauffenberg, Colonel Claus von, attempt to assassinate Hitler, 320–2

Steinberg, Paul Hans (alias Thümmel), 127–8, 261

Stieff, General Helmut, 16, 298

Stohrer, Eberhard (German Ambassador to Spain), 8, 93–4, 97, 99, 291; Canaris's conversation in Salamanca with, 90–2; Operation